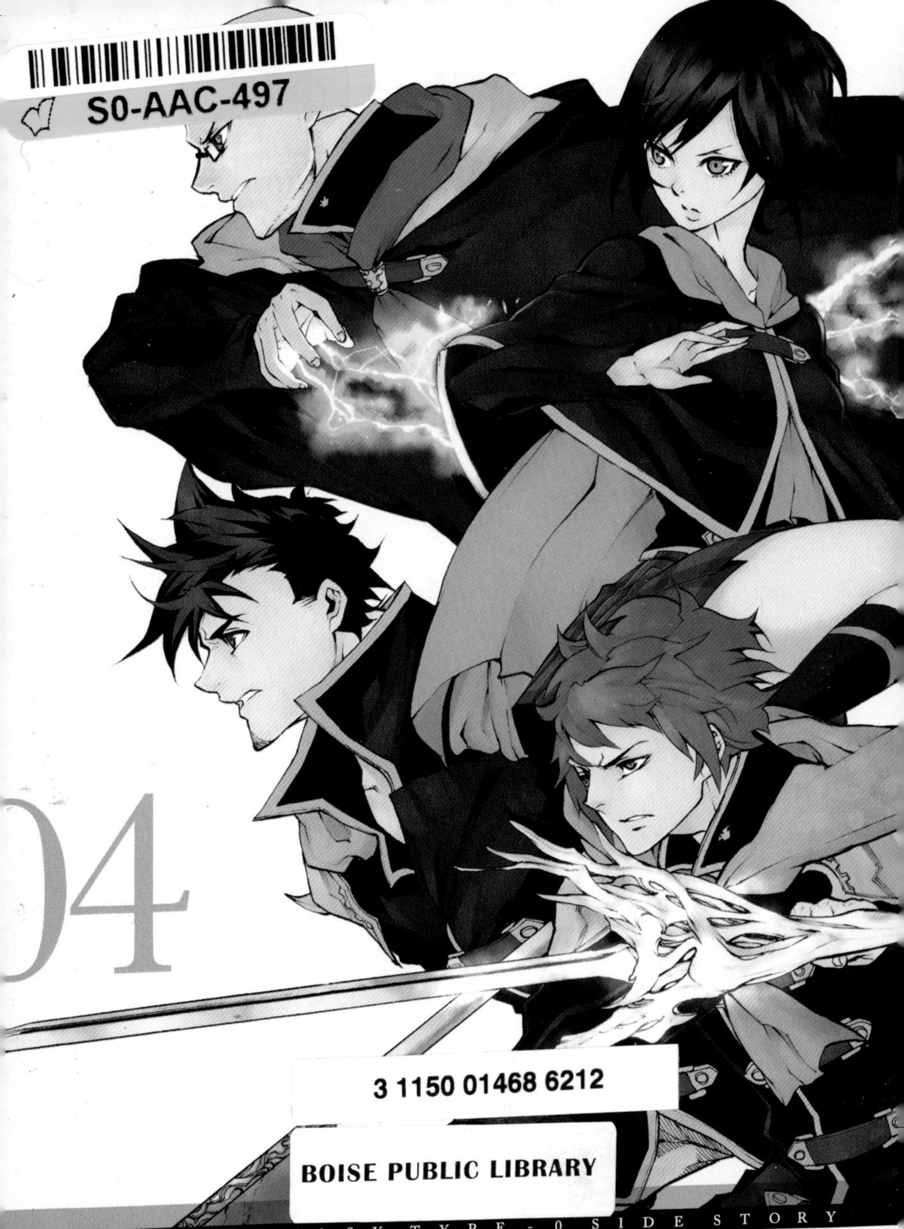
04

FINAL FANTASY TYPE-0 SIDE STORY

THE ICE REAPER

Takatoshi Shiozawa SUPERVISION: Tetsuya Nomura

CONTENTS

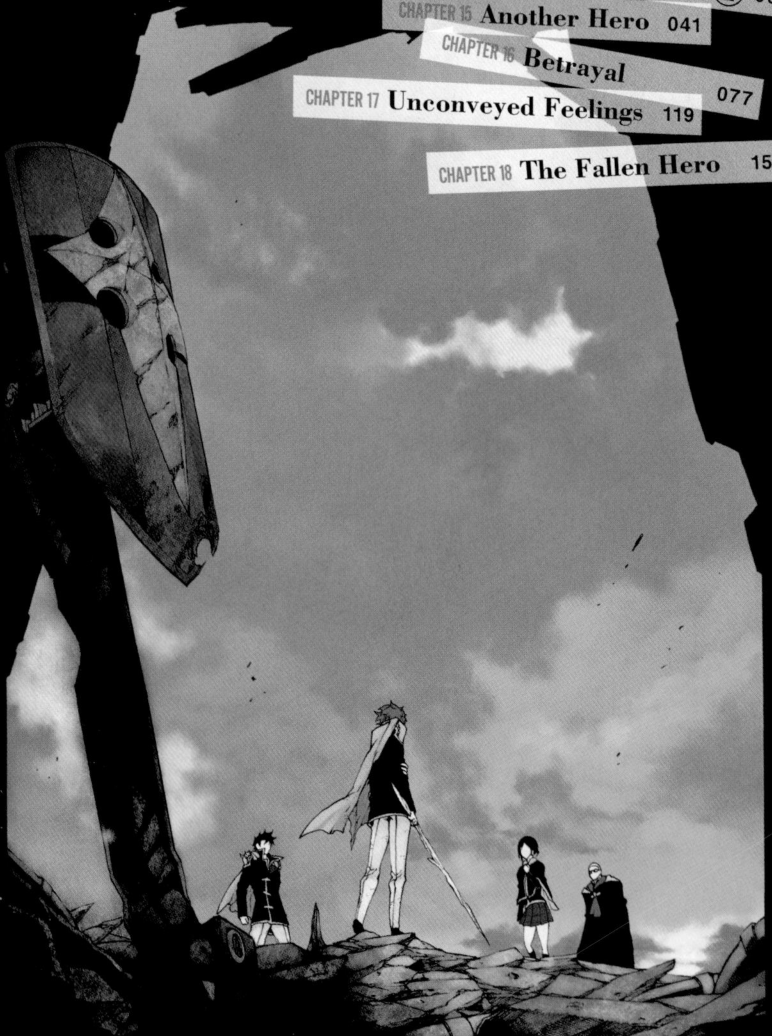

CHARACTER DESIGN:TETSUYA NOMURA

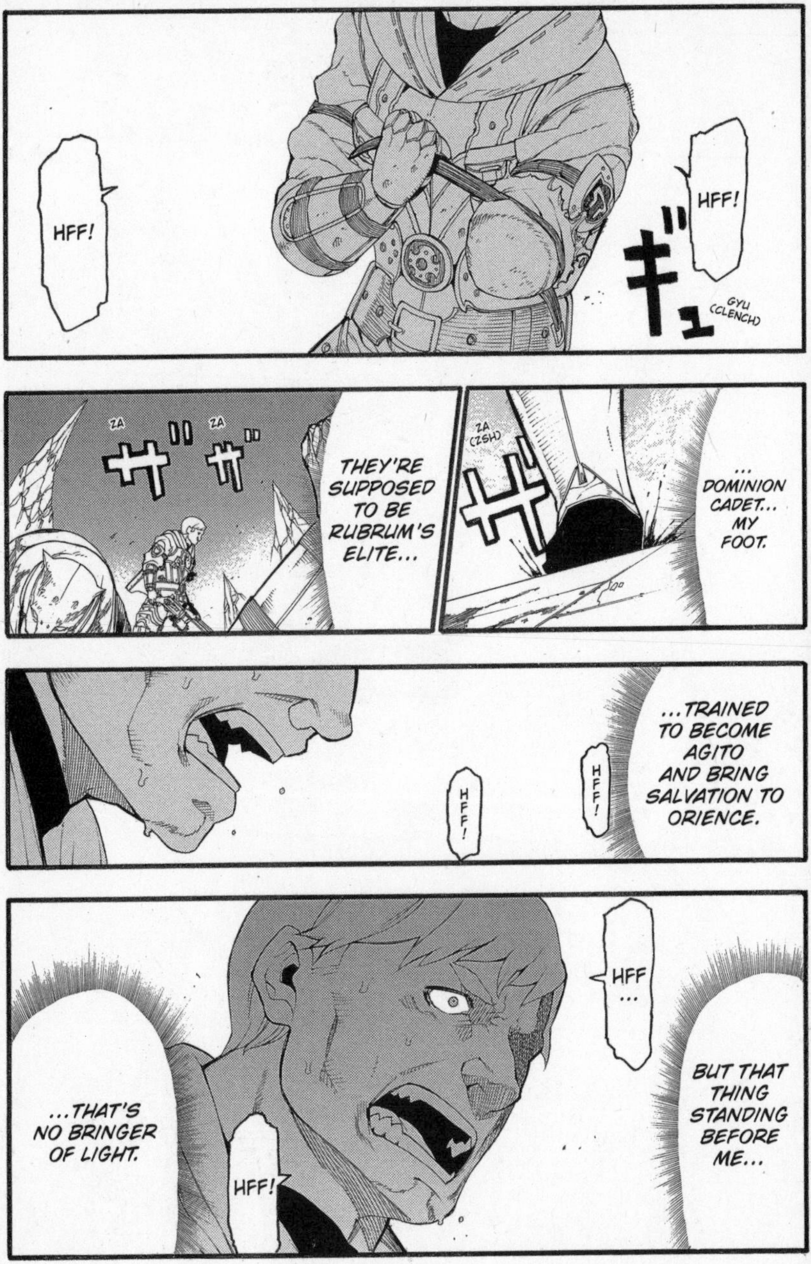
HFF!
ギュ
GYU (CLENCH)
HFF!
...DOMINION CADET... MY FOOT.
ザ
ZA (ZSH)
THEY'RE SUPPOSED TO BE RUBRUM'S ELITE...
ザ ザ
ZA ZA
...TRAINED TO BECOME AGITO AND BRING SALVATION TO ORIENCE.
HFF!
HFF!
HFF ...
BUT THAT THING STANDING BEFORE ME...
...THAT'S NO BRINGER OF LIGHT.
HFF!

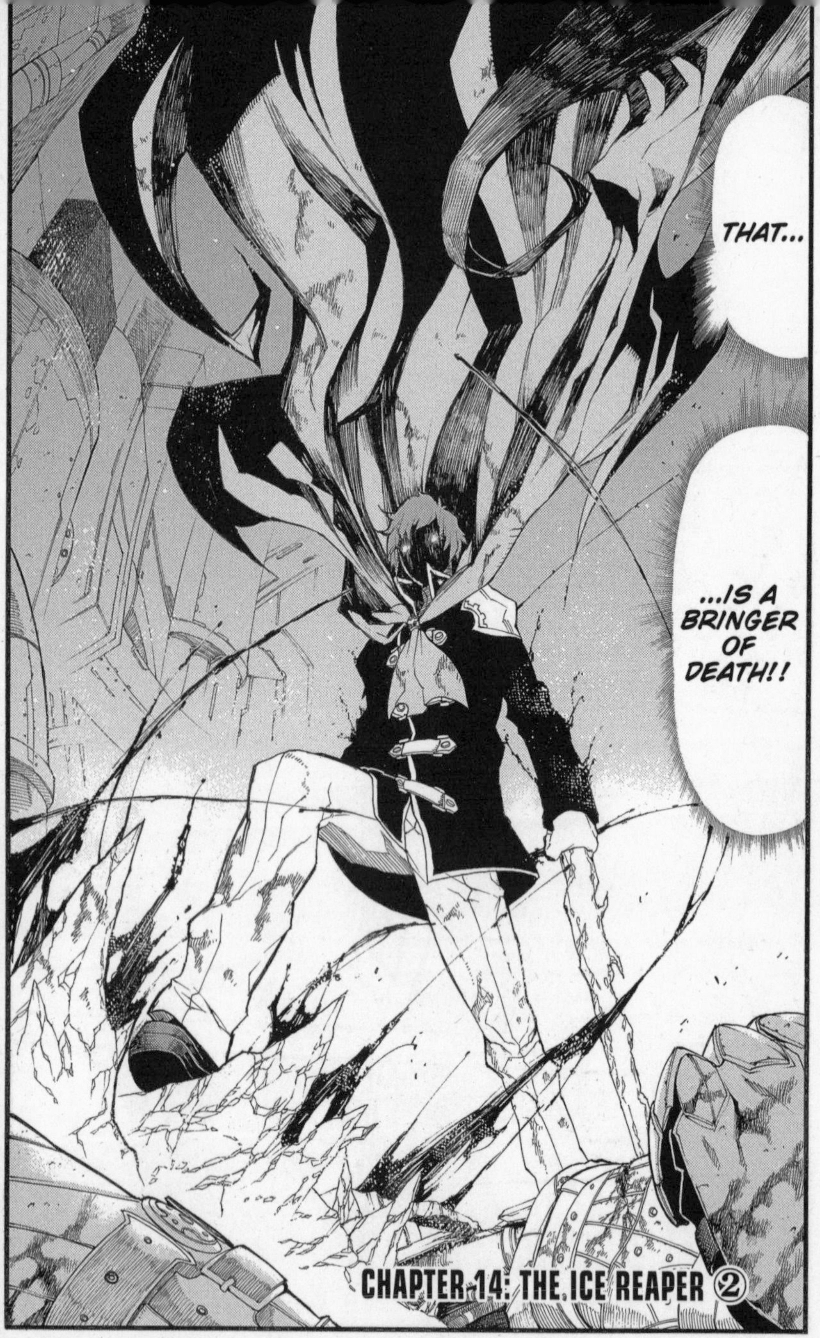
THAT...
...IS A BRINGER OF DEATH!!
CHAPTER 14: THE ICE REAPER ②

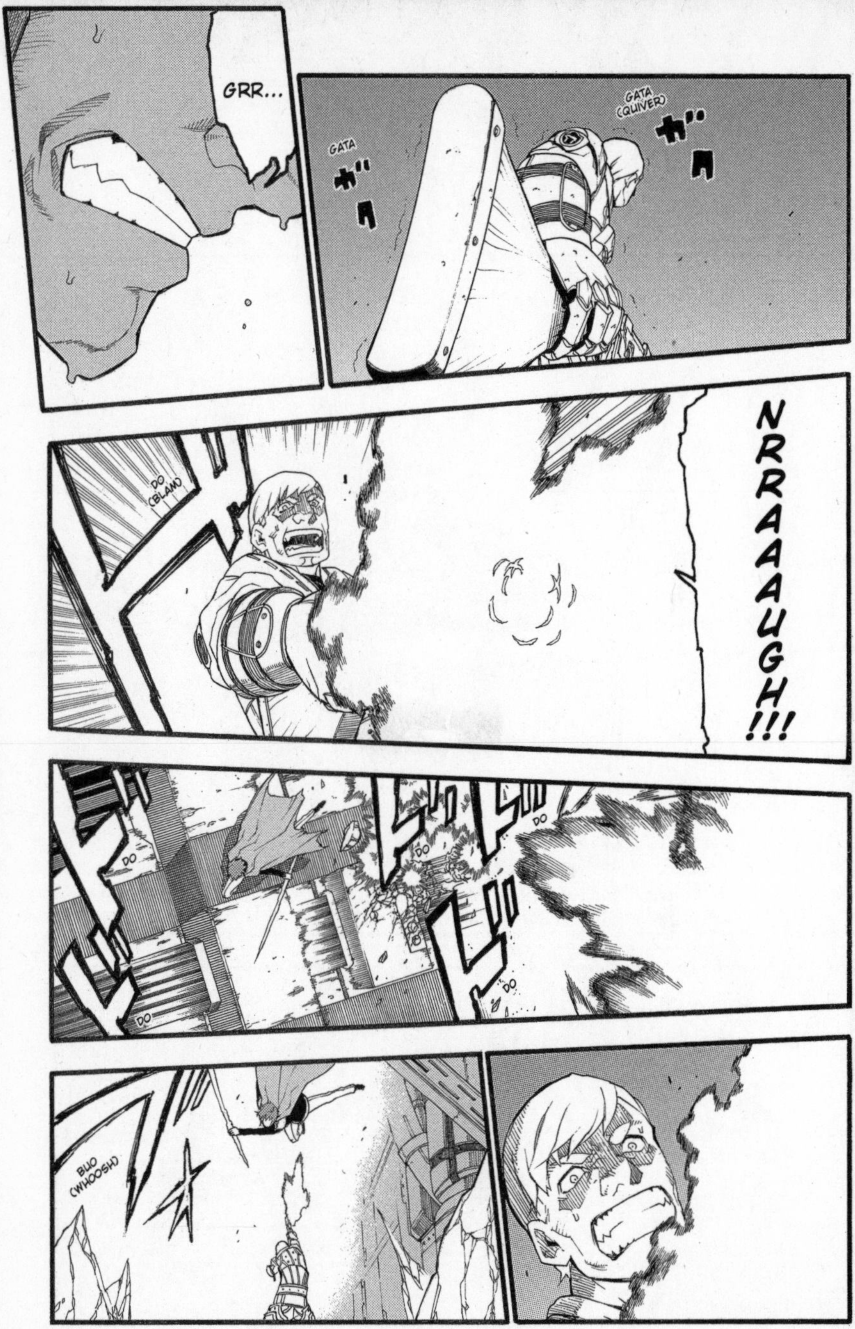
GATA (QUIVER)
GATA
GRR...
NRRAAAAUGH!!!
DO (BLAM)
DO
DO
DO
DO
BUO (WHOOSH)

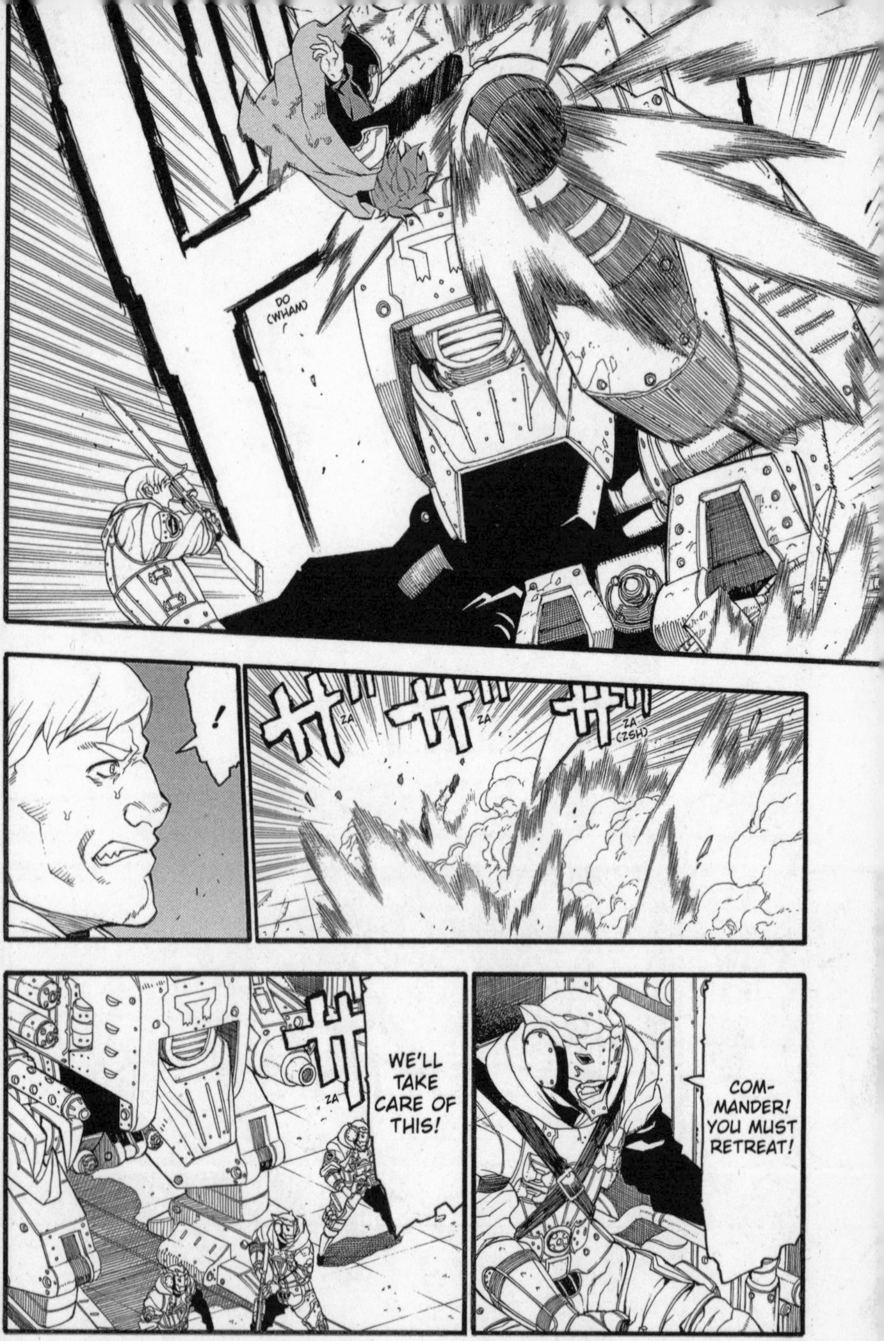
DO
(WHAM)
ZA
(ZSH)
ZA
ZA
!
COM-MANDER! YOU MUST RETREAT!
ZA
WE'LL TAKE CARE OF THIS!

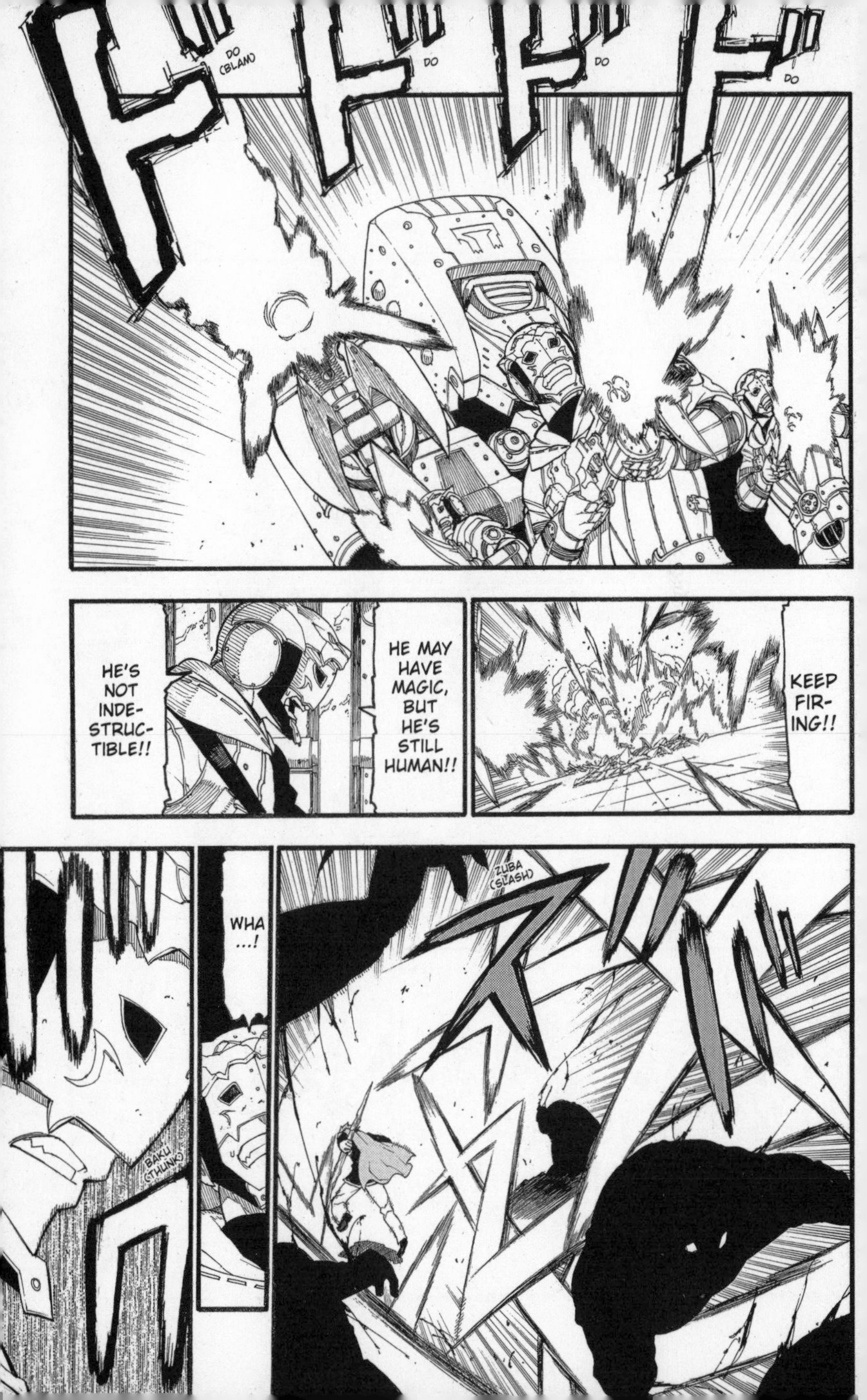
DO
DO
DO
DO (BLAM)
KEEP FIR-ING!!
HE MAY HAVE MAGIC, BUT HE'S STILL HUMAN!!
HE'S NOT INDE-STRUC-TIBLE!!
ZUBA (SLASH)
WHA ...!
BAKU (THUNK)

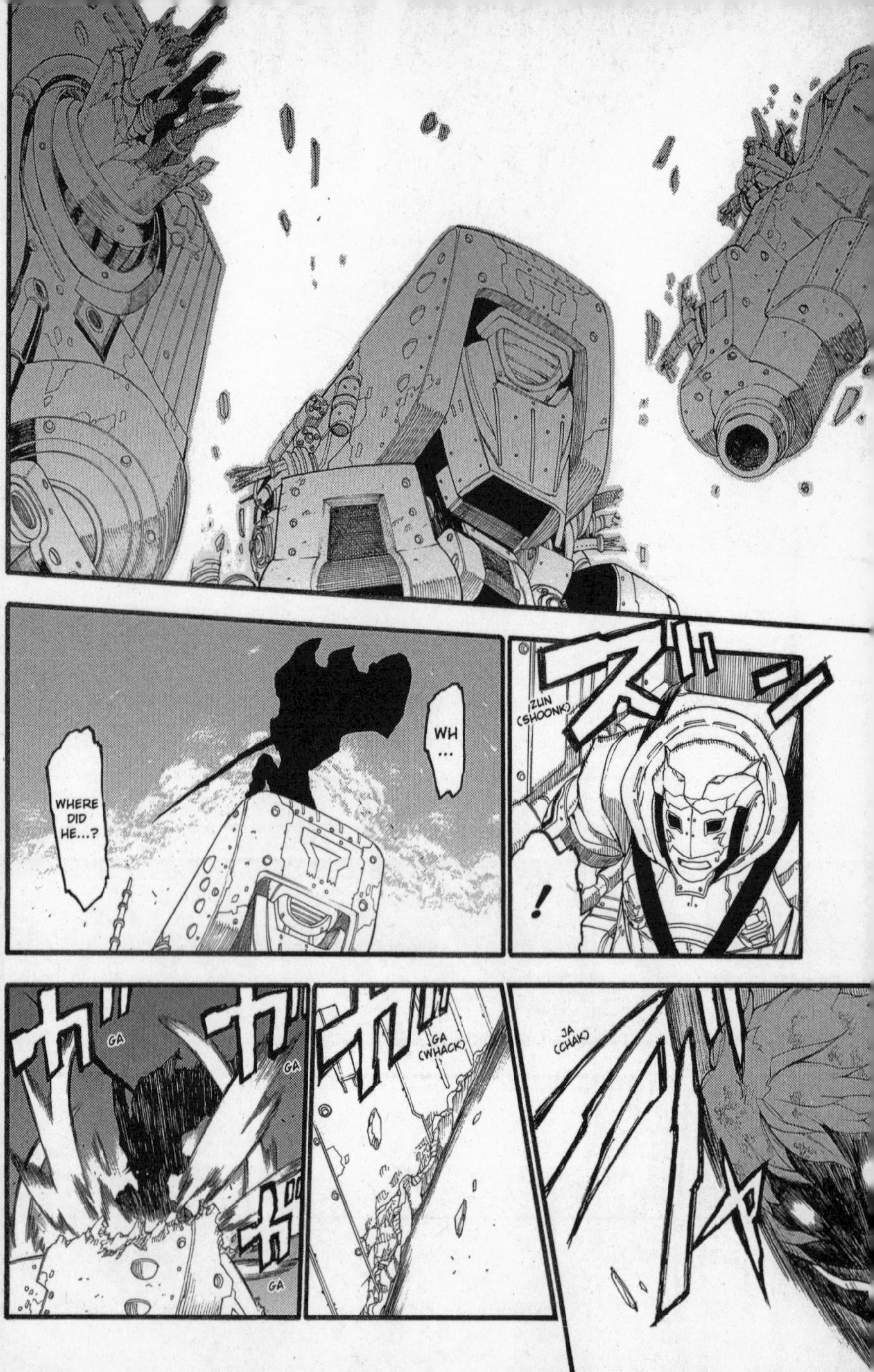
ZUN (SHOONK)
!
WH ...
WHERE DID HE...?
JA (CHAK)
GA (WHACK)
GA
GA
GA

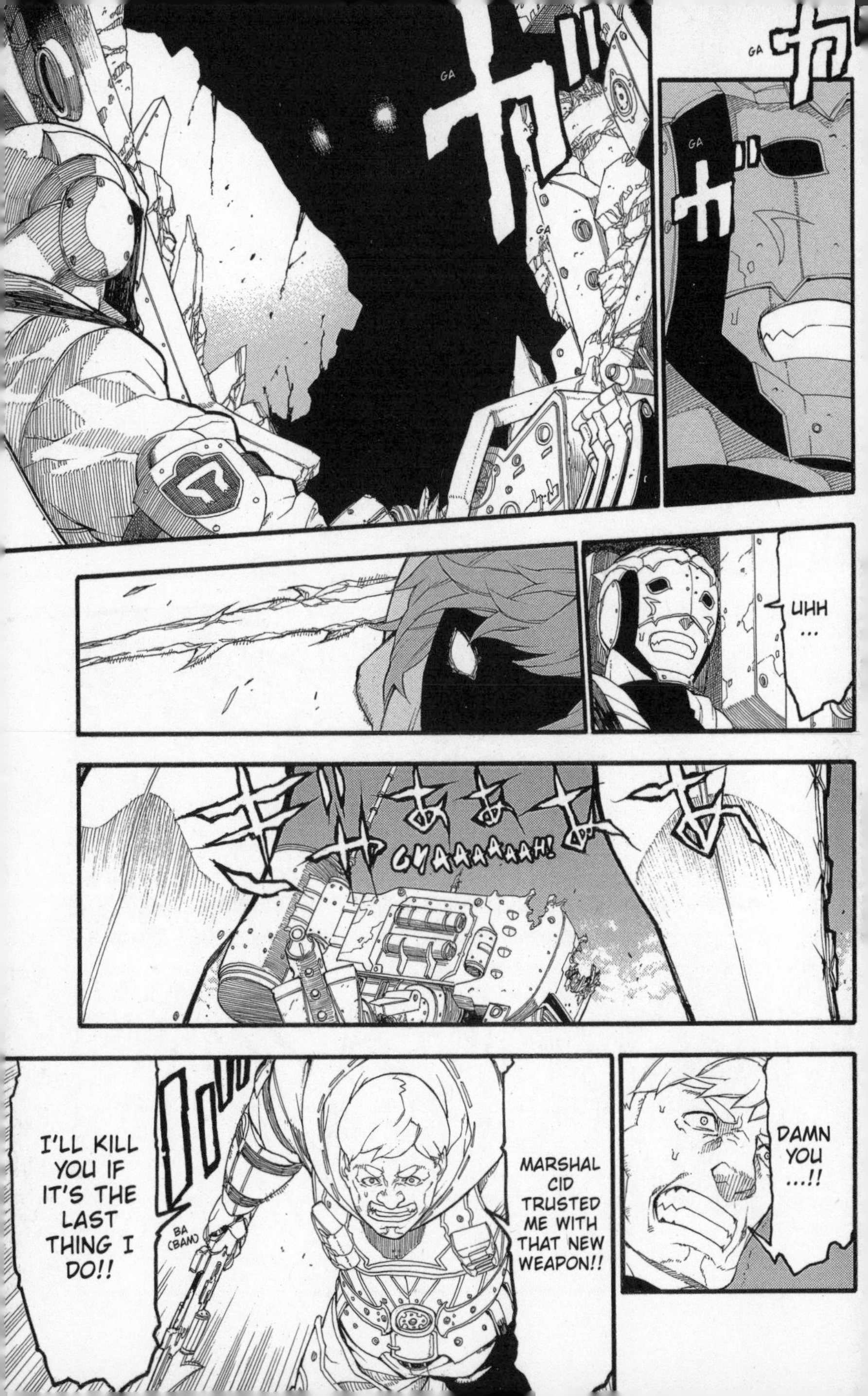
GA
GA
GA
GA
UHH ...
GYAAAAAAH!
DAMN YOU ...!!
MARSHAL CID TRUSTED ME WITH THAT NEW WEAPON!!
BA (BAM)
I'LL KILL YOU IF IT'S THE LAST THING I DO!!

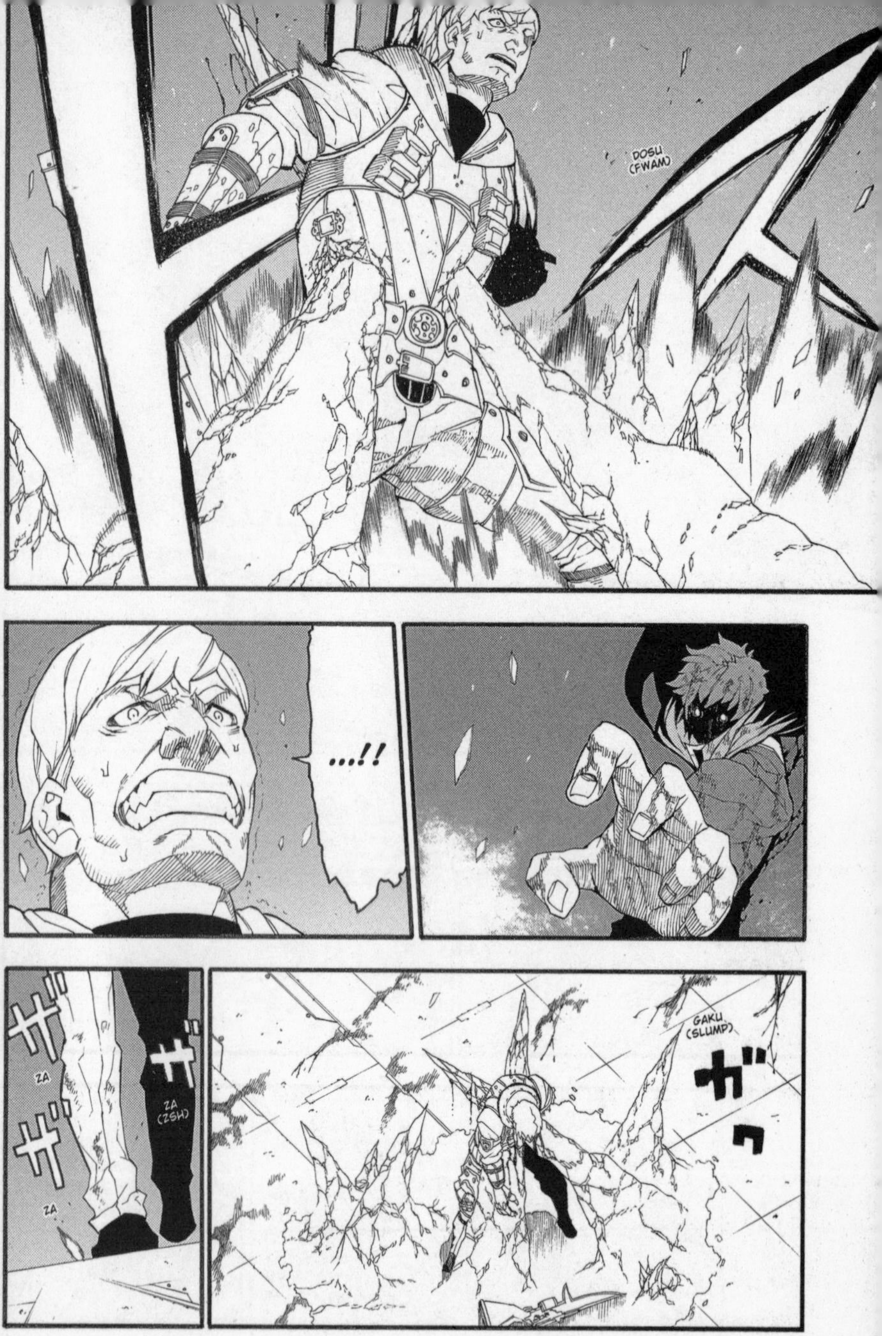
DOSU (FWAM)
...!!
ガク
GAKU (SLUMP)
ザ
ZA
ザ
ZA (ZSH)
ザ
ZA

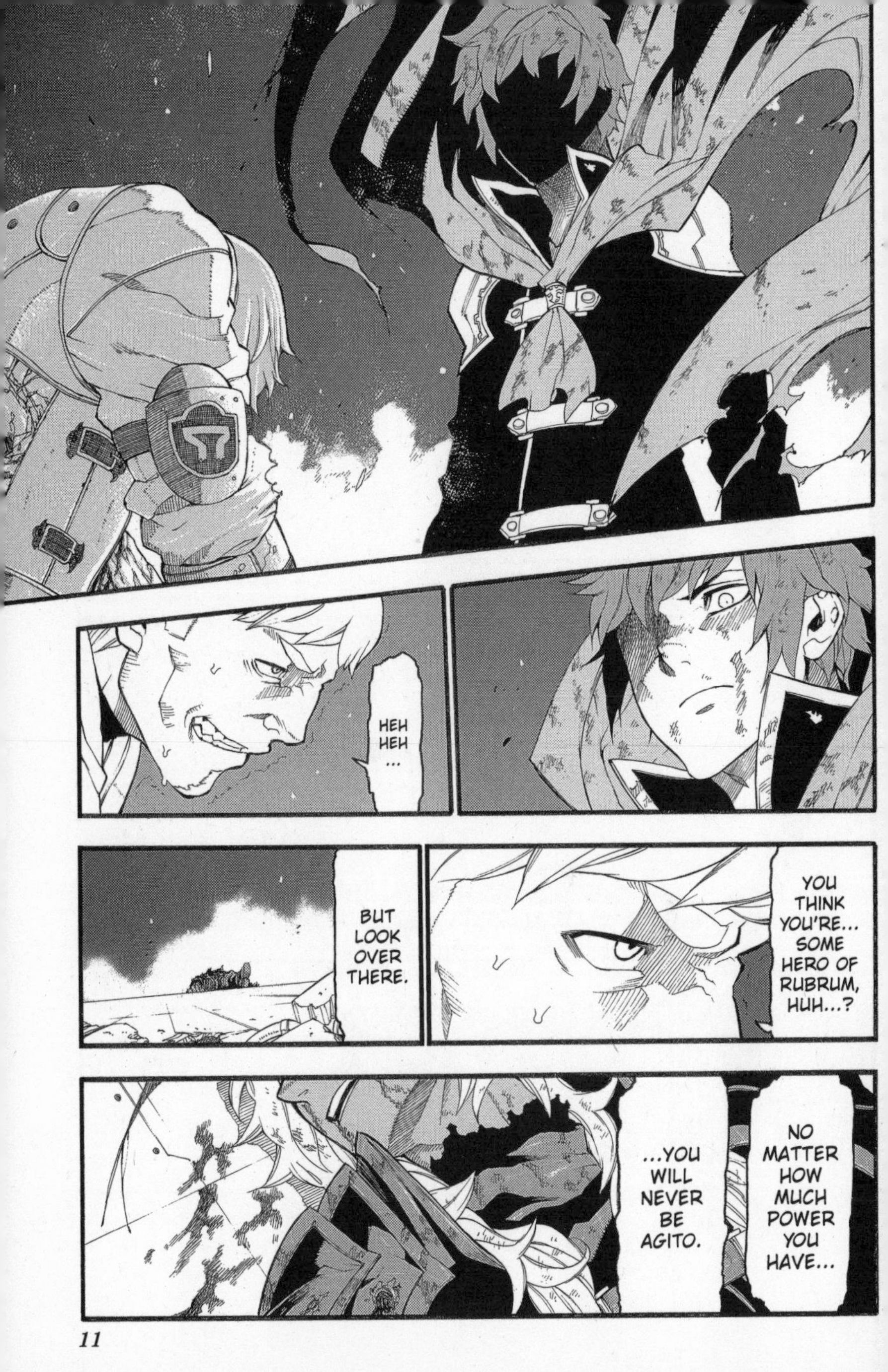
HEH HEH ...
YOU THINK YOU'RE... SOME HERO OF RUBRUM, HUH...?
BUT LOOK OVER THERE.
NO MATTER HOW MUCH POWER YOU HAVE...
...YOU WILL NEVER BE AGITO.

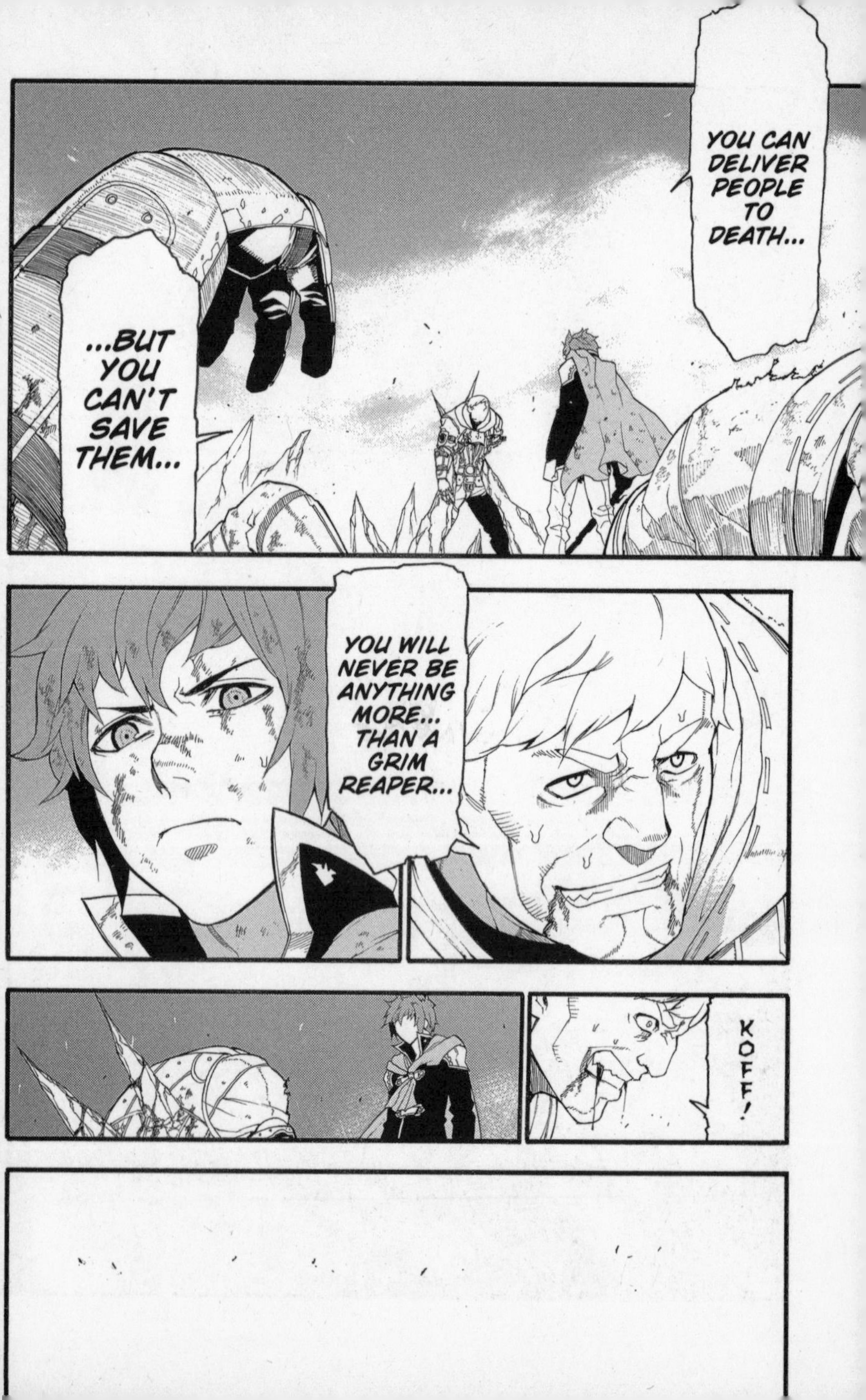
YOU CAN DELIVER PEOPLE TO DEATH...
...BUT YOU CAN'T SAVE THEM...
YOU WILL NEVER BE ANYTHING MORE... THAN A GRIM REAPER...
KOFF!

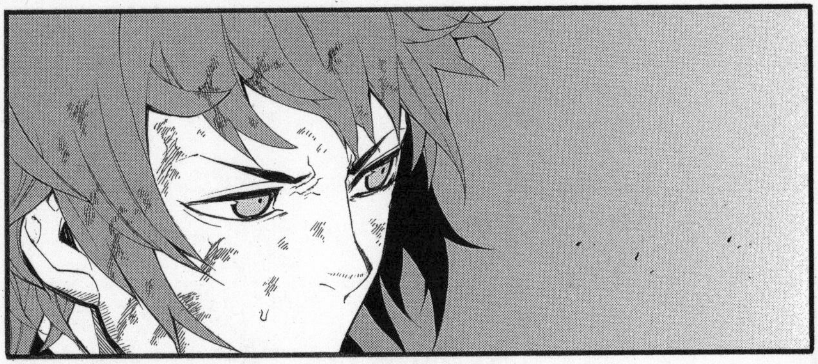
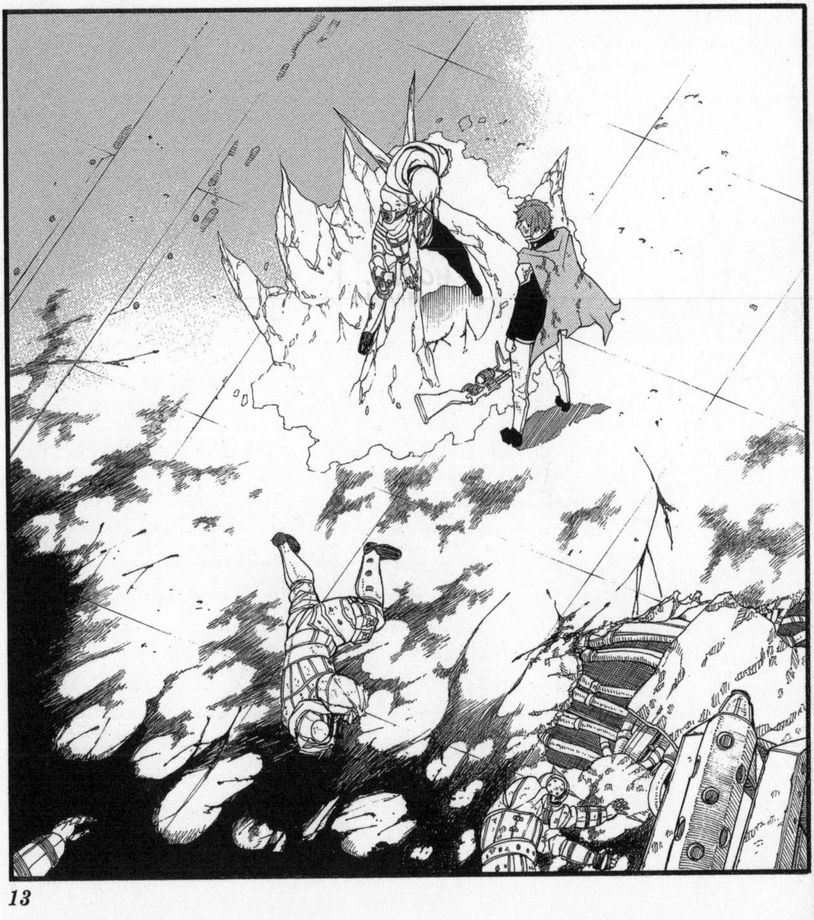

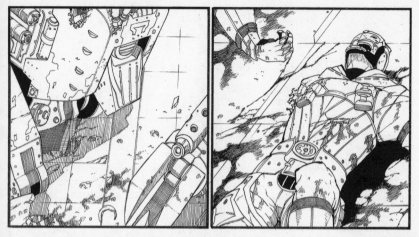

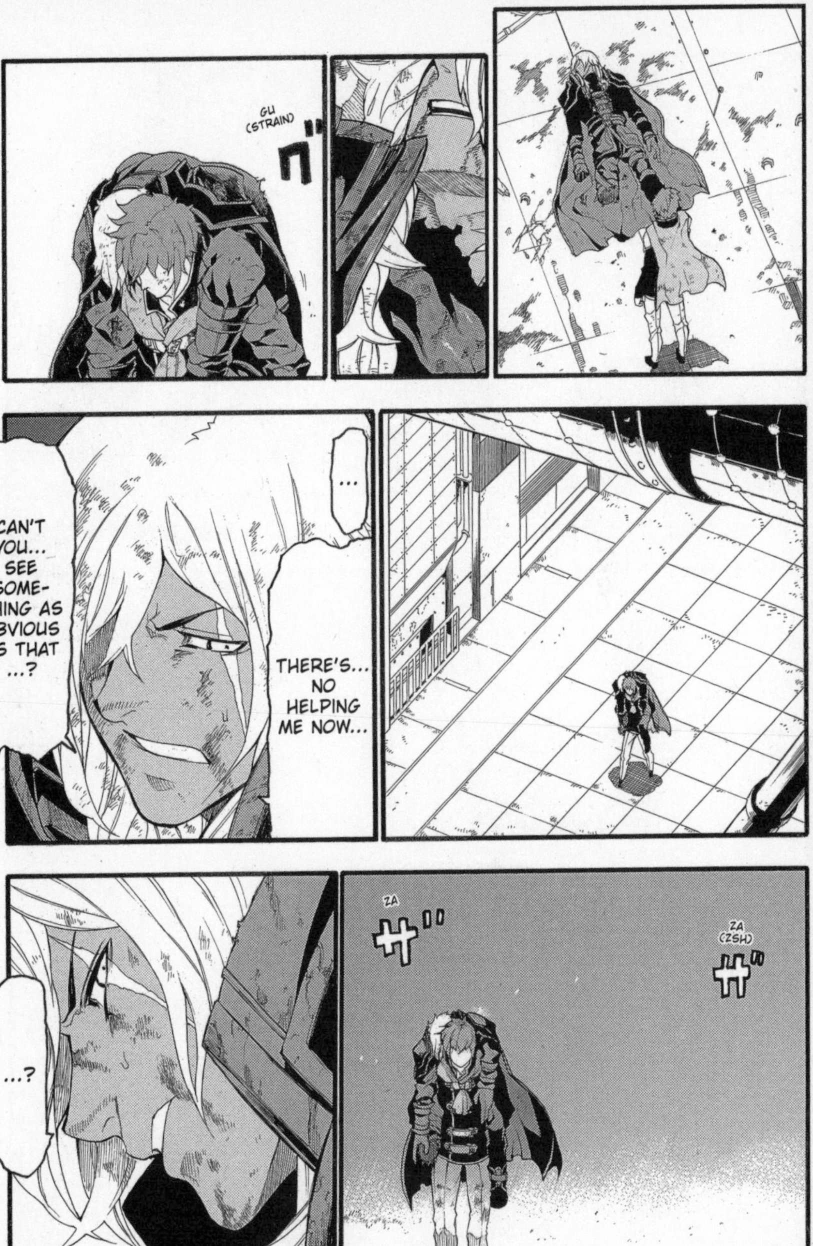
GU (STRAIN)
...
THERE'S... NO HELPING ME NOW...
CAN'T YOU... SEE SOME-THING AS OBVIOUS AS THAT ...?
ZA
ZA (ZSH)
...?

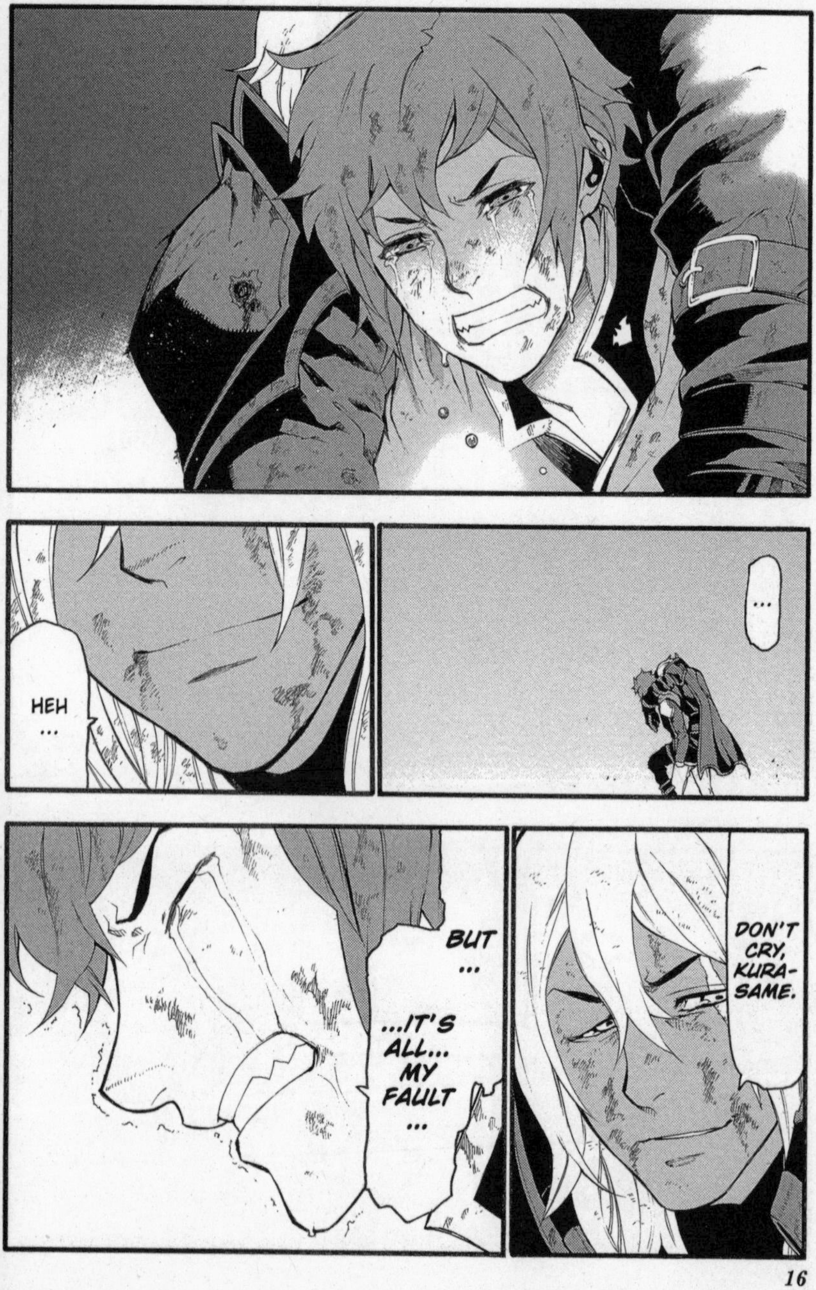
...
HEH ...
DON'T CRY, KURA-SAME.
BUT ...
...IT'S ALL... MY FAULT ...

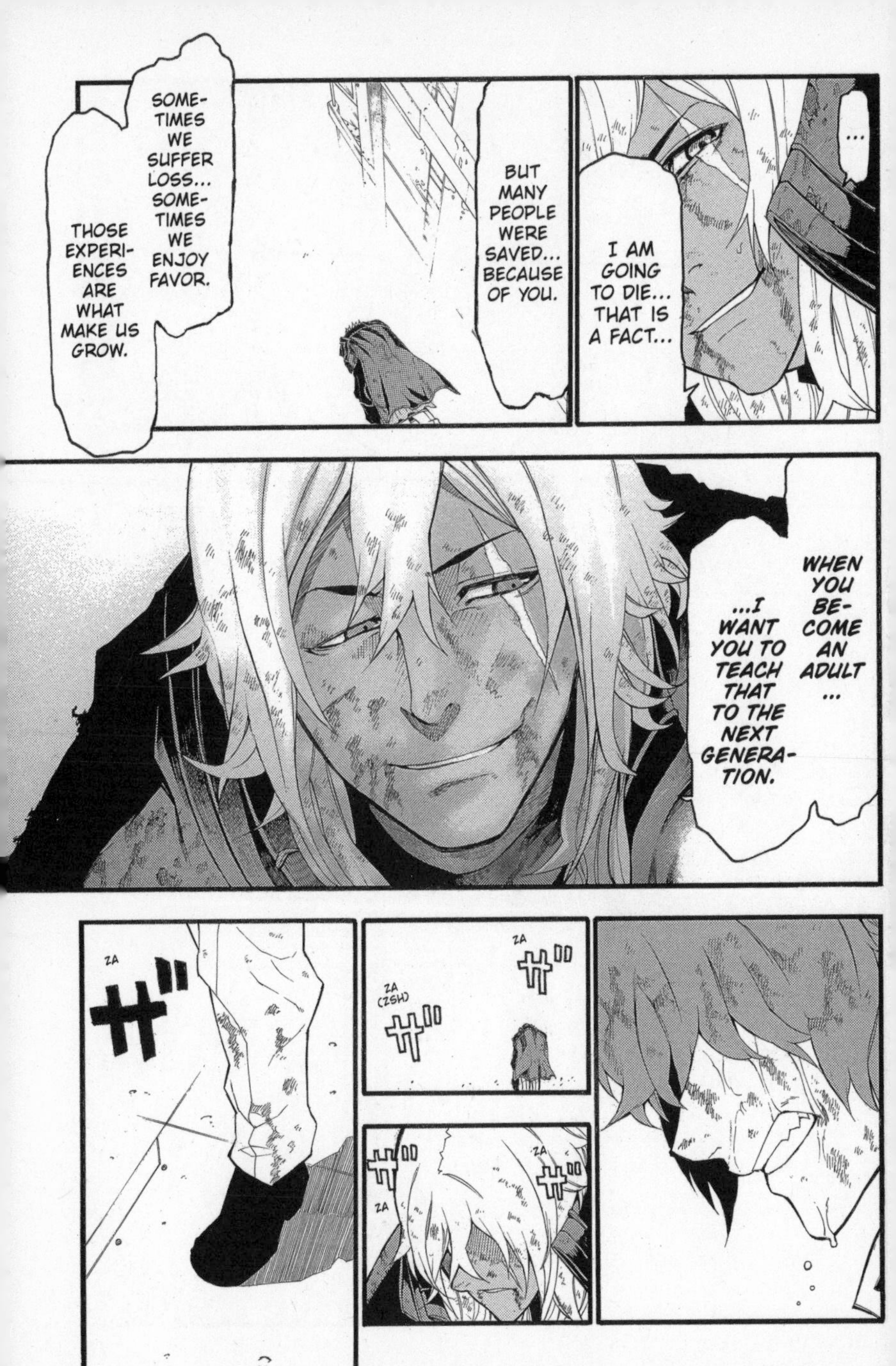
...
I AM GOING TO DIE... THAT IS A FACT...
BUT MANY PEOPLE WERE SAVED... BECAUSE OF YOU.
SOME-TIMES WE SUFFER LOSS... SOME-TIMES WE ENJOY FAVOR.
THOSE EXPERI-ENCES ARE WHAT MAKE US GROW.
WHEN YOU BE-COME AN ADULT...
...I WANT YOU TO TEACH THAT TO THE NEXT GENERA-TION.
ザッ
ZA
ザッ
ZA (ZSH)
ザッ
ZA
ザッ
ZA
ザッ
ZA

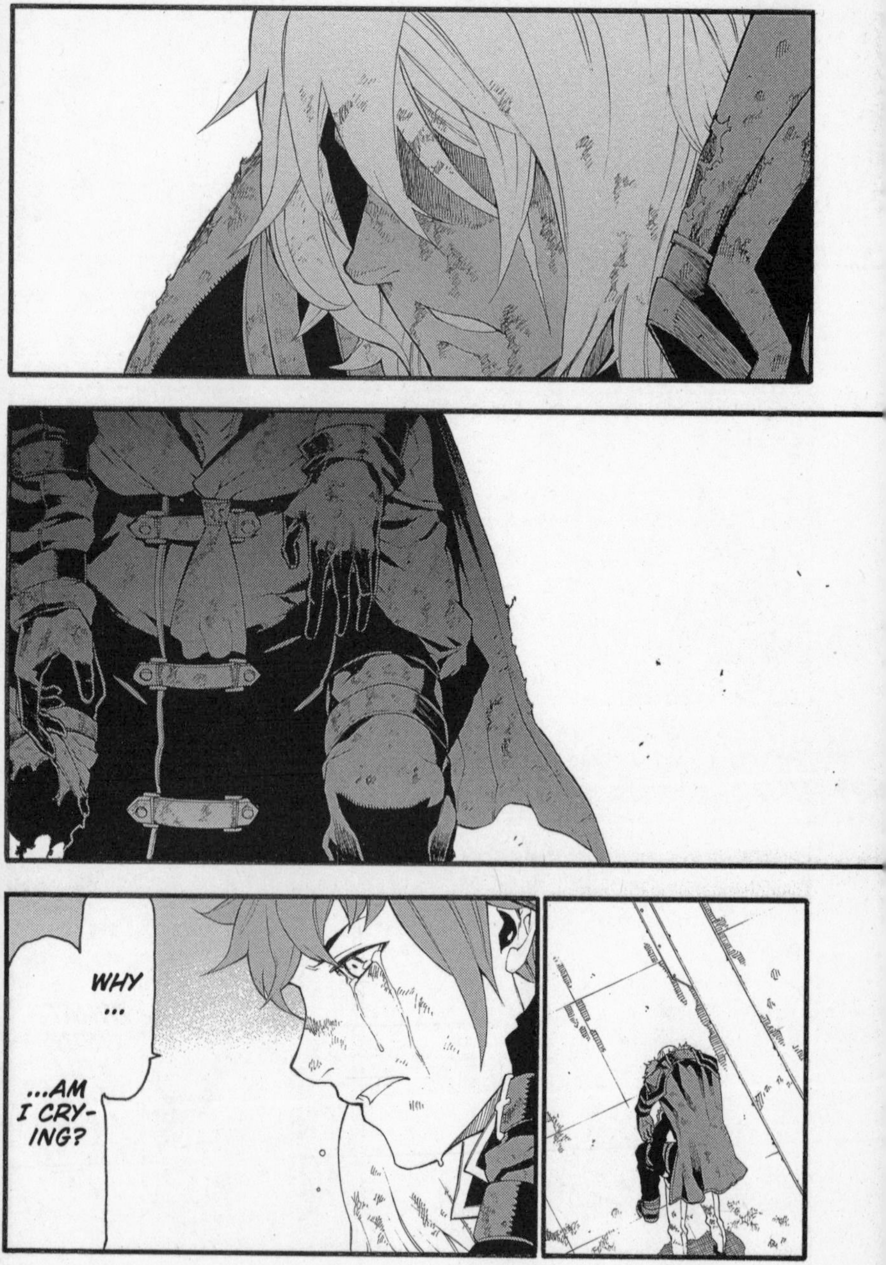
WHY ...
...AM I CRY-ING?

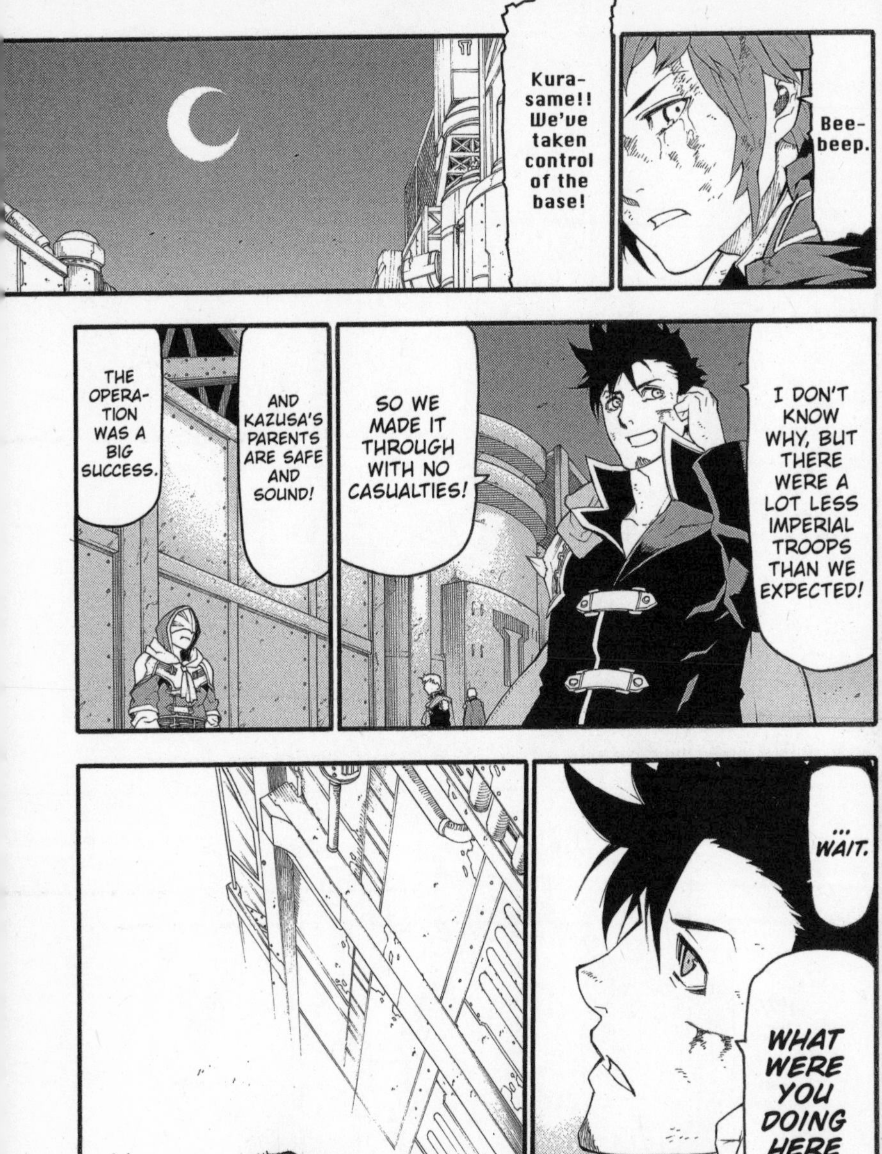
Bee-beep.
Kura-same!! We've taken control of the base!
I DON'T KNOW WHY, BUT THERE WERE A LOT LESS IMPERIAL TROOPS THAN WE EXPECTED!
SO WE MADE IT THROUGH WITH NO CASUALTIES!
AND KAZUSA'S PARENTS ARE SAFE AND SOUND!
THE OPERATION WAS A BIG SUCCESS.
...WAIT.
WHAT WERE YOU DOING HERE AGAIN ...?

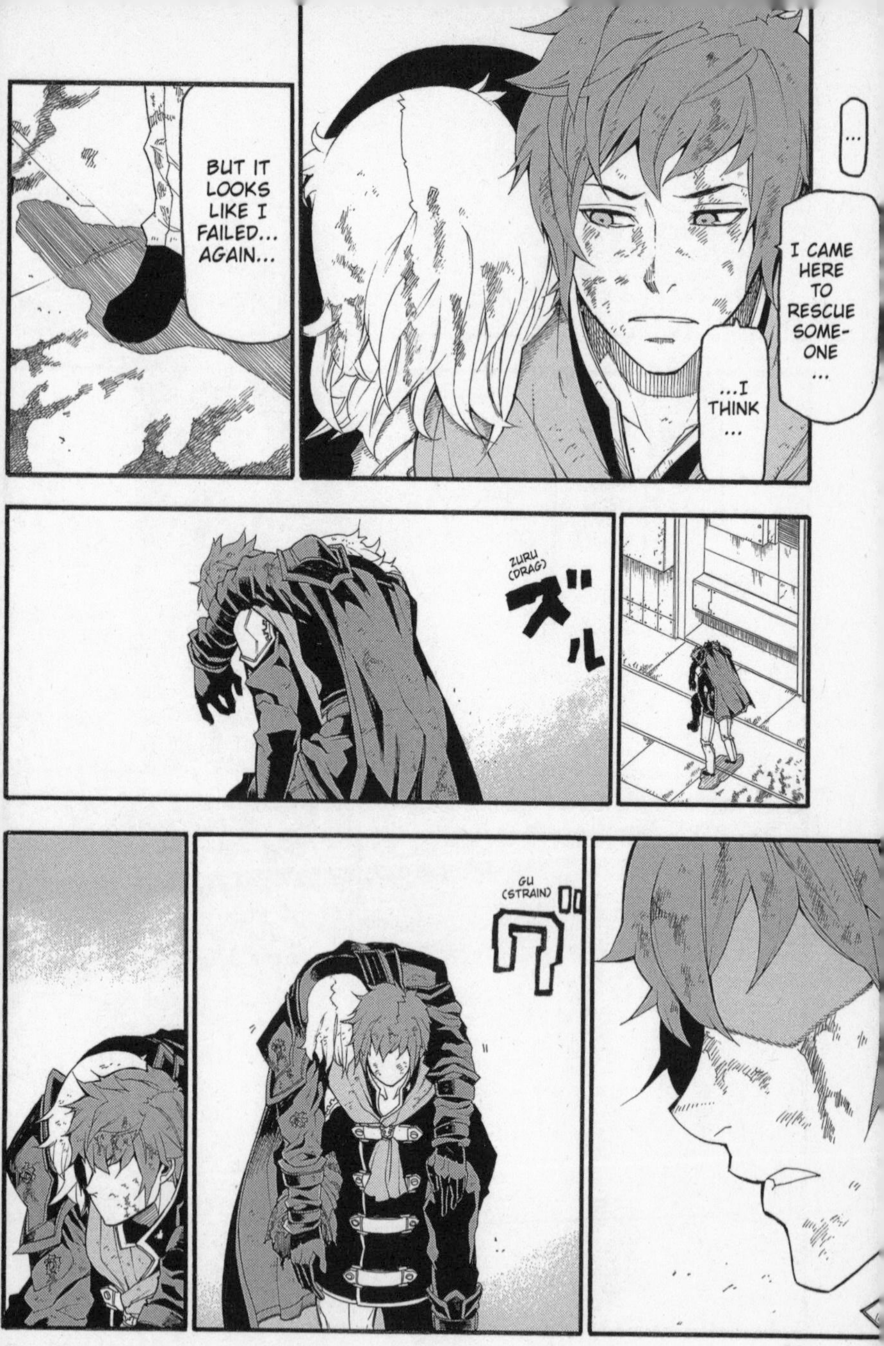
...
I CAME HERE TO RESCUE SOME-ONE...
...I THINK...
BUT IT LOOKS LIKE I FAILED... AGAIN...
ZURU (DRAG)
ズル
GU (STRAIN)
グ

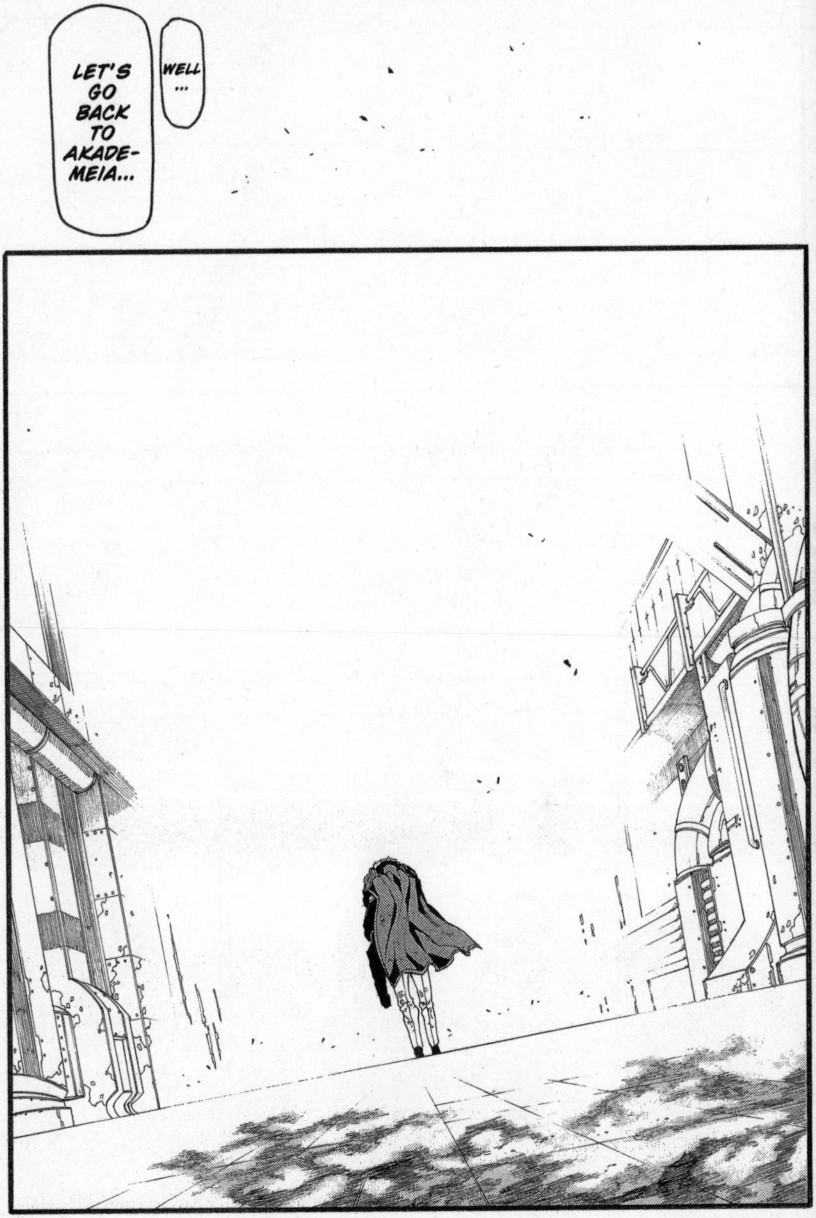
WELL...
LET'S GO BACK TO AKADE-MEIA...

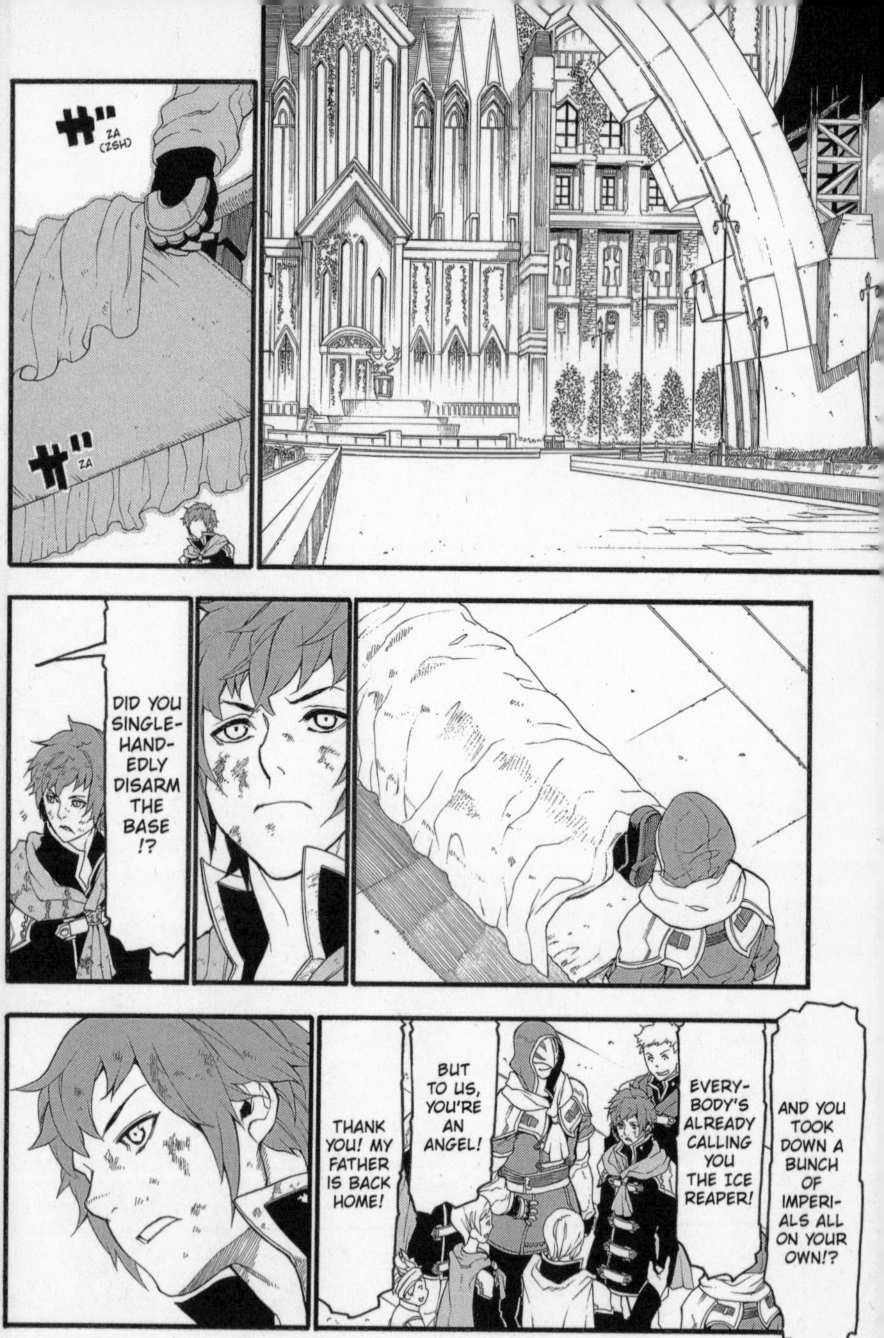
ザッ
ZA (ZSH)
ザッ
ZA
DID YOU SINGLE-HANDEDLY DISARM THE BASE!?
AND YOU TOOK DOWN A BUNCH OF IMPERIALS ALL ON YOUR OWN!?
EVERYBODY'S ALREADY CALLING YOU THE ICE REAPER!
...
BUT TO US, YOU'RE AN ANGEL!
THANK YOU! MY FATHER IS BACK HOME!

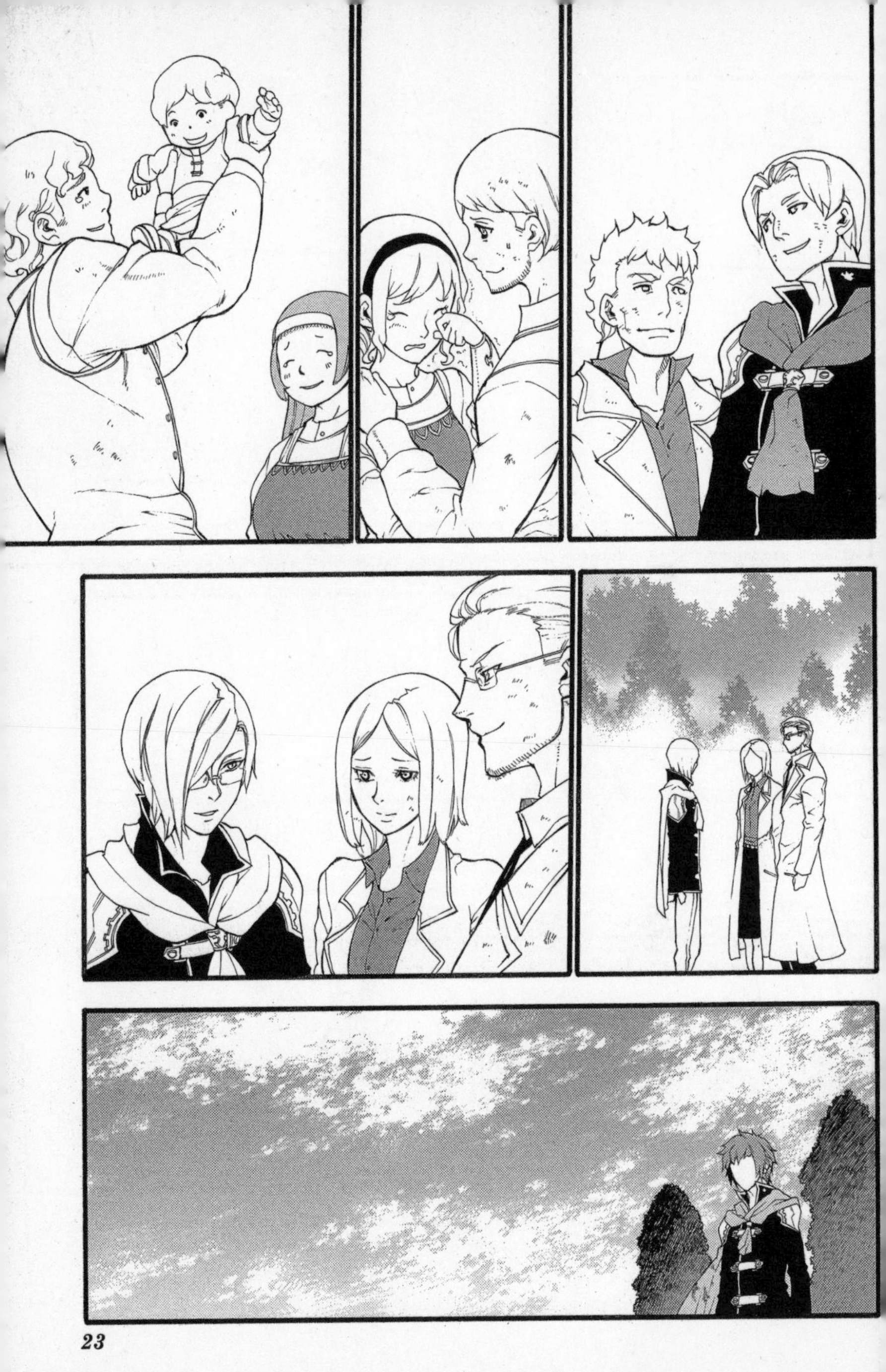

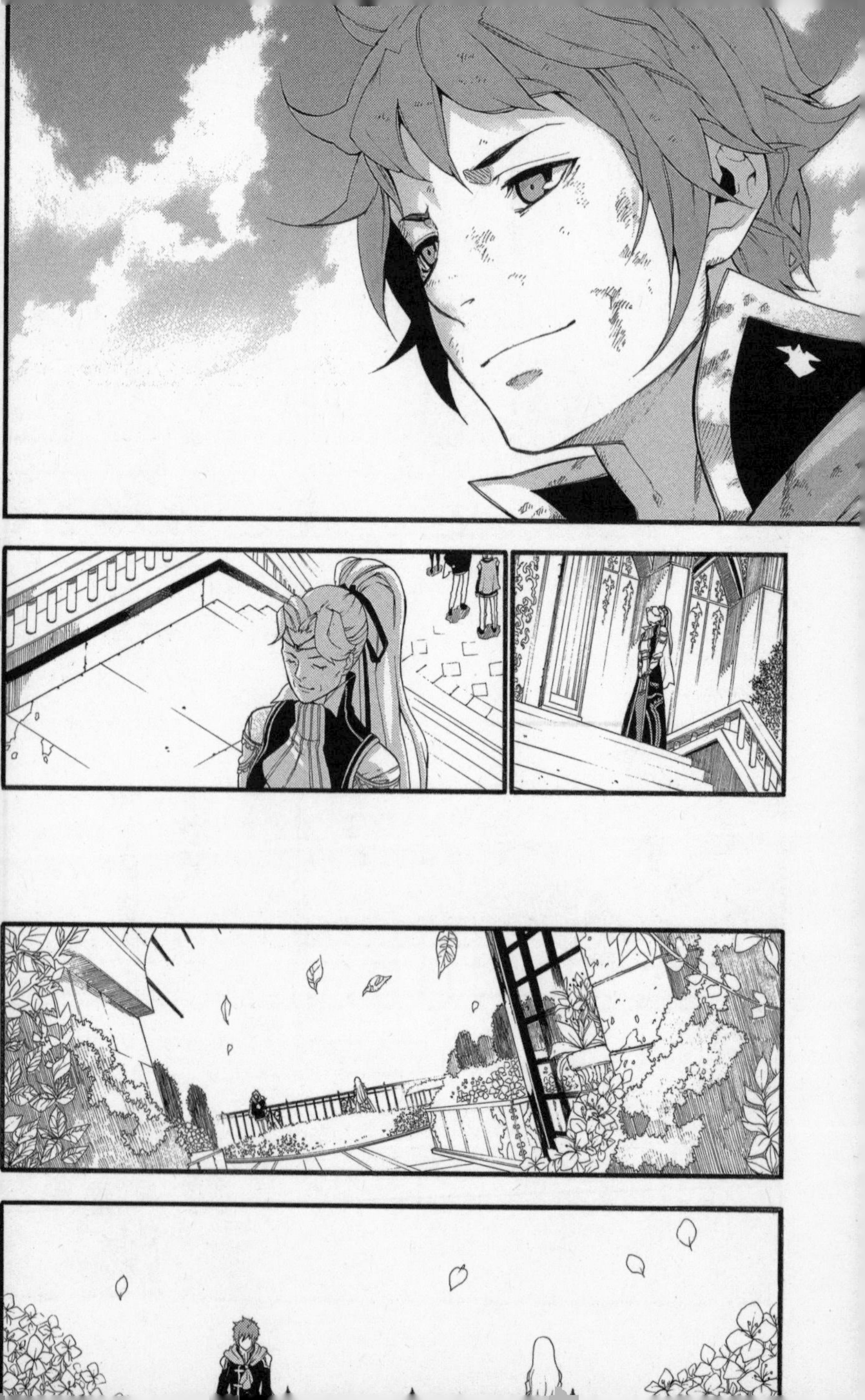

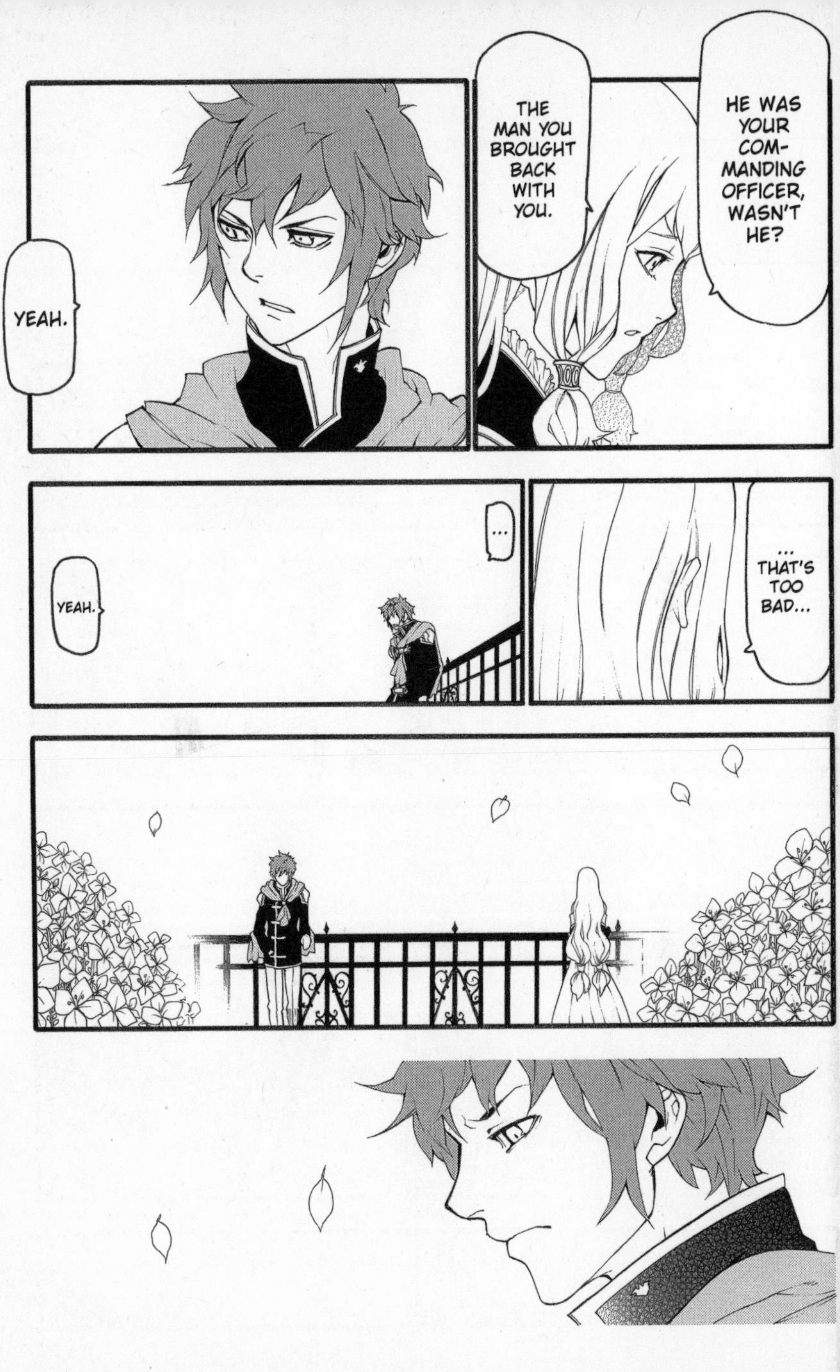
HE WAS YOUR COM-MANDING OFFICER, WASN'T HE?
THE MAN YOU BROUGHT BACK WITH YOU.
YEAH.
... THAT'S TOO BAD...
...
YEAH.

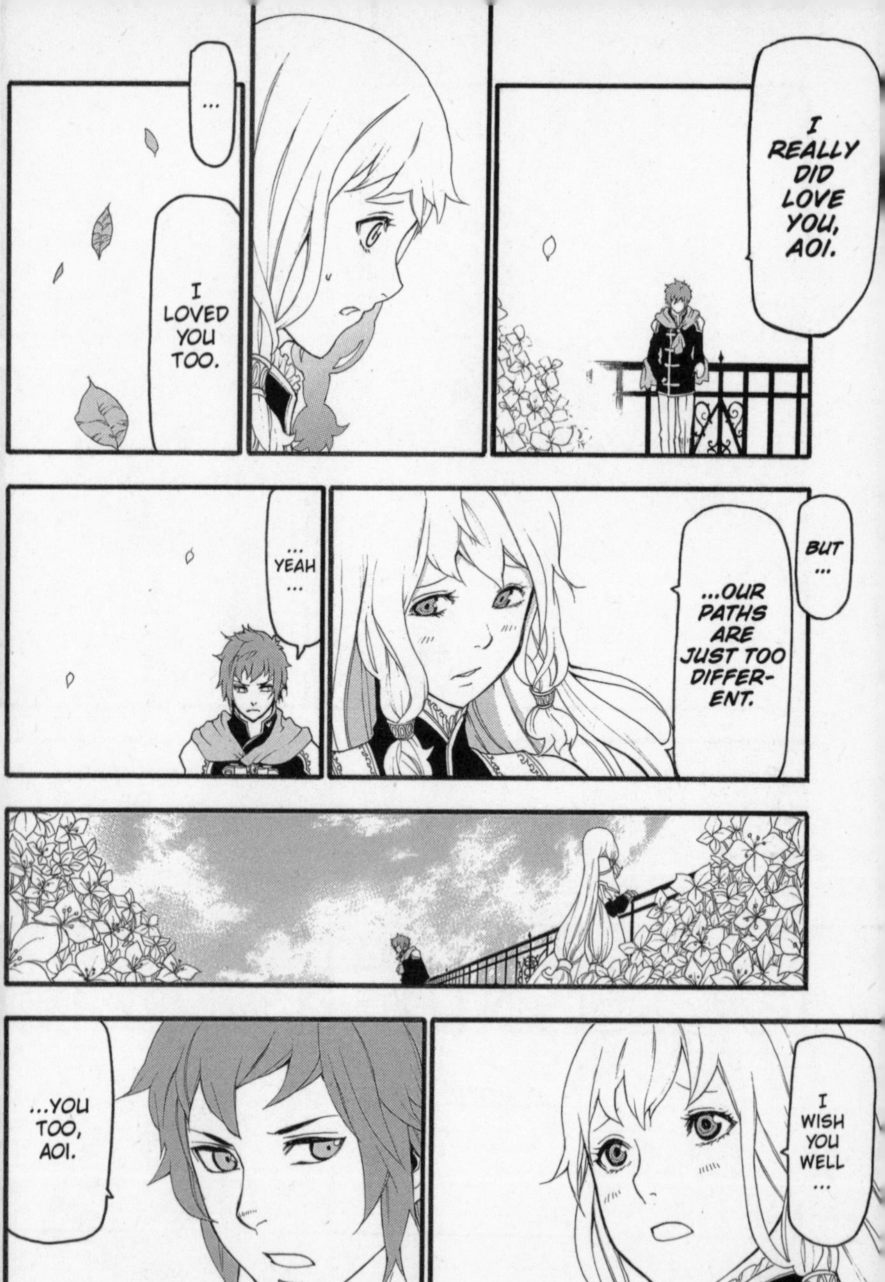
I REALLY DID LOVE YOU, AOI.
...
I LOVED YOU TOO.
BUT ...
...OUR PATHS ARE JUST TOO DIFFER-ENT.
... YEAH ...
I WISH YOU WELL ...
...YOU TOO, AOI.

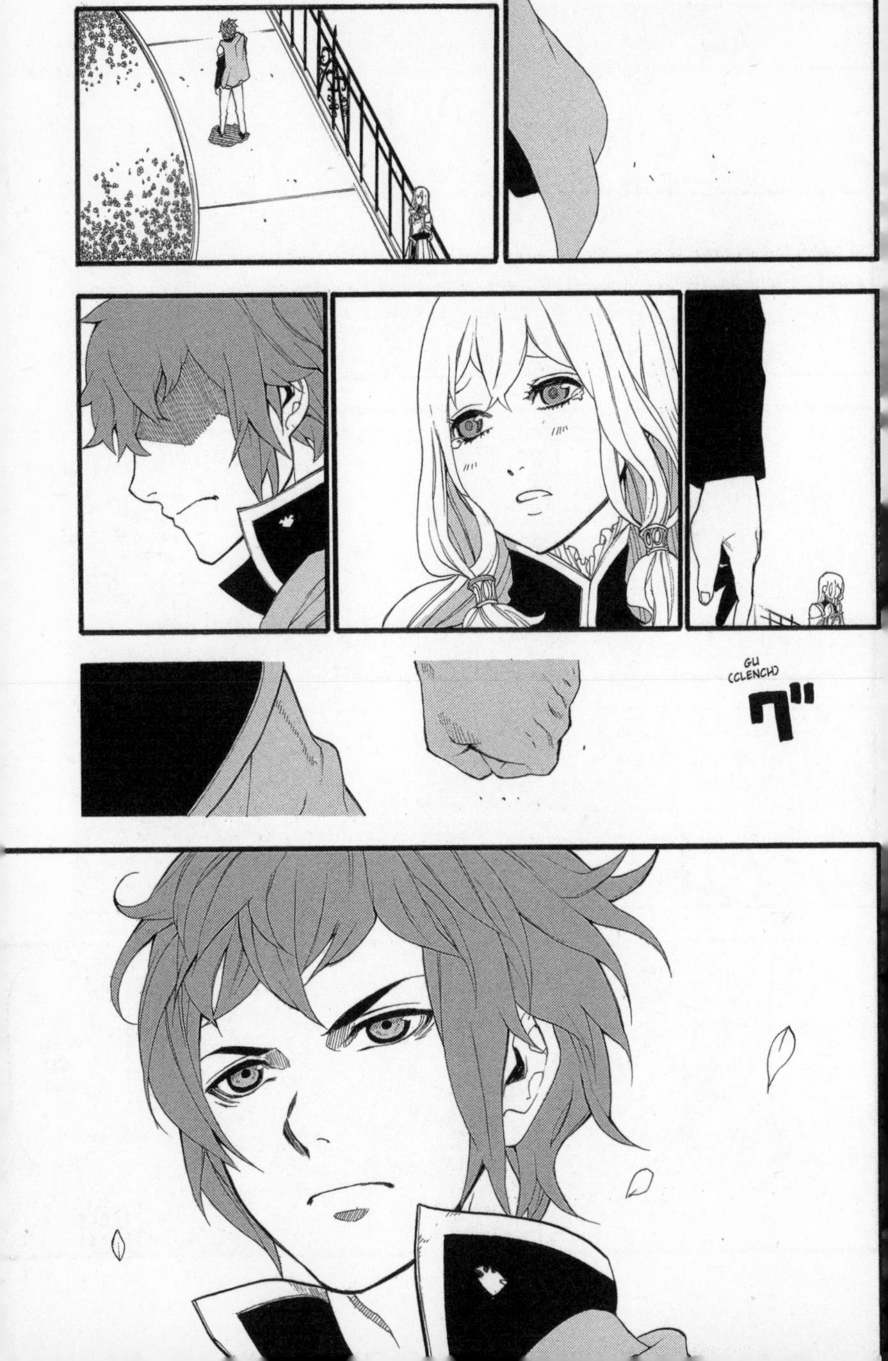
GU
(CLENCH)
グ

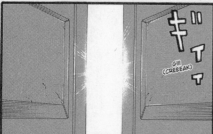

GIII
(CREEEAK)

THE GUEST OF HONOR ISN'T SUPPOSED TO BE LATE.

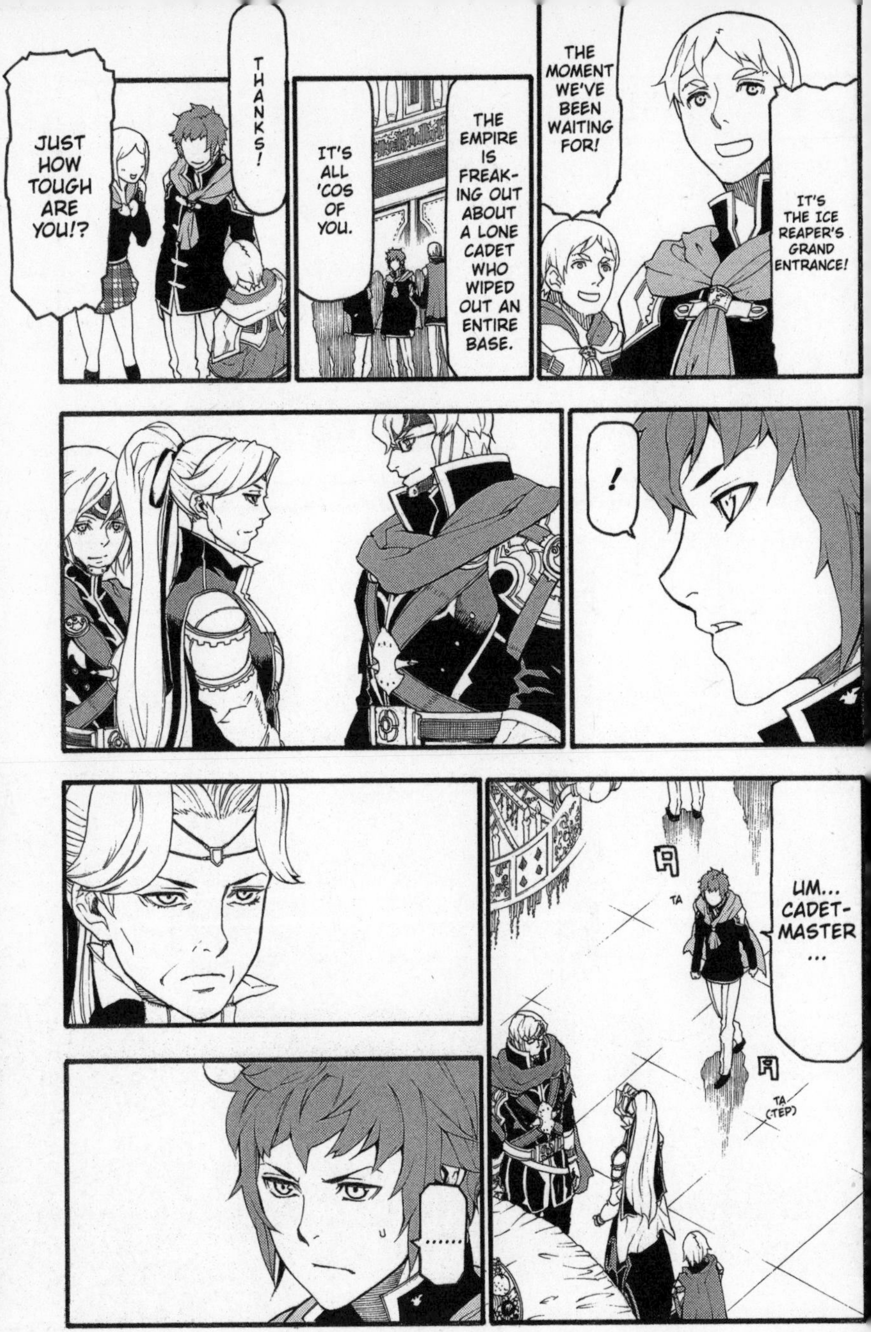
THE MOMENT WE'VE BEEN WAITING FOR!
IT'S THE ICE REAPER'S GRAND ENTRANCE!
THE EMPIRE IS FREAKING OUT ABOUT A LONE CADET WHO WIPED OUT AN ENTIRE BASE.
IT'S ALL 'COS OF YOU.
THANKS!
JUST HOW TOUGH ARE YOU!?
!
TA
UM... CADET-MASTER...
TA (TEP)
......

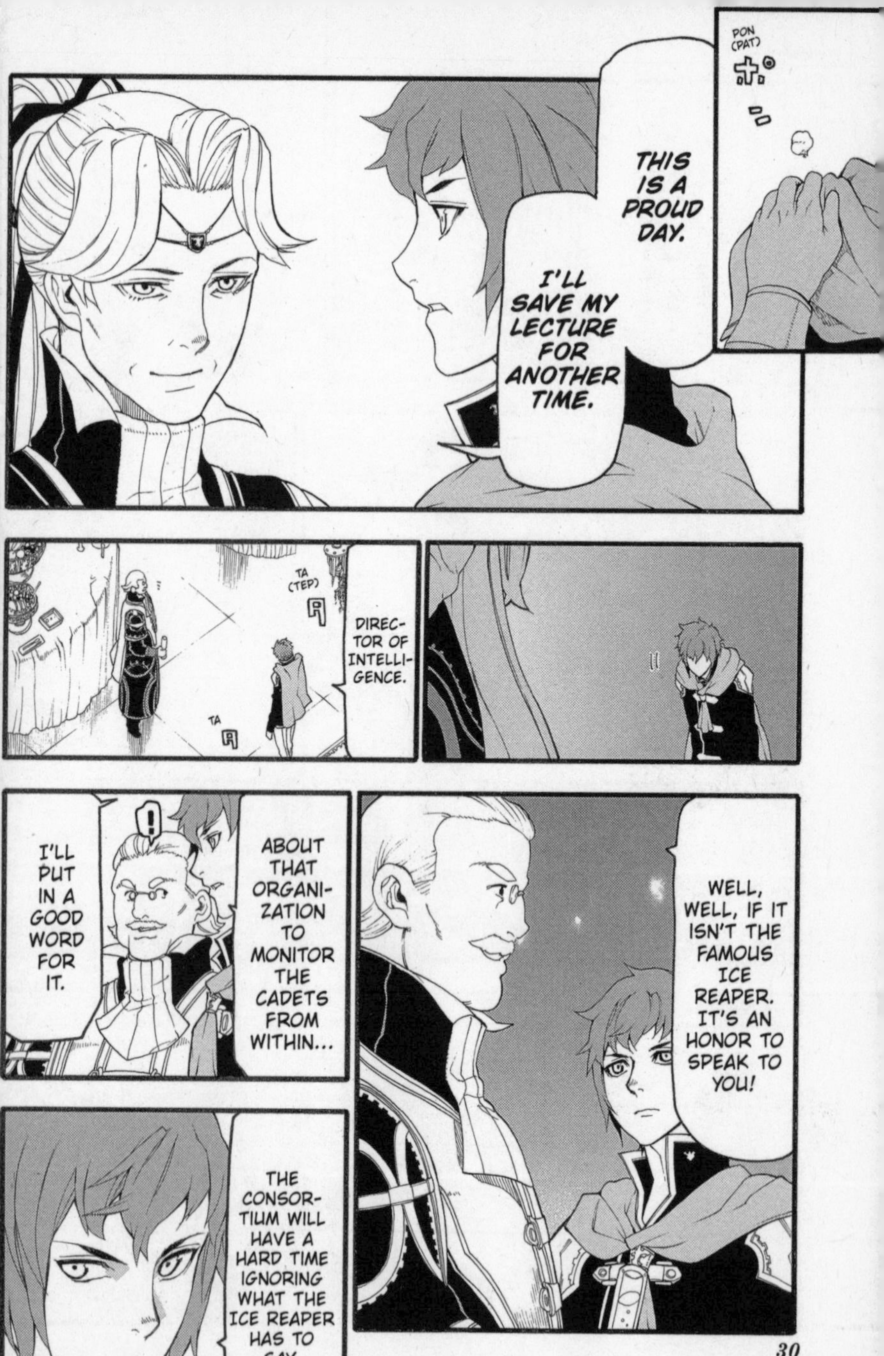
PON (PAT)
THIS IS A PROUD DAY.
I'LL SAVE MY LECTURE FOR ANOTHER TIME.
TA (TEP)
DIRECTOR OF INTELLIGENCE.
TA
WELL, WELL, IF IT ISN'T THE FAMOUS ICE REAPER. IT'S AN HONOR TO SPEAK TO YOU!
ABOUT THAT ORGANIZATION TO MONITOR THE CADETS FROM WITHIN...
I'LL PUT IN A GOOD WORD FOR IT.
THE CONSORTIUM WILL HAVE A HARD TIME IGNORING WHAT THE ICE REAPER HAS TO SAY.

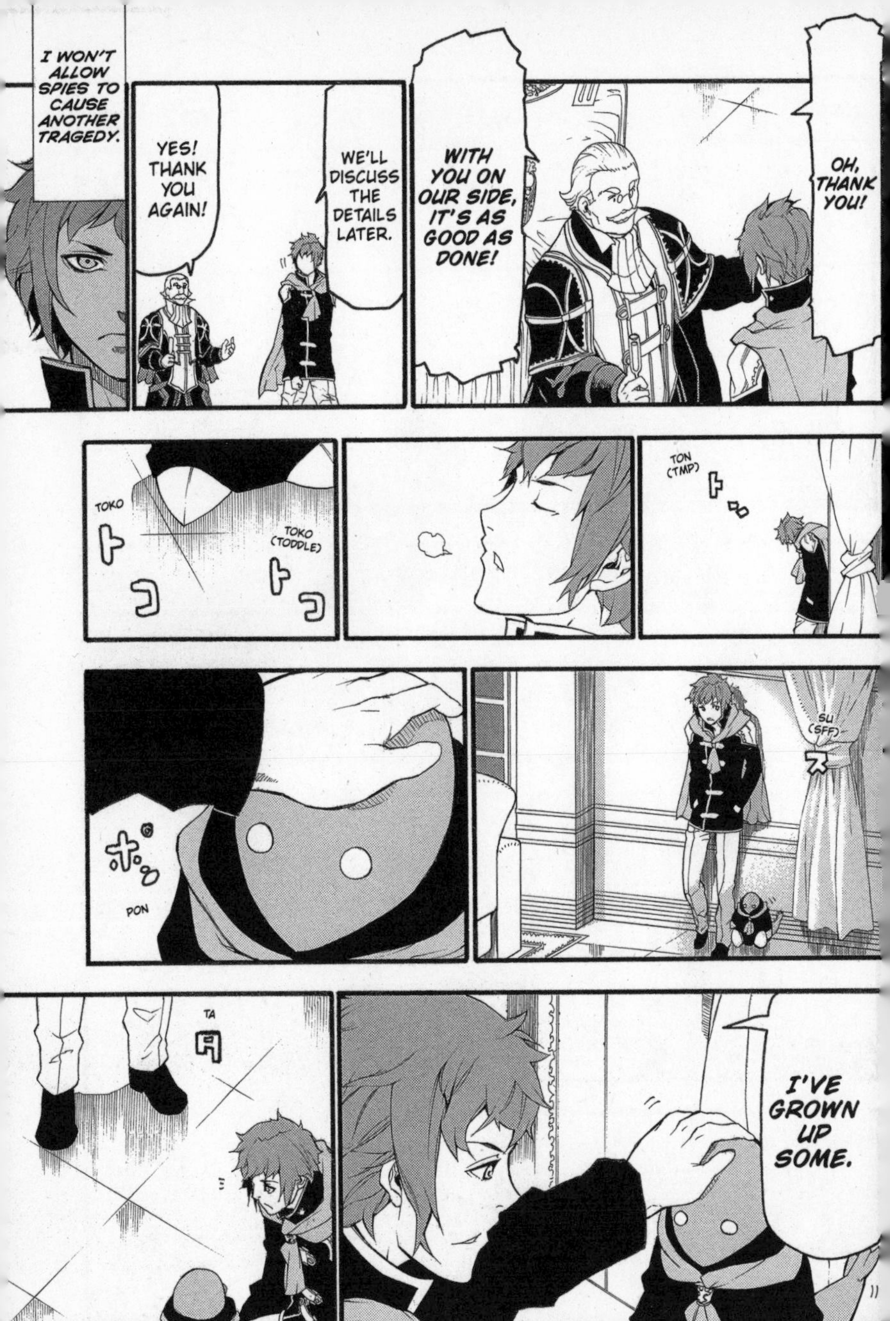
OH, THANK YOU!
WITH YOU ON OUR SIDE, IT'S AS GOOD AS DONE!
WE'LL DISCUSS THE DETAILS LATER.
YES! THANK YOU AGAIN!
I WON'T ALLOW SPIES TO CAUSE ANOTHER TRAGEDY.
TON (TMP)
TOKO
TOKO (TODDLE)
SU (SFF)
PON
I'VE GROWN UP SOME.
TA

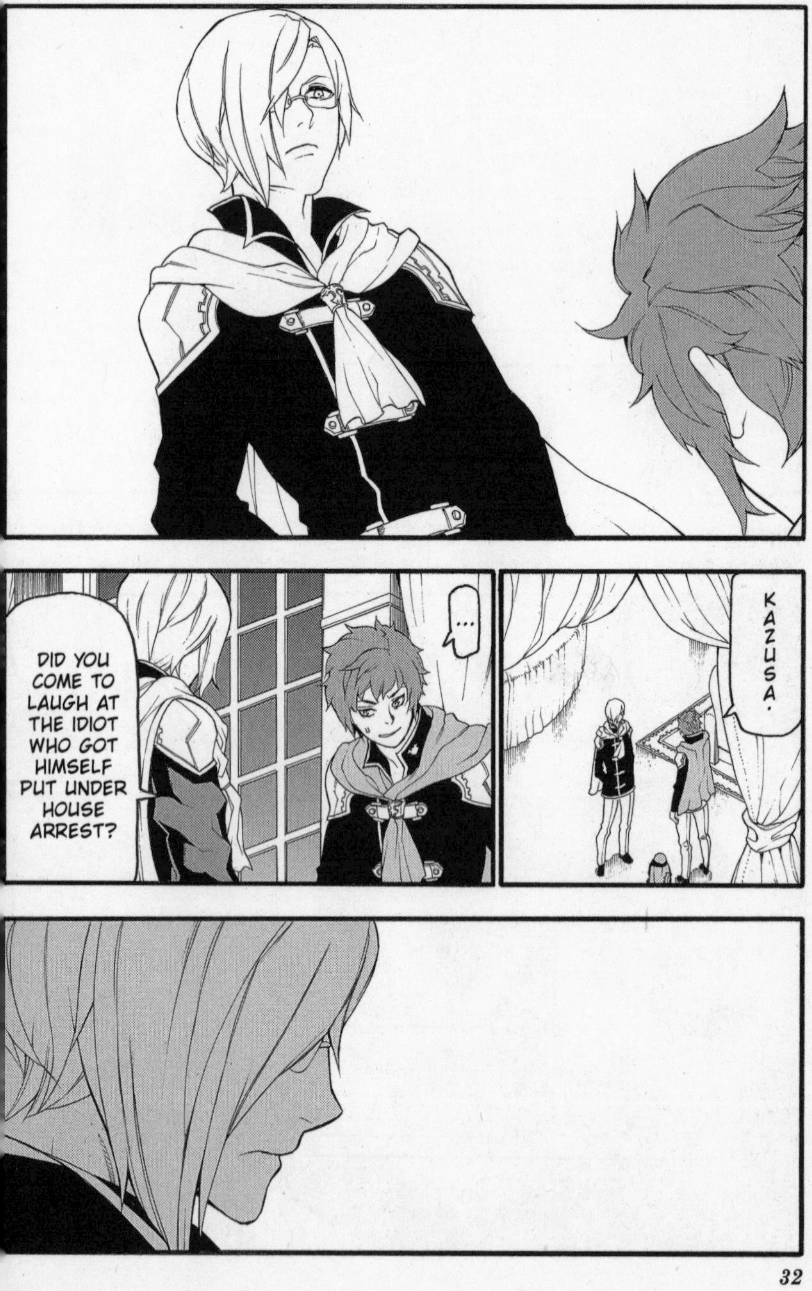
KAZUSA.
...
DID YOU COME TO LAUGH AT THE IDIOT WHO GOT HIMSELF PUT UNDER HOUSE ARREST?

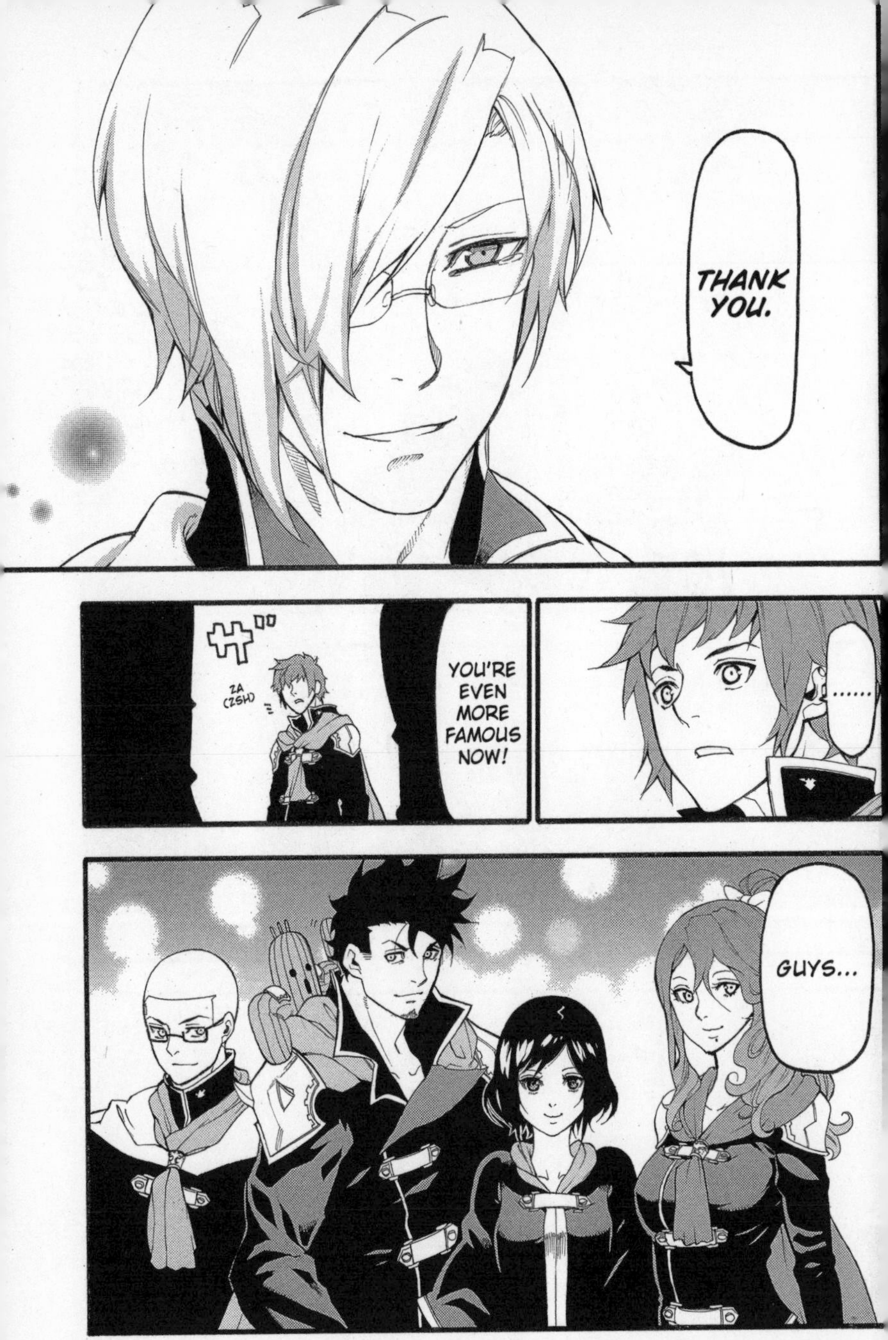
THANK YOU.
......
YOU'RE EVEN MORE FAMOUS NOW!
ZA (ZSH)
GUYS...

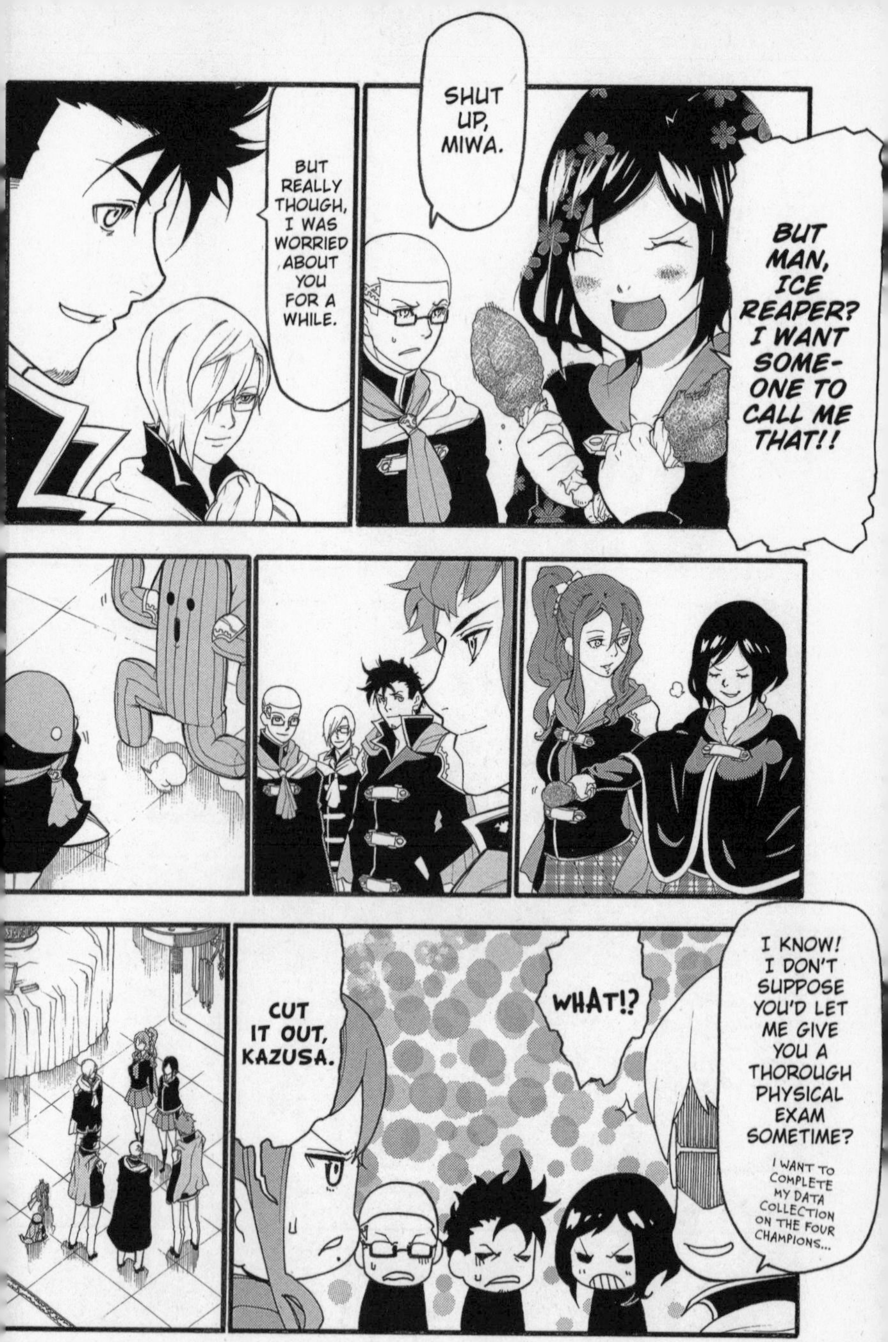
BUT MAN, ICE REAPER? I WANT SOMEONE TO CALL ME THAT!!
SHUT UP, MIWA.
BUT REALLY THOUGH, I WAS WORRIED ABOUT YOU FOR A WHILE.
I KNOW! I DON'T SUPPOSE YOU'D LET ME GIVE YOU A THOROUGH PHYSICAL EXAM SOMETIME?
I WANT TO COMPLETE MY DATA COLLECTION ON THE FOUR CHAMPIONS...
WHAT!?
CUT IT OUT, KAZUSA.

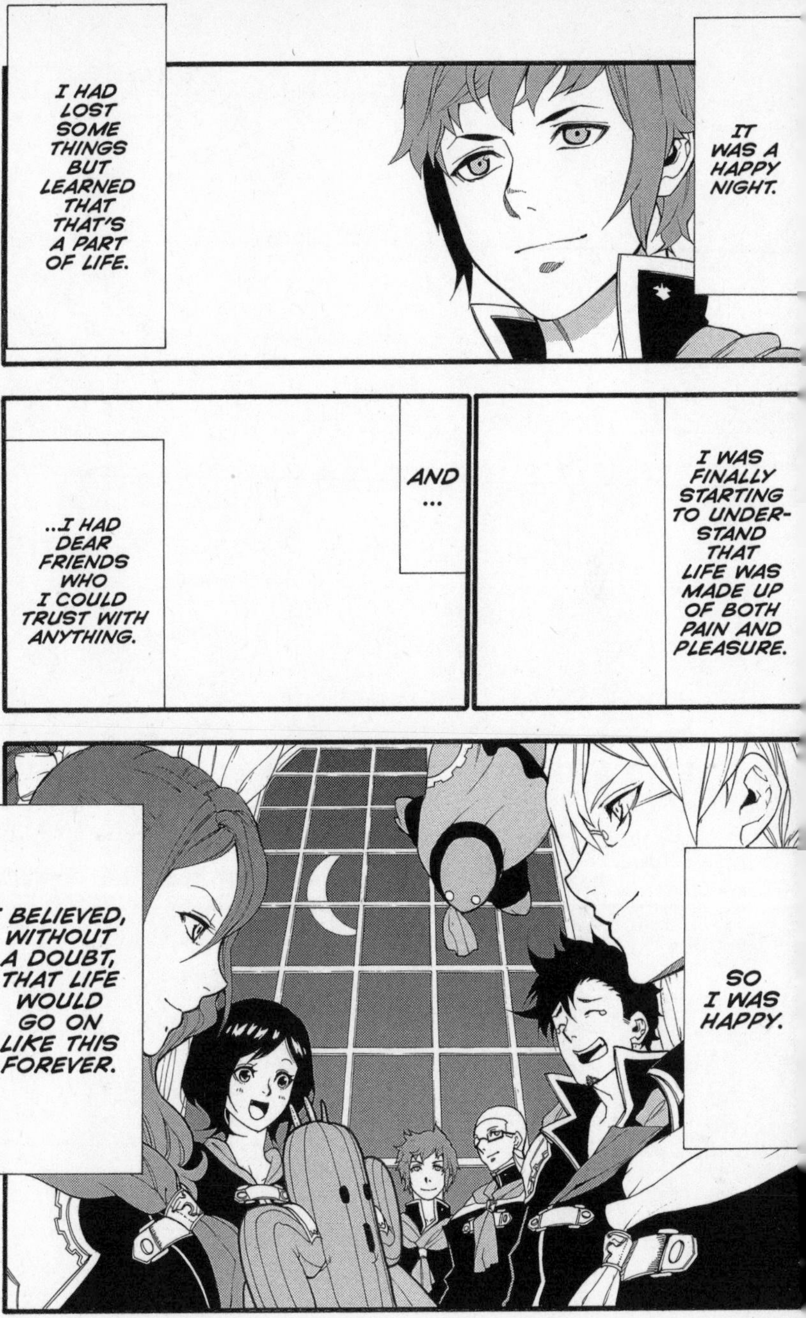
IT WAS A HAPPY NIGHT.
I HAD LOST SOME THINGS BUT LEARNED THAT THAT'S A PART OF LIFE.
I WAS FINALLY STARTING TO UNDER-STAND THAT LIFE WAS MADE UP OF BOTH PAIN AND PLEASURE.
AND...
...I HAD DEAR FRIENDS WHO I COULD TRUST WITH ANYTHING.
SO I WAS HAPPY.
I BELIEVED, WITHOUT A DOUBT, THAT LIFE WOULD GO ON LIKE THIS FOREVER.

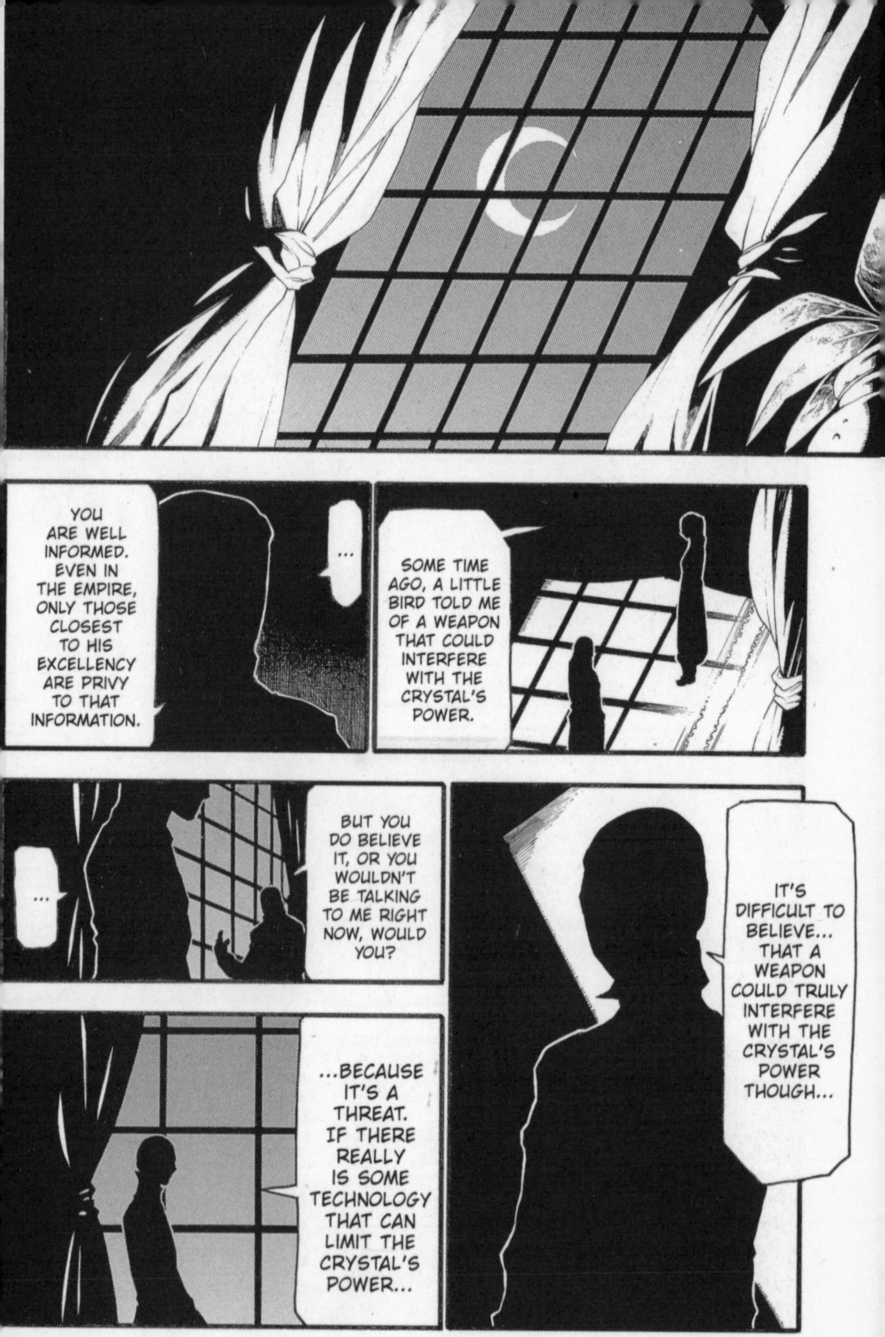
SOME TIME AGO, A LITTLE BIRD TOLD ME OF A WEAPON THAT COULD INTERFERE WITH THE CRYSTAL'S POWER.
...
YOU ARE WELL INFORMED. EVEN IN THE EMPIRE, ONLY THOSE CLOSEST TO HIS EXCELLENCY ARE PRIVY TO THAT INFORMATION.
IT'S DIFFICULT TO BELIEVE... THAT A WEAPON COULD TRULY INTERFERE WITH THE CRYSTAL'S POWER THOUGH...
BUT YOU DO BELIEVE IT, OR YOU WOULDN'T BE TALKING TO ME RIGHT NOW, WOULD YOU?
...
...BECAUSE IT'S A THREAT. IF THERE REALLY IS SOME TECHNOLOGY THAT CAN LIMIT THE CRYSTAL'S POWER...

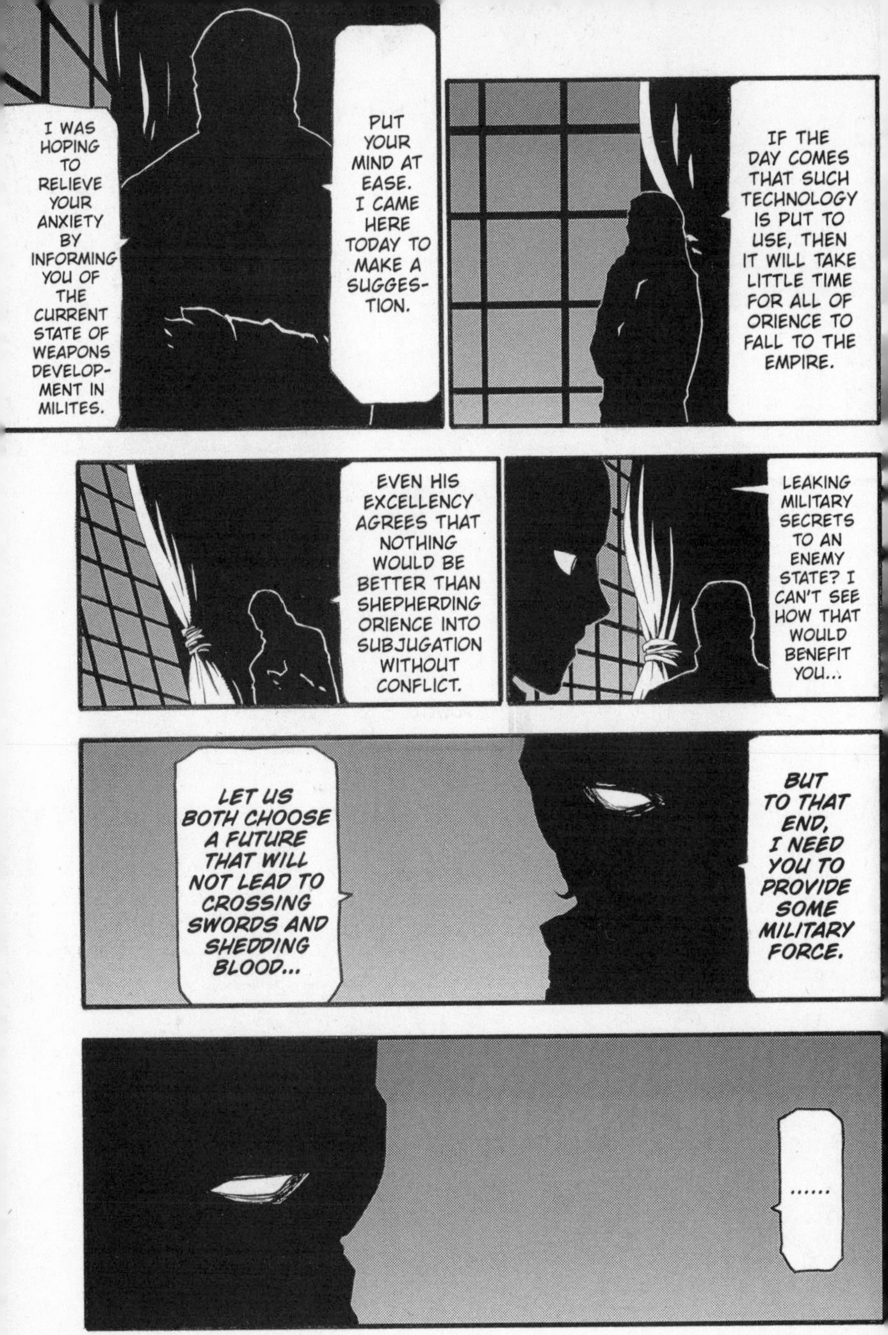
IF THE DAY COMES THAT SUCH TECHNOLOGY IS PUT TO USE, THEN IT WILL TAKE LITTLE TIME FOR ALL OF ORIENCE TO FALL TO THE EMPIRE.
PUT YOUR MIND AT EASE. I CAME HERE TODAY TO MAKE A SUGGES-TION.
I WAS HOPING TO RELIEVE YOUR ANXIETY BY INFORMING YOU OF THE CURRENT STATE OF WEAPONS DEVELOP-MENT IN MILITES.
LEAKING MILITARY SECRETS TO AN ENEMY STATE? I CAN'T SEE HOW THAT WOULD BENEFIT YOU...
EVEN HIS EXCELLENCY AGREES THAT NOTHING WOULD BE BETTER THAN SHEPHERDING ORIENCE INTO SUBJUGATION WITHOUT CONFLICT.
BUT TO THAT END, I NEED YOU TO PROVIDE SOME MILITARY FORCE.
LET US BOTH CHOOSE A FUTURE THAT WILL NOT LEAD TO CROSSING SWORDS AND SHEDDING BLOOD...
......

...I'M SORRY...

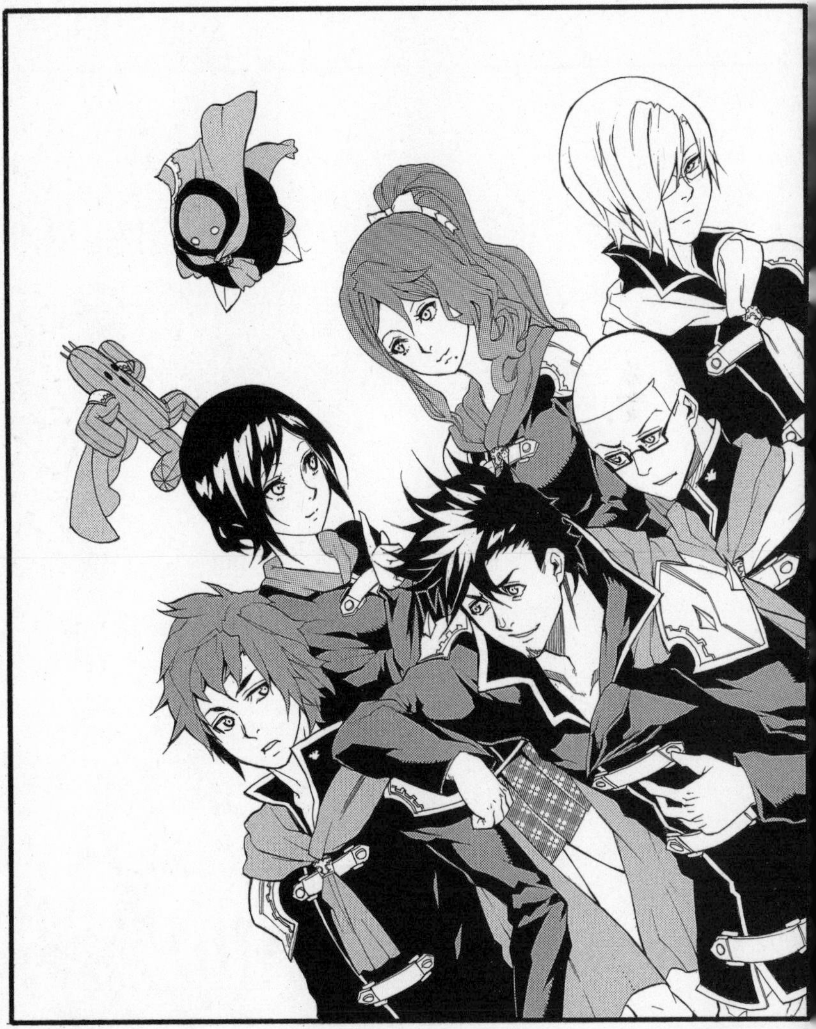

FINAL FANTASY 零式 TYPE-0™

SIDE STORY

The Ice Reaper

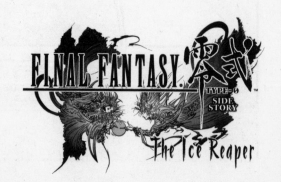

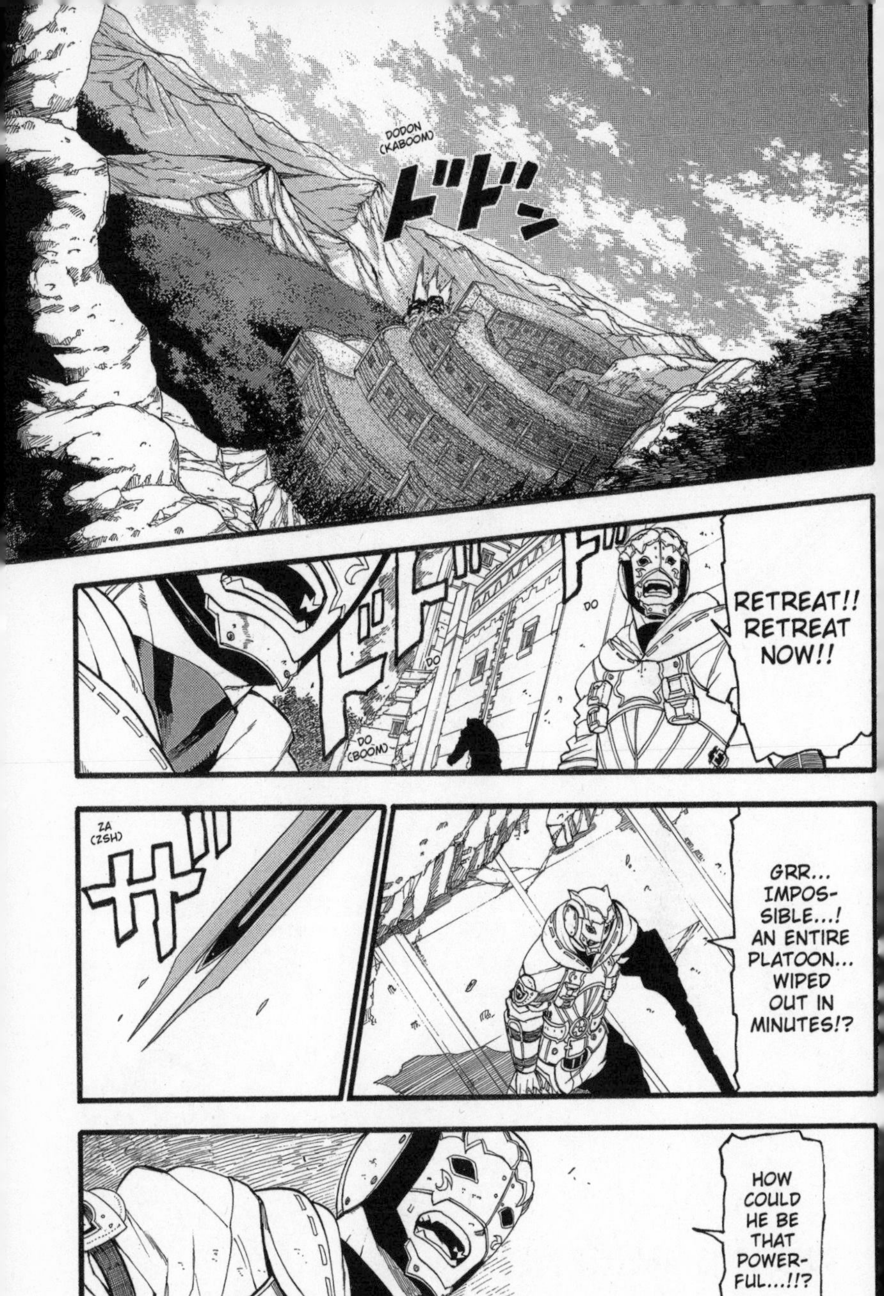
DODON (KABOOM)
RETREAT!! RETREAT NOW!!
DO
DO
DO (BOOM)
GRR... IMPOSSIBLE...! AN ENTIRE PLATOON... WIPED OUT IN MINUTES!?
ZA (ZSH)
HOW COULD HE BE THAT POWERFUL...!!?

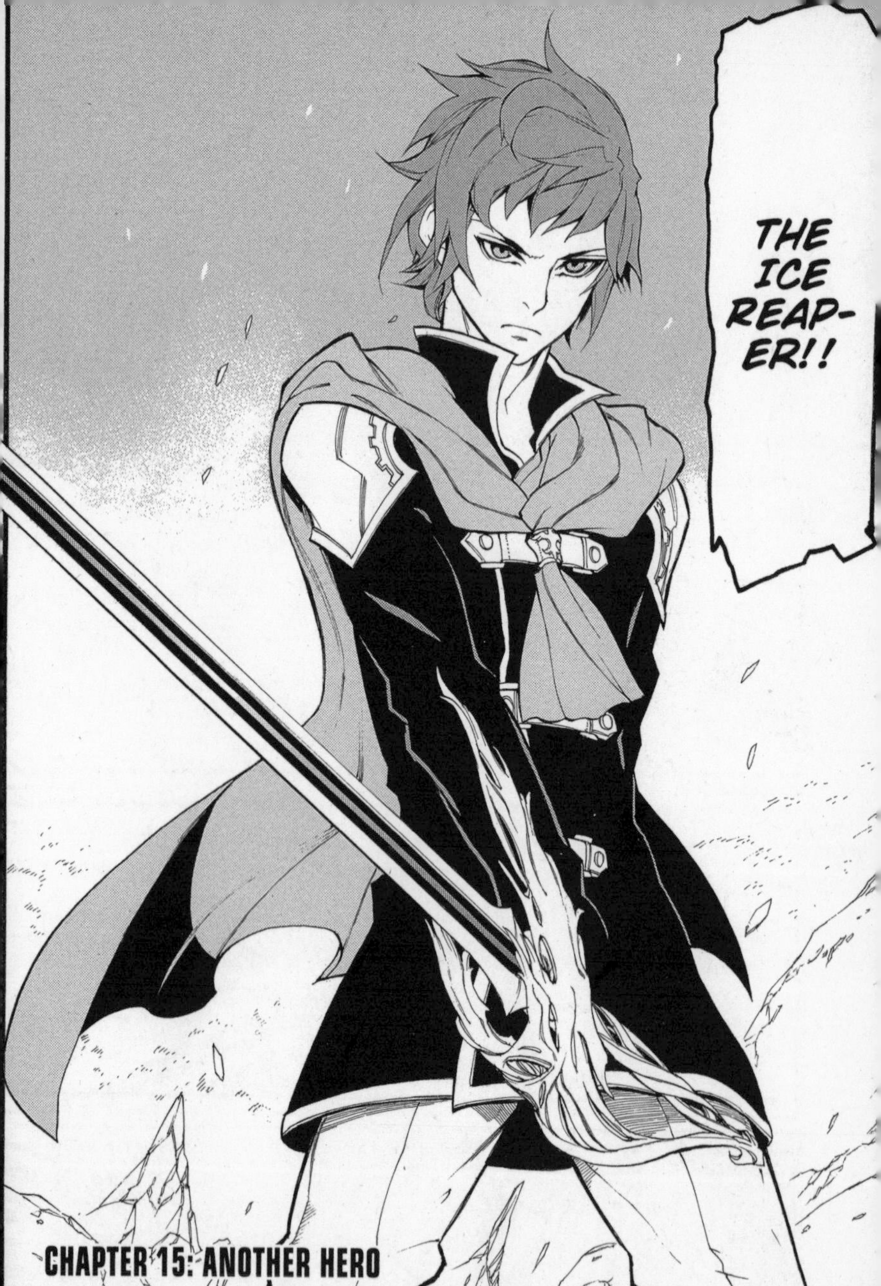
THE ICE REAP-ER!!

CHAPTER 15: ANOTHER HERO

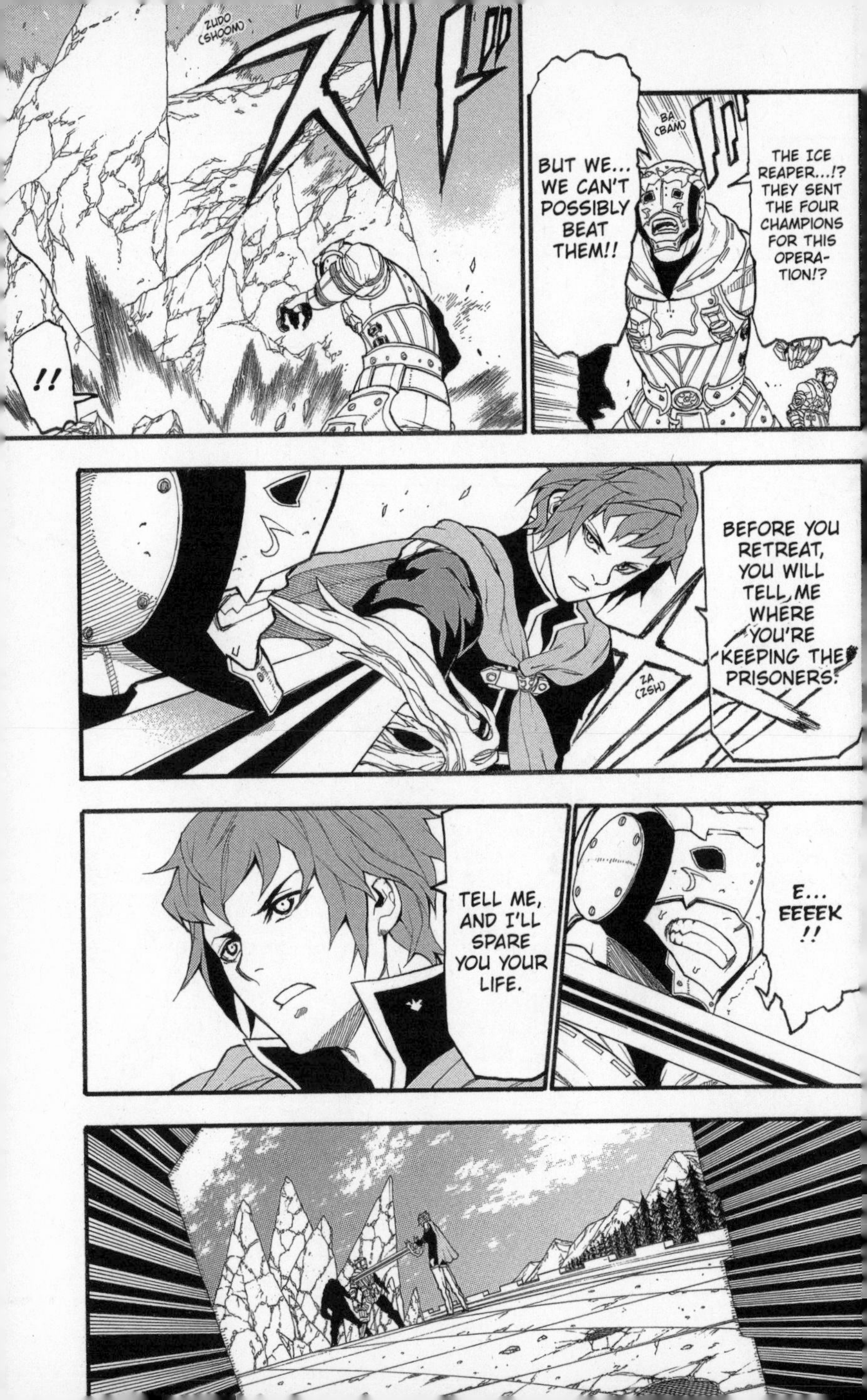
BA (BAM)
THE ICE REAPER...!? THEY SENT THE FOUR CHAMPIONS FOR THIS OPERATION!?
BUT WE... WE CAN'T POSSIBLY BEAT THEM!!
ZUDO (SHOOM)
!!
BEFORE YOU RETREAT, YOU WILL TELL ME WHERE YOU'RE KEEPING THE PRISONERS.
ZA (ZSH)
E... EEEEK!!
TELL ME, AND I'LL SPARE YOU YOUR LIFE.

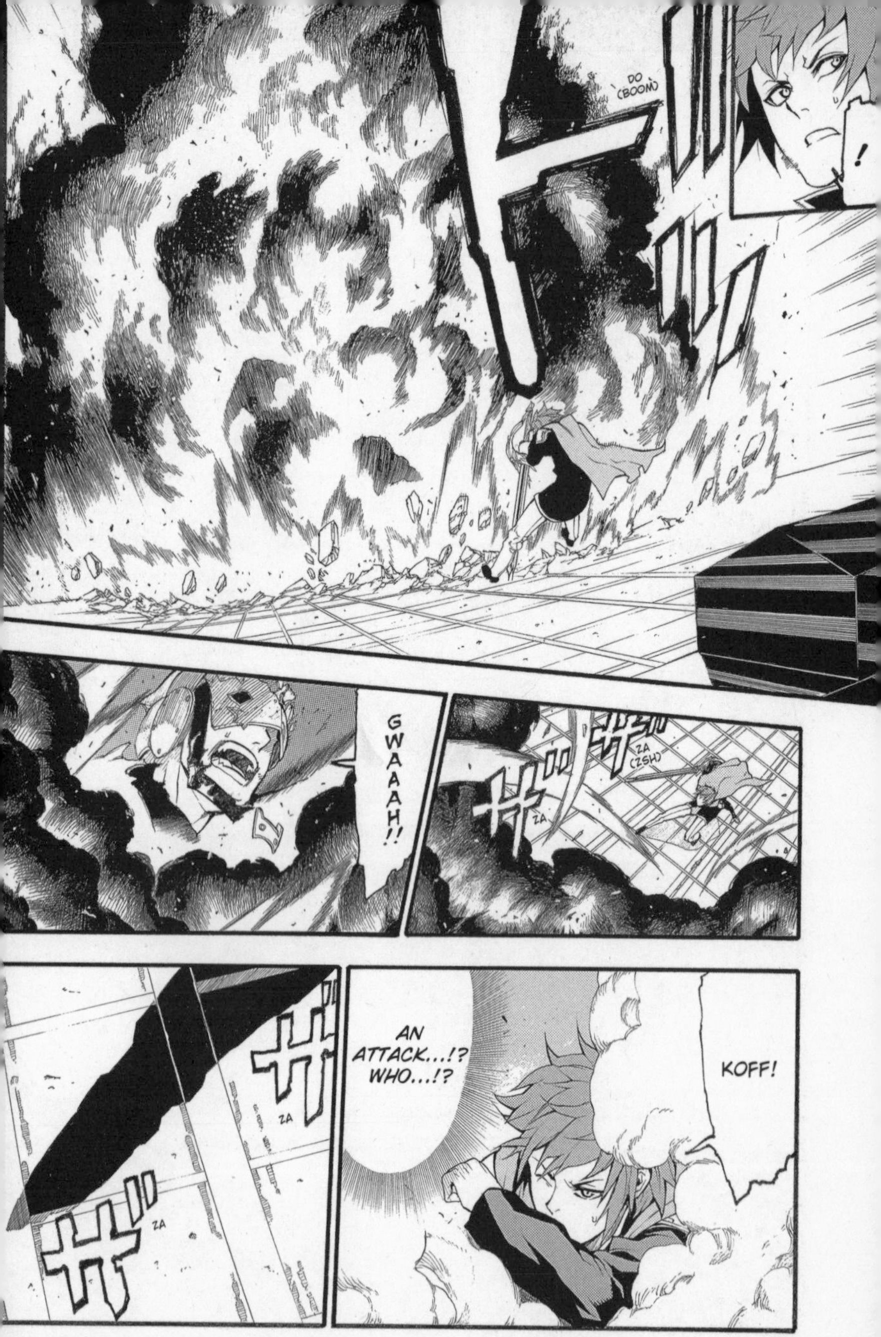
!
DO (BOOM)
GWAAAAH!!
ZA (ZSH)
ZA
KOFF!
AN ATTACK...!? WHO...!?
ZA
ZA

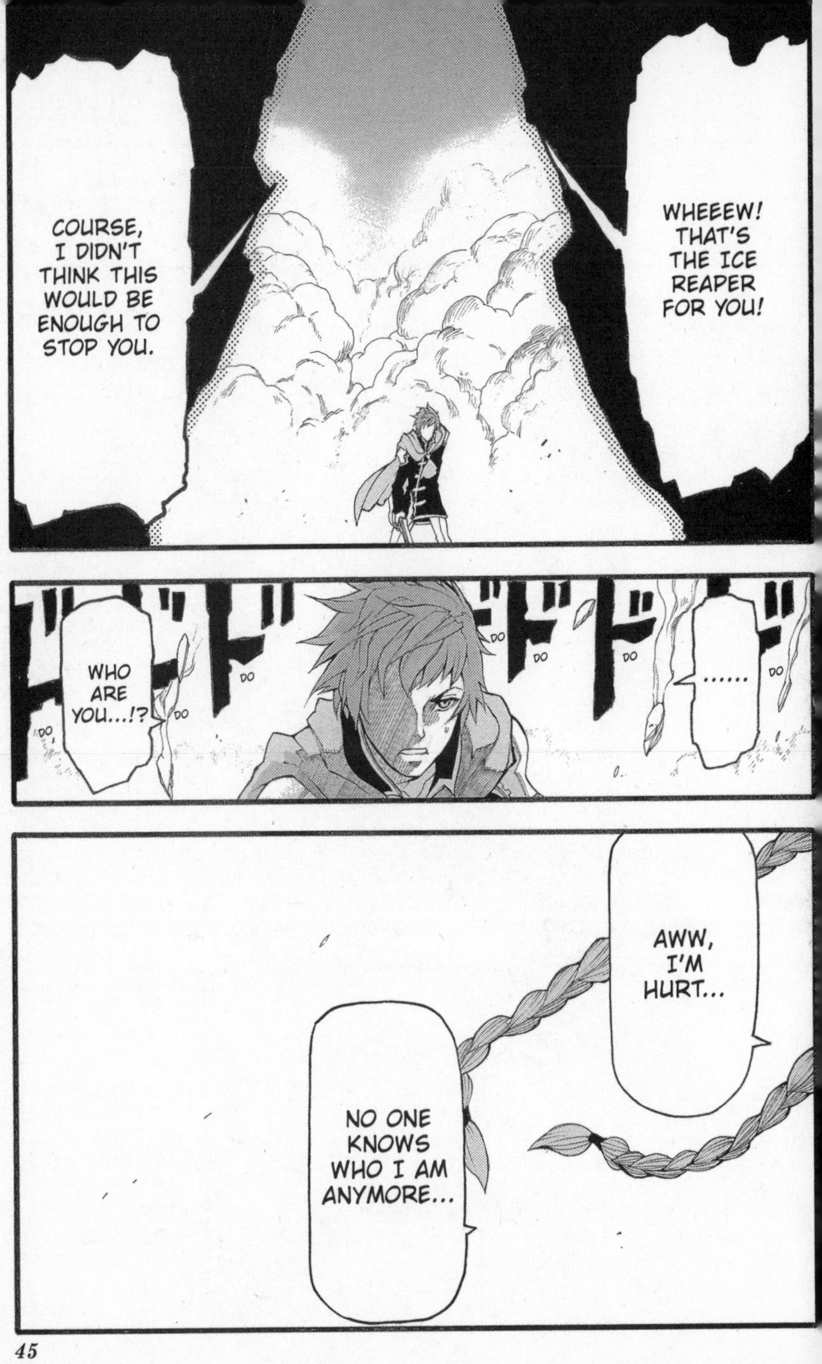
WHEEEW! THAT'S THE ICE REAPER FOR YOU!
COURSE, I DIDN'T THINK THIS WOULD BE ENOUGH TO STOP YOU.
DO
DO
DO
......
DO
DO
WHO ARE YOU...!?
DO
AWW, I'M HURT...
NO ONE KNOWS WHO I AM ANYMORE...

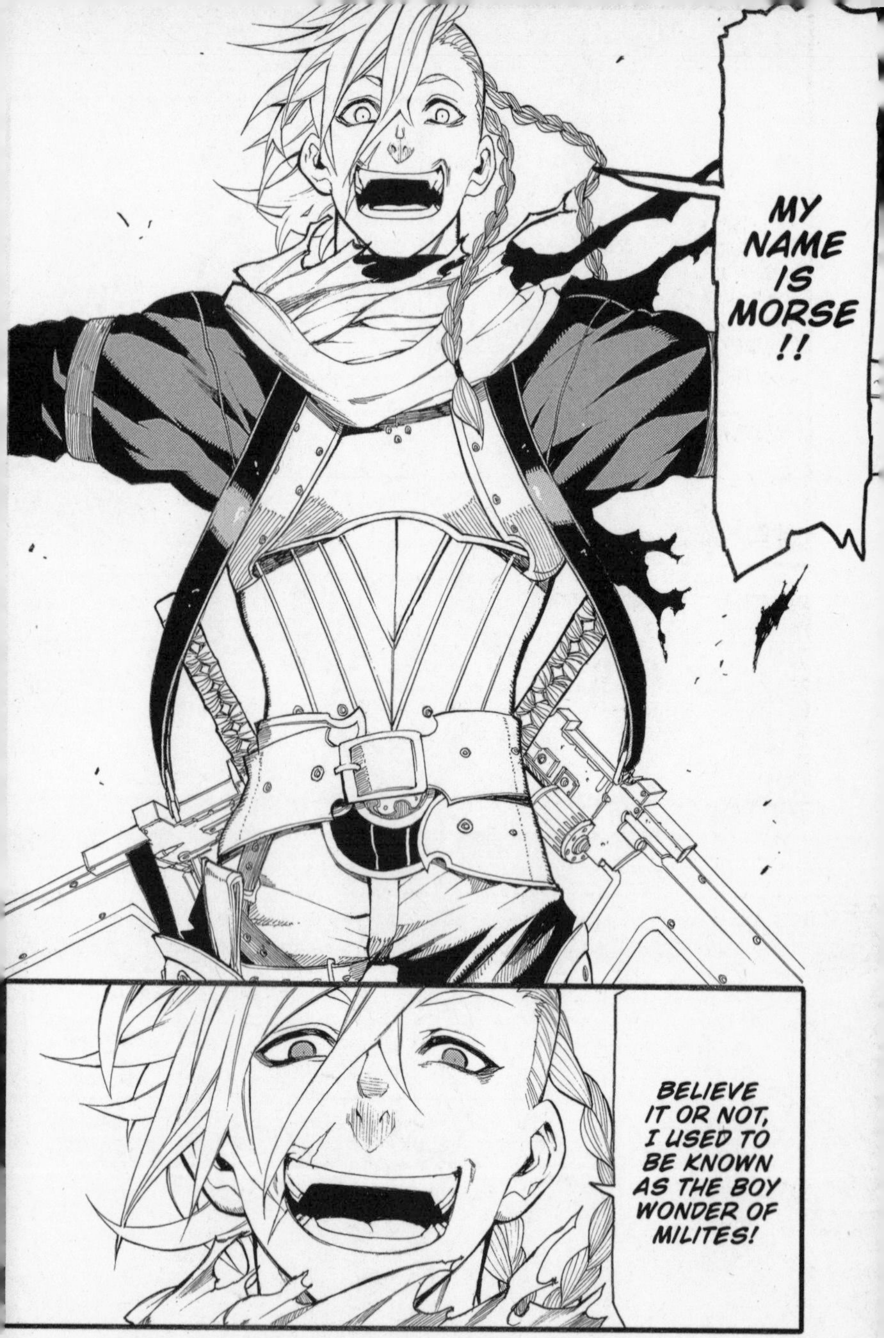
MY NAME IS MORSE!!
BELIEVE IT OR NOT, I USED TO BE KNOWN AS THE BOY WONDER OF MILITES!

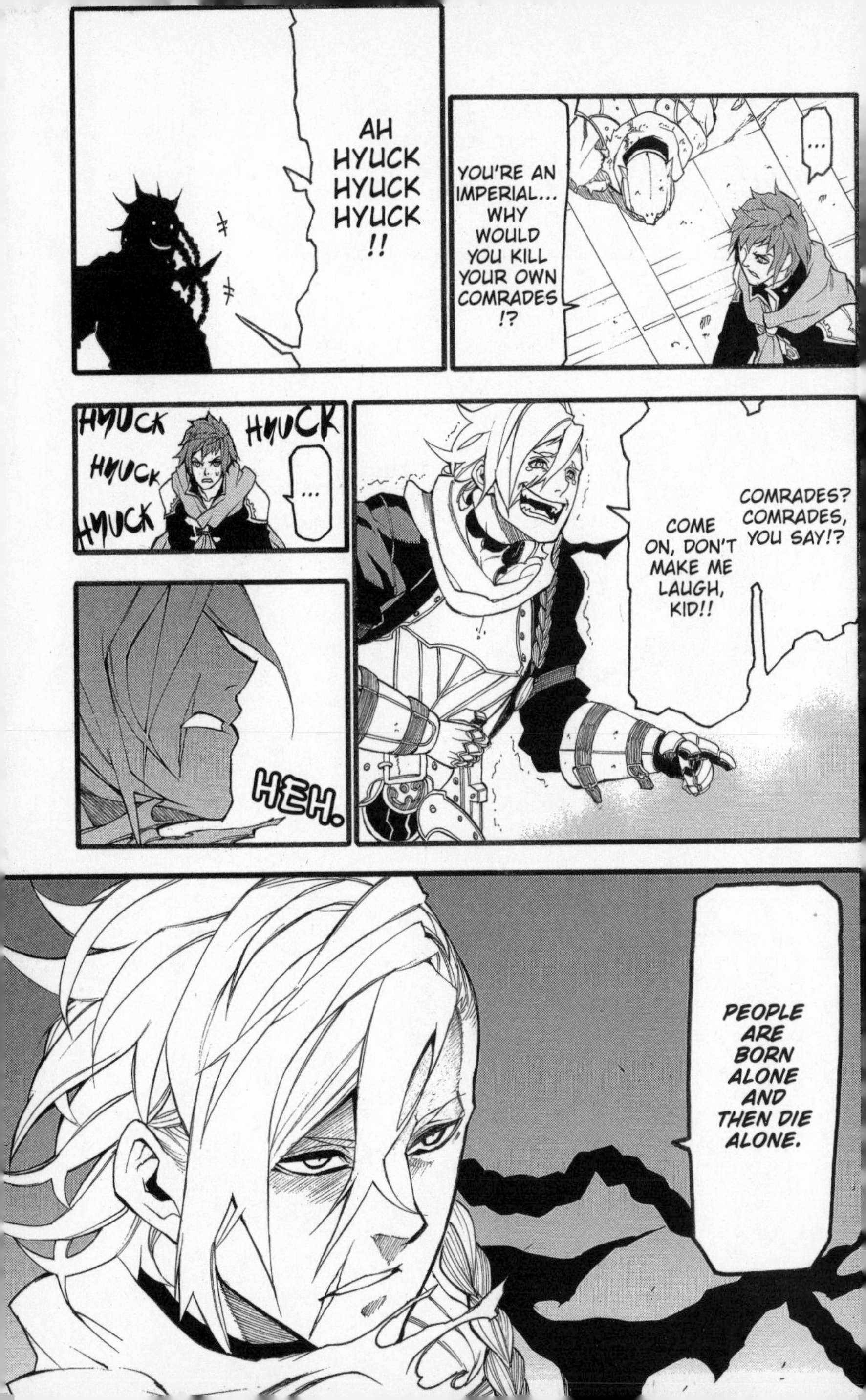
...
YOU'RE AN IMPERIAL... WHY WOULD YOU KILL YOUR OWN COMRADES!?
AH HYUCK HYUCK HYUCK!!
COMRADES? COMRADES, YOU SAY!?
COME ON, DON'T MAKE ME LAUGH, KID!!
HYUCK
HYUCK
HYUCK
HYUCK
...
HEH.
PEOPLE ARE BORN ALONE AND THEN DIE ALONE.

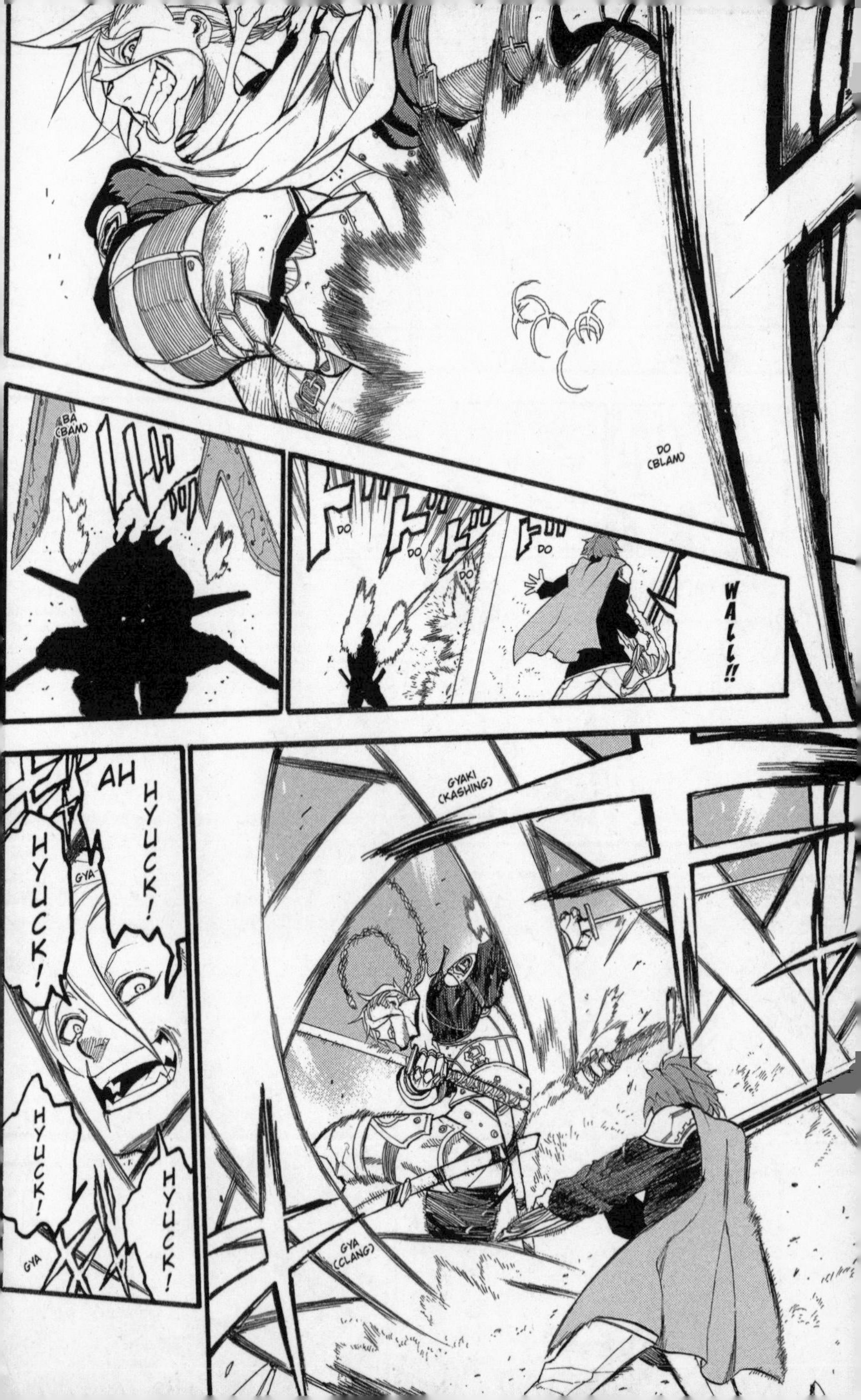
DO
(BLAM)
WALL!!
DO
DO
DO
DO
BA
(BAM)
GYAKI
(KASHING)
GYA
(CLANG)
AH
HYUCK!
HYUCK!
GYA
HYUCK!
HYUCK!
GYA

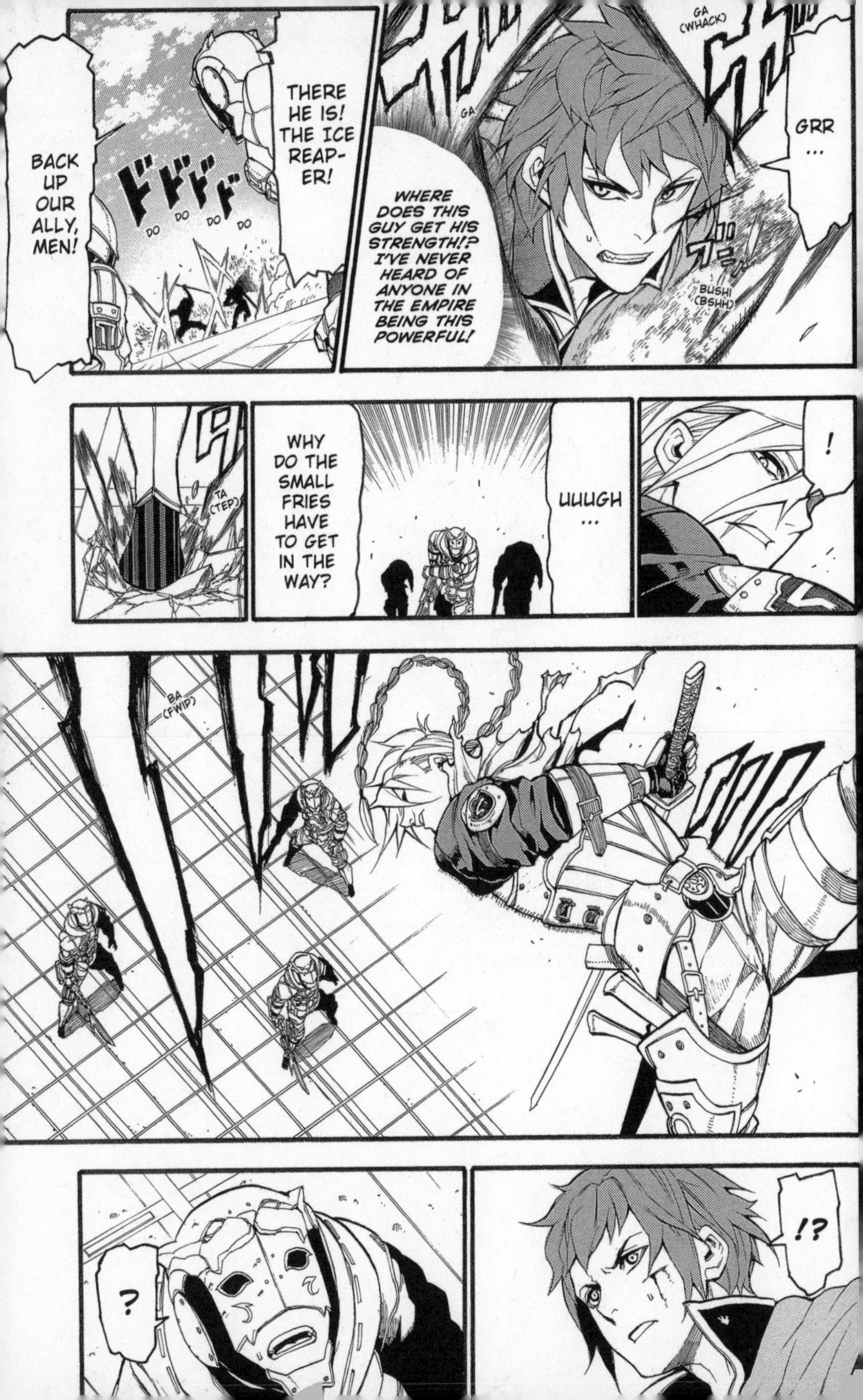
GA (WHACK)
GRR ...
GA
WHERE DOES THIS GUY GET HIS STRENGTH!? I'VE NEVER HEARD OF ANYONE IN THE EMPIRE BEING THIS POWERFUL!
BUSHI (BSHH)
THERE HE IS! THE ICE REAPER!
BACK UP OUR ALLY, MEN!
DO DO DO DO
!
UUUGH ...
WHY DO THE SMALL FRIES HAVE TO GET IN THE WAY?
TA (TEP)
BA (FWIP)
!?
?

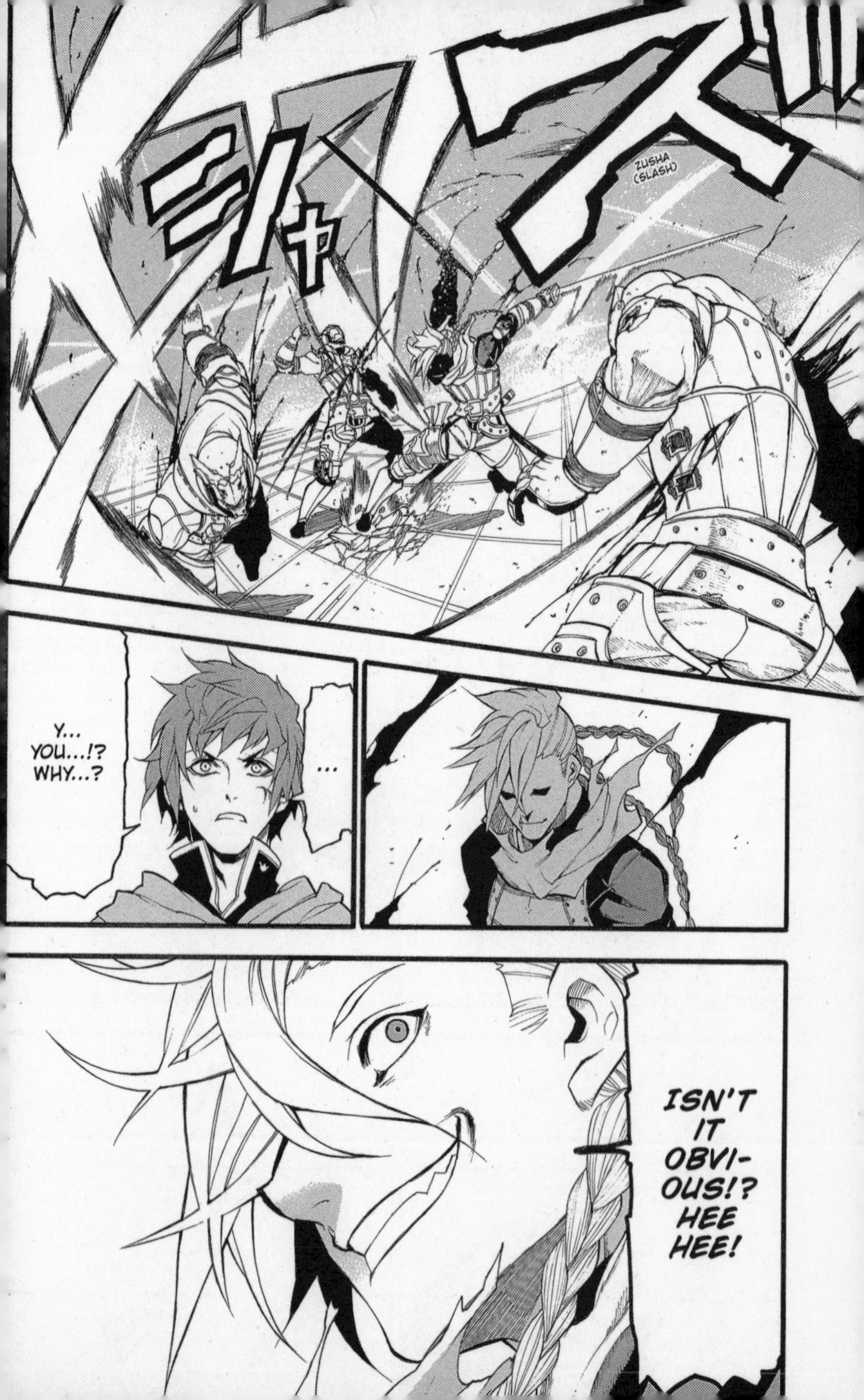
ZUSHA (SLASH)
...
Y... YOU...!? WHY...?
ISN'T IT OBVI-OUS!? HEE HEE!

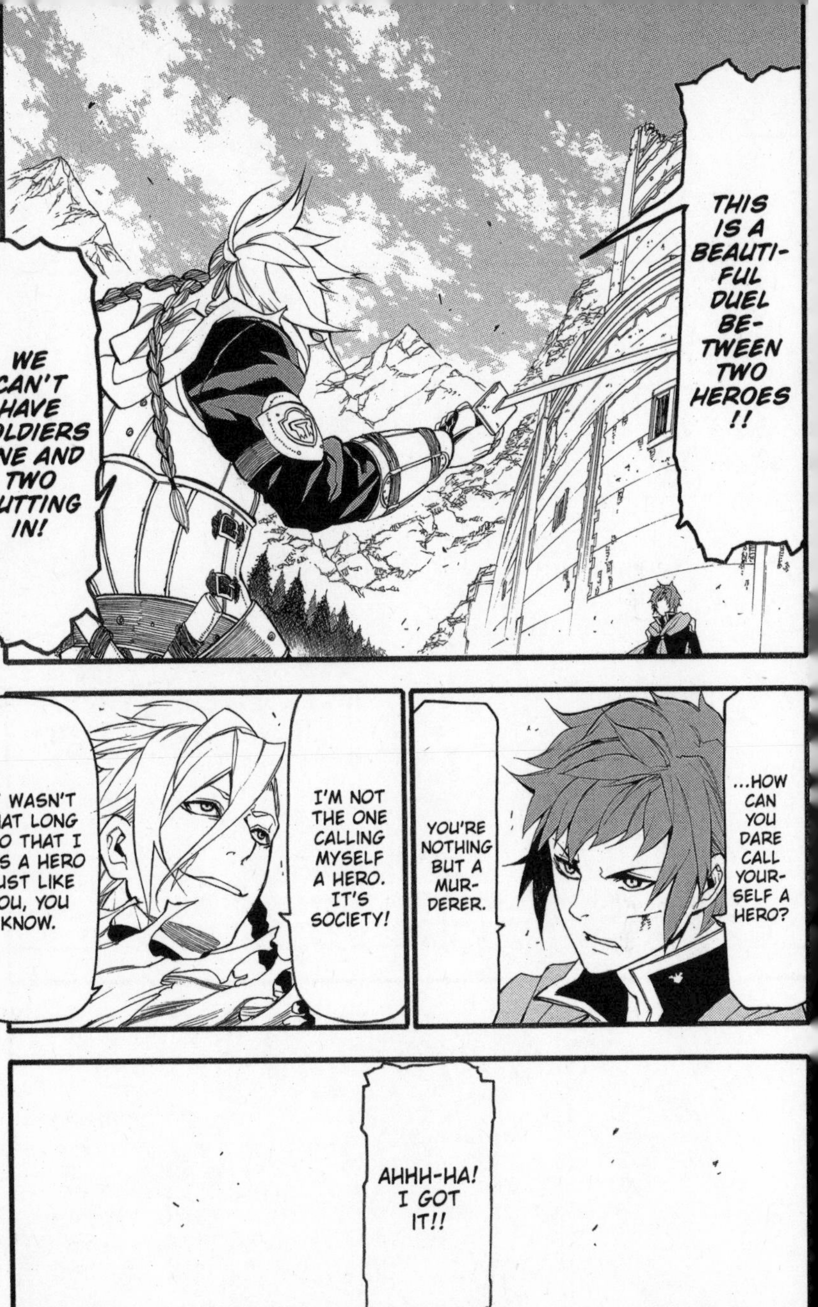
THIS IS A BEAUTIFUL DUEL BETWEEN TWO HEROES!!
WE CAN'T HAVE SOLDIERS ONE AND TWO BUTTING IN!
...HOW CAN YOU DARE CALL YOURSELF A HERO?
YOU'RE NOTHING BUT A MURDERER.
I'M NOT THE ONE CALLING MYSELF A HERO. IT'S SOCIETY!
IT WASN'T THAT LONG AGO THAT I WAS A HERO JUST LIKE YOU, YOU KNOW.
AHHH-HA! I GOT IT!!

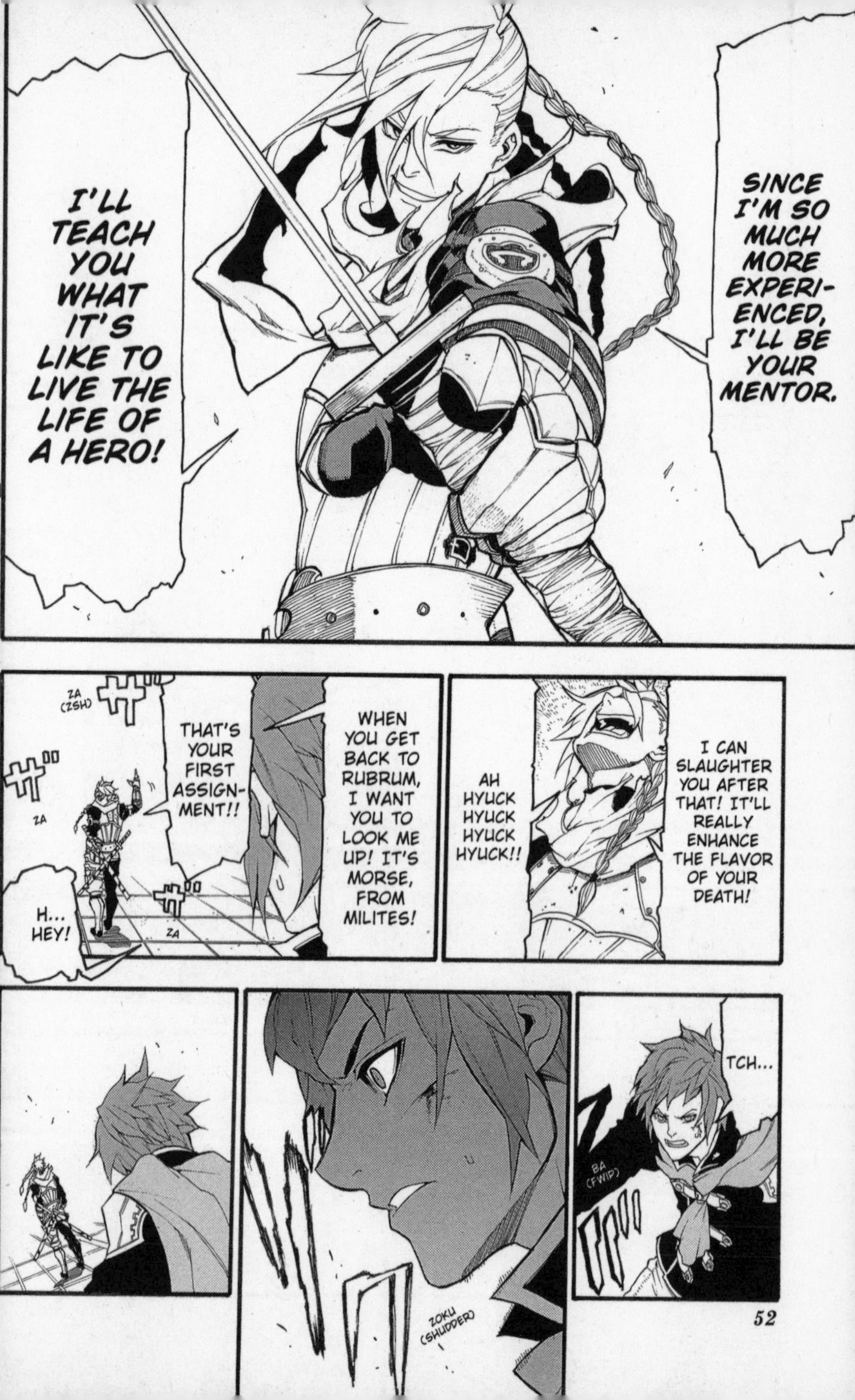
SINCE I'M SO MUCH MORE EXPERI-ENCED, I'LL BE YOUR MENTOR.
I'LL TEACH YOU WHAT IT'S LIKE TO LIVE THE LIFE OF A HERO!
I CAN SLAUGHTER YOU AFTER THAT! IT'LL REALLY ENHANCE THE FLAVOR OF YOUR DEATH!
AH HYUCK HYUCK HYUCK HYUCK!!
WHEN YOU GET BACK TO RUBRUM, I WANT YOU TO LOOK ME UP! IT'S MORSE, FROM MILITES!
THAT'S YOUR FIRST ASSIGN-MENT!!
ZA (ZSH)
ZA
H... HEY!
ZA
TCH...
BA (FWIP)
ZOKU (SHUDDER)

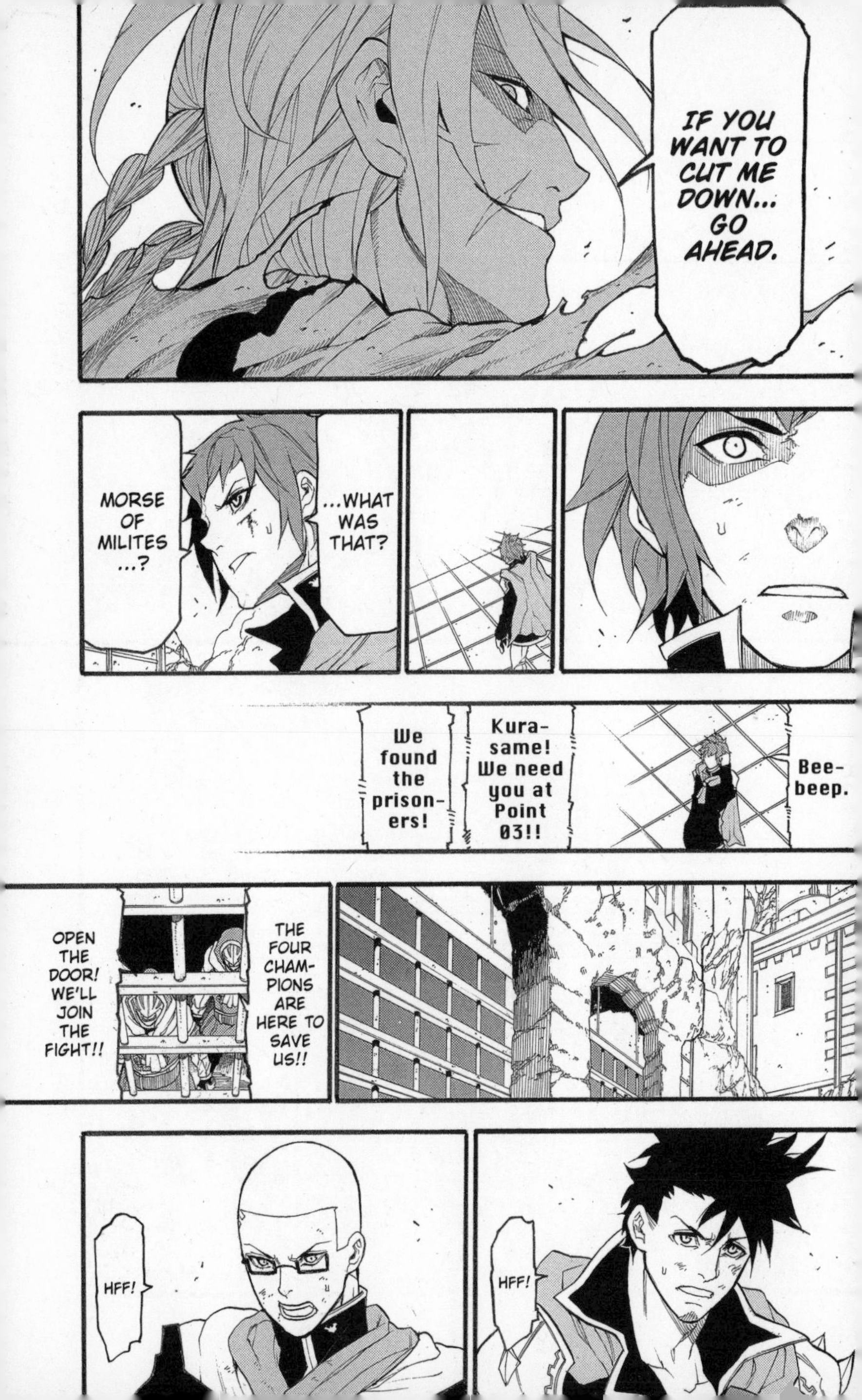
IF YOU WANT TO CUT ME DOWN... GO AHEAD.
...WHAT WAS THAT?
MORSE OF MILITES ...?
Bee-beep.
Kura-same! We need you at Point 03!!
We found the prison-ers!
THE FOUR CHAM-PIONS ARE HERE TO SAVE US!!
OPEN THE DOOR! WE'LL JOIN THE FIGHT!!
HFF!
HFF!

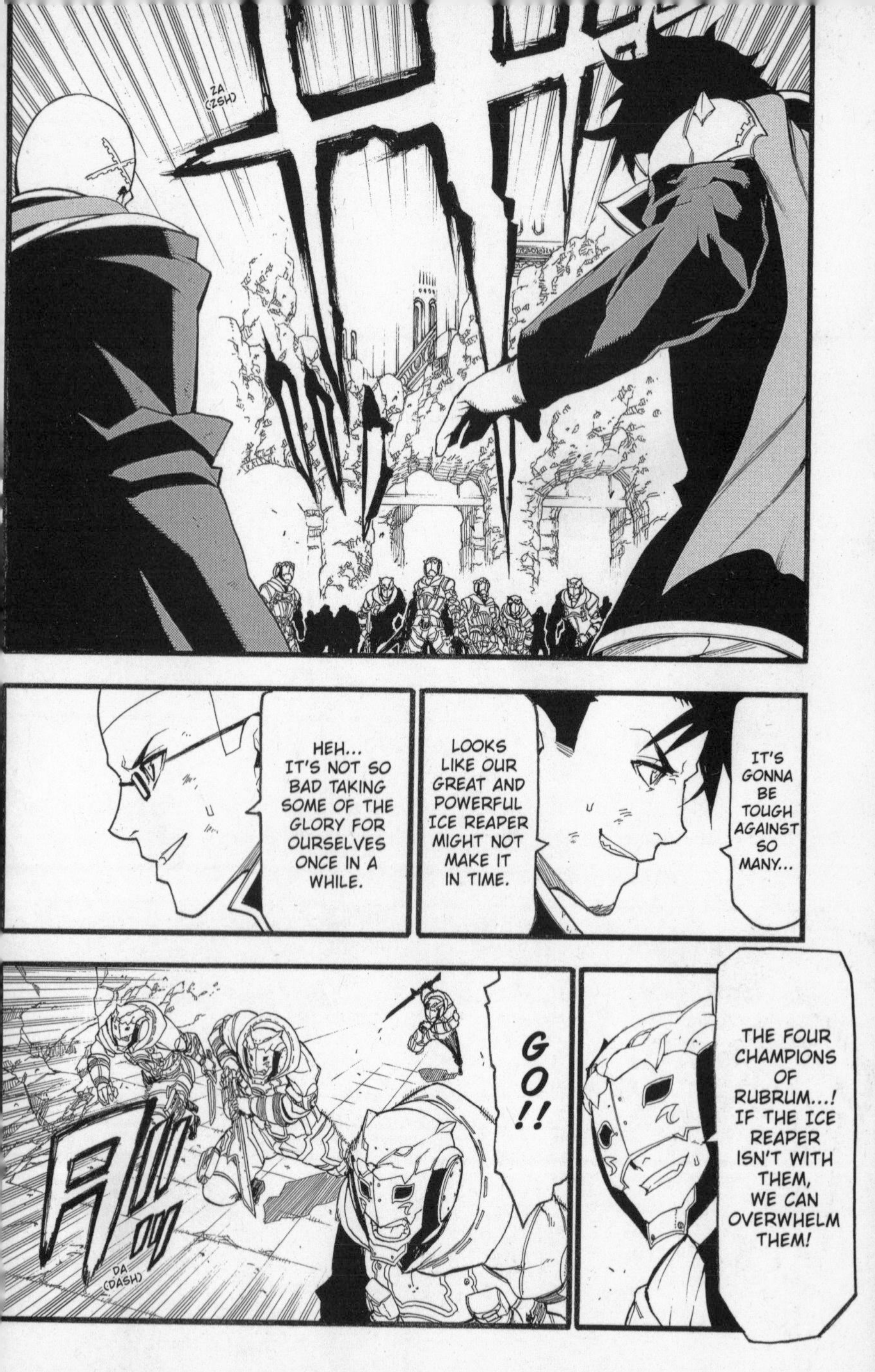
ZA (ZSH)
IT'S GONNA BE TOUGH AGAINST SO MANY...
LOOKS LIKE OUR GREAT AND POWERFUL ICE REAPER MIGHT NOT MAKE IT IN TIME.
HEH... IT'S NOT SO BAD TAKING SOME OF THE GLORY FOR OURSELVES ONCE IN A WHILE.
THE FOUR CHAMPIONS OF RUBRUM...! IF THE ICE REAPER ISN'T WITH THEM, WE CAN OVERWHELM THEM!
GO!!
DA (DASH)

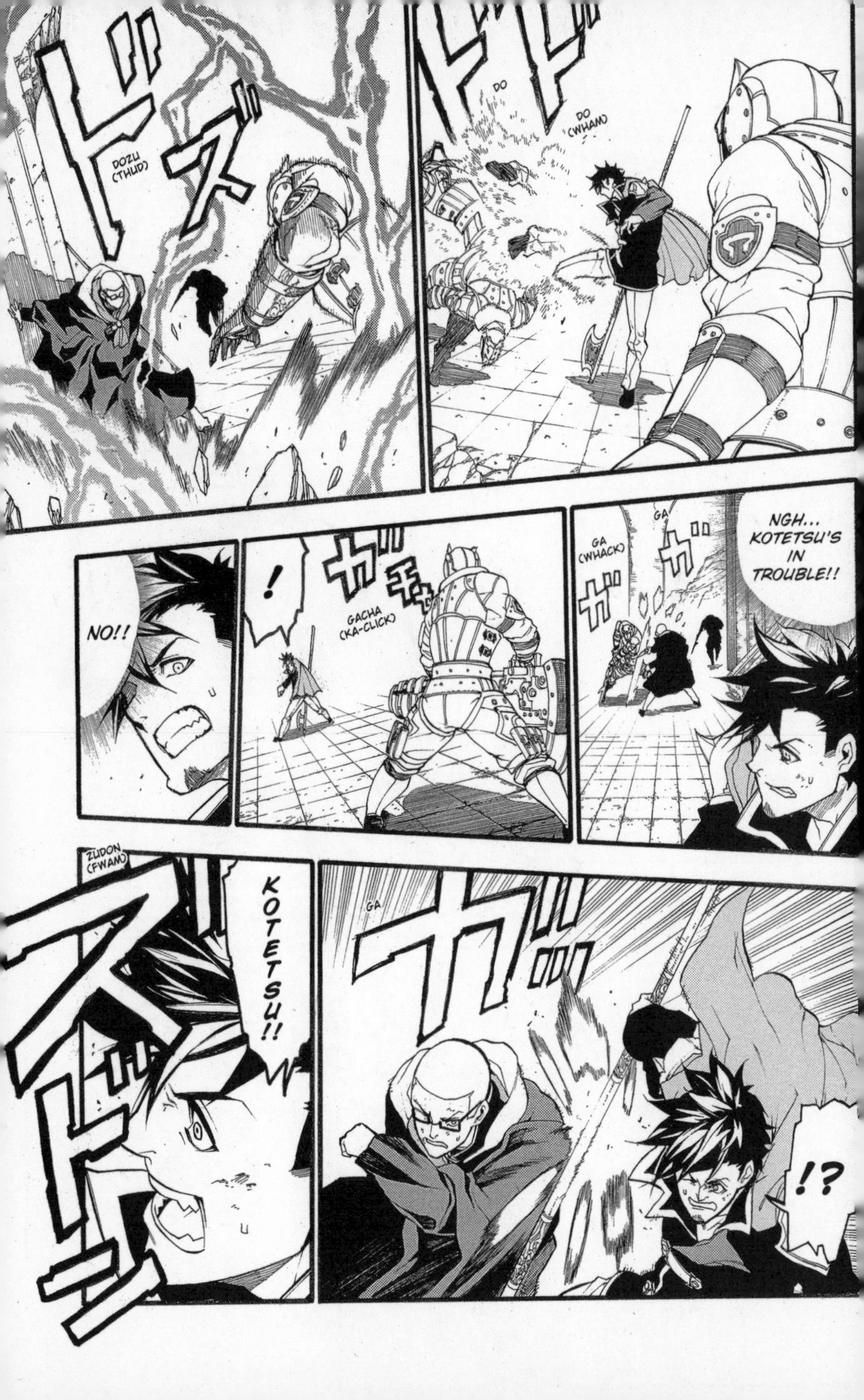
DO
DO (WHAM)
DOZU (THUD)
NGH... KOTETSU'S IN TROUBLE!!
GA (WHACK)
GA
!
GACHA (KA-CLICK)
NO!!
GA
!?
ZUDON (FWAM)
KOTETSU!!

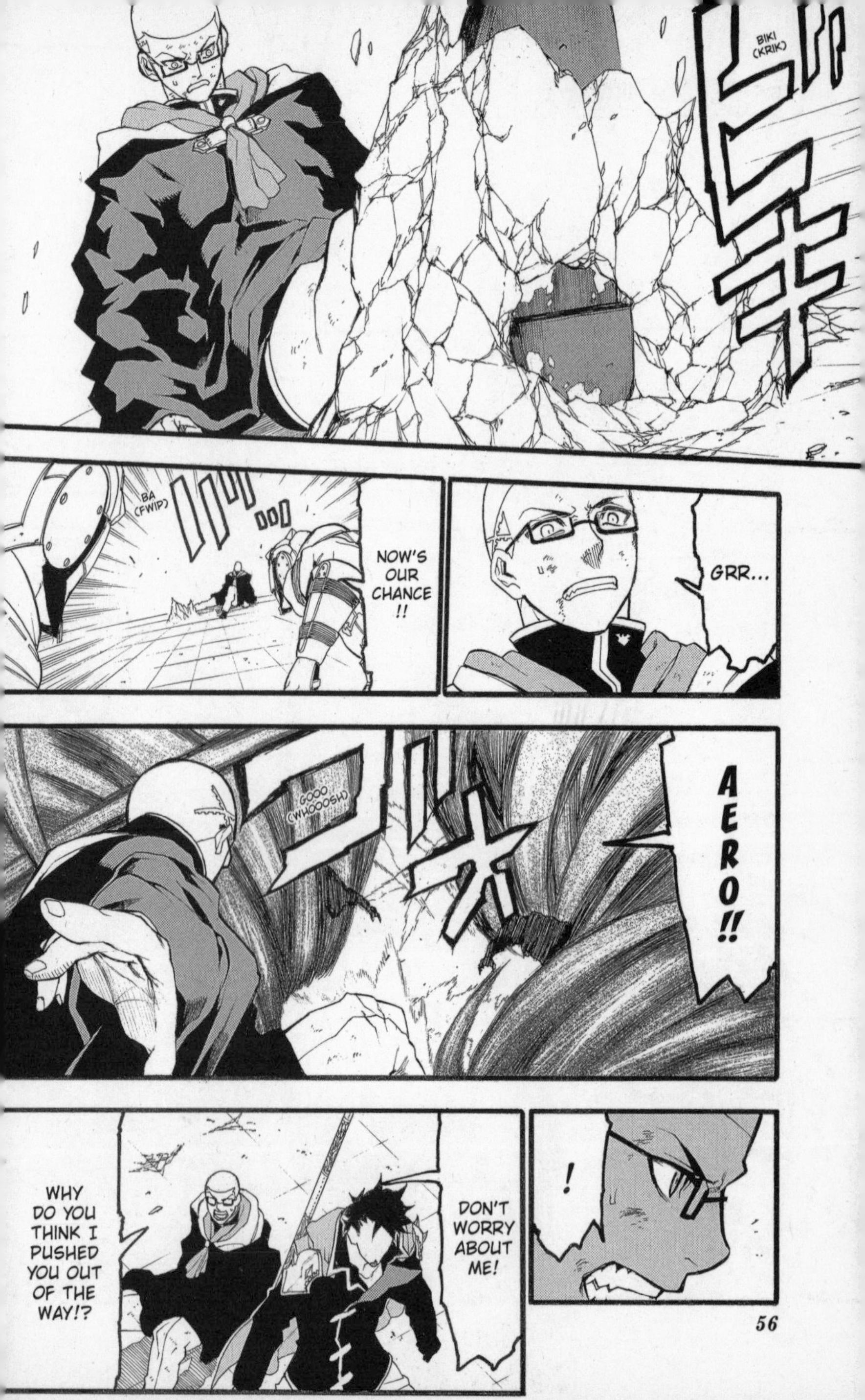

BIKI (KRIK)
GRR...
NOW'S OUR CHANCE!!
BA (FWIP)
DOD
AERO!!
GOOO (WHOOOSH)
!
DON'T WORRY ABOUT ME!
WHY DO YOU THINK I PUSHED YOU OUT OF THE WAY!?

I KNOW! BUT... BUT!!

BECAUSE I DETERMINED THAT YOU HAVE A GREATER CHANCE OF COMPLETING THE MISSION UNDER THESE CIRCUM- STANCES!

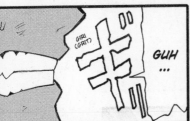

GIRI (GRIT)

GUH...

IT'S NO USE... GUREN CAN'T BRING HIMSELF TO ABANDON ME!

!?

BO (BWOH)

FIRE!!

GWAAAAHH!!

57

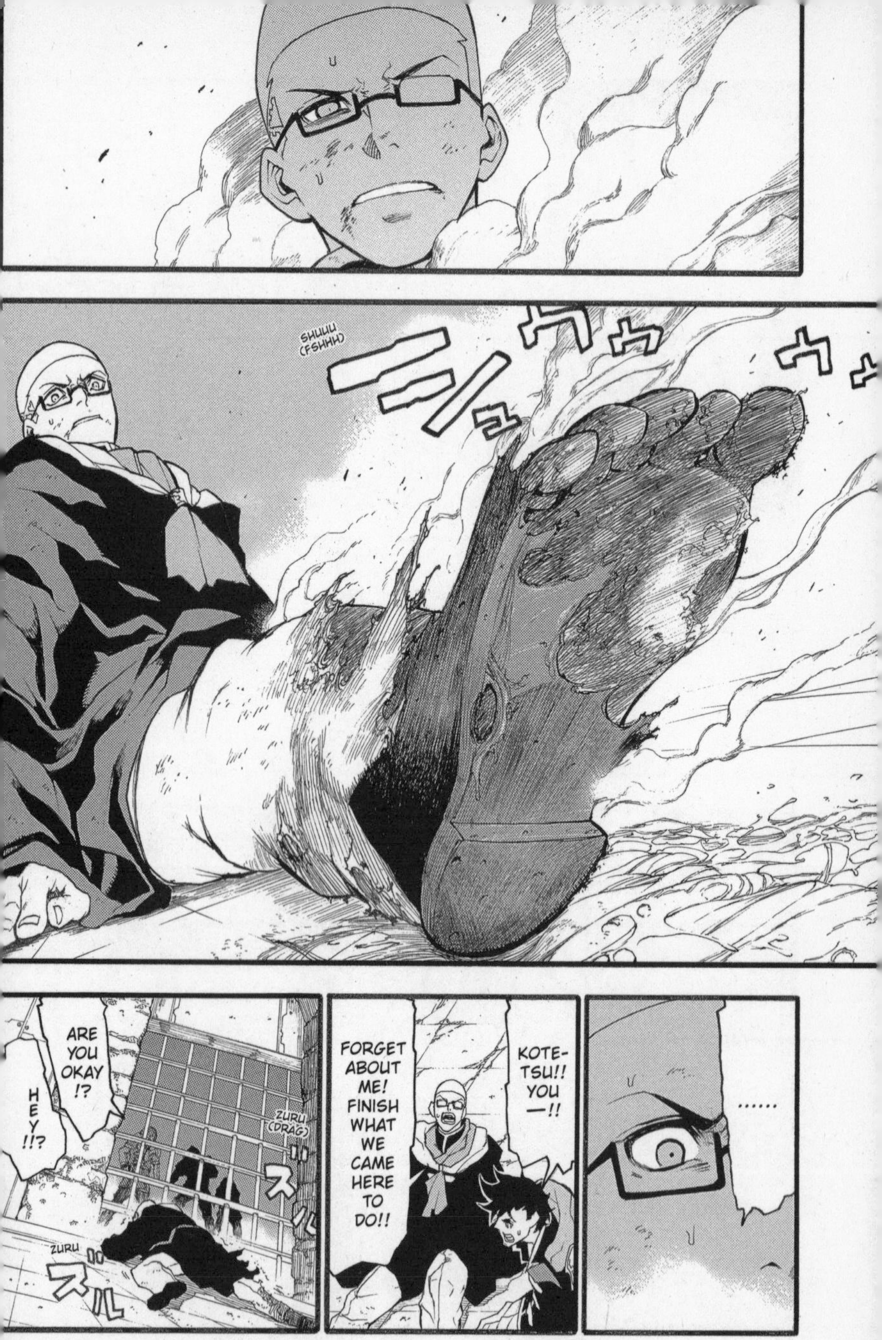
SHUUU (FSHHH)
......
KOTE-TSU!! YOU—!!
FORGET ABOUT ME! FINISH WHAT WE CAME HERE TO DO!!
ARE YOU OKAY!?
HEY!!?
ZURU (DRAG)
ズル
ZURU
ズル

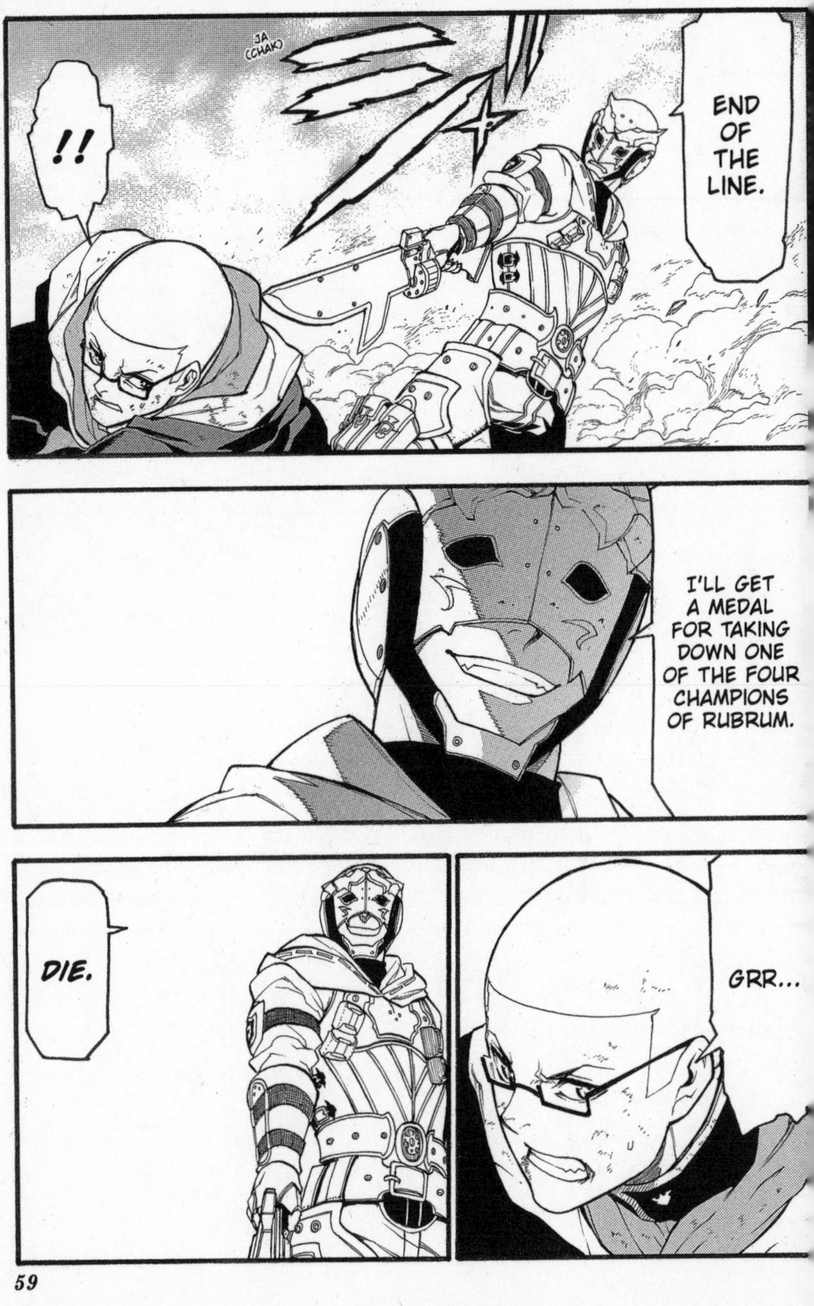
END OF THE LINE.
JA (CHAK)
!!
I'LL GET A MEDAL FOR TAKING DOWN ONE OF THE FOUR CHAMPIONS OF RUBRUM.
GRR...
DIE.

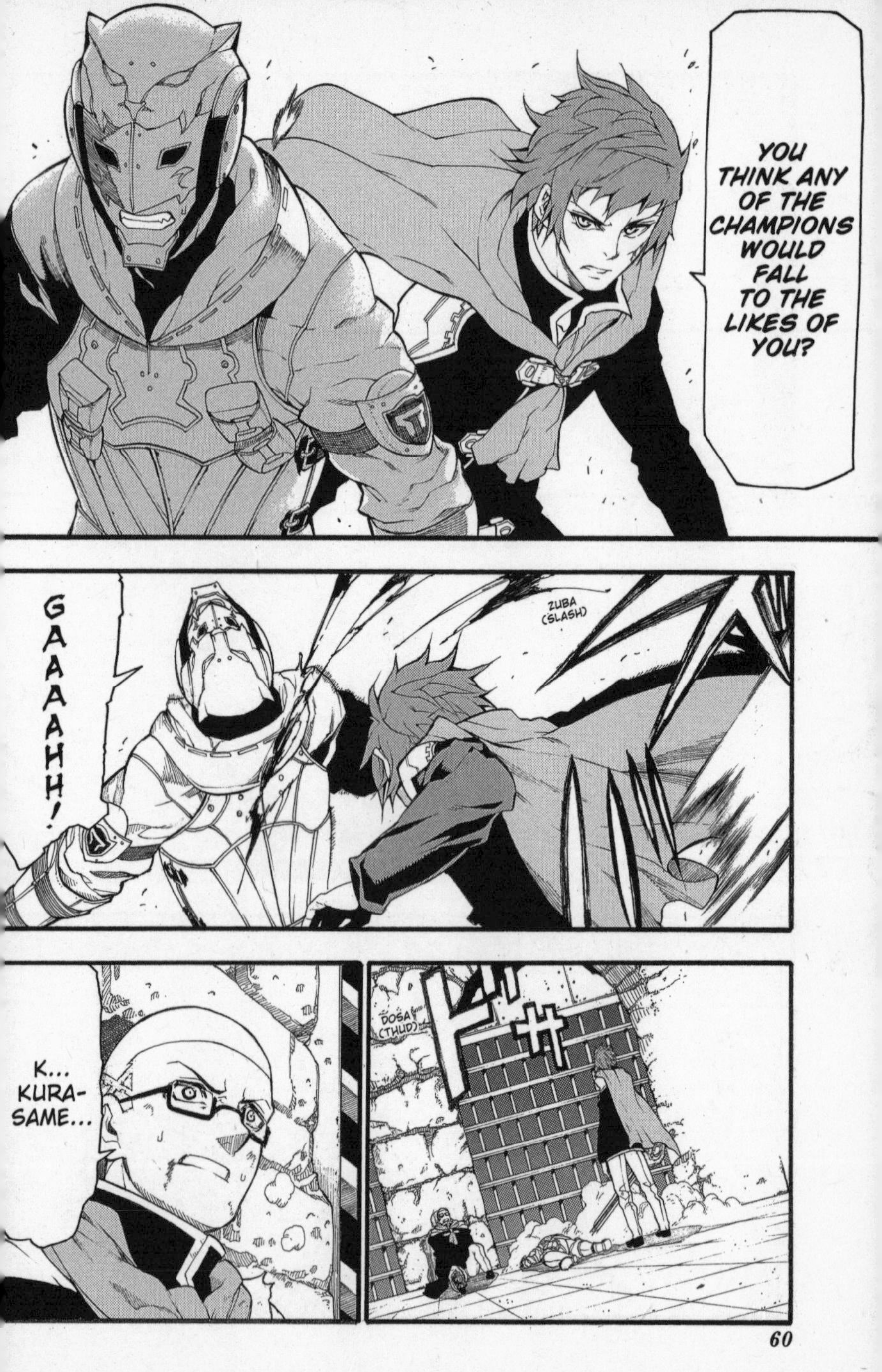
YOU THINK ANY OF THE CHAMPIONS WOULD FALL TO THE LIKES OF YOU?
ZUBA (SLASH)
GAAAAAHH!
DOSA (THUD)
K... KURA-SAME...

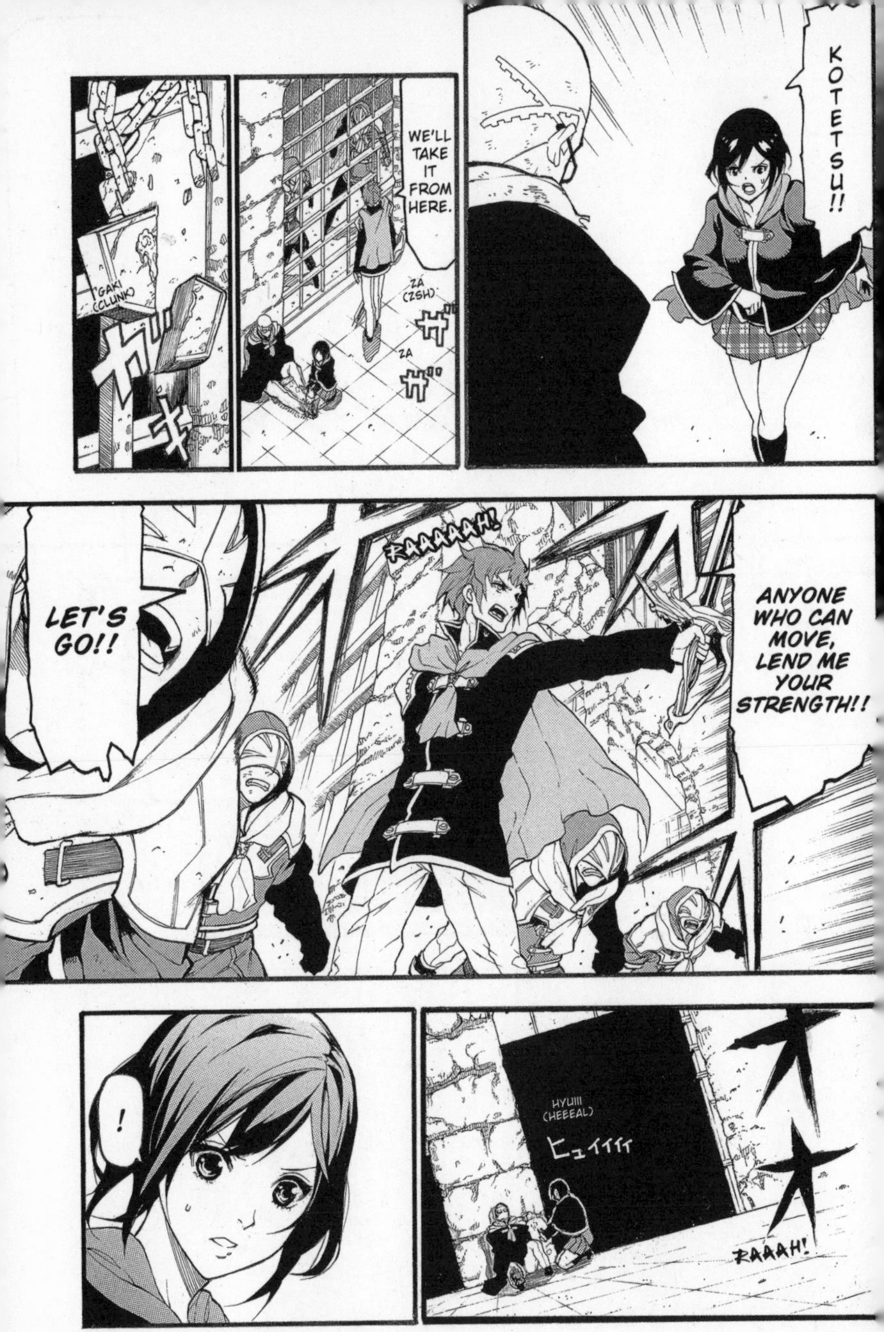
KOTETSU!!
WE'LL TAKE IT FROM HERE.
ZA (ZSH)
ザ
ZA
ザ
GAKI (CLUNK)
ガキ
ANYONE WHO CAN MOVE, LEND ME YOUR STRENGTH!!
RAAAAAH!
LET'S GO!!
HYUIII (HEEEAL)
ヒュイイイ
RAAAH!
!

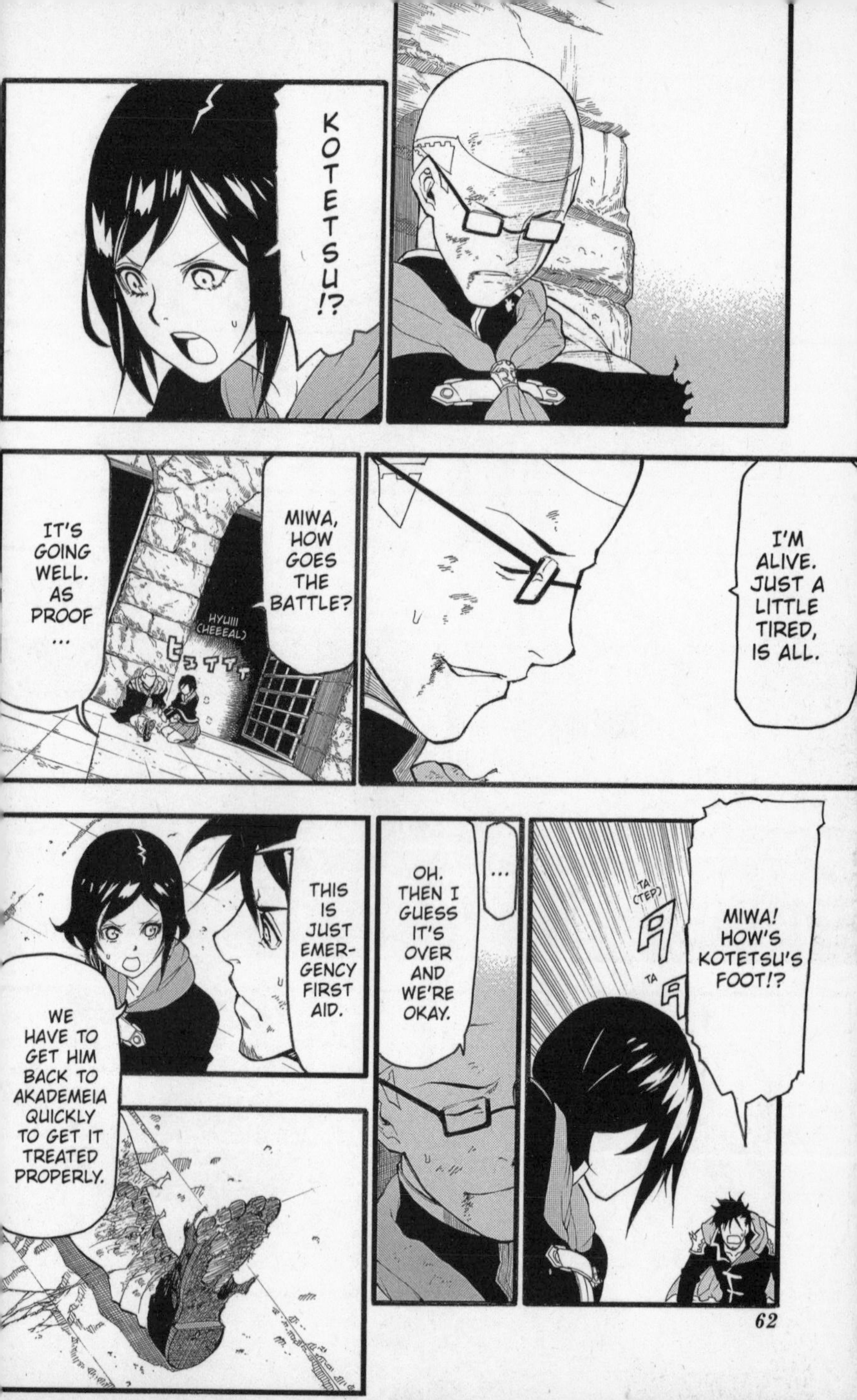
KOTETSU!?
I'M ALIVE. JUST A LITTLE TIRED, IS ALL.
MIWA, HOW GOES THE BATTLE?
IT'S GOING WELL. AS PROOF...
HYUIII (CHEEEAL)
MIWA! HOW'S KOTETSU'S FOOT!?
TA (TEP)
TA
...
OH. THEN I GUESS IT'S OVER AND WE'RE OKAY.
THIS IS JUST EMERGENCY FIRST AID.
WE HAVE TO GET HIM BACK TO AKADEMEIA QUICKLY TO GET IT TREATED PROPERLY.

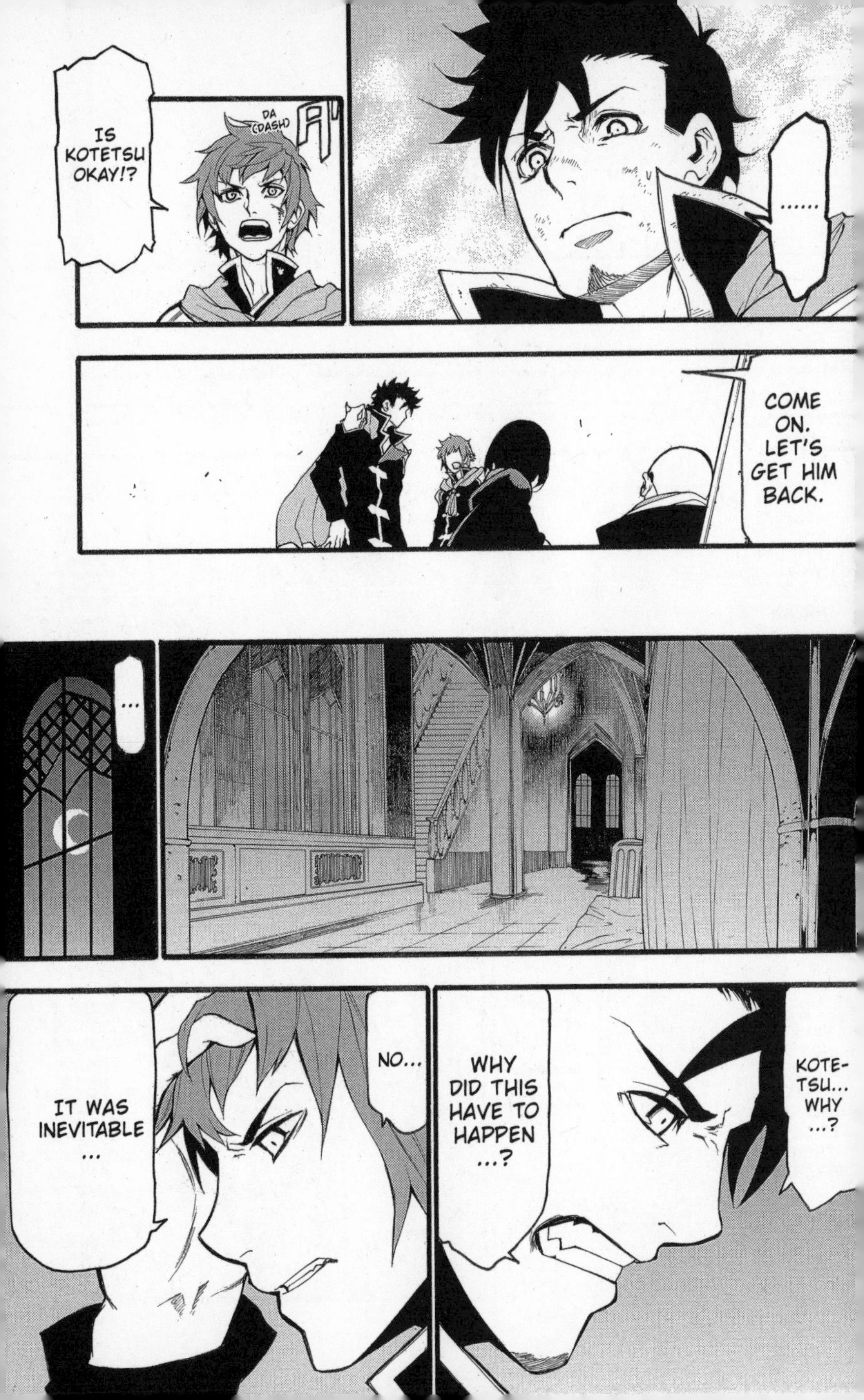
......
DA (DASH)
IS KOTETSU OKAY!?
COME ON. LET'S GET HIM BACK.
...
KOTE-TSU... WHY ...?
WHY DID THIS HAVE TO HAPPEN ...?
NO...
IT WAS INEVITABLE ...

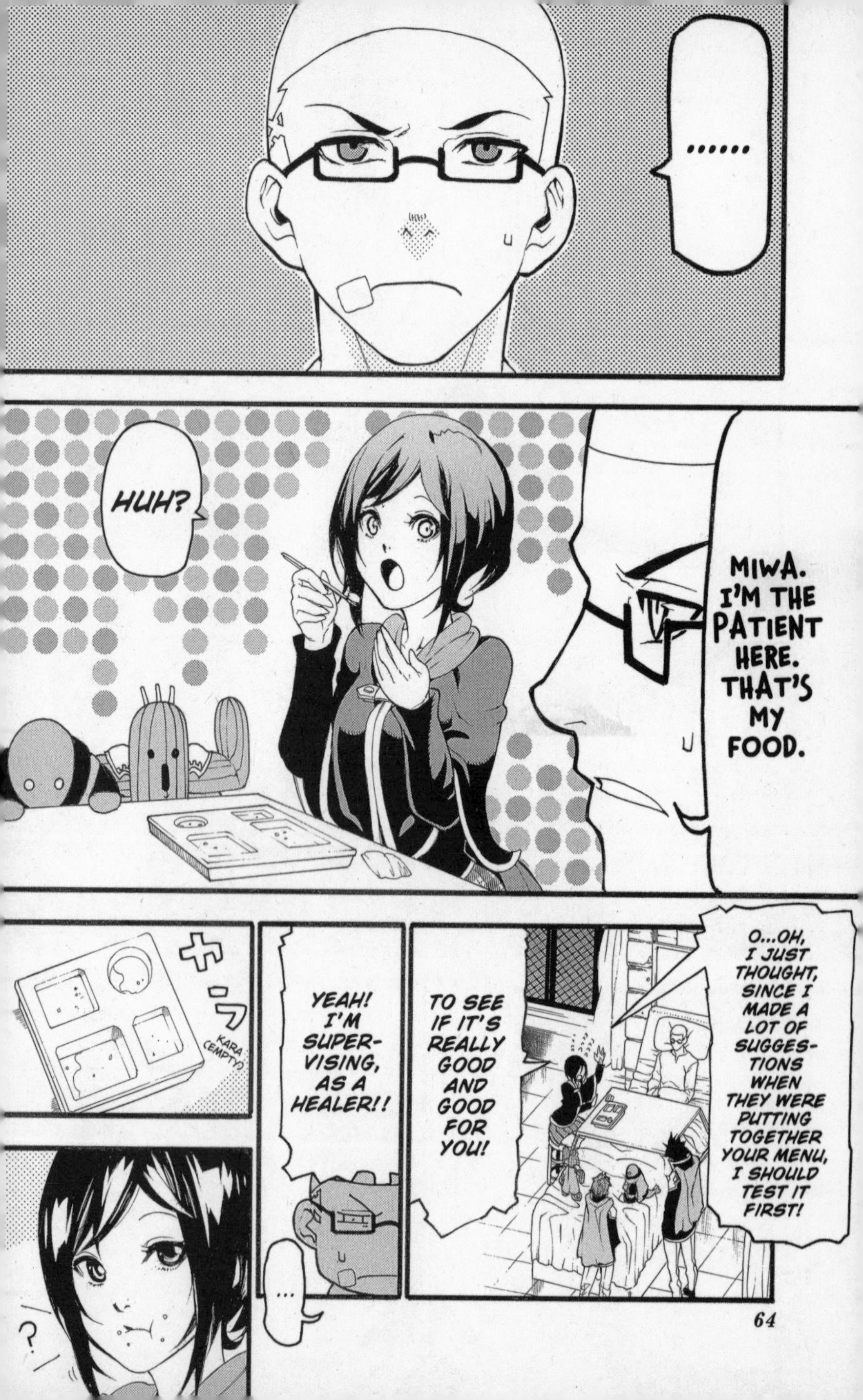
......
MIWA. I'M THE PATIENT HERE. THAT'S MY FOOD.
HUH?
O...OH, I JUST THOUGHT, SINCE I MADE A LOT OF SUGGES-TIONS WHEN THEY WERE PUTTING TOGETHER YOUR MENU, I SHOULD TEST IT FIRST!
TO SEE IF IT'S REALLY GOOD AND GOOD FOR YOU!
YEAH! I'M SUPER-VISING, AS A HEALER!!
...
カラ
KARA (EMPTY)
?

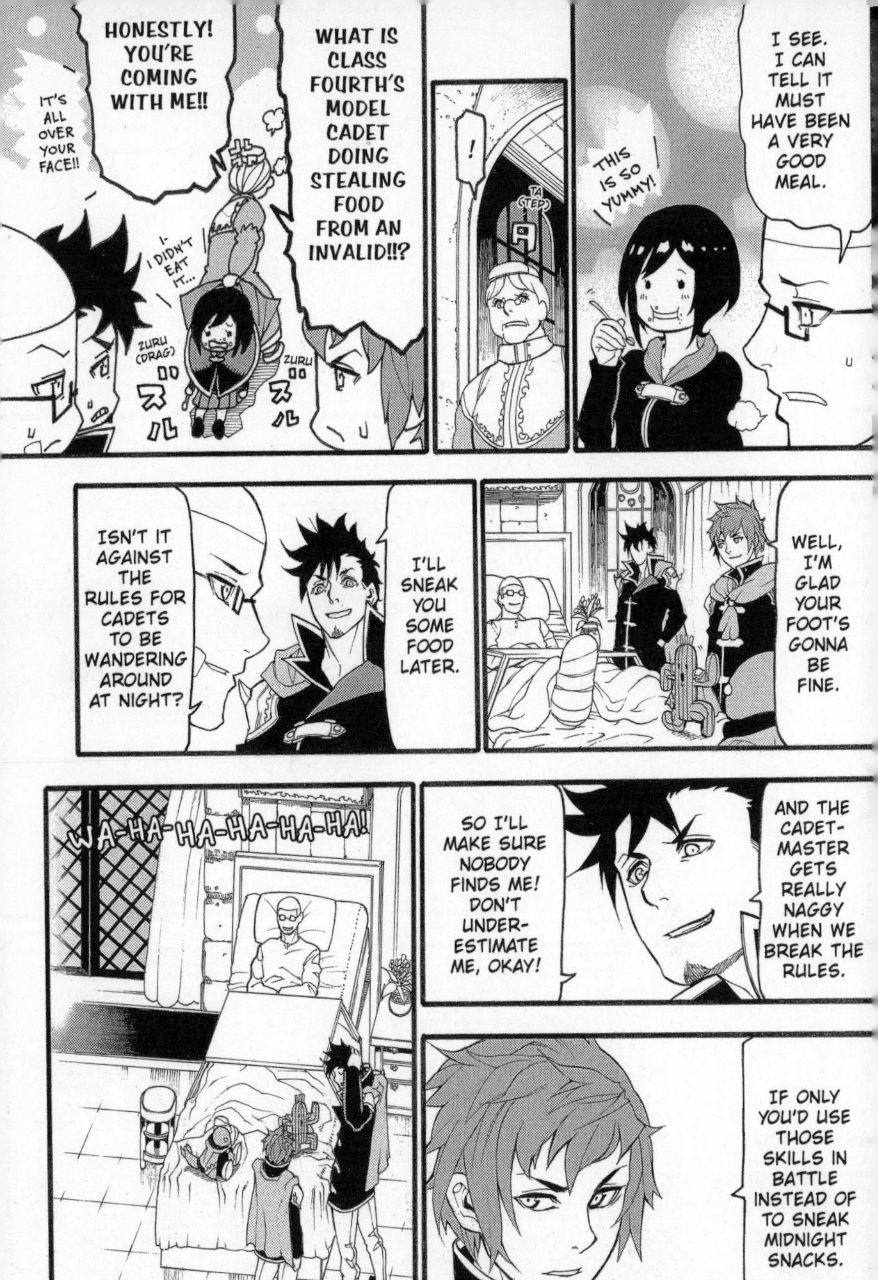
I SEE. I CAN TELL IT MUST HAVE BEEN A VERY GOOD MEAL.
THIS IS SO YUMMY!
!
TA (TEP)
WHAT IS CLASS FOURTH'S MODEL CADET DOING STEALING FOOD FROM AN INVALID!!?
HONESTLY! YOU'RE COMING WITH ME!!
IT'S ALL OVER YOUR FACE!!
I- I DIDN'T EAT IT...
ZURU (DRAG)
ZURU
WELL, I'M GLAD YOUR FOOT'S GONNA BE FINE.
I'LL SNEAK YOU SOME FOOD LATER.
ISN'T IT AGAINST THE RULES FOR CADETS TO BE WANDERING AROUND AT NIGHT?
AND THE CADET-MASTER GETS REALLY NAGGY WHEN WE BREAK THE RULES.
SO I'LL MAKE SURE NOBODY FINDS ME! DON'T UNDER-ESTIMATE ME, OKAY!
IF ONLY YOU'D USE THOSE SKILLS IN BATTLE INSTEAD OF TO SNEAK MIDNIGHT SNACKS.
WA-HA-HA-HA-HA-HA!

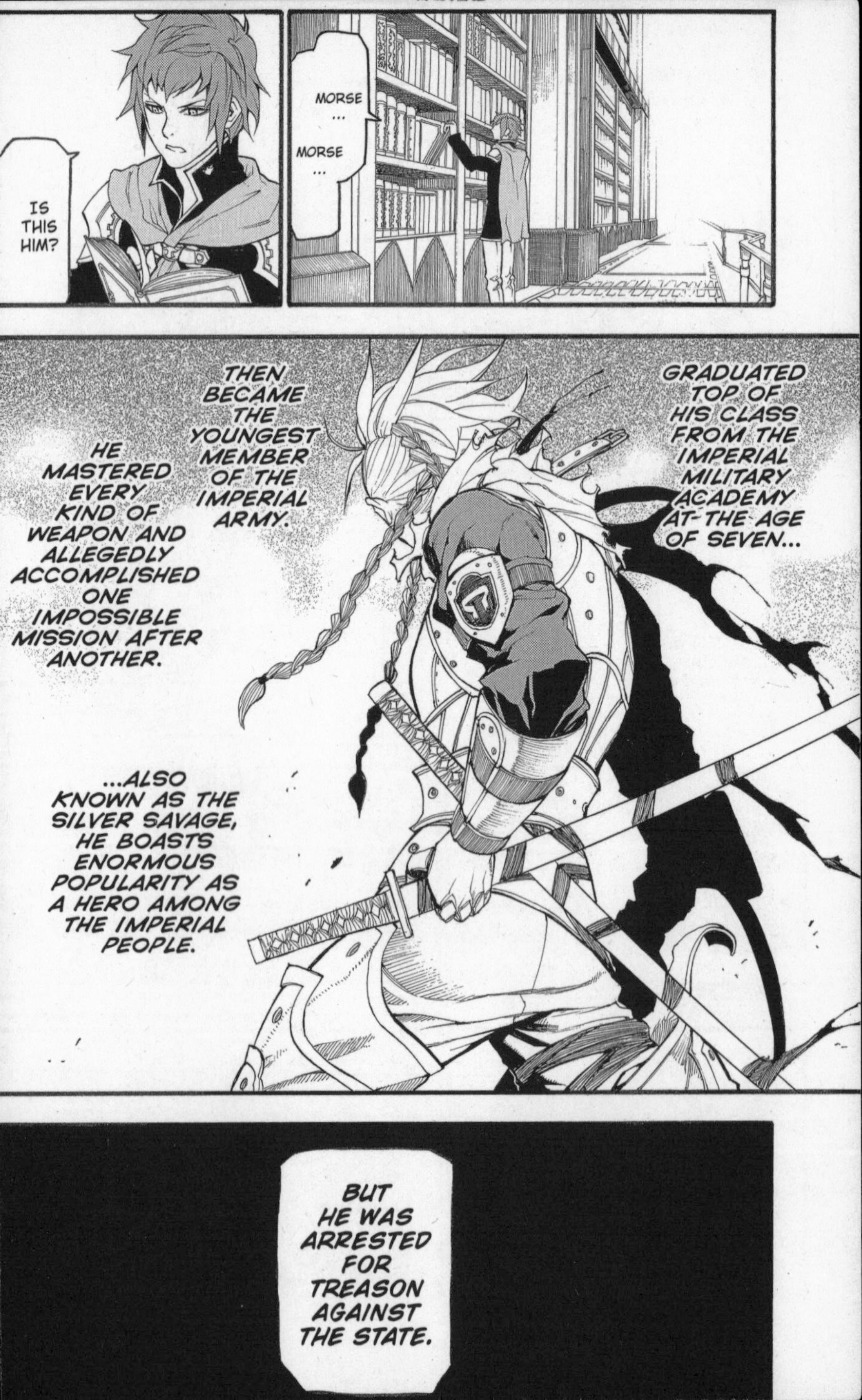
MORSE ... MORSE ...
IS THIS HIM?
GRADUATED TOP OF HIS CLASS FROM THE IMPERIAL MILITARY ACADEMY AT THE AGE OF SEVEN...
THEN BECAME THE YOUNGEST MEMBER OF THE IMPERIAL ARMY.
HE MASTERED EVERY KIND OF WEAPON AND ALLEGEDLY ACCOMPLISHED ONE IMPOSSIBLE MISSION AFTER ANOTHER.
...ALSO KNOWN AS THE SILVER SAVAGE, HE BOASTS ENORMOUS POPULARITY AS A HERO AMONG THE IMPERIAL PEOPLE.
BUT HE WAS ARRESTED FOR TREASON AGAINST THE STATE.

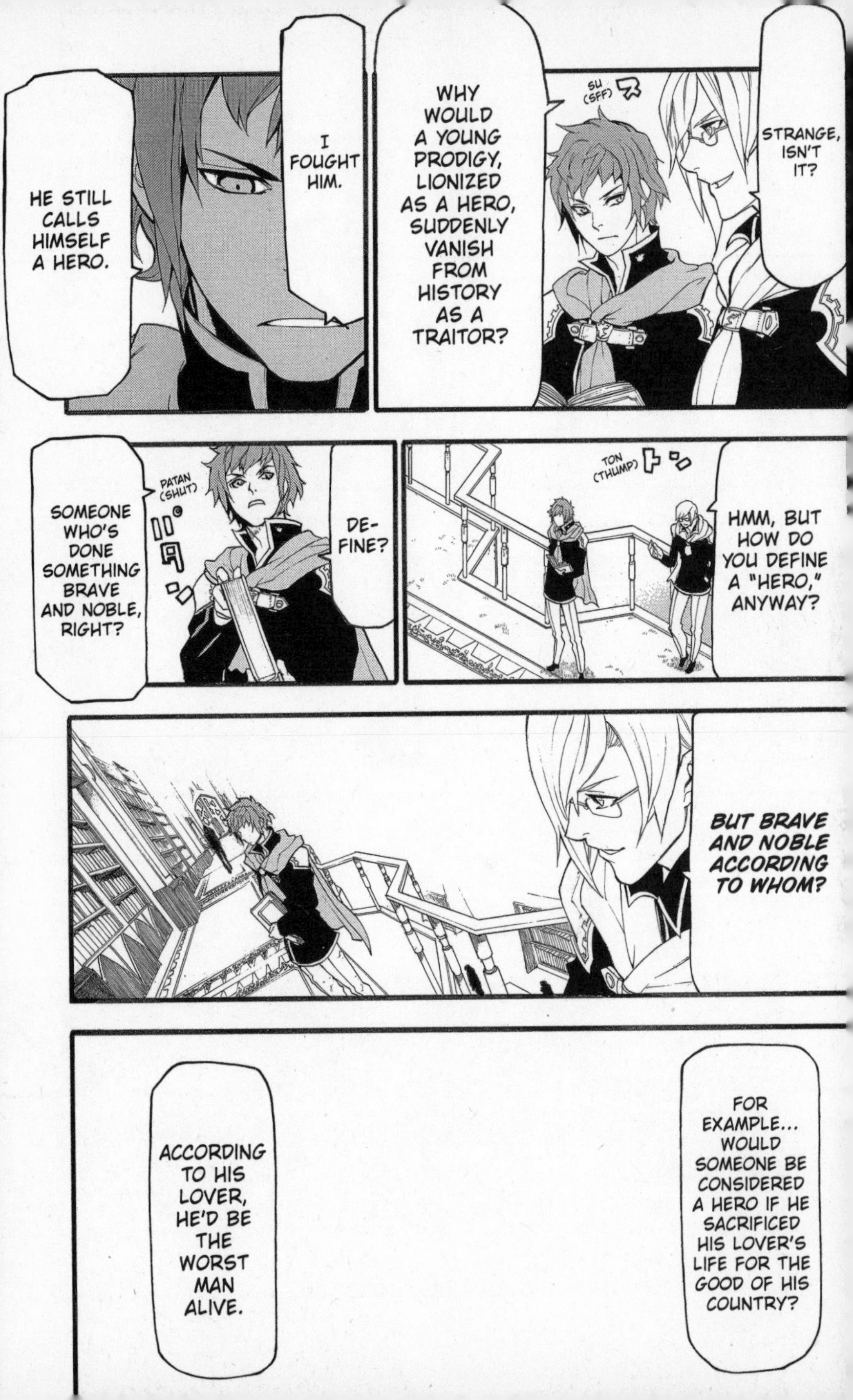
SU (SFF)
STRANGE, ISN'T IT?
WHY WOULD A YOUNG PRODIGY, LIONIZED AS A HERO, SUDDENLY VANISH FROM HISTORY AS A TRAITOR?
I FOUGHT HIM.
HE STILL CALLS HIMSELF A HERO.
TON (THUMP)
HMM, BUT HOW DO YOU DEFINE A "HERO," ANYWAY?
DE-FINE?
PATAN (SHUT)
SOMEONE WHO'S DONE SOMETHING BRAVE AND NOBLE, RIGHT?
BUT BRAVE AND NOBLE ACCORDING TO WHOM?
FOR EXAMPLE... WOULD SOMEONE BE CONSIDERED A HERO IF HE SACRIFICED HIS LOVER'S LIFE FOR THE GOOD OF HIS COUNTRY?
ACCORDING TO HIS LOVER, HE'D BE THE WORST MAN ALIVE.

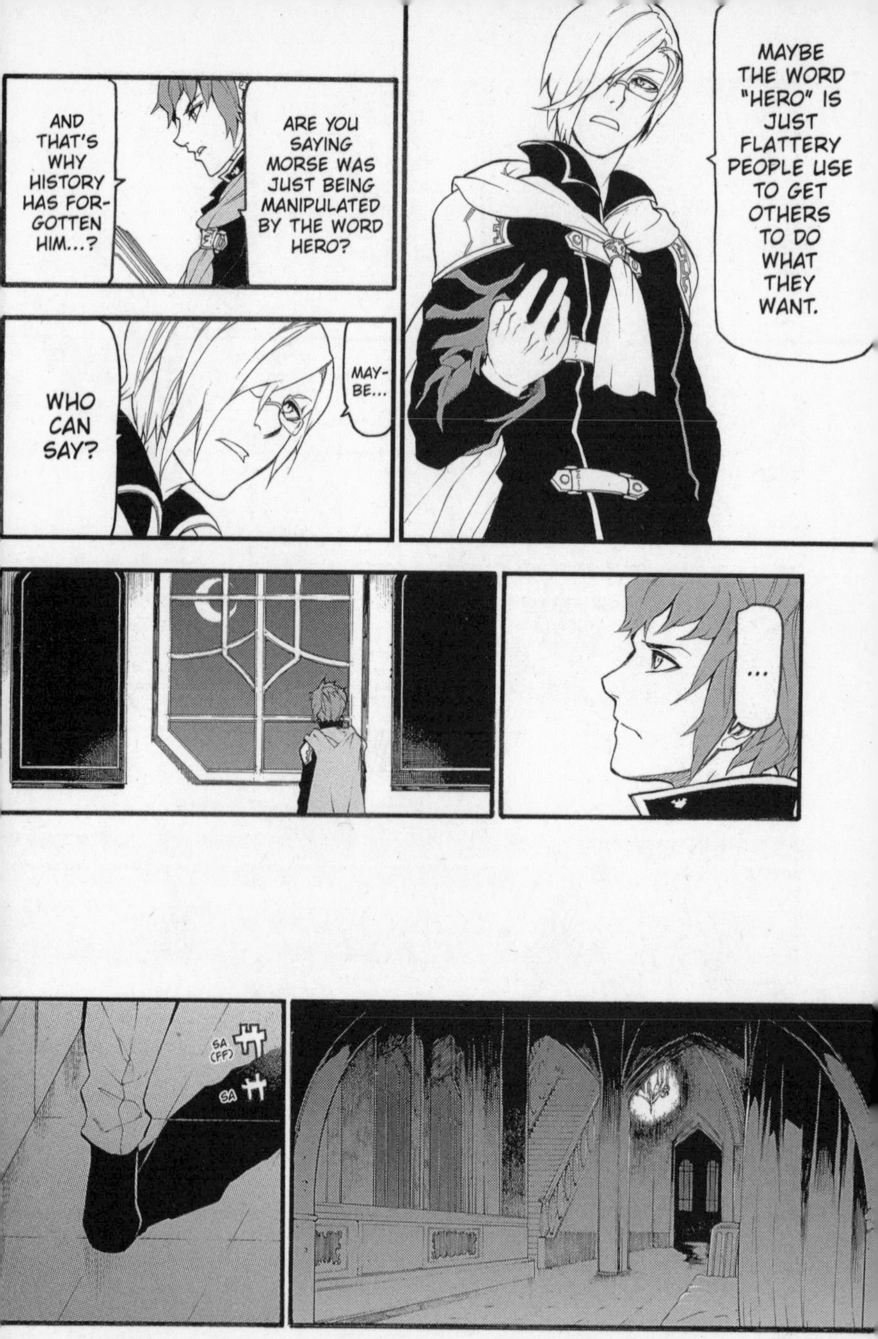
MAYBE THE WORD "HERO" IS JUST FLATTERY PEOPLE USE TO GET OTHERS TO DO WHAT THEY WANT.
ARE YOU SAYING MORSE WAS JUST BEING MANIPULATED BY THE WORD HERO?
AND THAT'S WHY HISTORY HAS FOR-GOTTEN HIM...?
MAY-BE...
WHO CAN SAY?
...
SA (FF)
SA

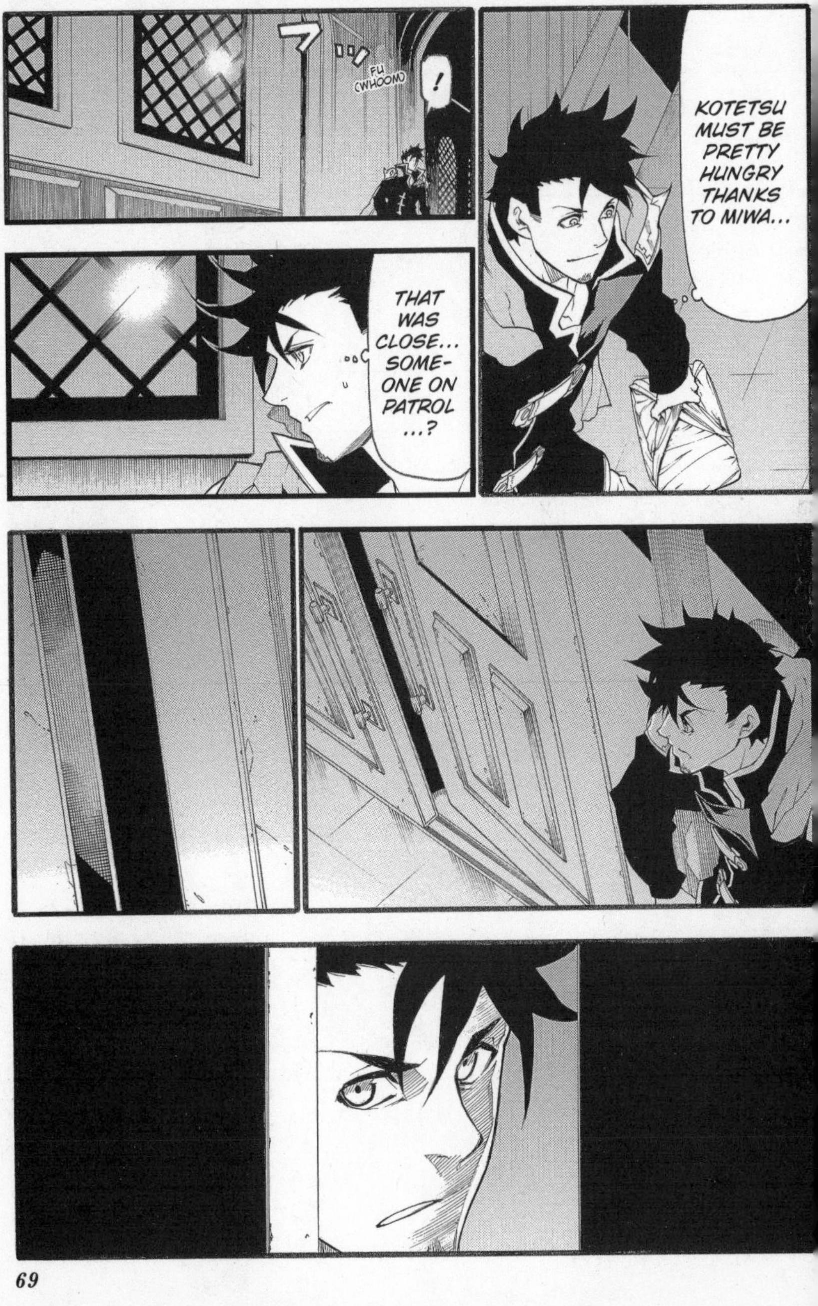
KOTETSU MUST BE PRETTY HUNGRY THANKS TO MIWA...
FU (WHOOM)
!
THAT WAS CLOSE... SOME-ONE ON PATROL ...?

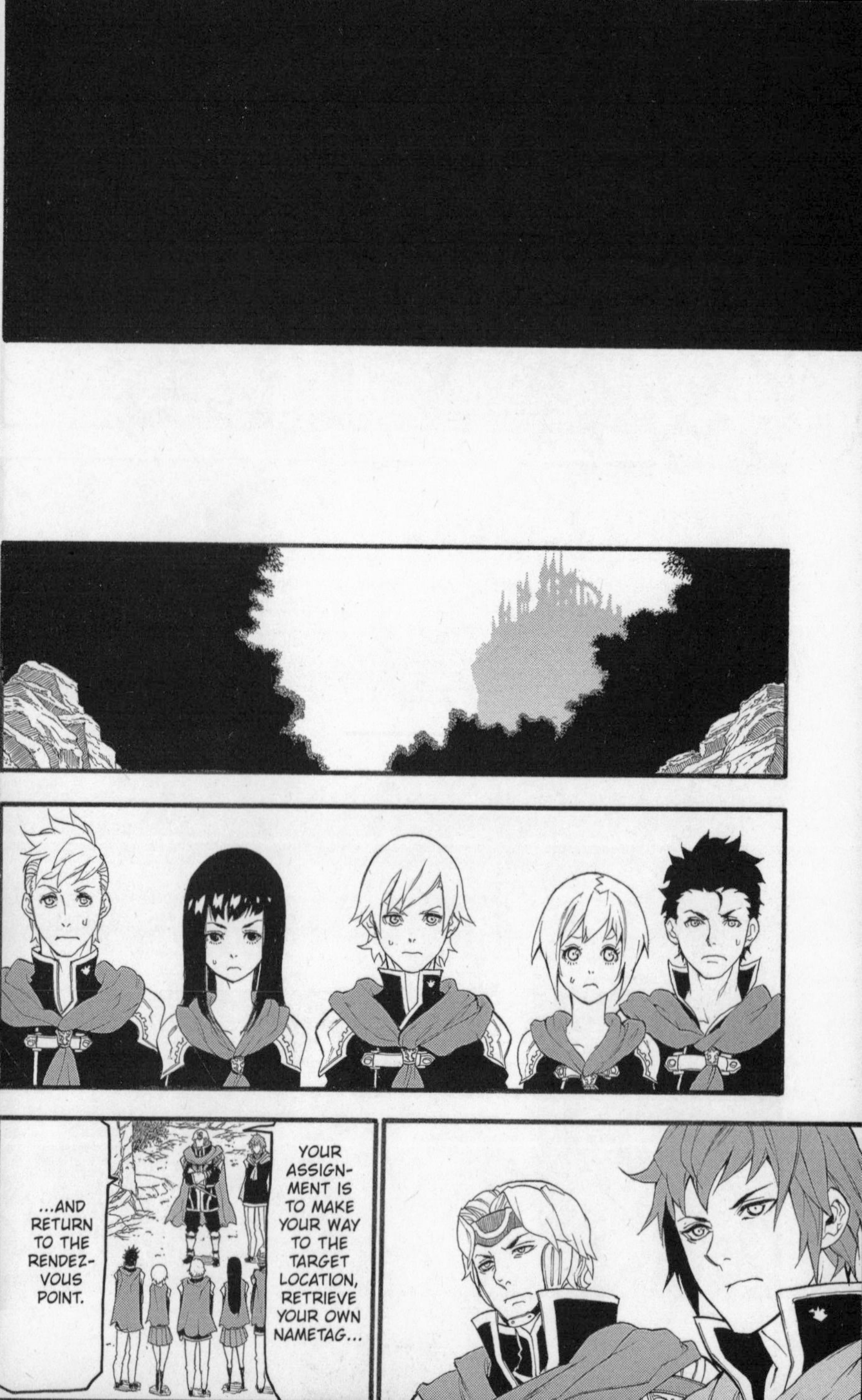
YOUR ASSIGN-MENT IS TO MAKE YOUR WAY TO THE TARGET LOCATION, RETRIEVE YOUR OWN NAMETAG...
...AND RETURN TO THE RENDEZ-VOUS POINT.

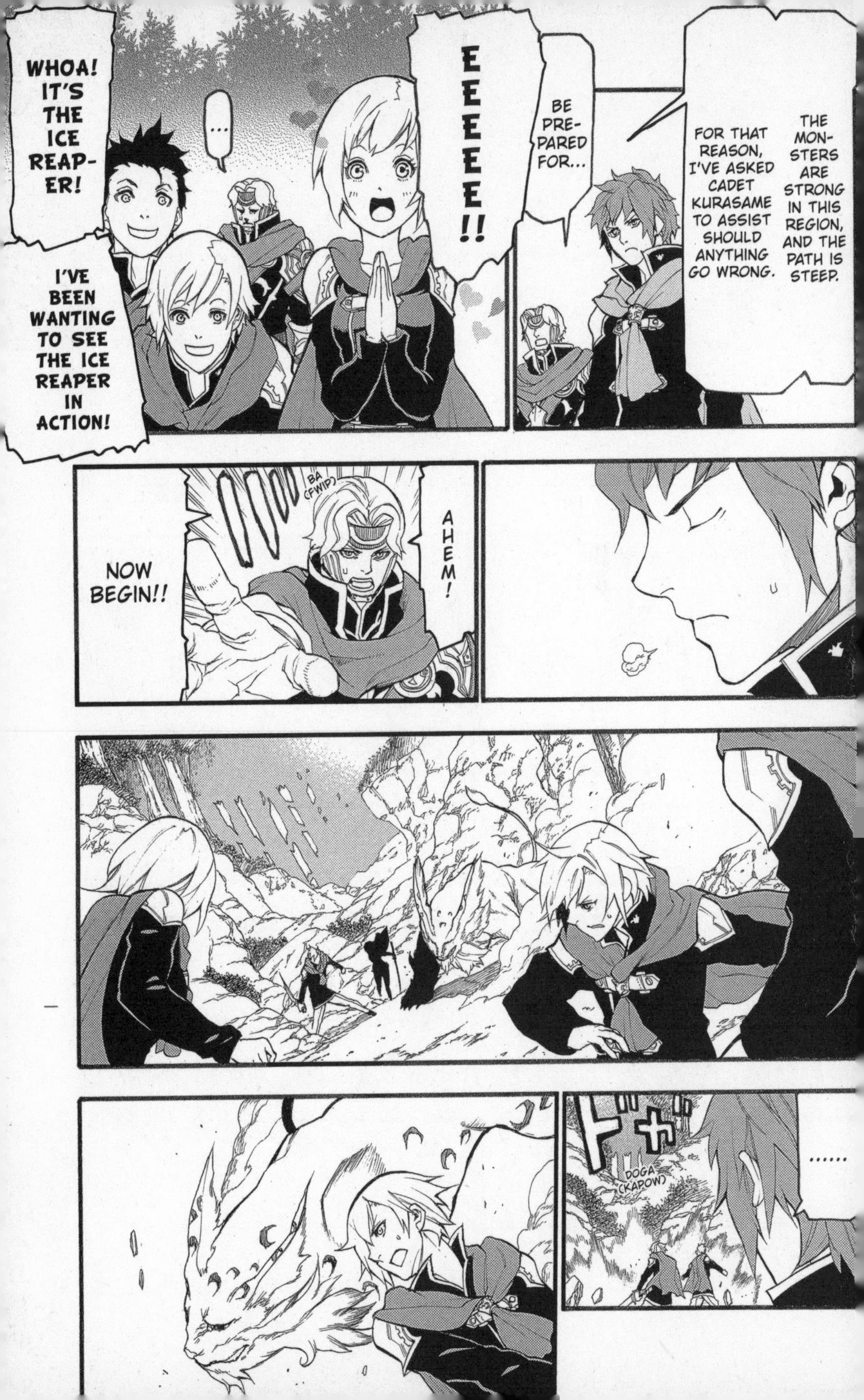
THE MONSTERS ARE STRONG IN THIS REGION, AND THE PATH IS STEEP.
FOR THAT REASON, I'VE ASKED CADET KURASAME TO ASSIST SHOULD ANYTHING GO WRONG.
BE PREPARED FOR...
EEEEEE!!
...
WHOA! IT'S THE ICE REAPER!
I'VE BEEN WANTING TO SEE THE ICE REAPER IN ACTION!
BA (FWIP)
AHEM!
NOW BEGIN!!
DOGA (KAPOW)
......

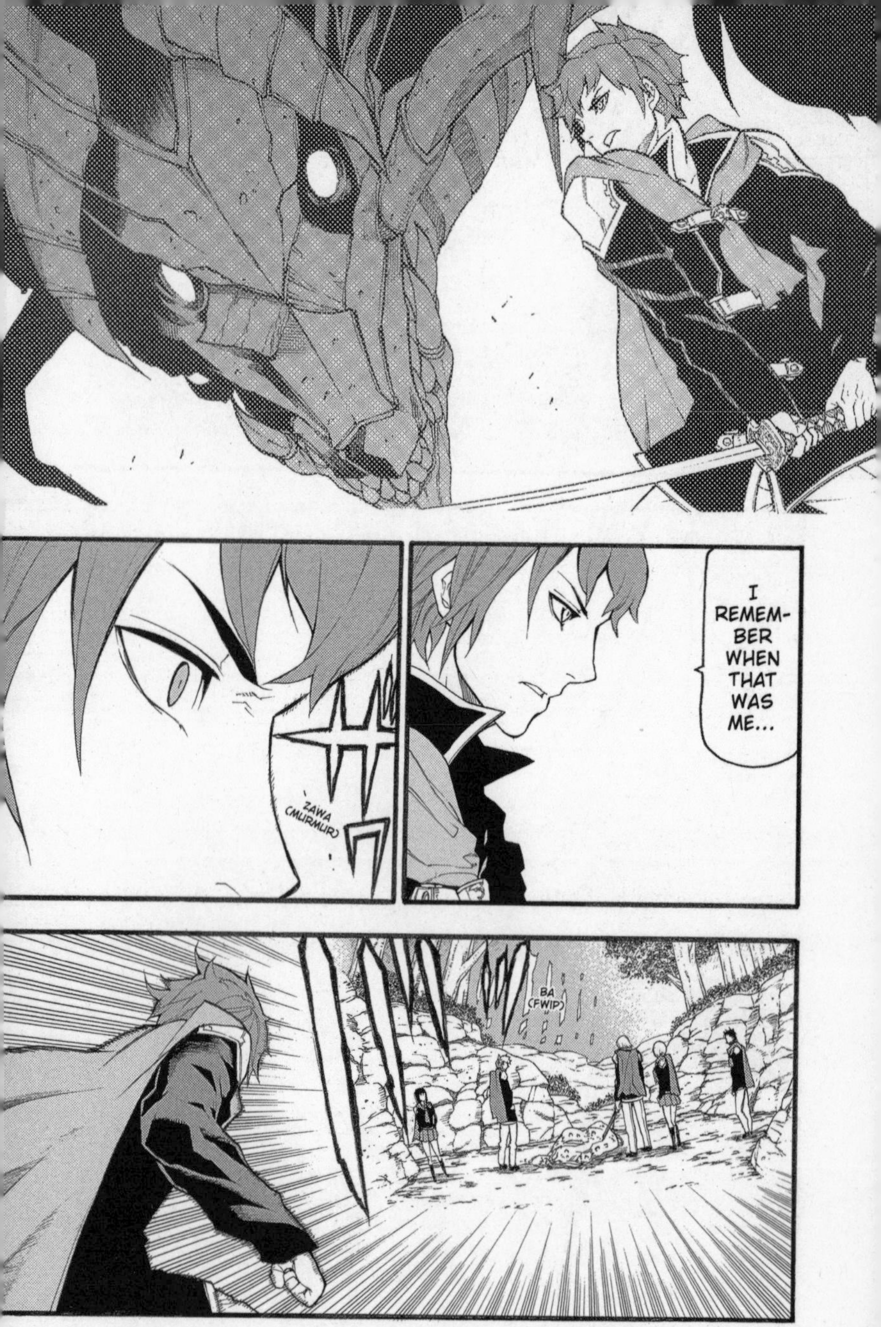
I REMEMBER WHEN THAT WAS ME...
ZAWA (MURMUR)
BA (FWIP)

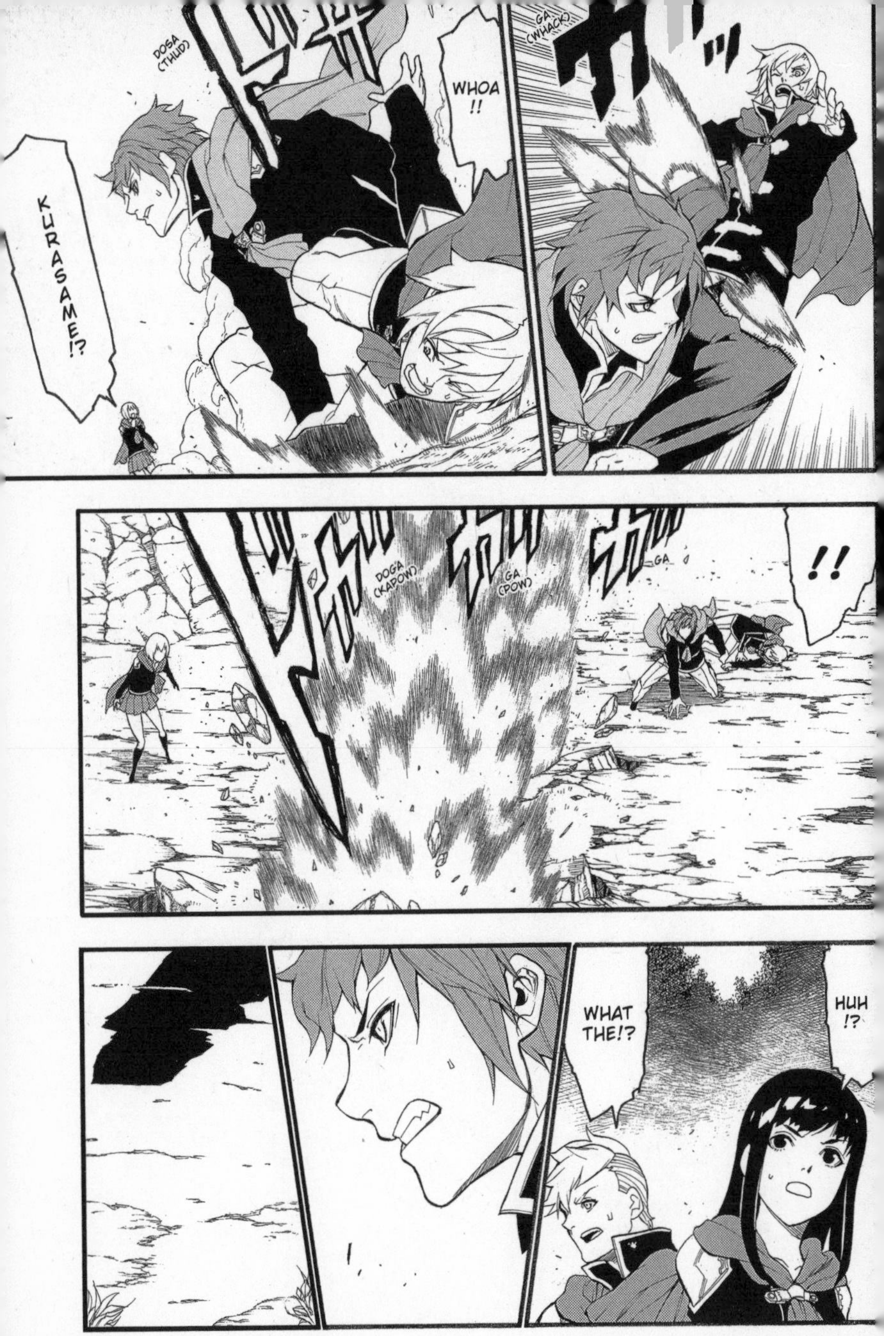
GA (WHACK)
WHOA !!
DOSA (THUD)
KURASAME!?
!!
GA
GA (POW)
DOGA (KAPOW)
HUH !?
WHAT THE!?
!

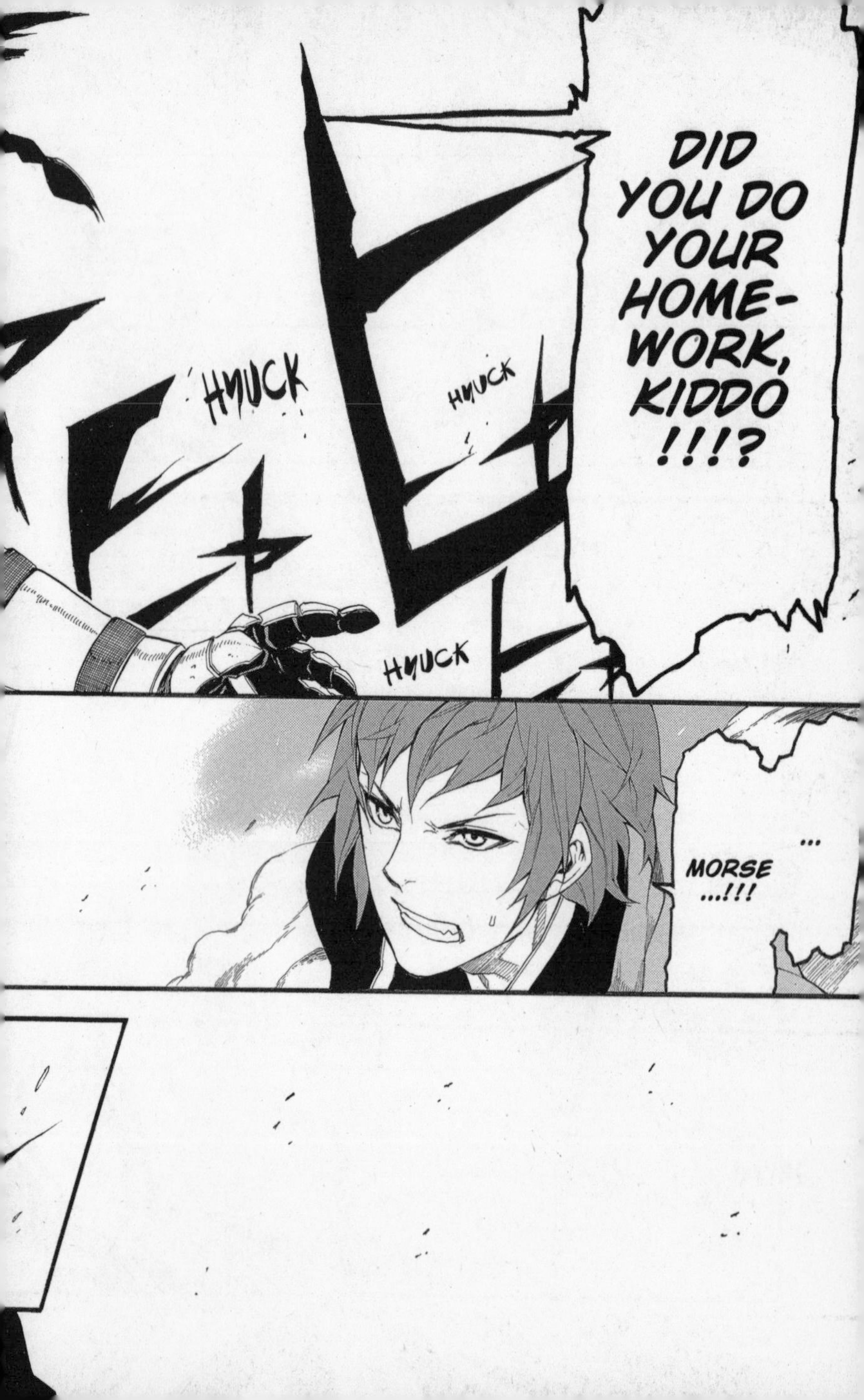
DID YOU DO YOUR HOME-WORK, KIDDO!!!?
HNUCK
HNUCK
HNUCK
... MORSE ...!!!

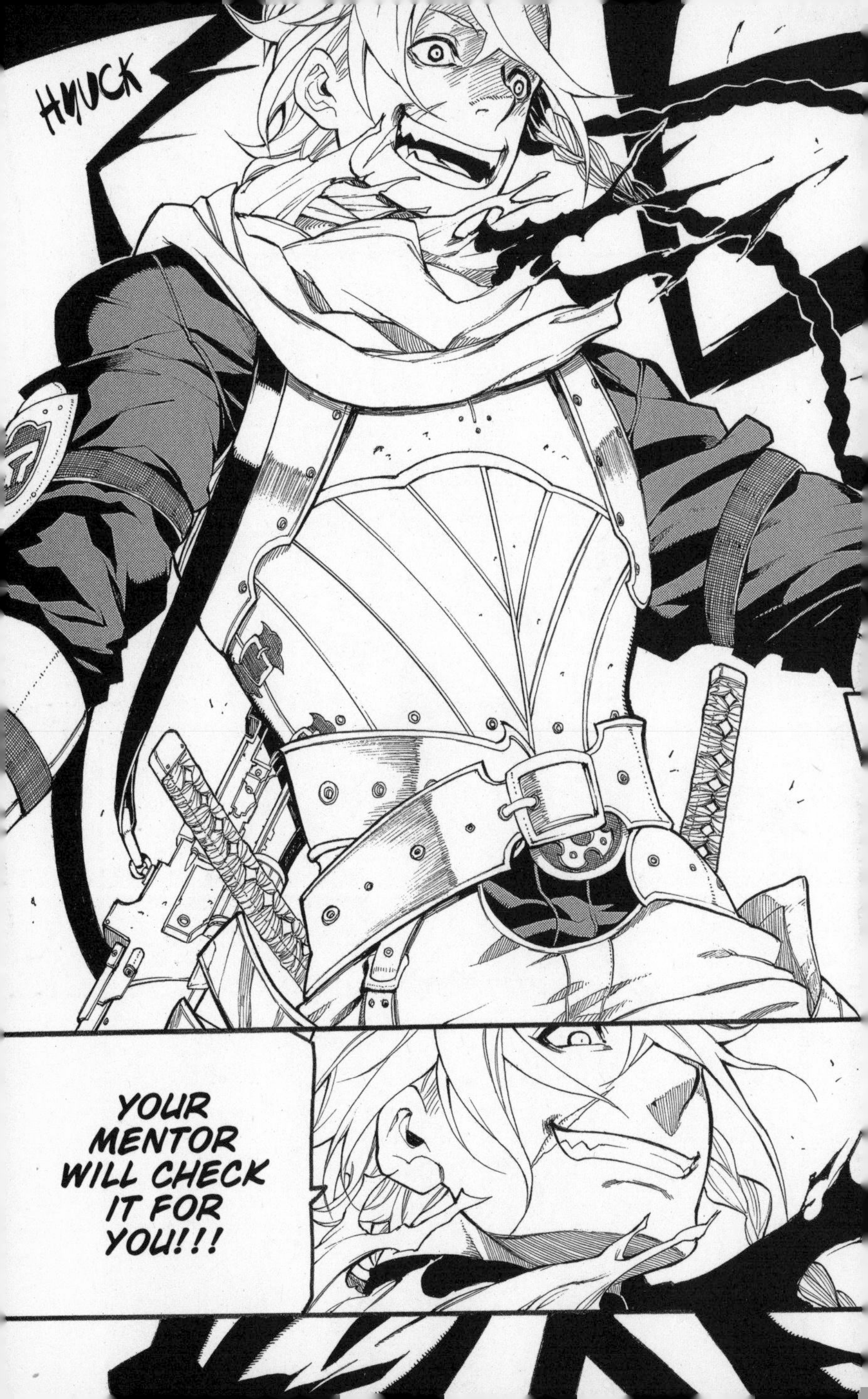
HNUCK
YOUR MENTOR WILL CHECK IT FOR YOU!!!

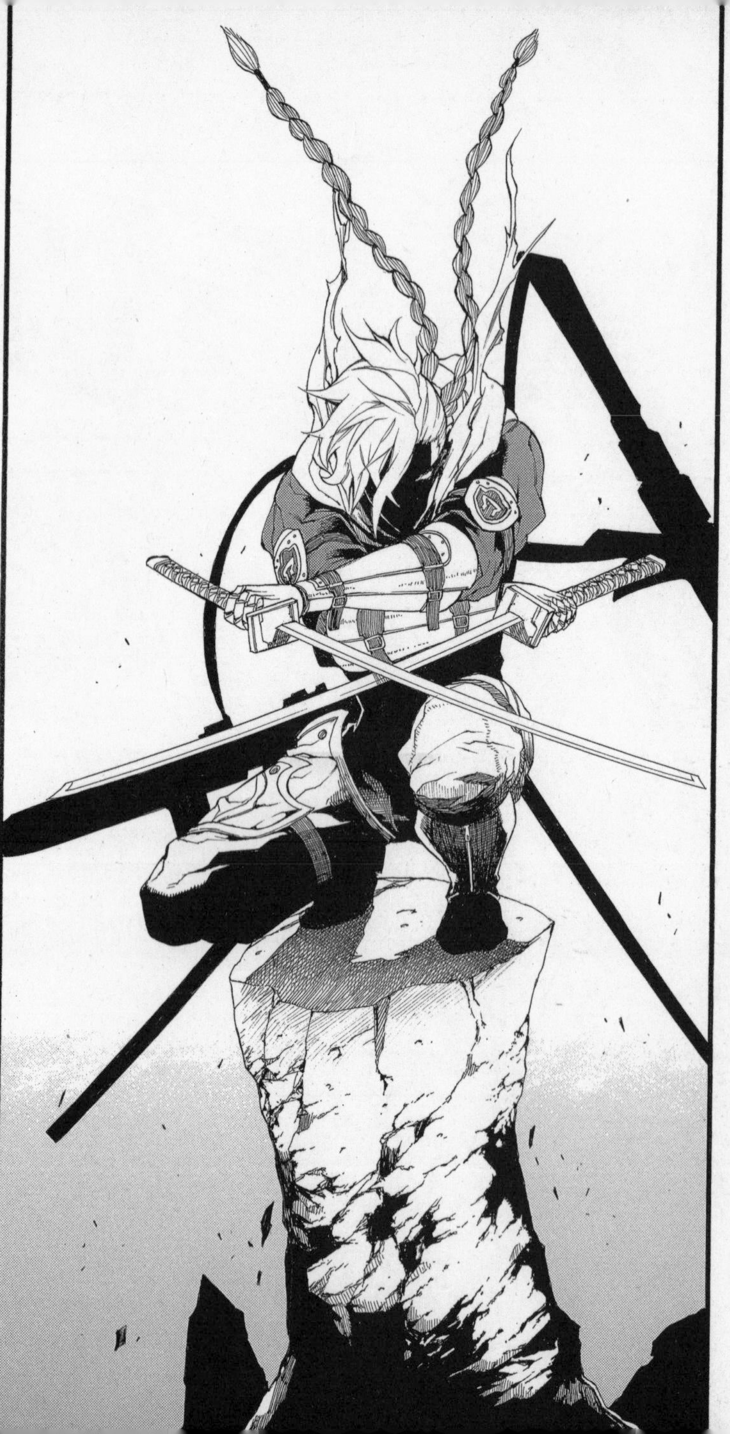

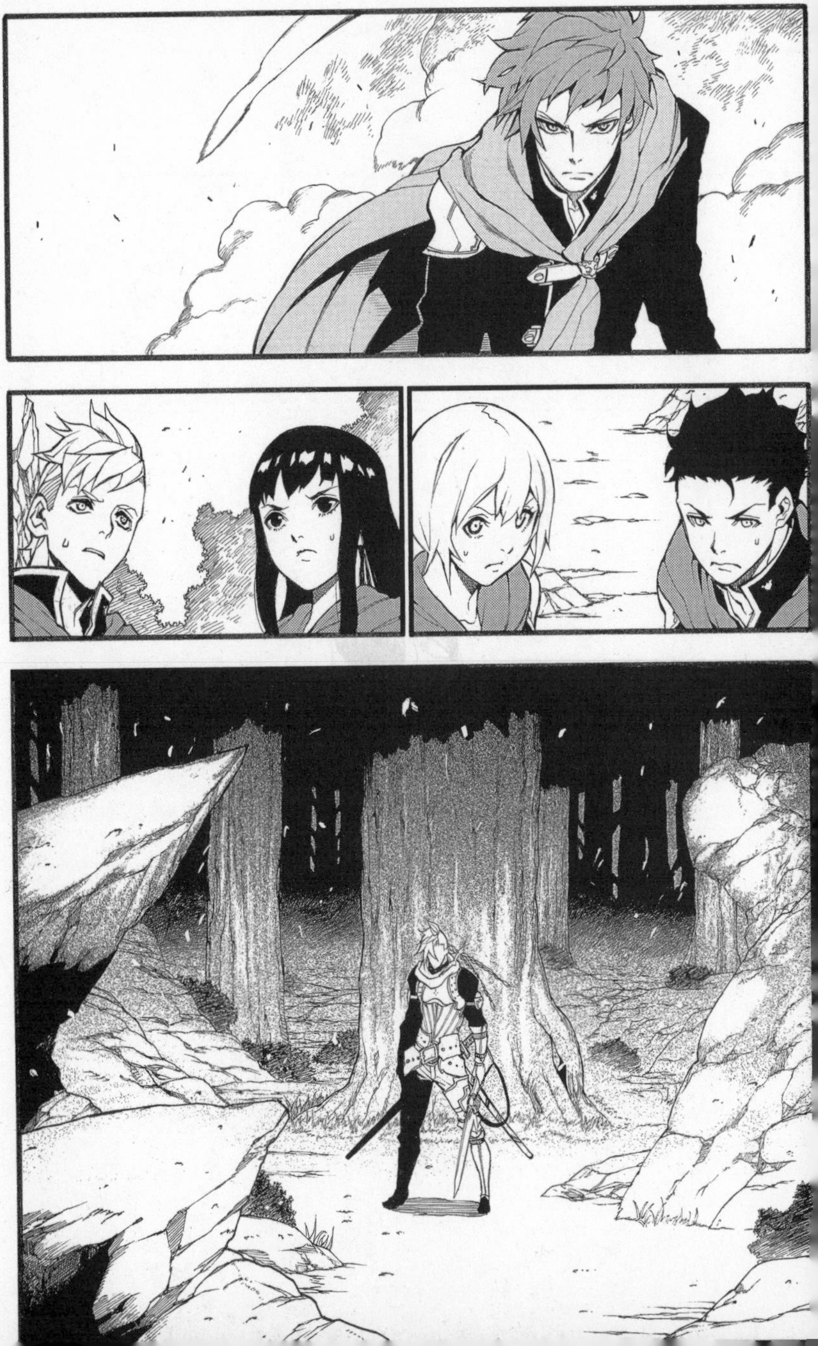

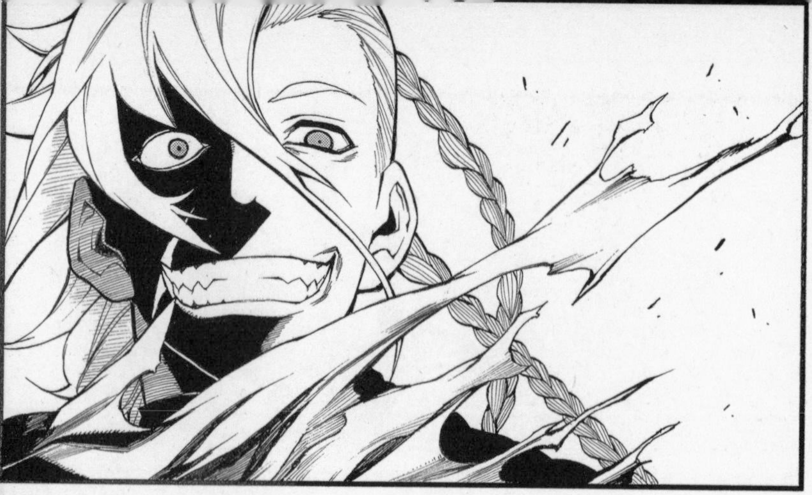

CHAPTER 16: BETRAYAL

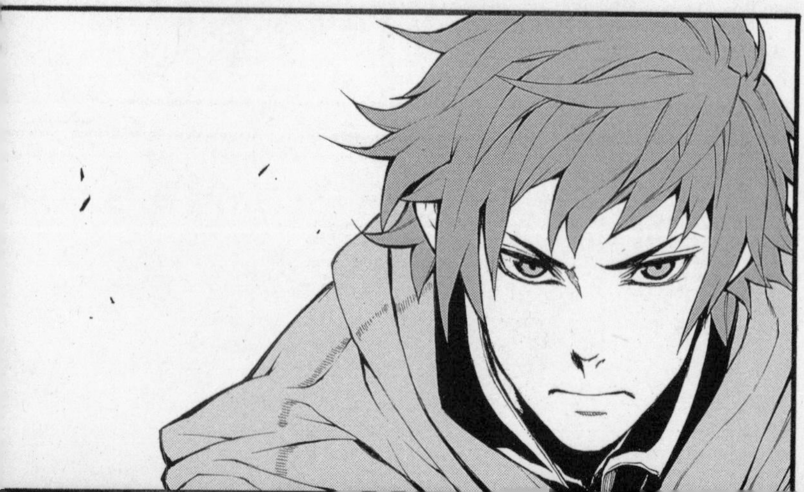

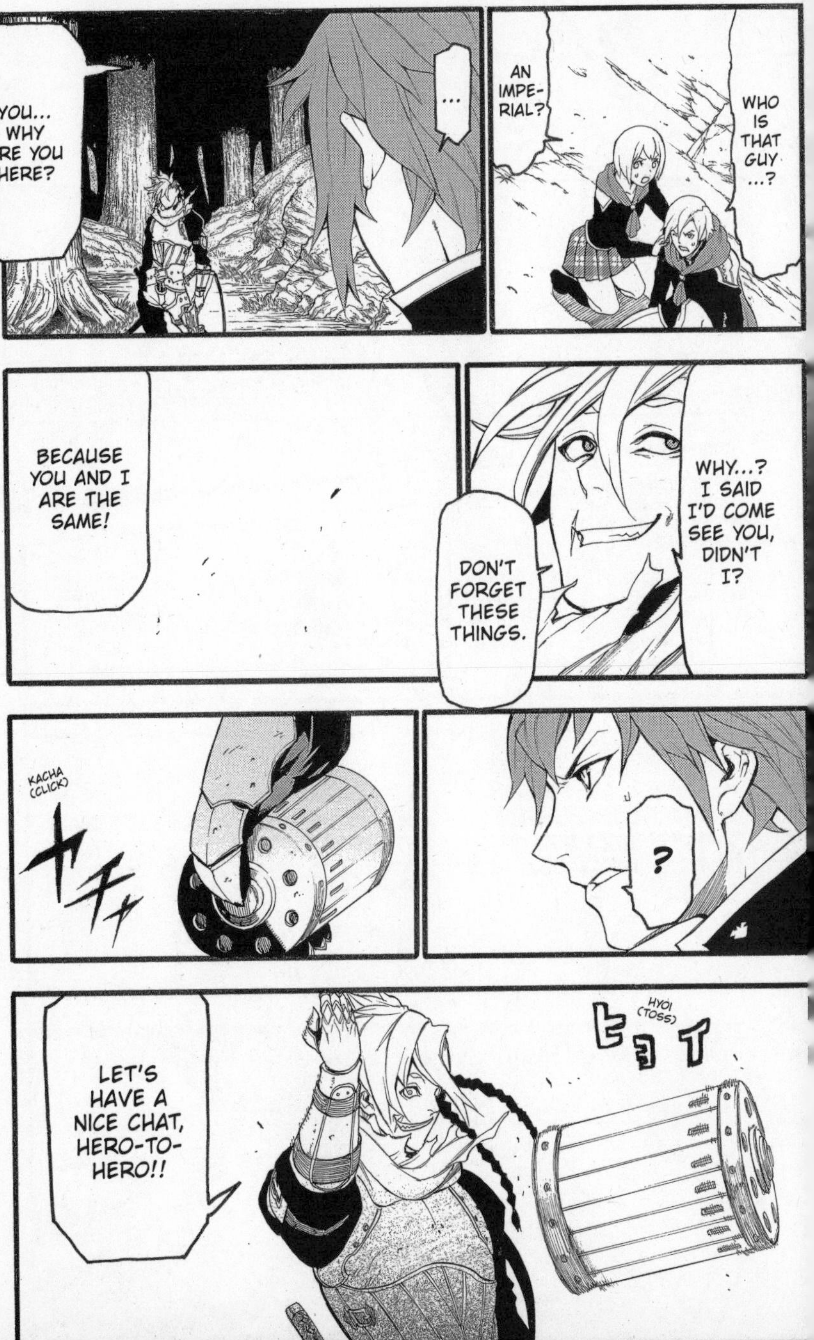
WHO IS THAT GUY ...?
AN IMPERIAL?
...
YOU... WHY ARE YOU HERE?
WHY...? I SAID I'D COME SEE YOU, DIDN'T I?
DON'T FORGET THESE THINGS.
BECAUSE YOU AND I ARE THE SAME!
?
KACHA (CLICK)
カチャ
HYOI (TOSS)
ヒョイ
LET'S HAVE A NICE CHAT, HERO-TO-HERO!!

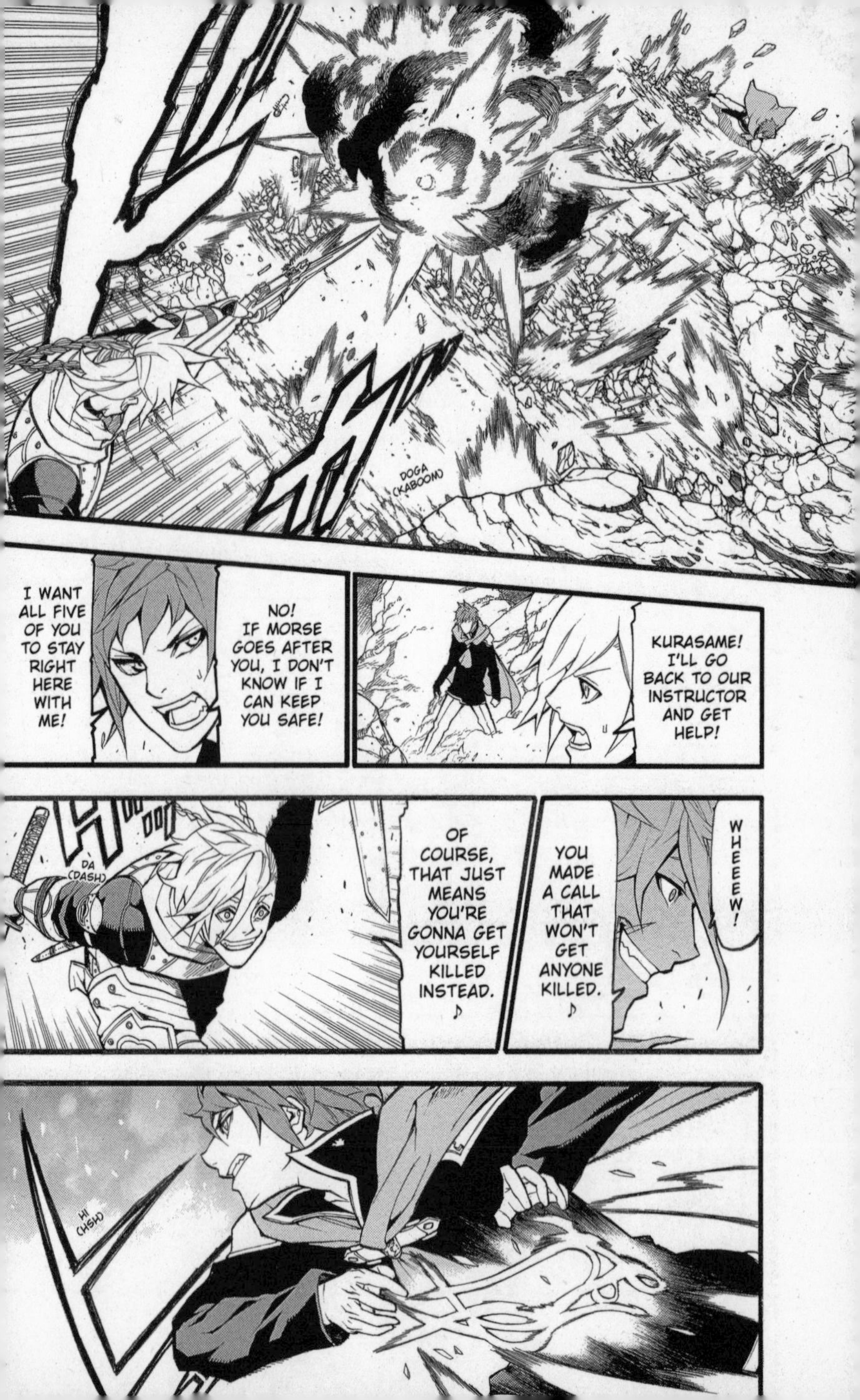
DOGA (KABOOM)
KURASAME! I'LL GO BACK TO OUR INSTRUCTOR AND GET HELP!
NO! IF MORSE GOES AFTER YOU, I DON'T KNOW IF I CAN KEEP YOU SAFE!
I WANT ALL FIVE OF YOU TO STAY RIGHT HERE WITH ME!
WHEEEW!
YOU MADE A CALL THAT WON'T GET ANYONE KILLED. ♪
OF COURSE, THAT JUST MEANS YOU'RE GONNA GET YOURSELF KILLED INSTEAD. ♪
DA (DASH)
HI (HSH)

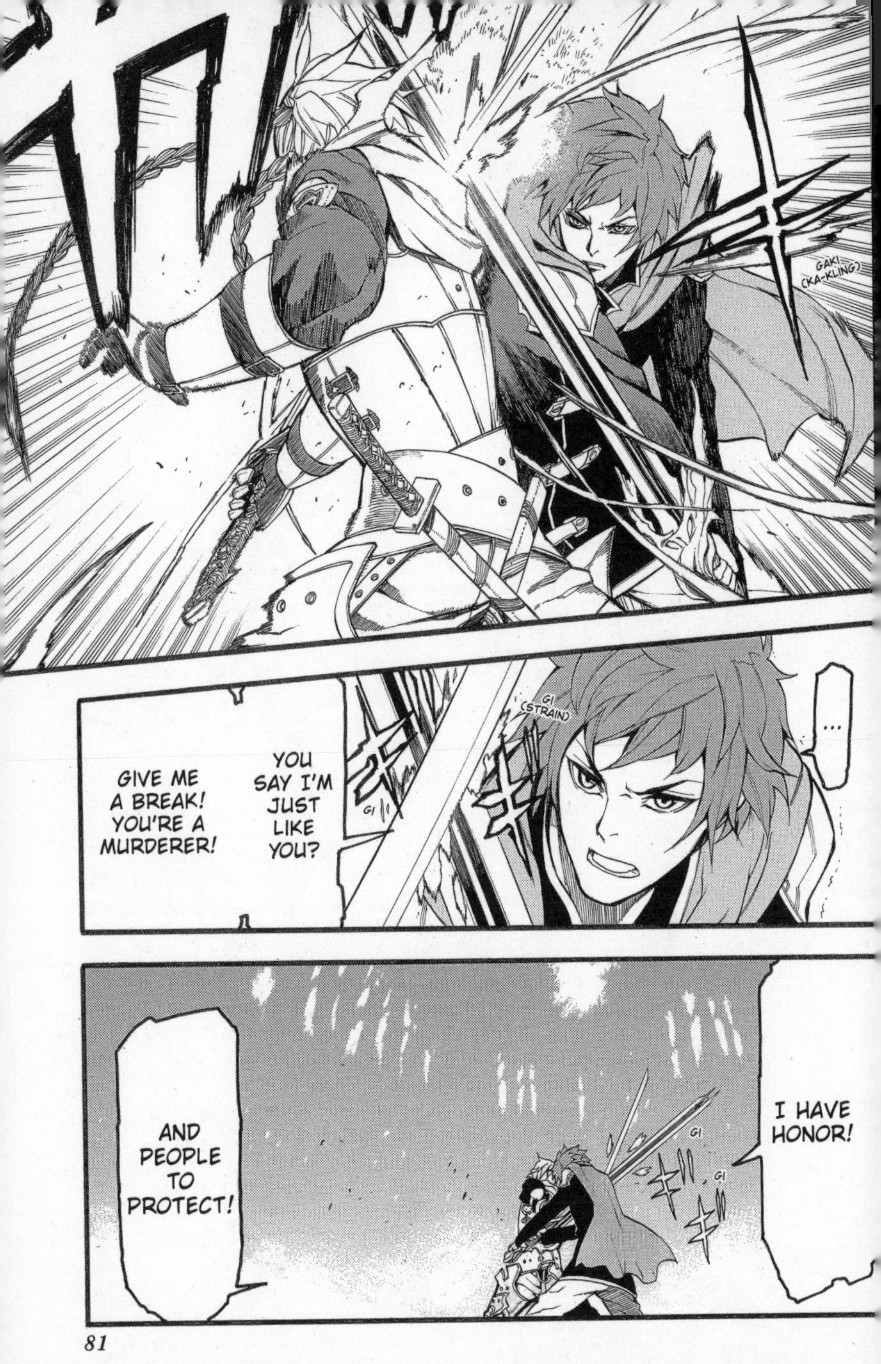
GAKI (KA-KLING)
...
GI (STRAIN)
GI
YOU SAY I'M JUST LIKE YOU?
GIVE ME A BREAK! YOU'RE A MURDERER!
I HAVE HONOR!
GI
GI
AND PEOPLE TO PROTECT!

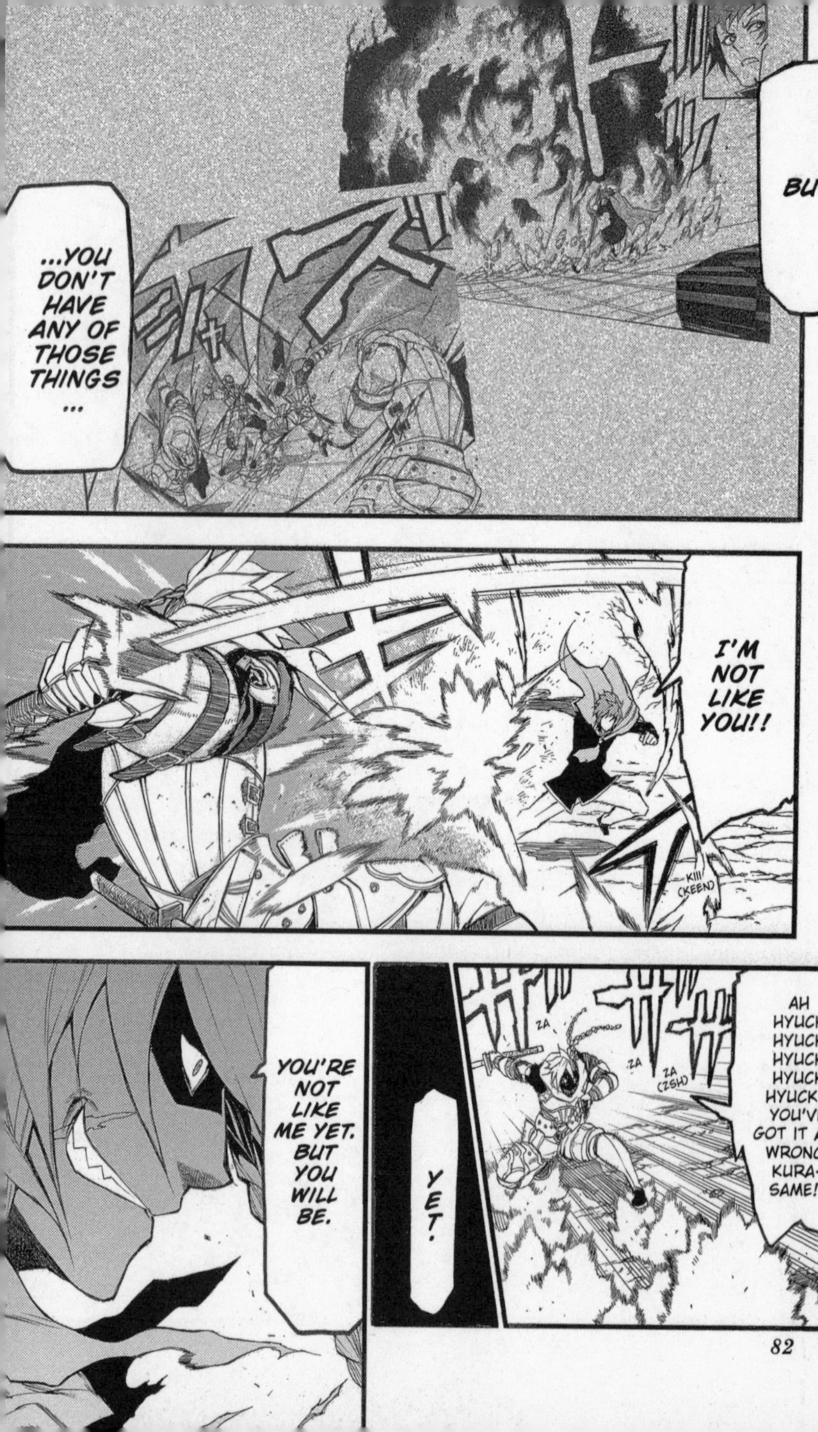
BUT...
...YOU DON'T HAVE ANY OF THOSE THINGS...
I'M NOT LIKE YOU!!
KIII (KEEN)
AH HYUCK HYUCK HYUCK HYUCK HYUCK!! YOU'VE GOT IT ALL WRONG, KURA-SAME!!
ZA
ZA
ZA (ZSH)
YET.
YOU'RE NOT LIKE ME YET. BUT YOU WILL BE.

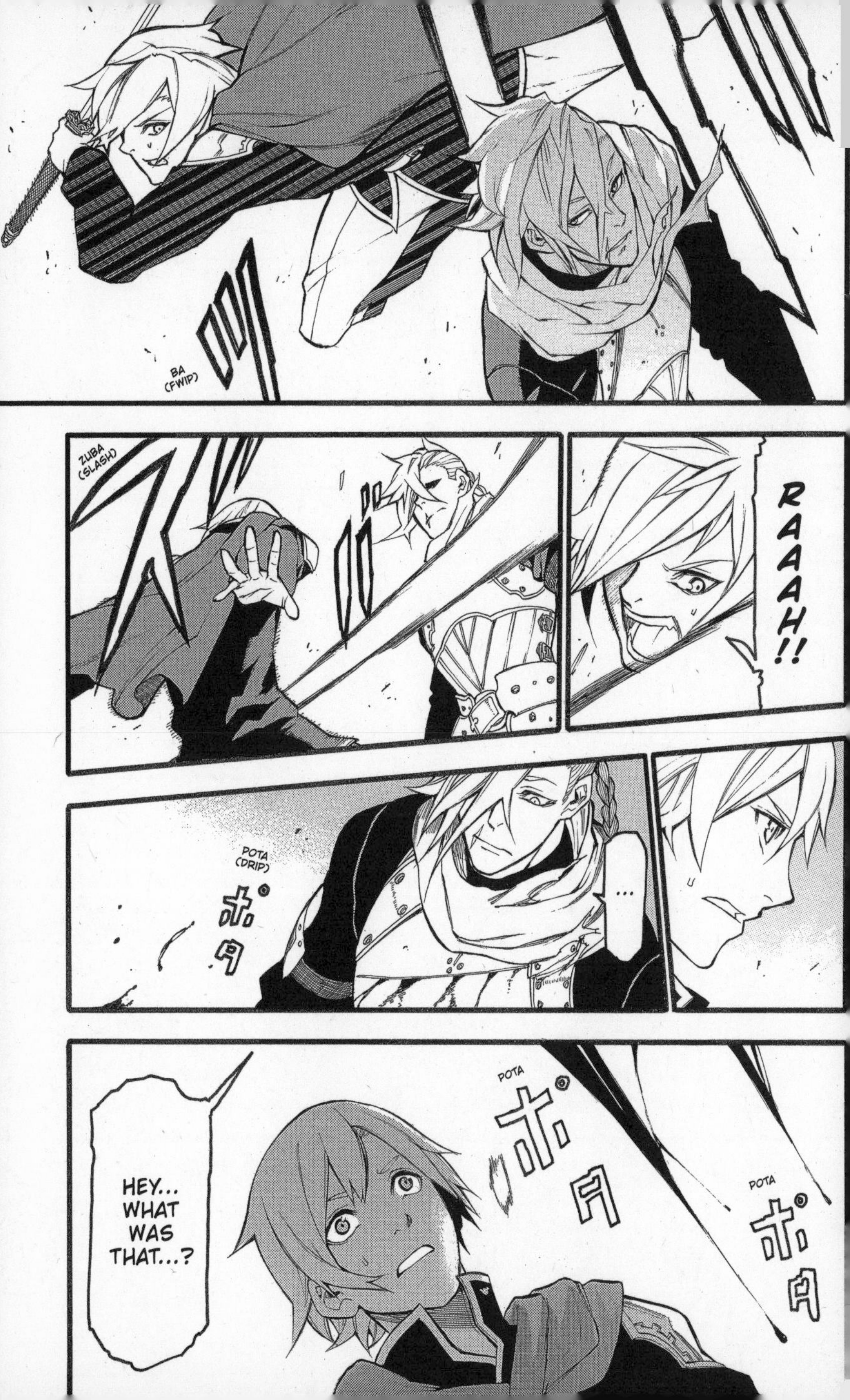
BA (FWIP)
RAAAAH!!
ZUBA (SLASH)
...
POTA (DRIP)
POTA
POTA
HEY... WHAT WAS THAT...?

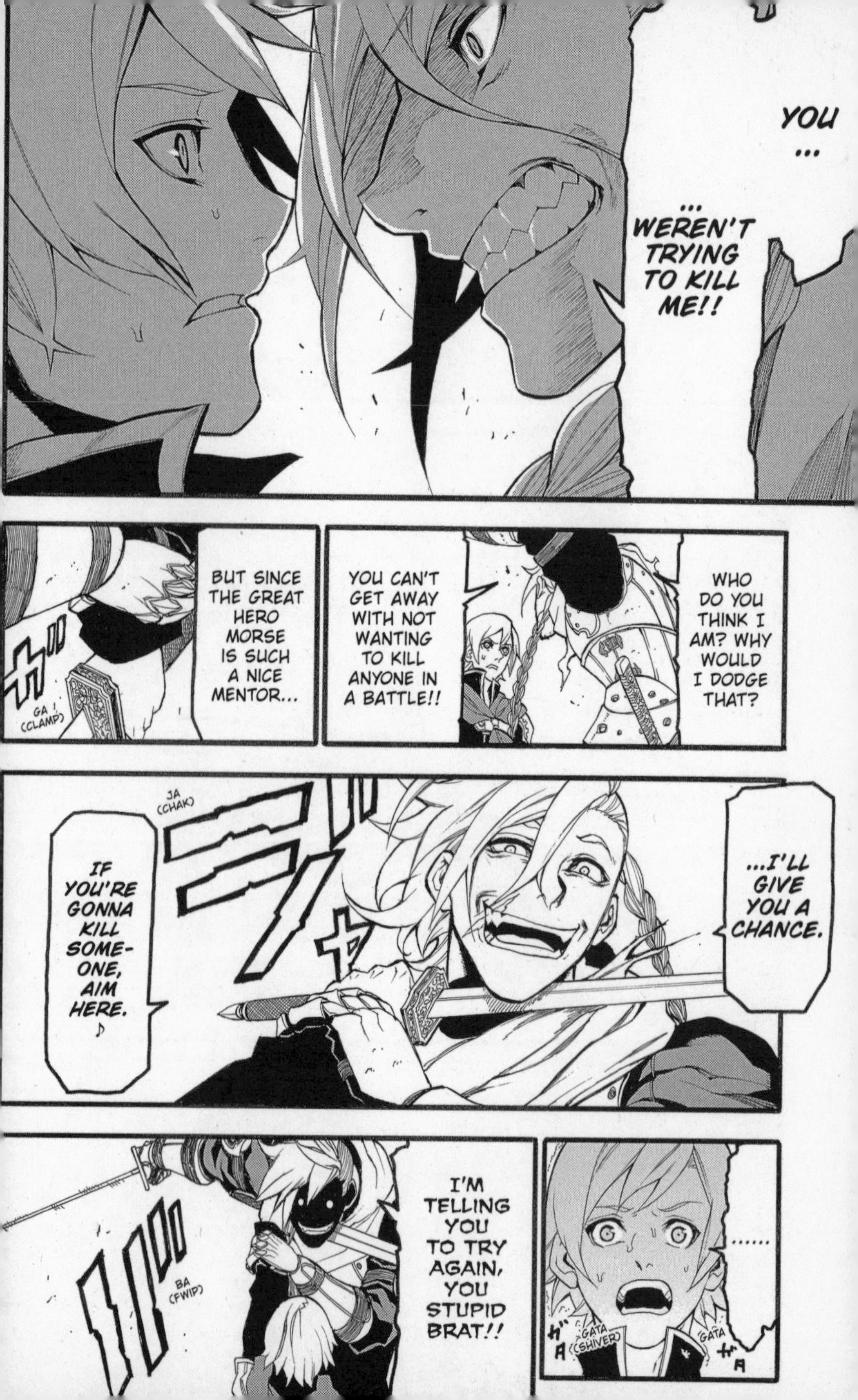
YOU ...
... WEREN'T TRYING TO KILL ME!!
WHO DO YOU THINK I AM? WHY WOULD I DODGE THAT?
YOU CAN'T GET AWAY WITH NOT WANTING TO KILL ANYONE IN A BATTLE!!
BUT SINCE THE GREAT HERO MORSE IS SUCH A NICE MENTOR...
GA (CLAMP)
...I'LL GIVE YOU A CHANCE.
JA (CHAK)
IF YOU'RE GONNA KILL SOME-ONE, AIM HERE. ♪
......
GATA (SHIVER)
GATA
I'M TELLING YOU TO TRY AGAIN, YOU STUPID BRAT!!
BA (FWIP)

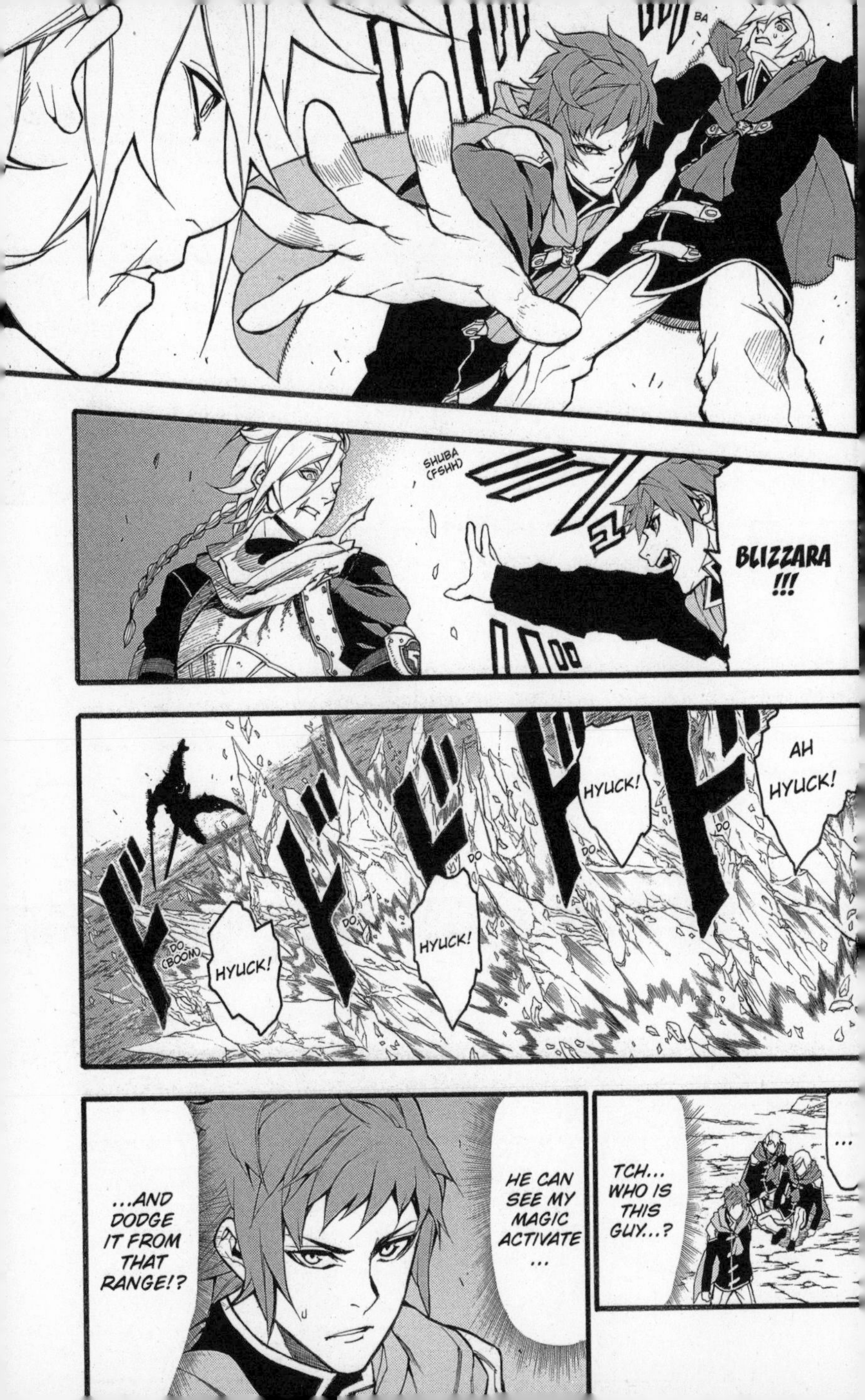
BA
SHUBA (FSHH)
BLIZZARA !!!
AH HYUCK!
HYUCK!
DO
DO
DO
HYUCK!
DO
DO (BOOM)
HYUCK!
...
TCH... WHO IS THIS GUY...?
HE CAN SEE MY MAGIC ACTIVATE ...
...AND DODGE IT FROM THAT RANGE!?

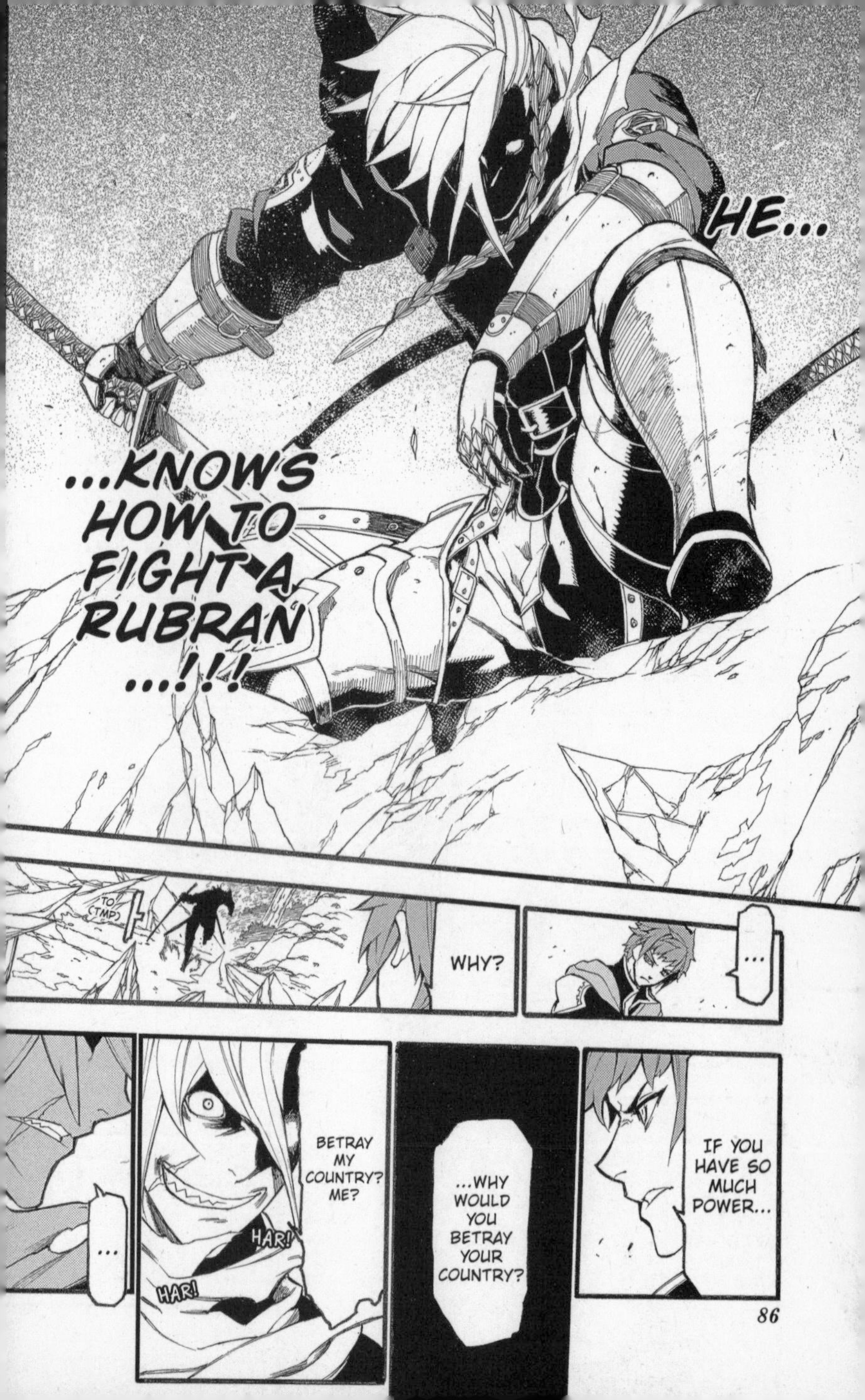
HE...
...KNOWS HOW TO FIGHT A RUBRAN ...!!!
...
WHY?
TO (TMP)
IF YOU HAVE SO MUCH POWER...
...WHY WOULD YOU BETRAY YOUR COUNTRY?
BETRAY MY COUNTRY? ME?
HAR!
HAR!
...

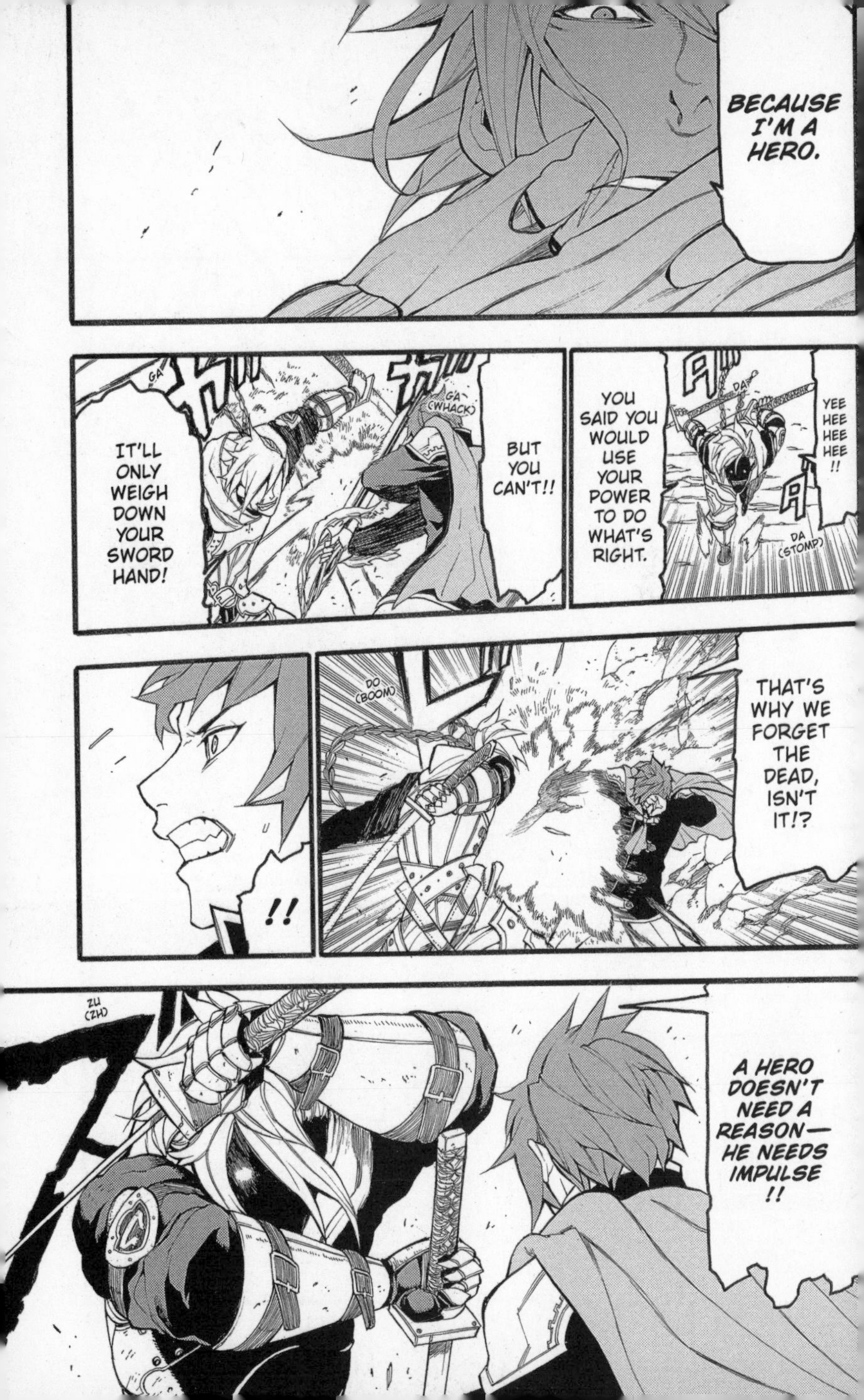
BECAUSE I'M A HERO.
YEE HEE HEE HEE!!
DA (STOMP)
YOU SAID YOU WOULD USE YOUR POWER TO DO WHAT'S RIGHT.
GA (WHACK)
BUT YOU CAN'T!!
GA
IT'LL ONLY WEIGH DOWN YOUR SWORD HAND!
DO (BOOM)
THAT'S WHY WE FORGET THE DEAD, ISN'T IT!?
!!
ZU (ZH)
A HERO DOESN'T NEED A REASON— HE NEEDS IMPULSE!!

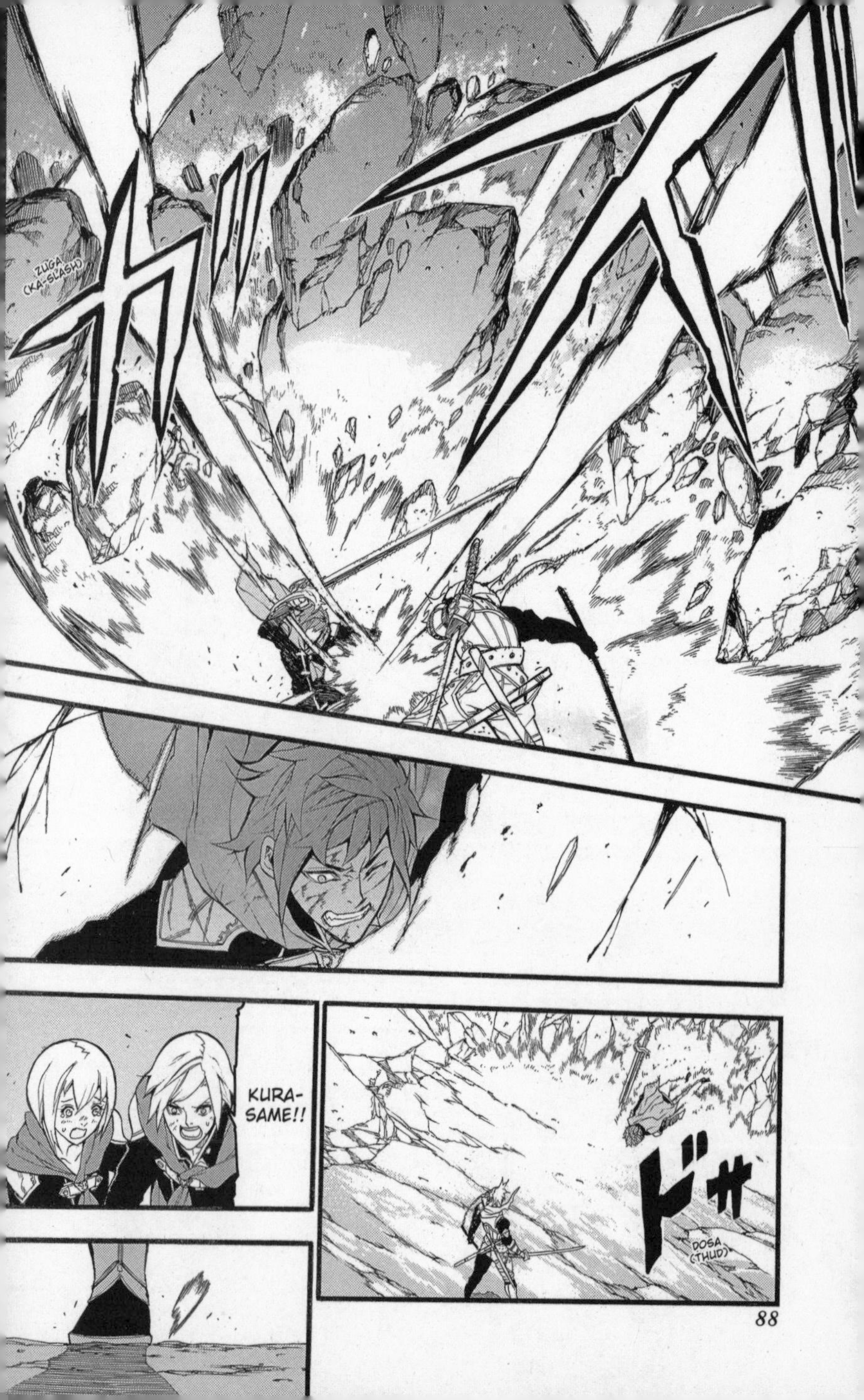
ZUGA (KA-SLASH)
DOSA (THUD)
KURA-SAME!!

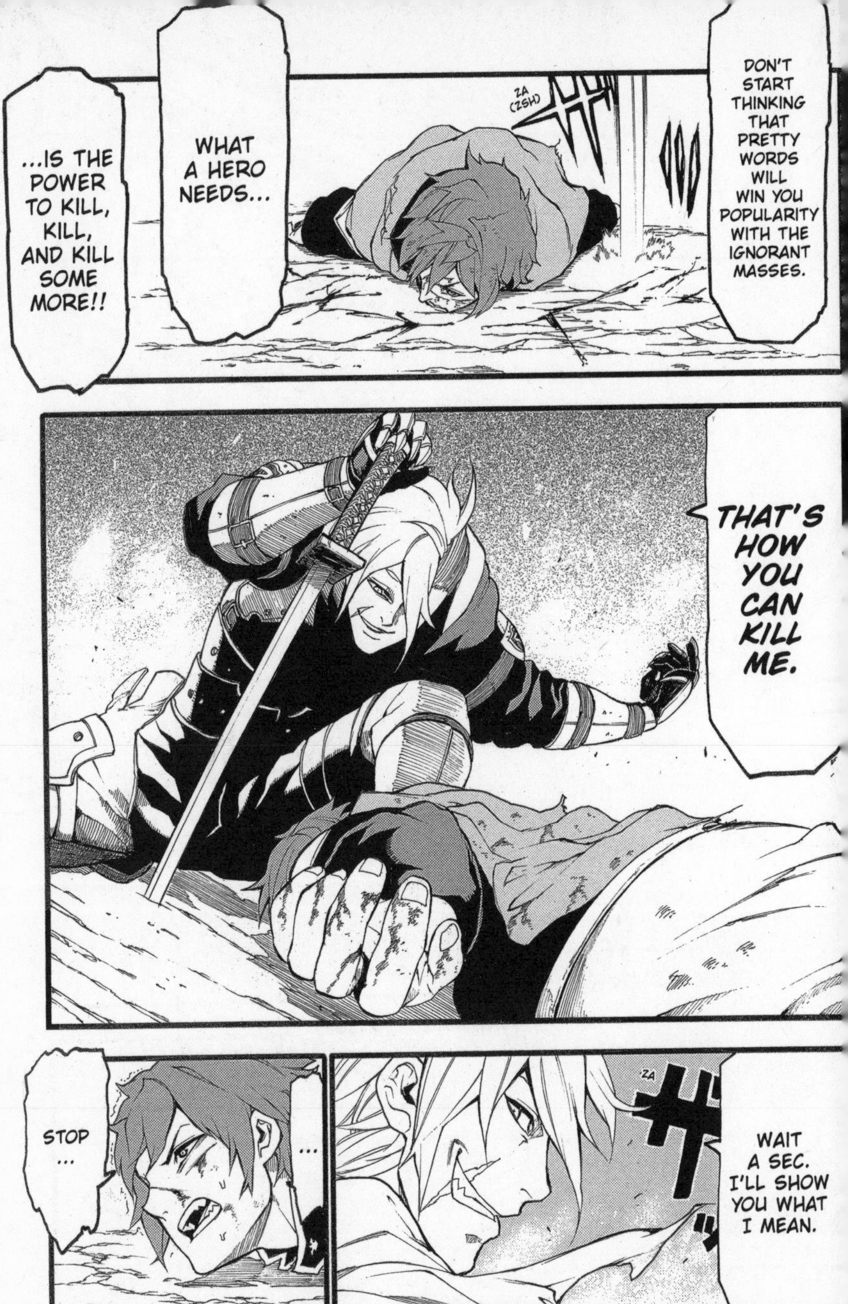
DON'T START THINKING THAT PRETTY WORDS WILL WIN YOU POPULARITY WITH THE IGNORANT MASSES.
ZA (ZSH)
WHAT A HERO NEEDS...
...IS THE POWER TO KILL, KILL, AND KILL SOME MORE!!
THAT'S HOW YOU CAN KILL ME.
WAIT A SEC. I'LL SHOW YOU WHAT I MEAN.
ZA
...
STOP ...

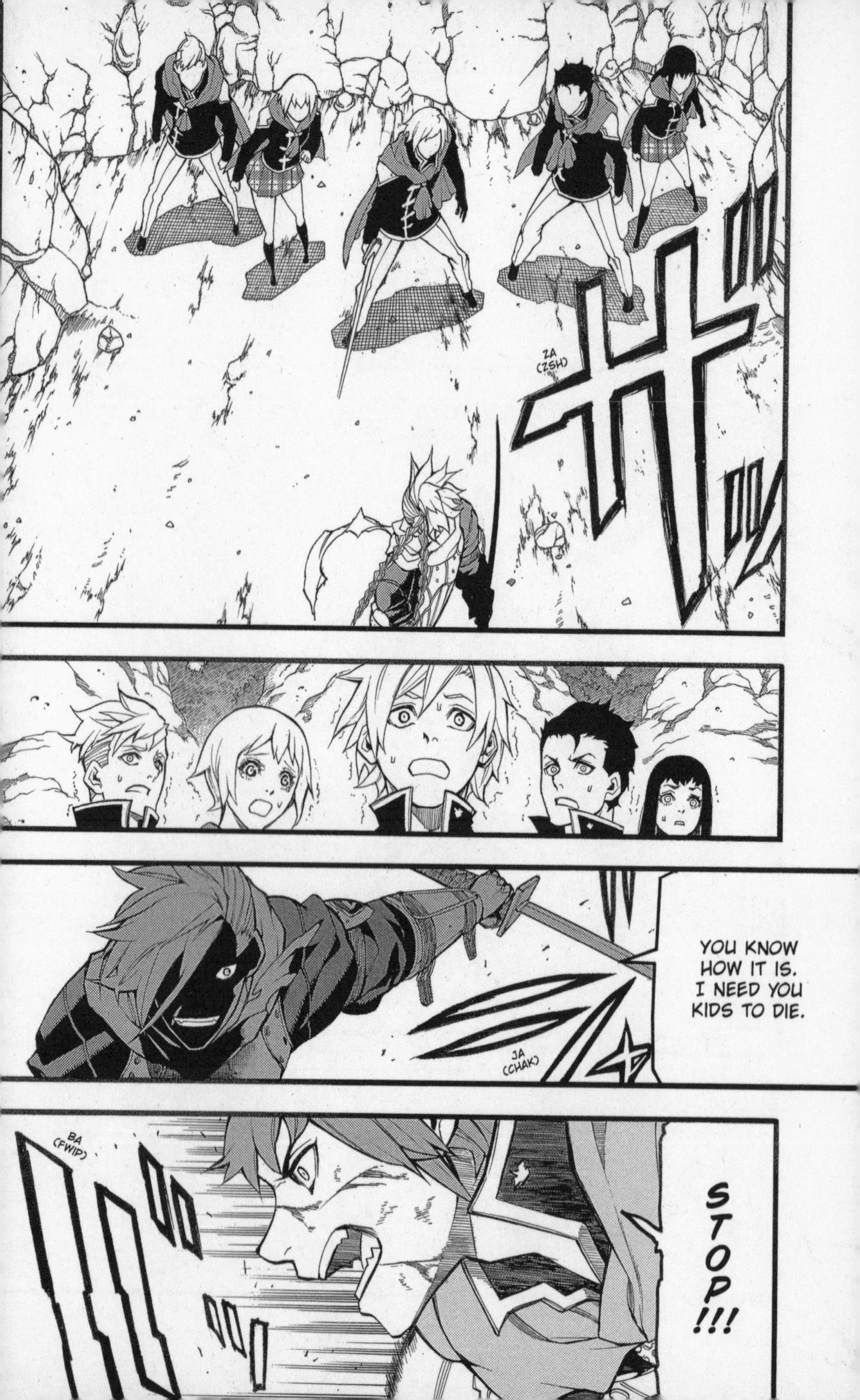
ZA (ZSH)
YOU KNOW HOW IT IS. I NEED YOU KIDS TO DIE.
JA (CHAK)
BA (FWIP)
STOP!!!

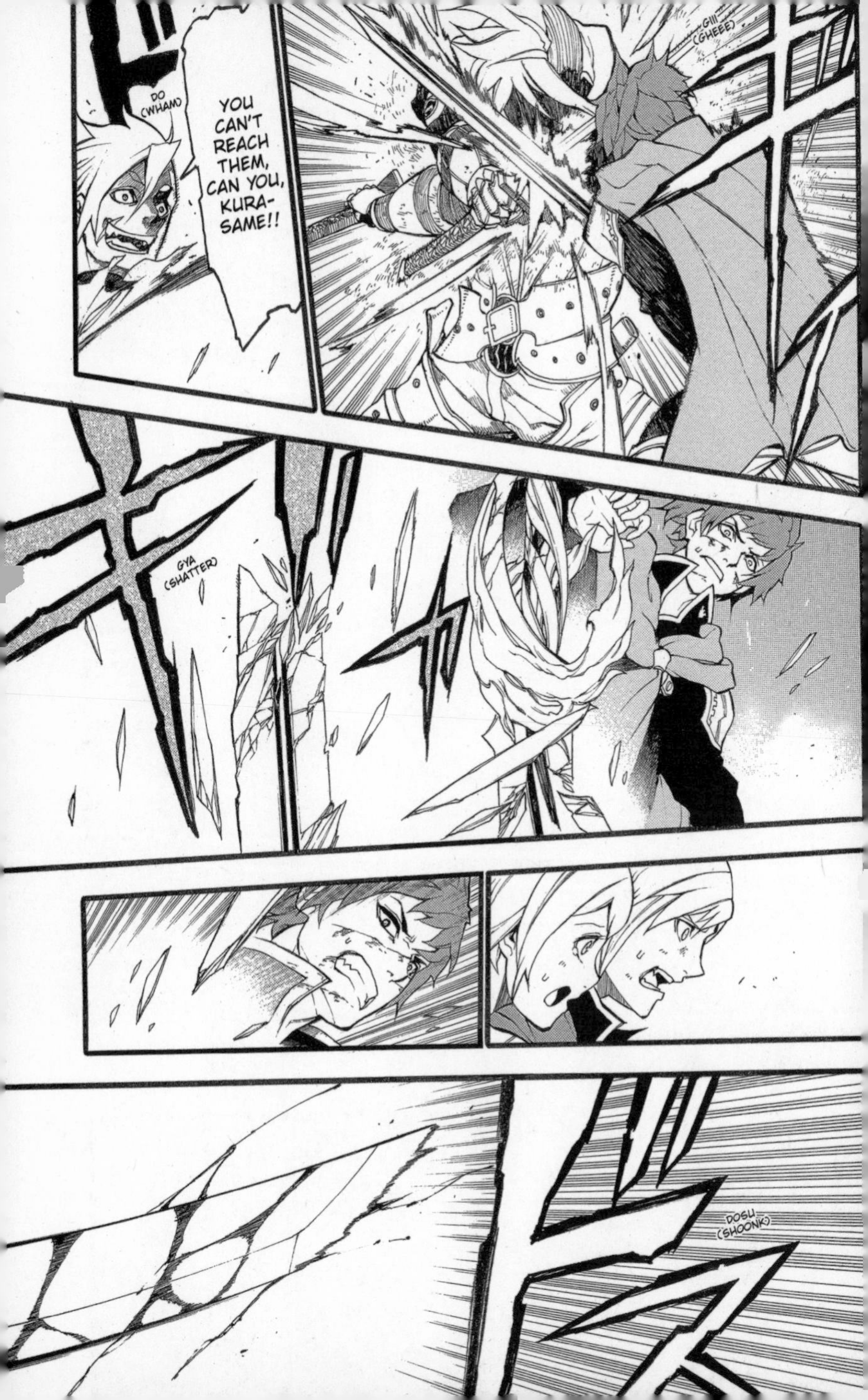
GIII (GHEEE)
DO (WHAM)
YOU CAN'T REACH THEM, CAN YOU, KURA-SAME!!
GYA (SHATTER)
DOSU (SHOONK)

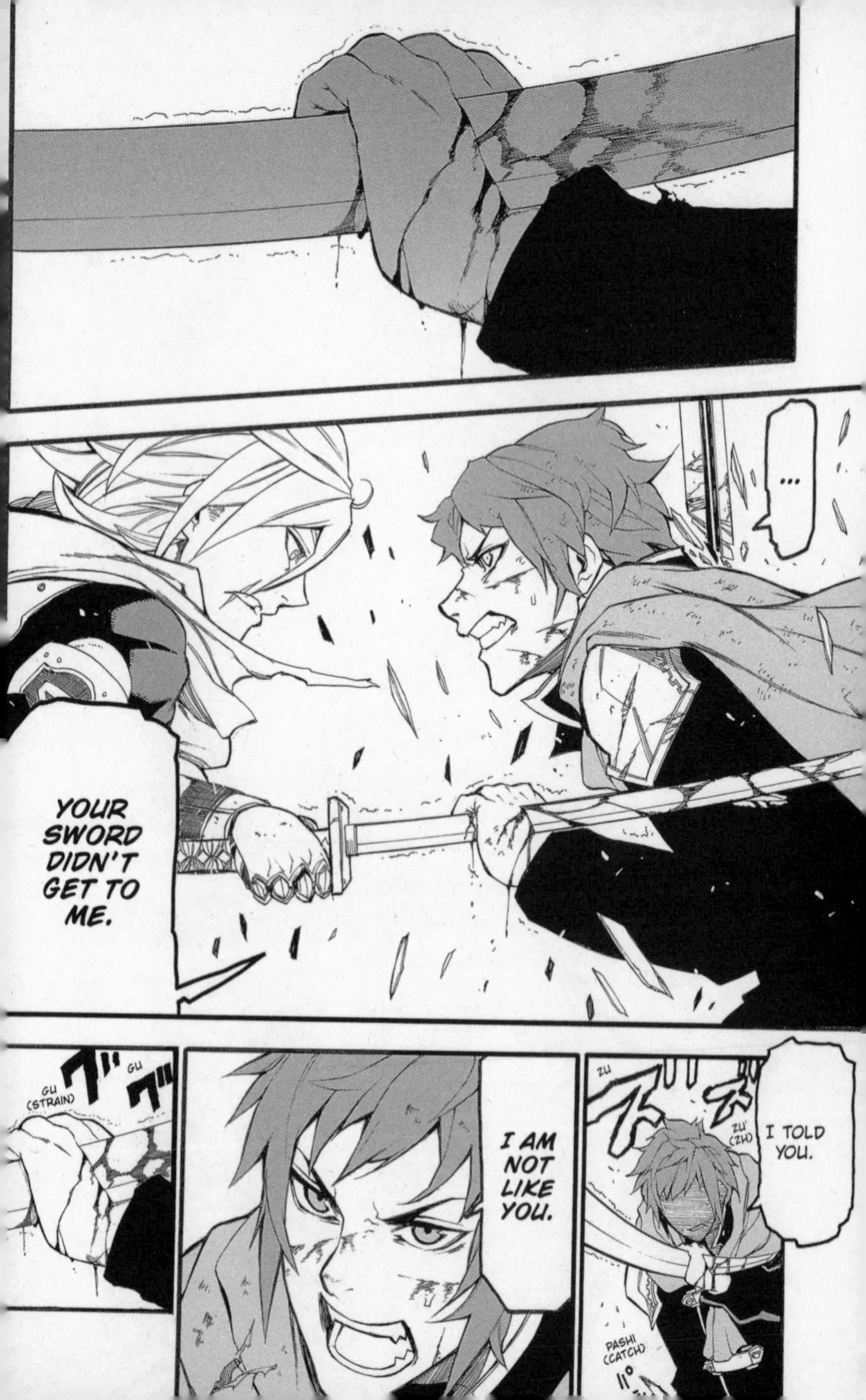
...
YOUR SWORD DIDN'T GET TO ME.
I TOLD YOU.
ZU
ZU' (ZH)
PASHI (CATCH)
I AM NOT LIKE YOU.
GU
GU (STRAIN)

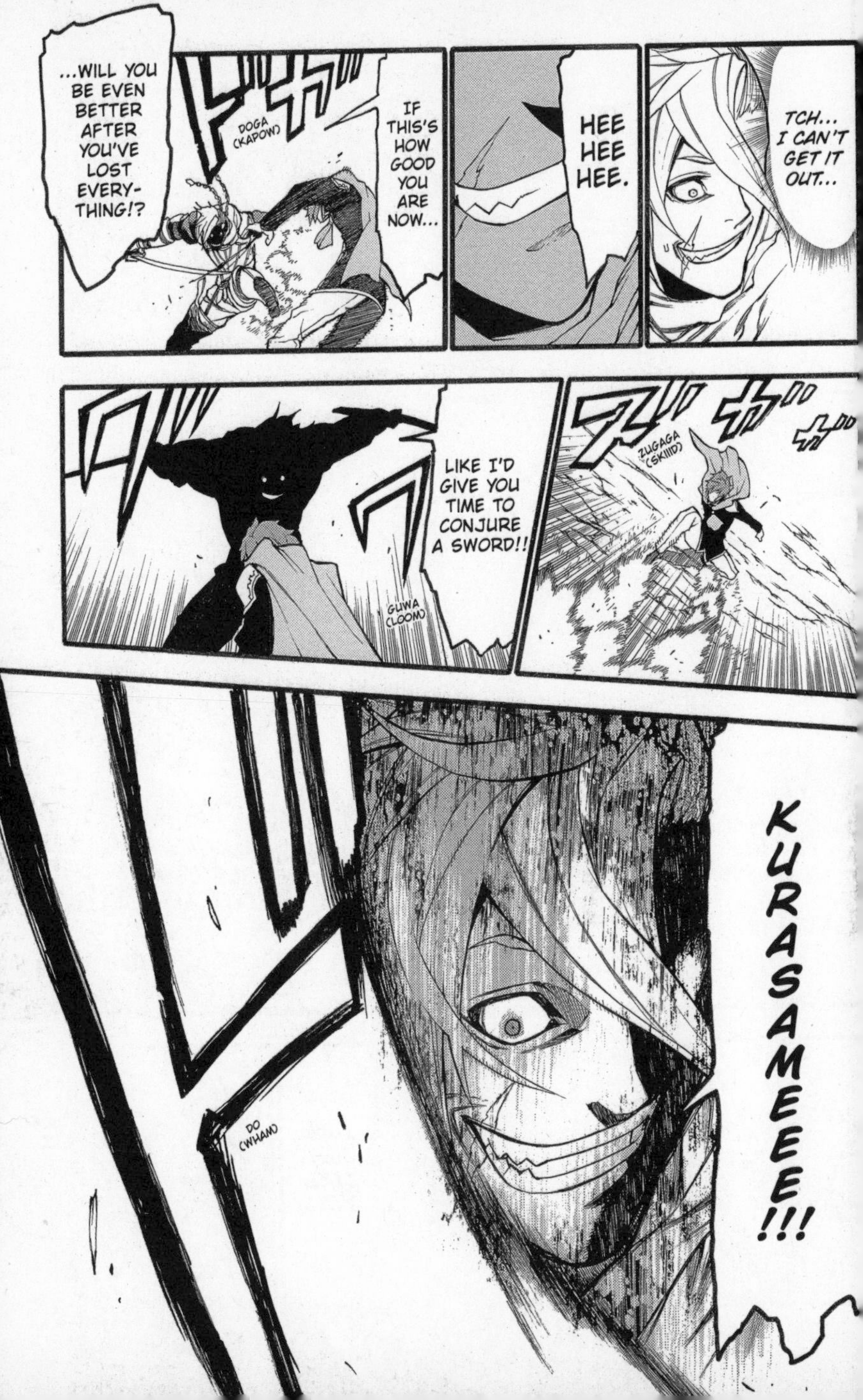
TCH... I CAN'T GET IT OUT...
HEE HEE HEE.
IF THIS'S HOW GOOD YOU ARE NOW...
...WILL YOU BE EVEN BETTER AFTER YOU'VE LOST EVERY-THING!?
DOGA (KAPOW)
ZUGAGA (SKIIID)
LIKE I'D GIVE YOU TIME TO CONJURE A SWORD!!
GUWA (LOOM)
KURASAMEEEE!!!
DO (WHAM)

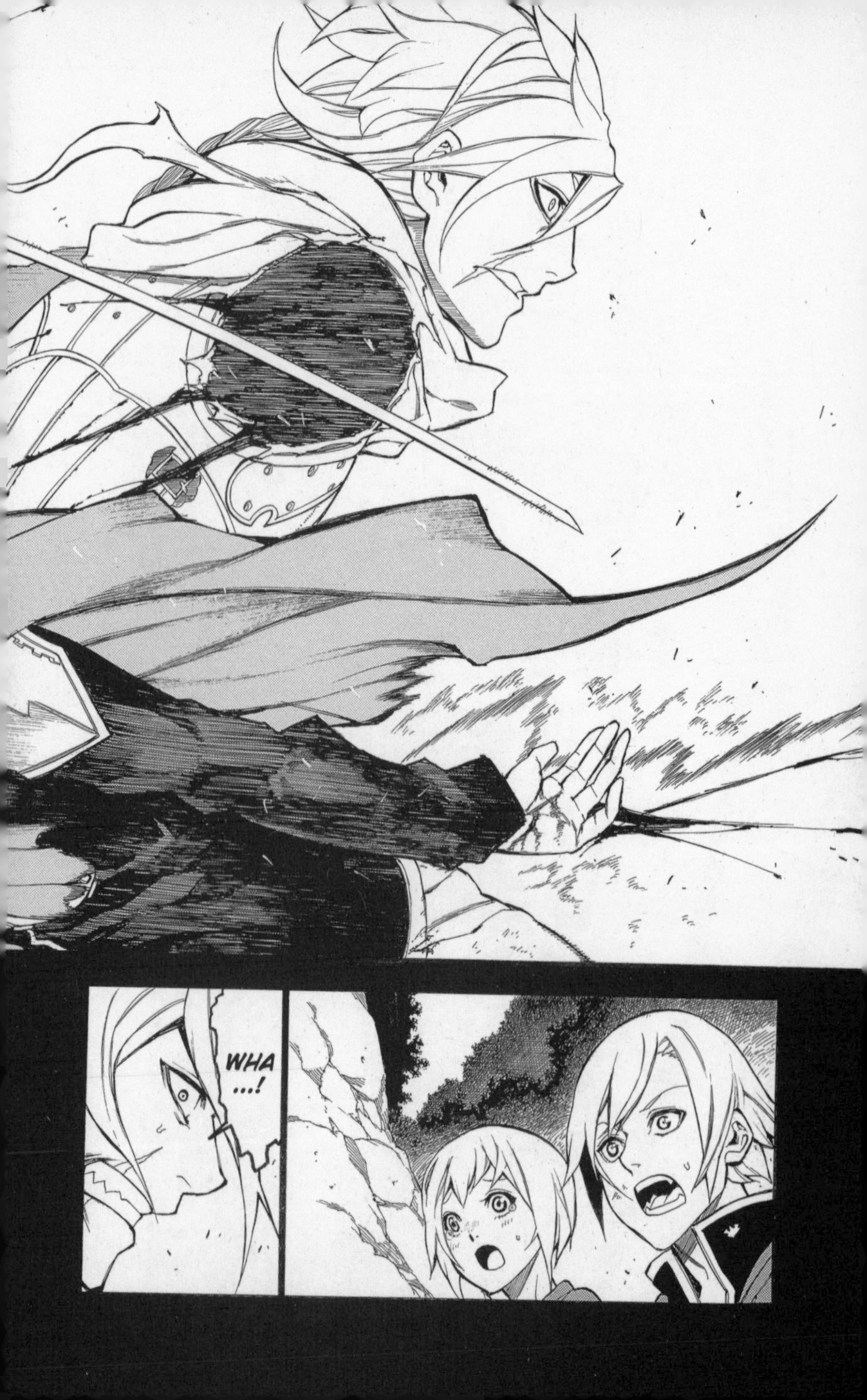
WHA ...!

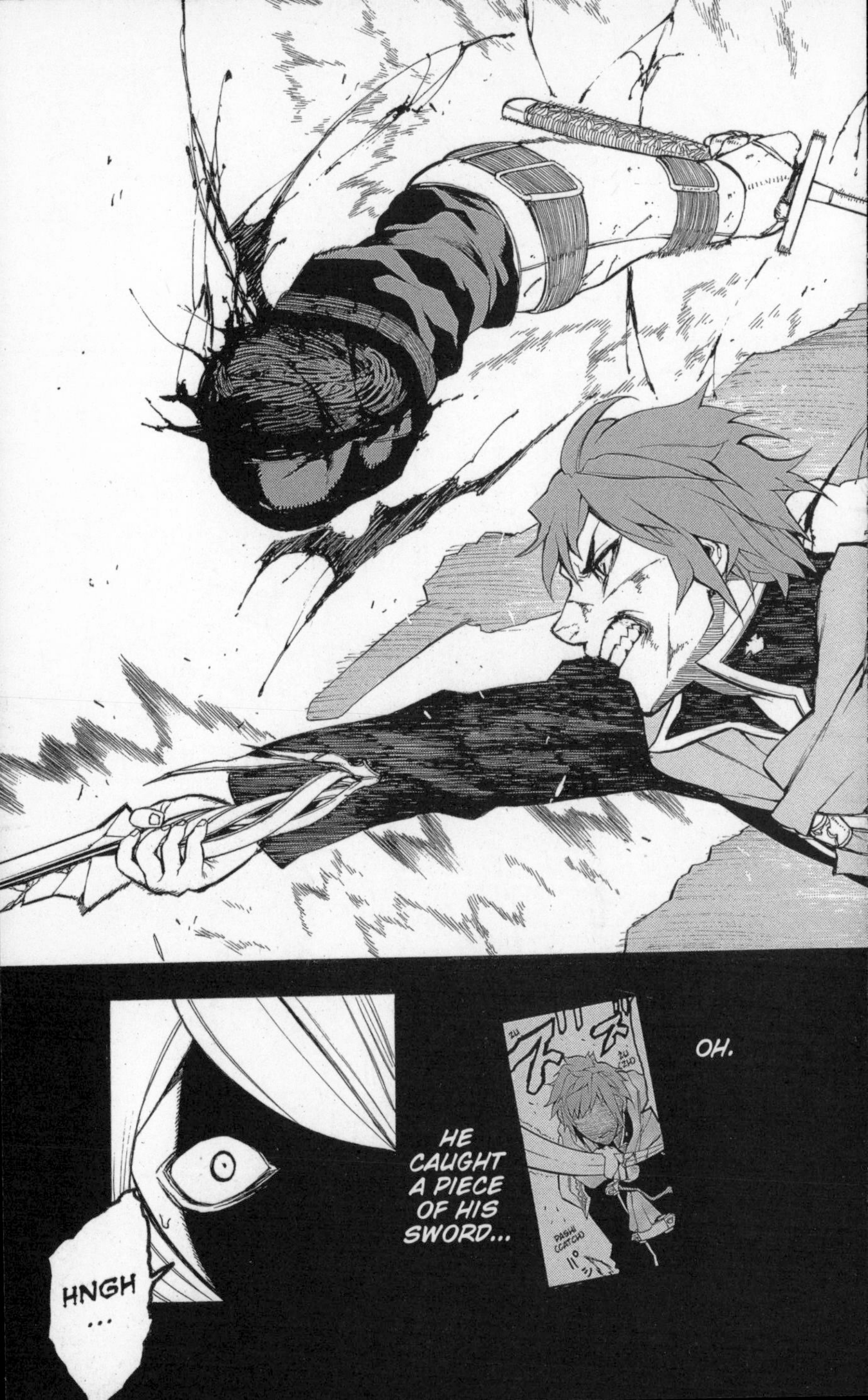
OH.
ZU ZUO
ZU
PASHI (CATCH)
HE CAUGHT A PIECE OF HIS SWORD...
HNGH ...

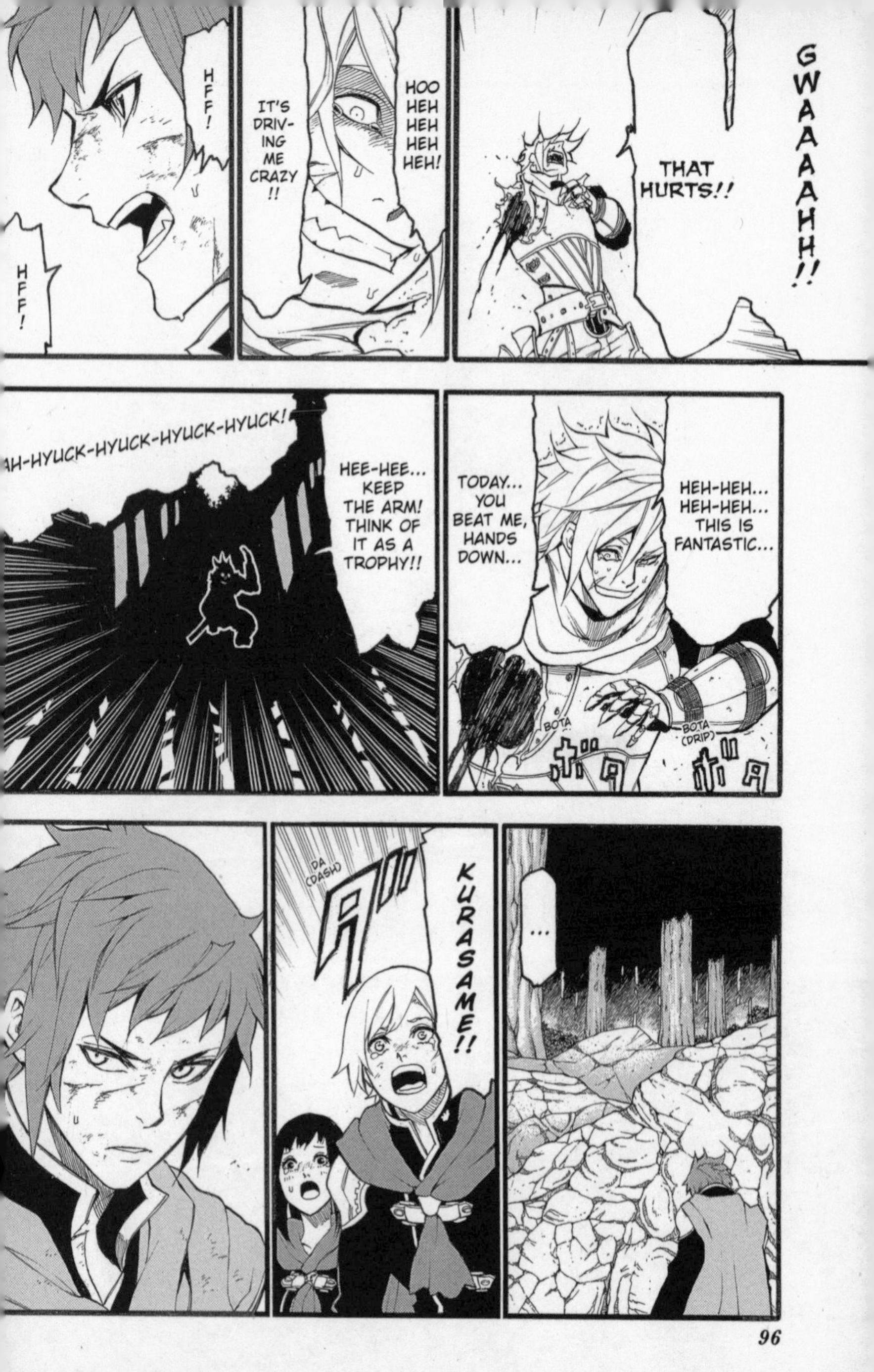
GWAAAAAHH!!
THAT HURTS!!
HOO HEH HEH HEH HEH!
IT'S DRIV-ING ME CRAZY!!
HFF!
HFF!
HEH-HEH... HEH-HEH... THIS IS FANTASTIC...
TODAY... YOU BEAT ME, HANDS DOWN...
BOTA
BOTA (DRIP)
HEE-HEE... KEEP THE ARM! THINK OF IT AS A TROPHY!!
AH-HYUCK-HYUCK-HYUCK-HYUCK!
...
KURASAME!!
DA (DASH)

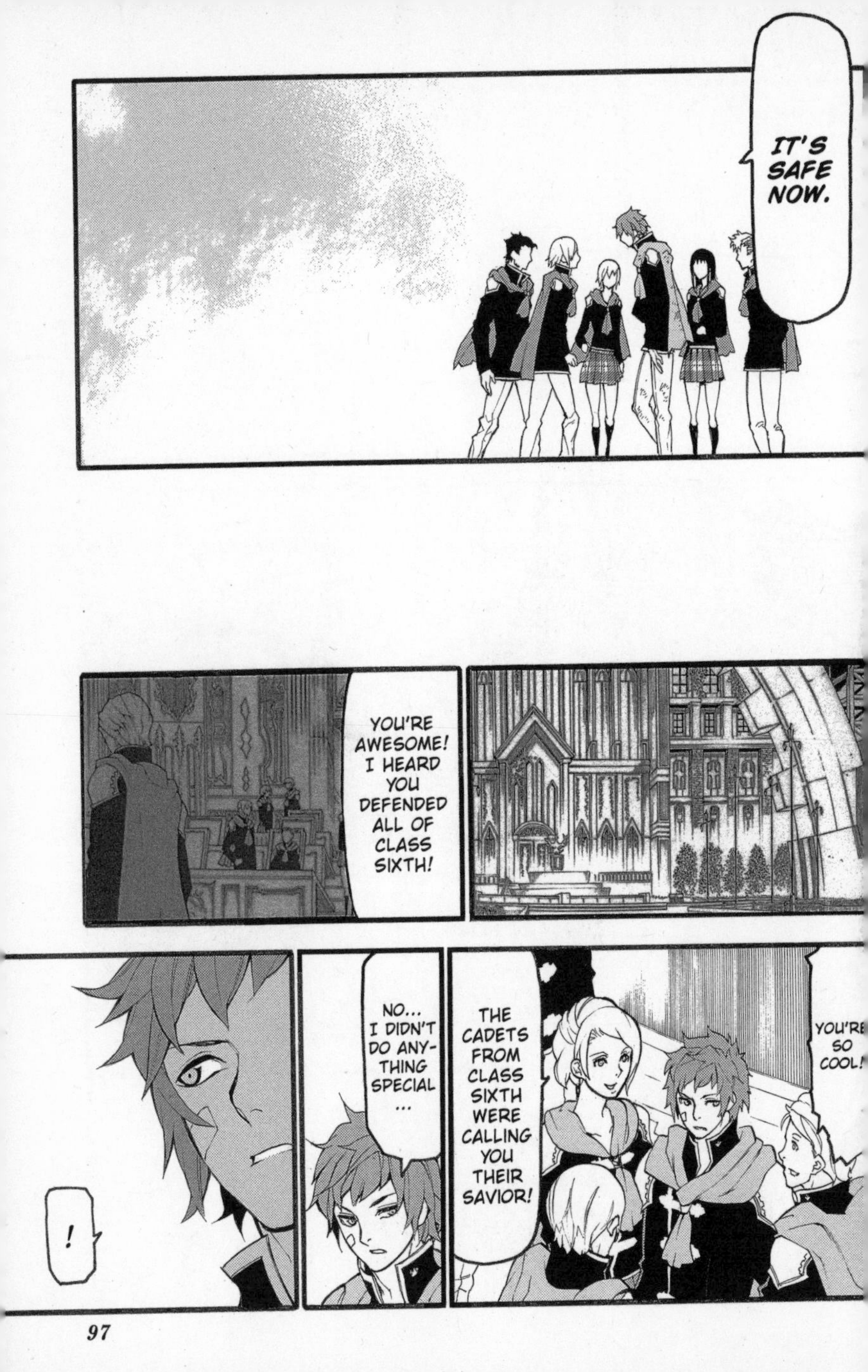
IT'S SAFE NOW.
YOU'RE AWESOME! I HEARD YOU DEFENDED ALL OF CLASS SIXTH!
YOU'RE SO COOL!
THE CADETS FROM CLASS SIXTH WERE CALLING YOU THEIR SAVIOR!
NO... I DIDN'T DO ANY-THING SPECIAL...
!

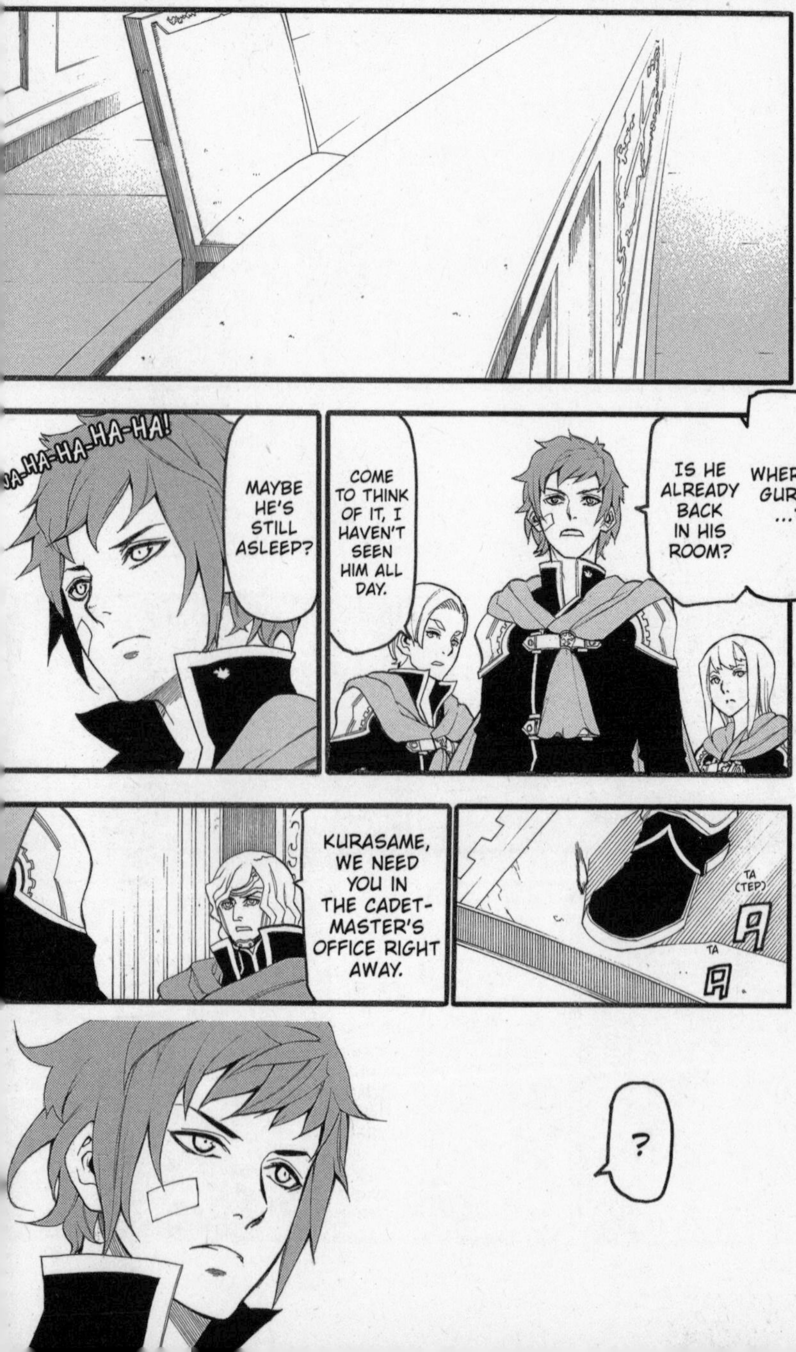
WHERE'S GUREN ...?
IS HE ALREADY BACK IN HIS ROOM?
COME TO THINK OF IT, I HAVEN'T SEEN HIM ALL DAY.
MAYBE HE'S STILL ASLEEP?
HA-HA-HA-HA!
TA (TEP)
TA
KURASAME, WE NEED YOU IN THE CADET-MASTER'S OFFICE RIGHT AWAY.
?

ZA
(ZSH)

ZA

ZA

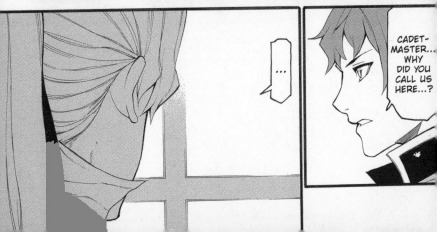

...

CADET-
MASTER...
WHY
DID YOU
CALL US
HERE...?

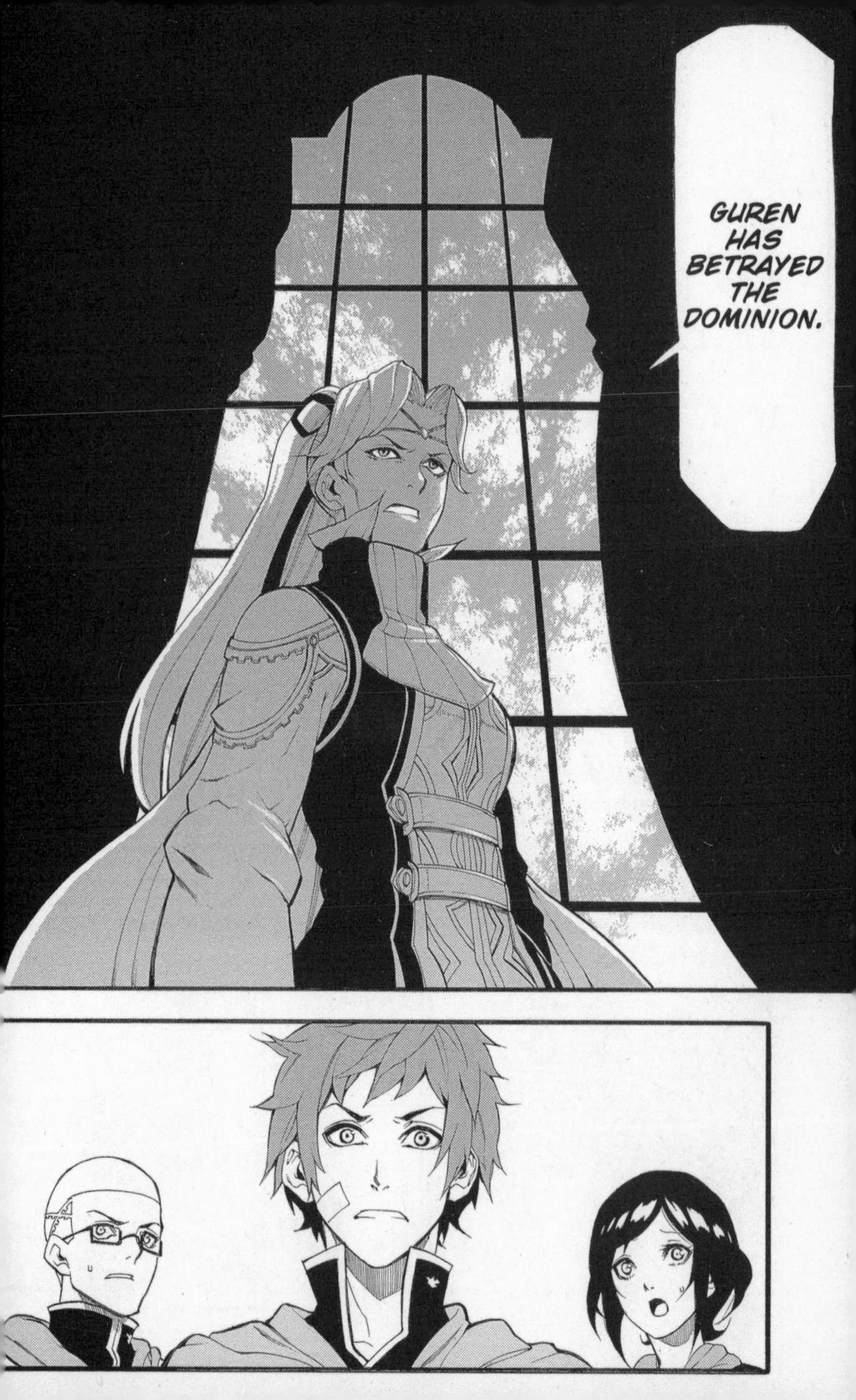
GUREN HAS BETRAYED THE DOMINION.

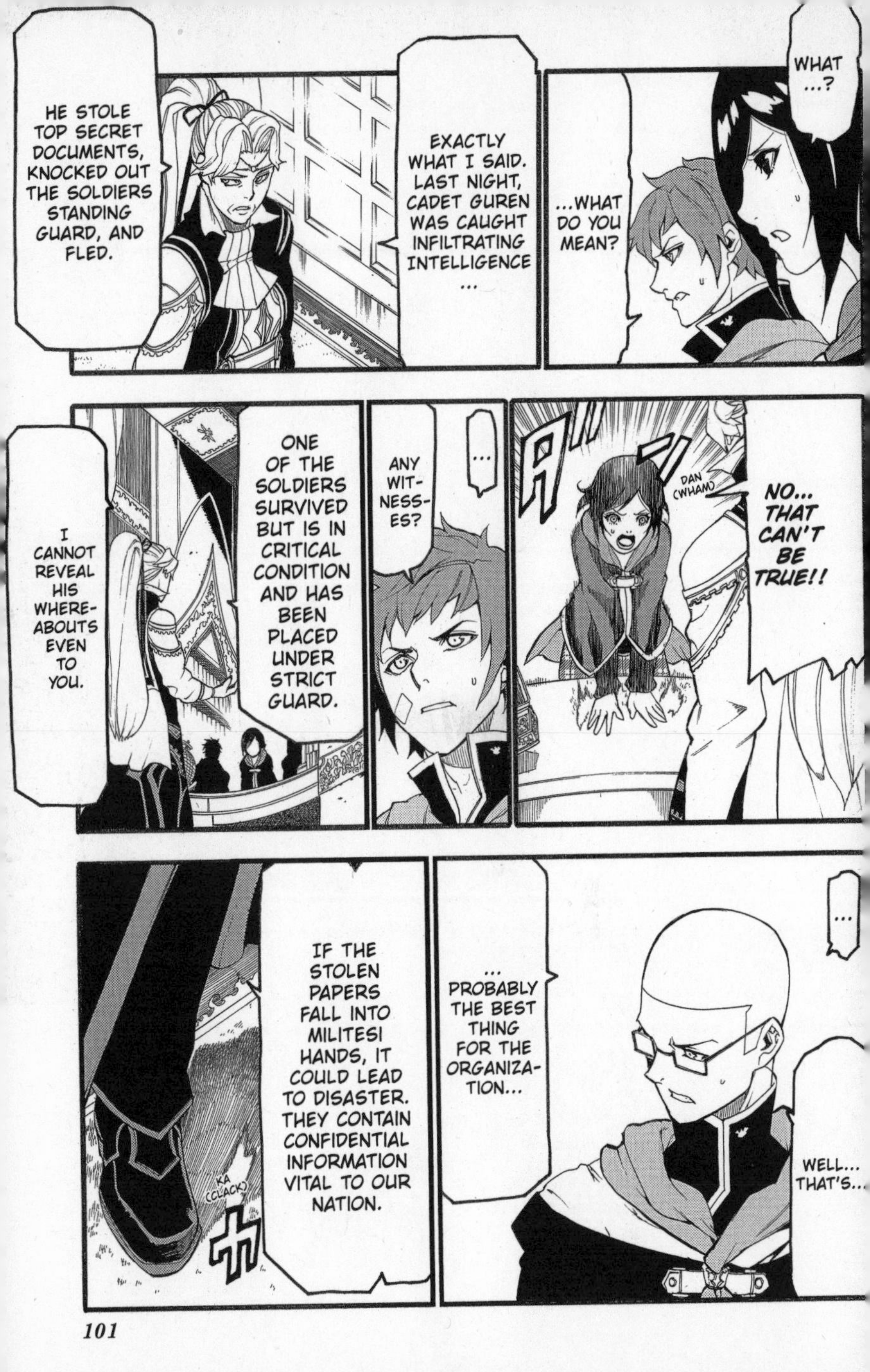
WHAT ...?
...WHAT DO YOU MEAN?
EXACTLY WHAT I SAID. LAST NIGHT, CADET GUREN WAS CAUGHT INFILTRATING INTELLIGENCE ...
HE STOLE TOP SECRET DOCUMENTS, KNOCKED OUT THE SOLDIERS STANDING GUARD, AND FLED.
NO... THAT CAN'T BE TRUE!!
DAN (WHAM)
...
ANY WIT-NESS-ES?
ONE OF THE SOLDIERS SURVIVED BUT IS IN CRITICAL CONDITION AND HAS BEEN PLACED UNDER STRICT GUARD.
I CANNOT REVEAL HIS WHERE-ABOUTS EVEN TO YOU.
...
WELL... THAT'S...
... PROBABLY THE BEST THING FOR THE ORGANIZA-TION...
IF THE STOLEN PAPERS FALL INTO MILITESI HANDS, IT COULD LEAD TO DISASTER. THEY CONTAIN CONFIDENTIAL INFORMATION VITAL TO OUR NATION.
KA (CLACK)

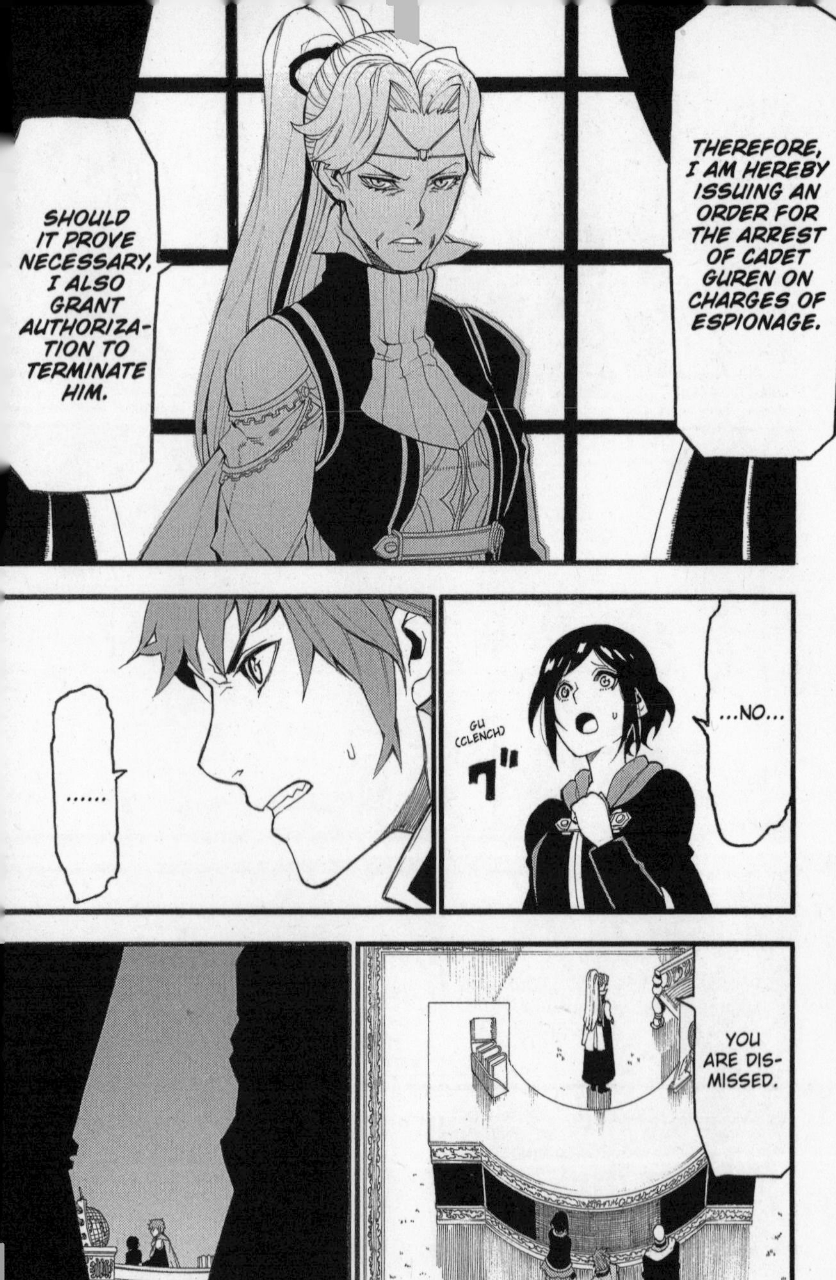
THEREFORE, I AM HEREBY ISSUING AN ORDER FOR THE ARREST OF CADET GUREN ON CHARGES OF ESPIONAGE.
SHOULD IT PROVE NECESSARY, I ALSO GRANT AUTHORIZATION TO TERMINATE HIM.
...NO...
GU (CLENCH)
......
YOU ARE DISMISSED.

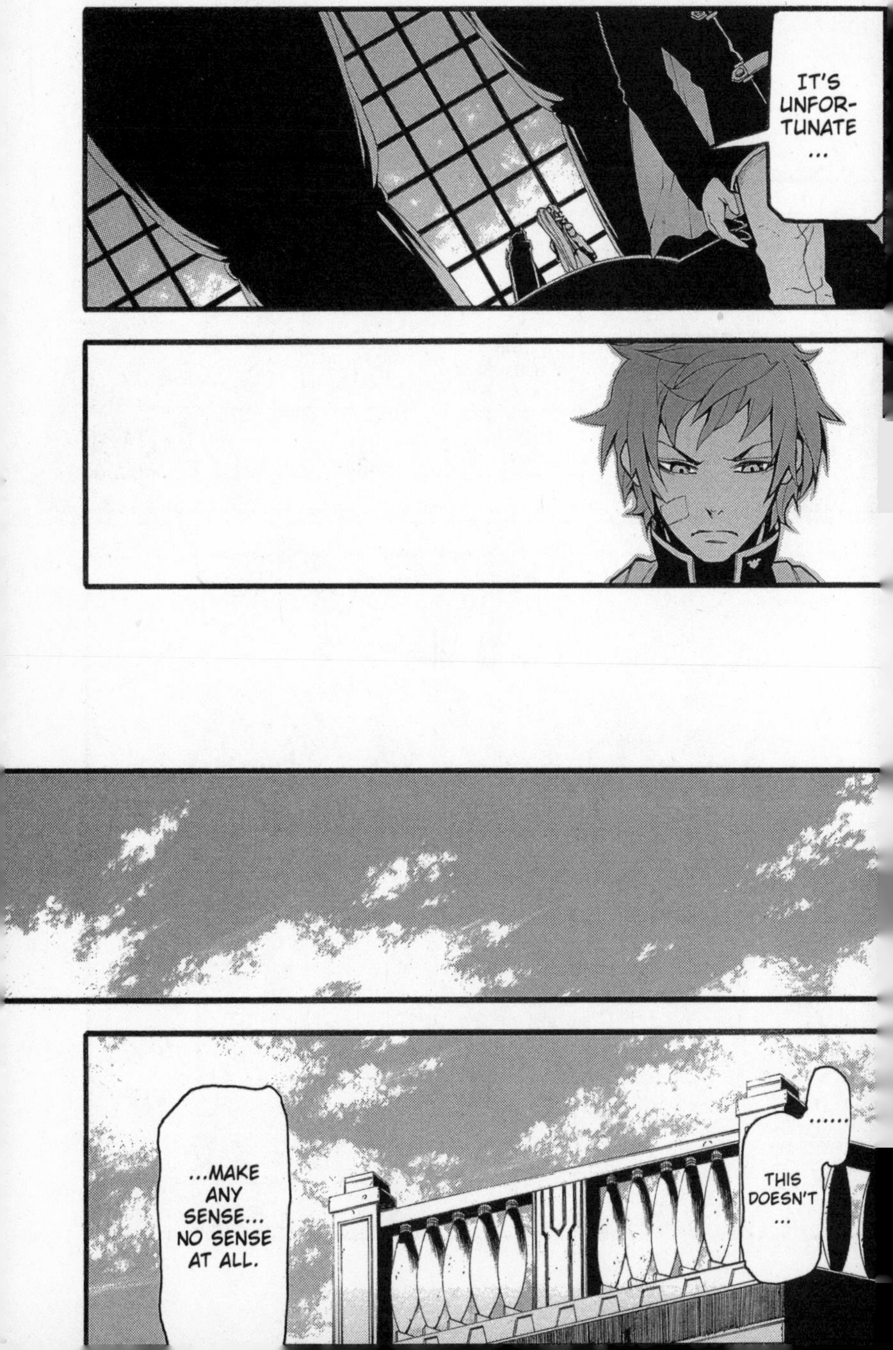
IT'S UNFORTUNATE...
......
THIS DOESN'T...
...MAKE ANY SENSE... NO SENSE AT ALL.

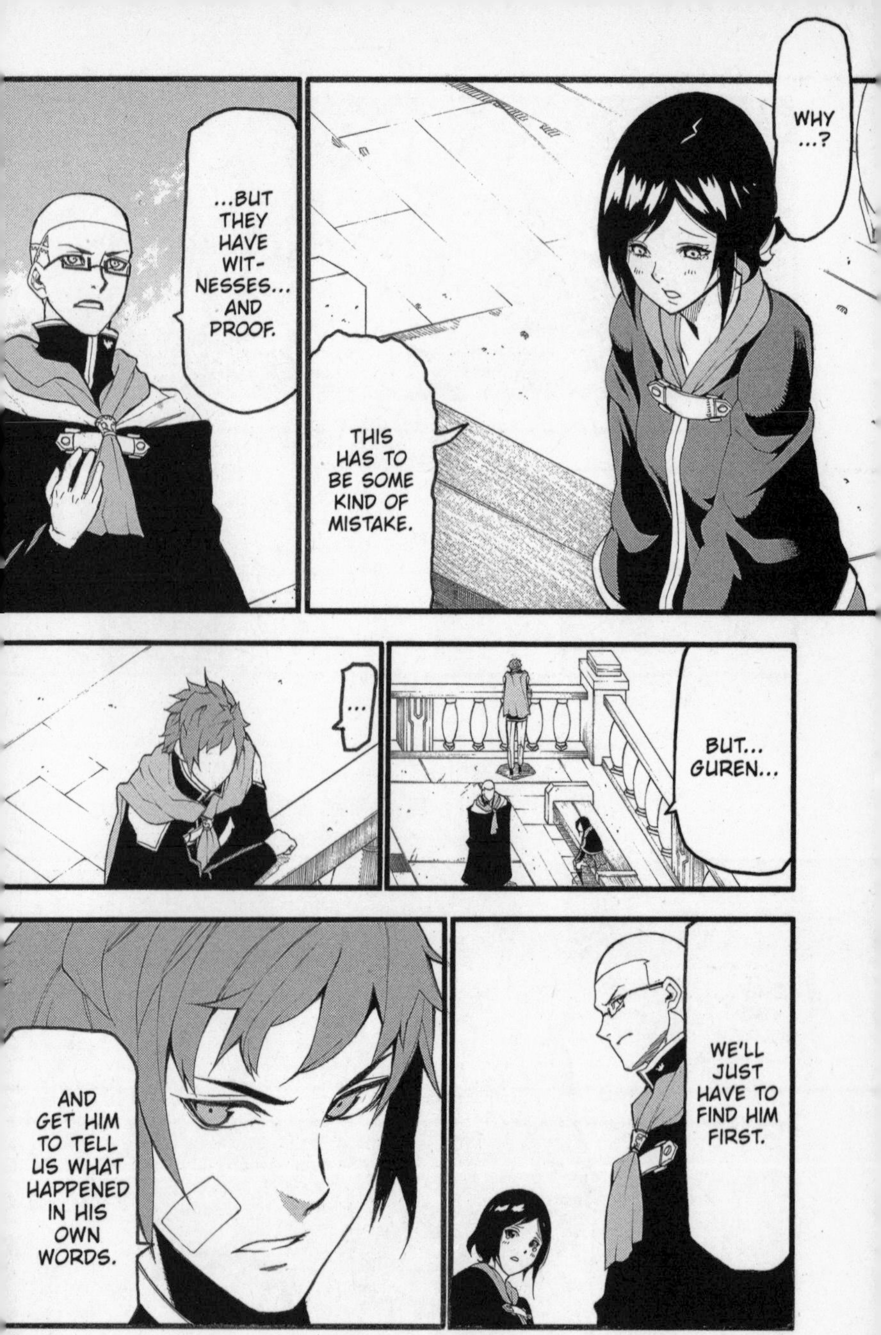
WHY ...?
THIS HAS TO BE SOME KIND OF MISTAKE.
...BUT THEY HAVE WIT-NESSES... AND PROOF.
BUT... GUREN...
...
WE'LL JUST HAVE TO FIND HIM FIRST.
AND GET HIM TO TELL US WHAT HAPPENED IN HIS OWN WORDS.

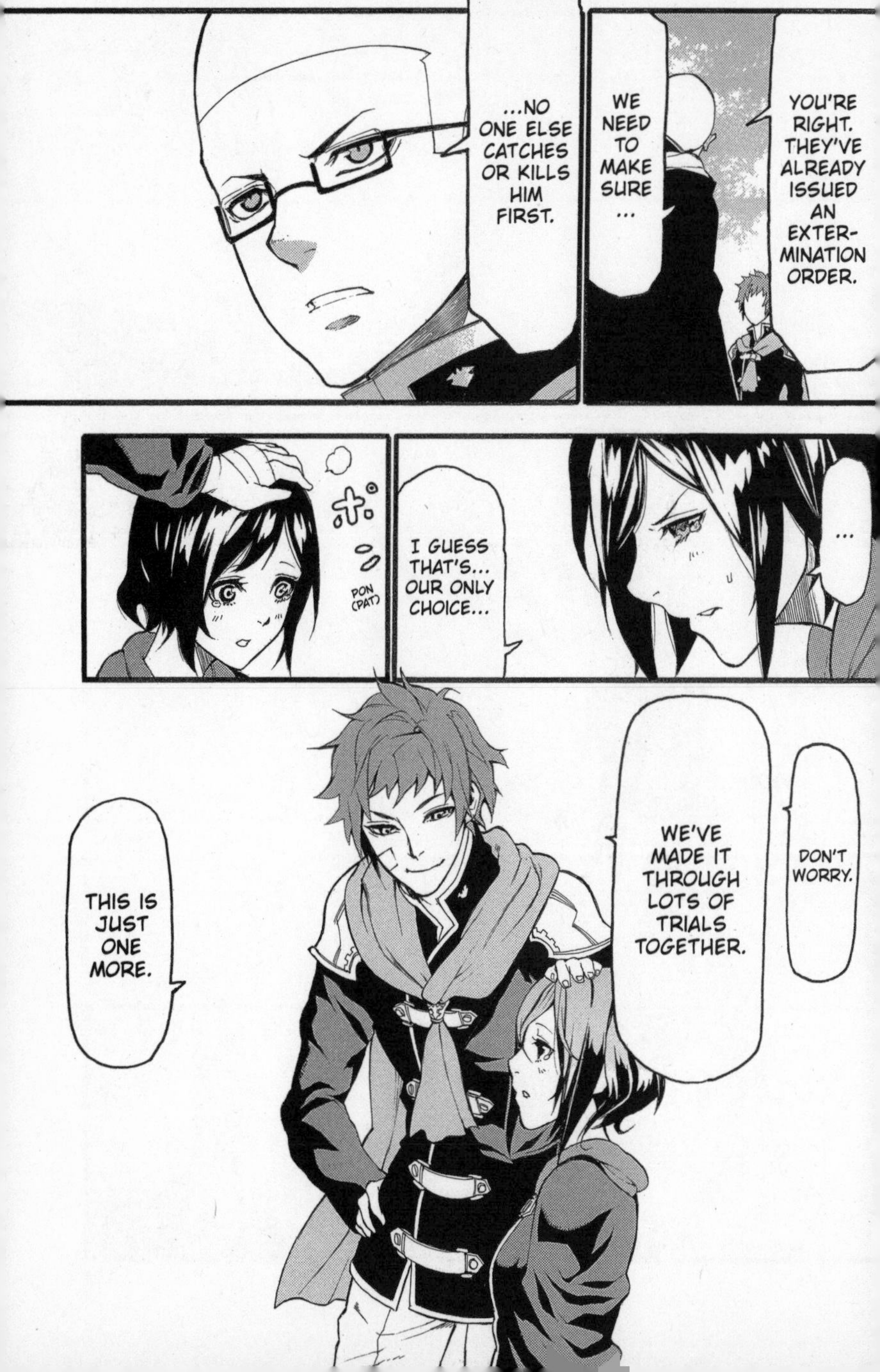
YOU'RE RIGHT. THEY'VE ALREADY ISSUED AN EXTER-MINATION ORDER.
WE NEED TO MAKE SURE ...
...NO ONE ELSE CATCHES OR KILLS HIM FIRST.
...
I GUESS THAT'S... OUR ONLY CHOICE...
PON (PAT)
DON'T WORRY.
WE'VE MADE IT THROUGH LOTS OF TRIALS TOGETHER.
THIS IS JUST ONE MORE.

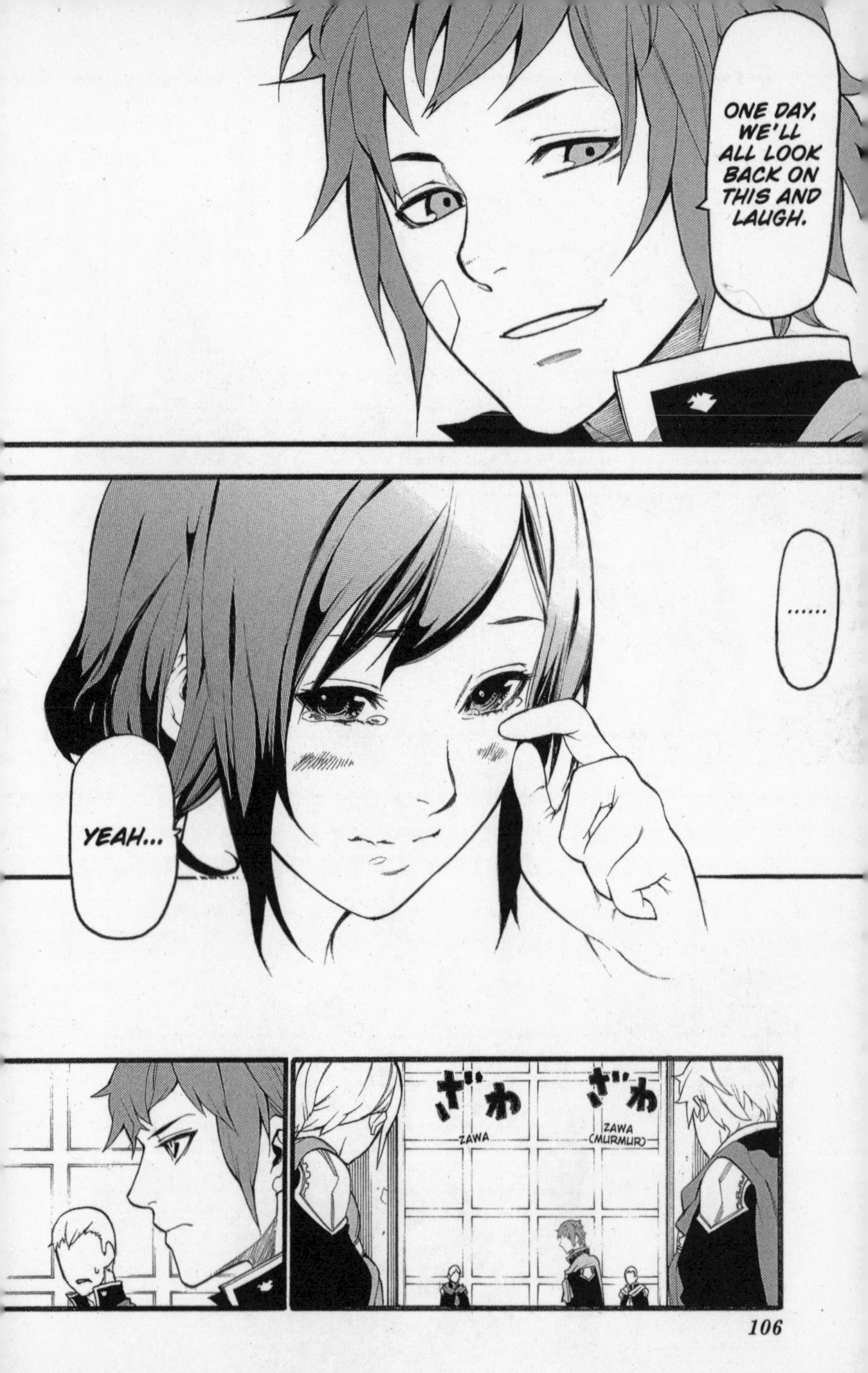
ONE DAY, WE'LL ALL LOOK BACK ON THIS AND LAUGH.
......
YEAH...
ざわ ざわ
ZAWA
ZAWA (MURMUR)

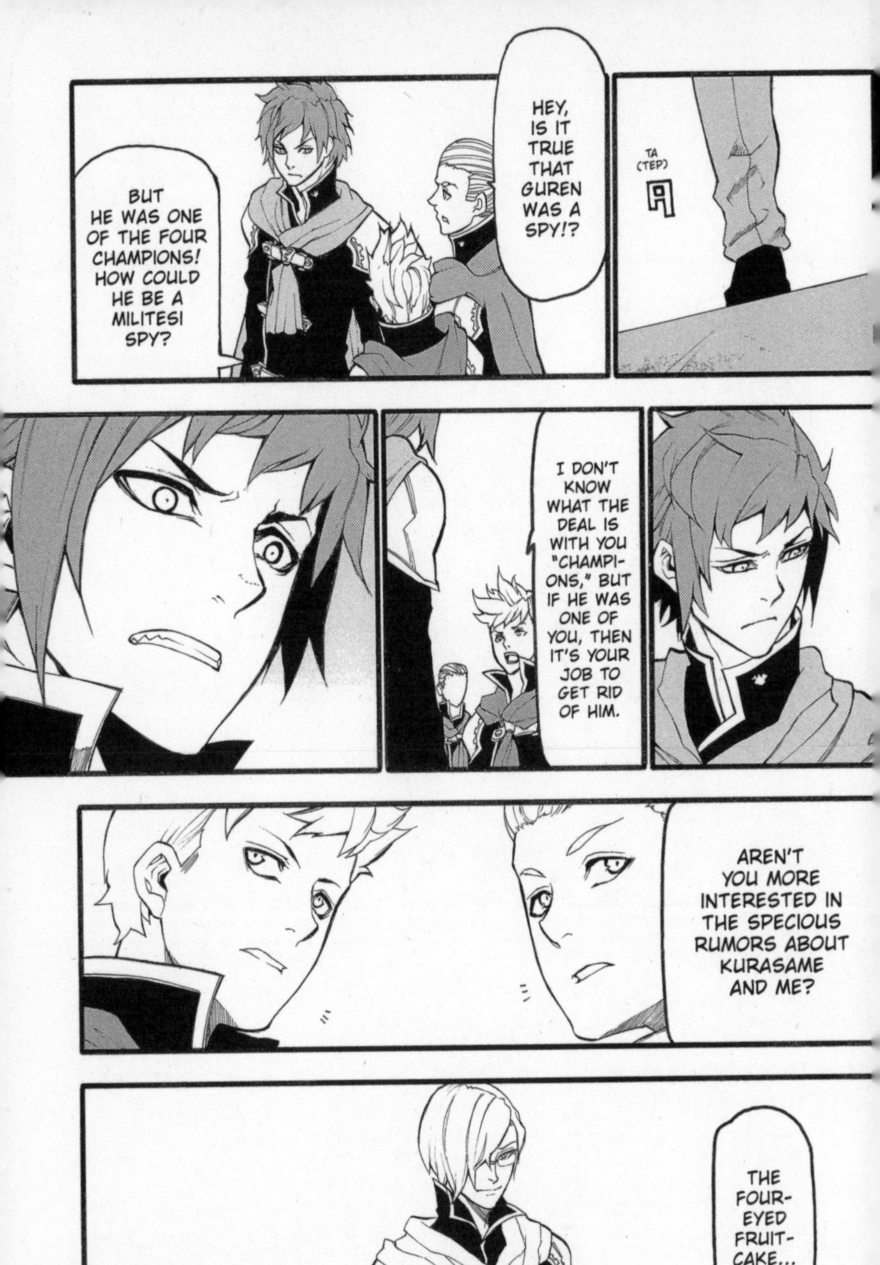
TA (TEP)
HEY, IS IT TRUE THAT GUREN WAS A SPY!?
BUT HE WAS ONE OF THE FOUR CHAMPIONS! HOW COULD HE BE A MILITESI SPY?
I DON'T KNOW WHAT THE DEAL IS WITH YOU "CHAMPIONS," BUT IF HE WAS ONE OF YOU, THEN IT'S YOUR JOB TO GET RID OF HIM.
AREN'T YOU MORE INTERESTED IN THE SPECIOUS RUMORS ABOUT KURASAME AND ME?
THE FOUR-EYED FRUIT-CAKE...

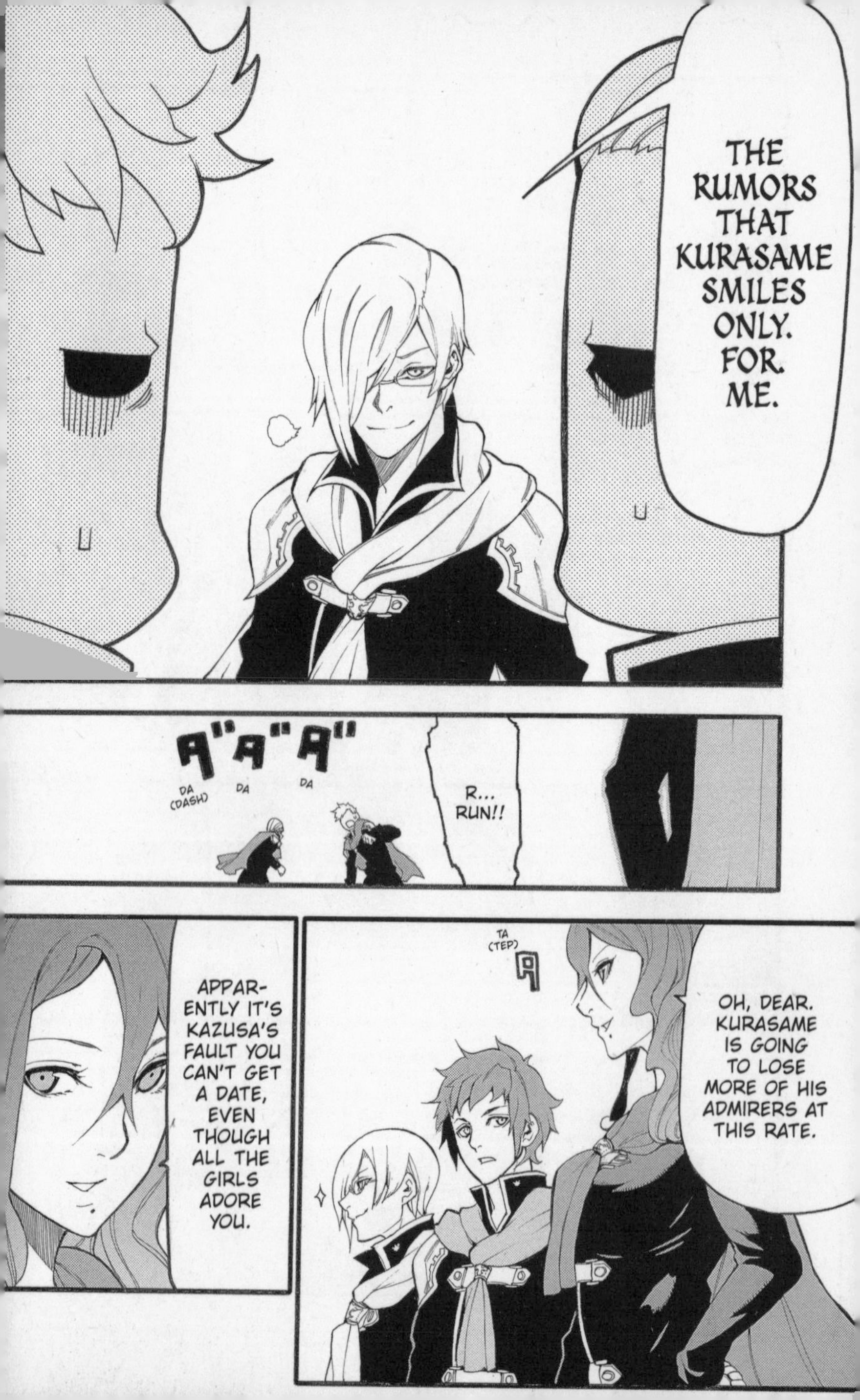
THE RUMORS THAT KURASAME SMILES ONLY. FOR ME.
R... RUN!!
DA (DASH) DA DA
OH, DEAR. KURASAME IS GOING TO LOSE MORE OF HIS ADMIRERS AT THIS RATE.
TA (TEP)
APPAR-ENTLY IT'S KAZUSA'S FAULT YOU CAN'T GET A DATE, EVEN THOUGH ALL THE GIRLS ADORE YOU.

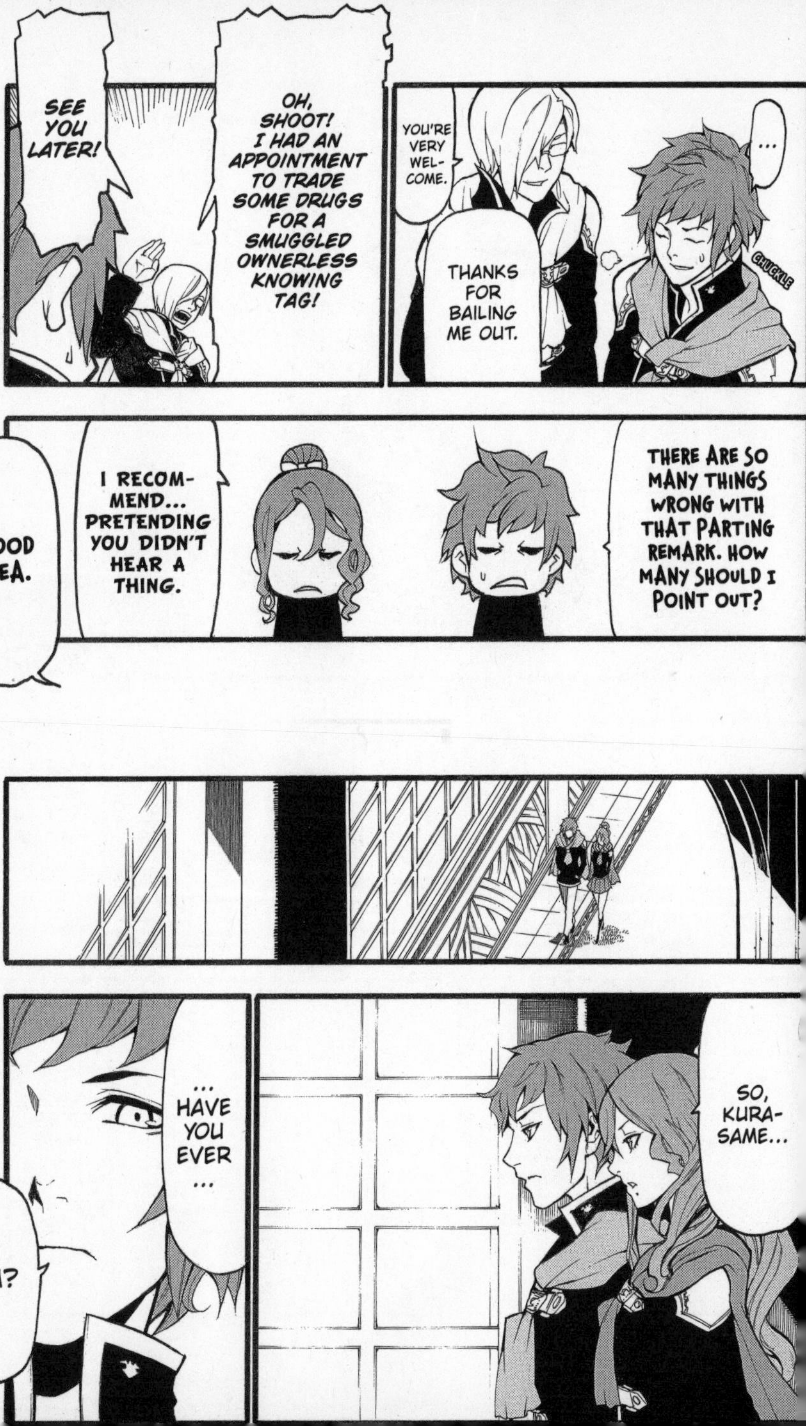
...
THANKS FOR BAILING ME OUT.
CHUCKLE
YOU'RE VERY WEL-COME.
OH, SHOOT! I HAD AN APPOINTMENT TO TRADE SOME DRUGS FOR A SMUGGLED OWNERLESS KNOWING TAG!
SEE YOU LATER!
THERE ARE SO MANY THINGS WRONG WITH THAT PARTING REMARK. HOW MANY SHOULD I POINT OUT?
I RECOM-MEND... PRETENDING YOU DIDN'T HEAR A THING.
GOOD IDEA.
SO, KURA-SAME...
HM?
...HAVE YOU EVER...

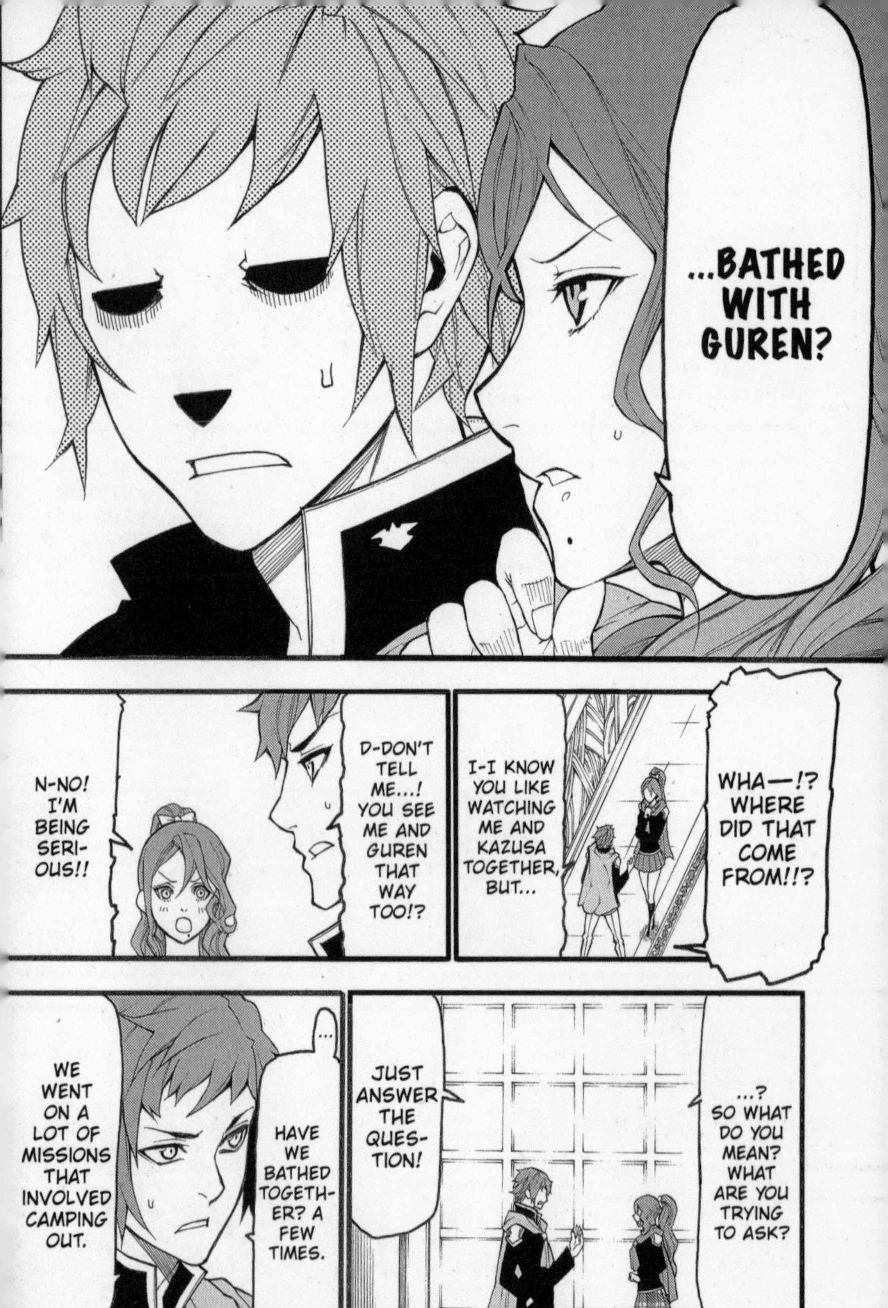
...BATHED WITH GUREN?
WHA—!? WHERE DID THAT COME FROM!!?
I-I KNOW YOU LIKE WATCHING ME AND KAZUSA TOGETHER, BUT...
D-DON'T TELL ME...! YOU SEE ME AND GUREN THAT WAY TOO!?
N-NO! I'M BEING SERI-OUS!!
...? SO WHAT DO YOU MEAN? WHAT ARE YOU TRYING TO ASK?
JUST ANSWER THE QUES-TION!
...
HAVE WE BATHED TOGETH-ER? A FEW TIMES.
WE WENT ON A LOT OF MISSIONS THAT INVOLVED CAMPING OUT.

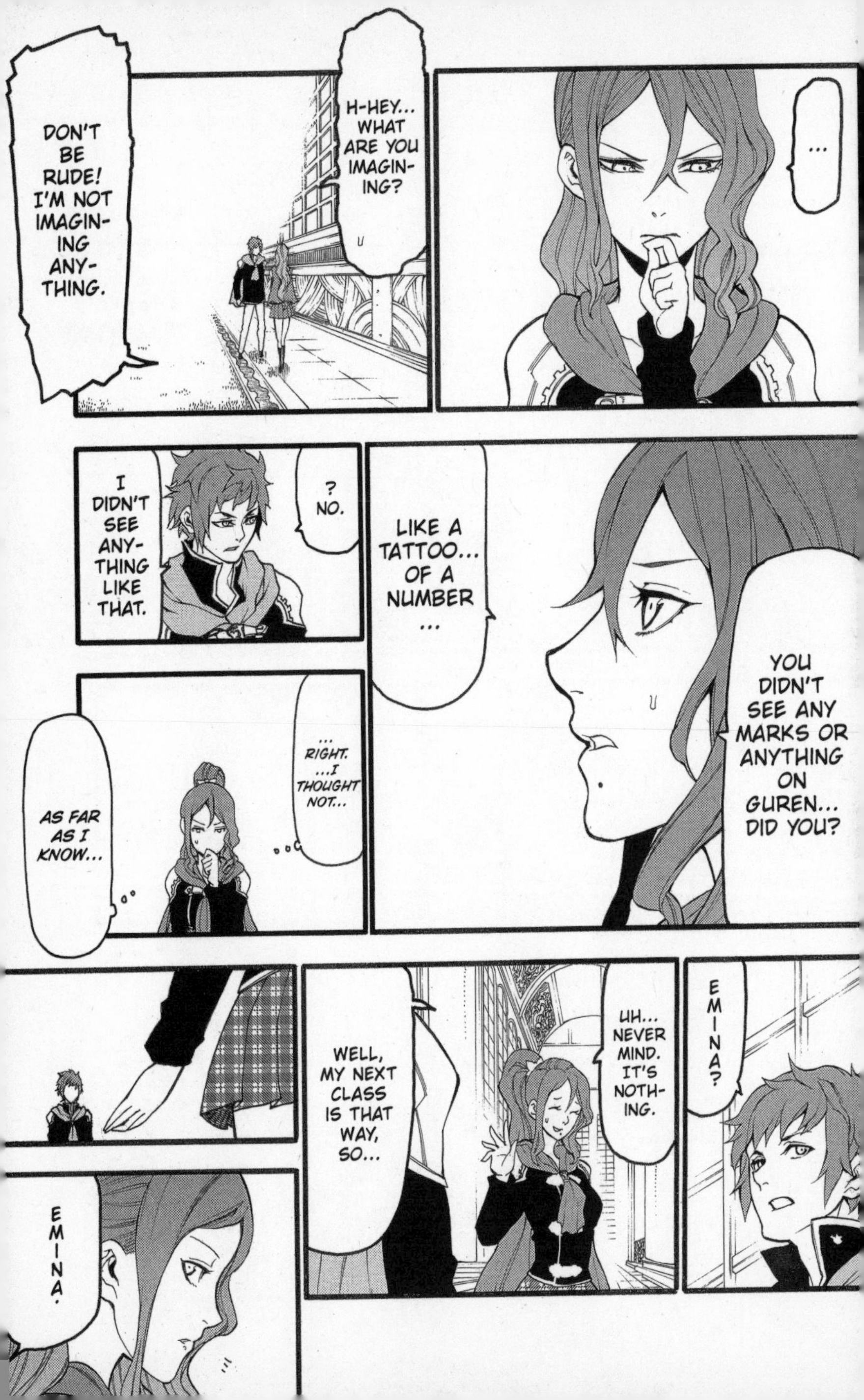
...
H-HEY... WHAT ARE YOU IMAGINING?
DON'T BE RUDE! I'M NOT IMAGINING ANYTHING.
YOU DIDN'T SEE ANY MARKS OR ANYTHING ON GUREN... DID YOU?
LIKE A TATTOO... OF A NUMBER...
? NO.
I DIDN'T SEE ANYTHING LIKE THAT.
...RIGHT. ...I THOUGHT NOT...
AS FAR AS I KNOW...
EMINA?
UH... NEVER MIND. IT'S NOTHING.
WELL, MY NEXT CLASS IS THAT WAY, SO...
EMINA.

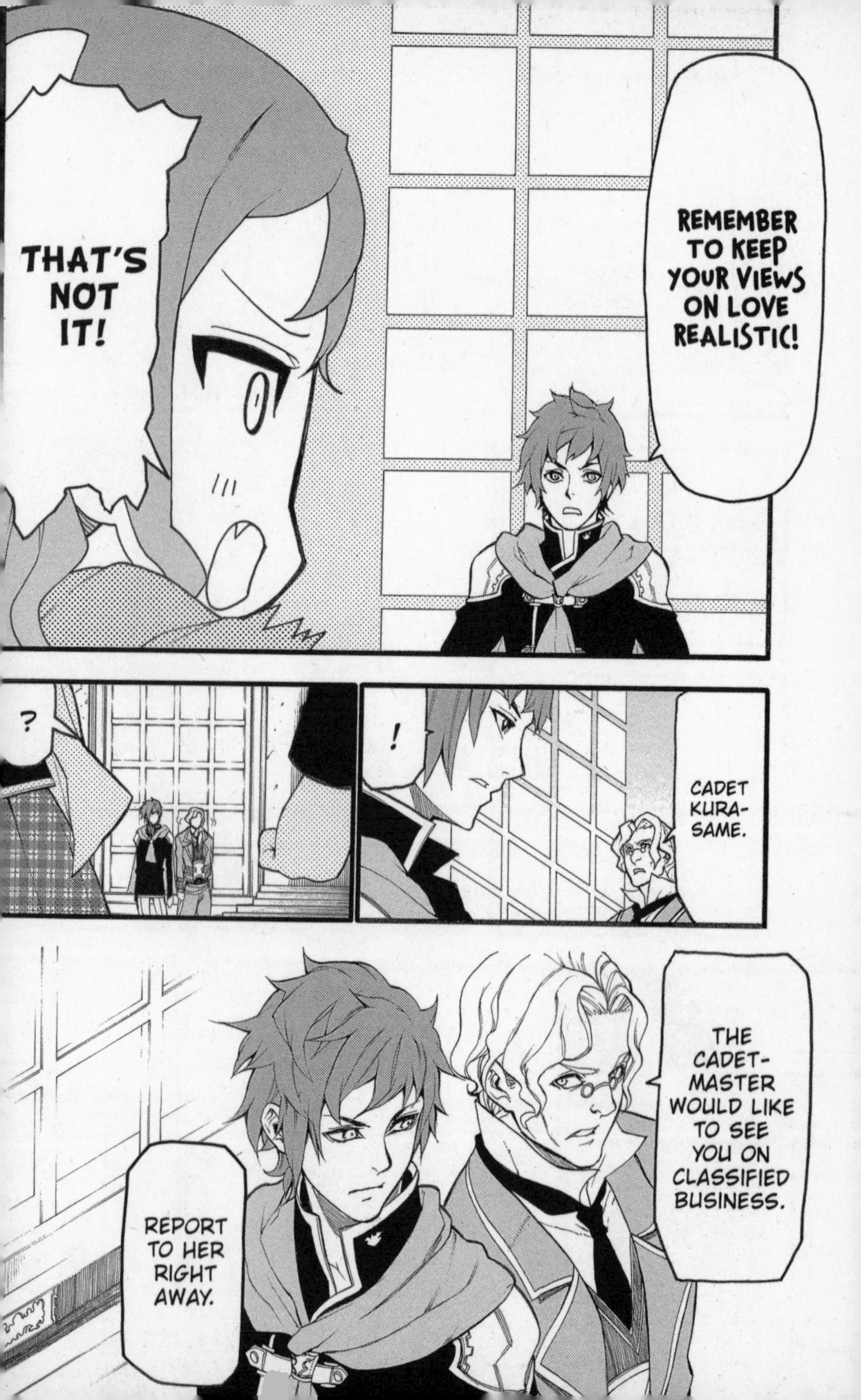
REMEMBER TO KEEP YOUR VIEWS ON LOVE REALISTIC!
THAT'S NOT IT!
!
CADET KURA-SAME.
?
THE CADET-MASTER WOULD LIKE TO SEE YOU ON CLASSIFIED BUSINESS.
REPORT TO HER RIGHT AWAY.

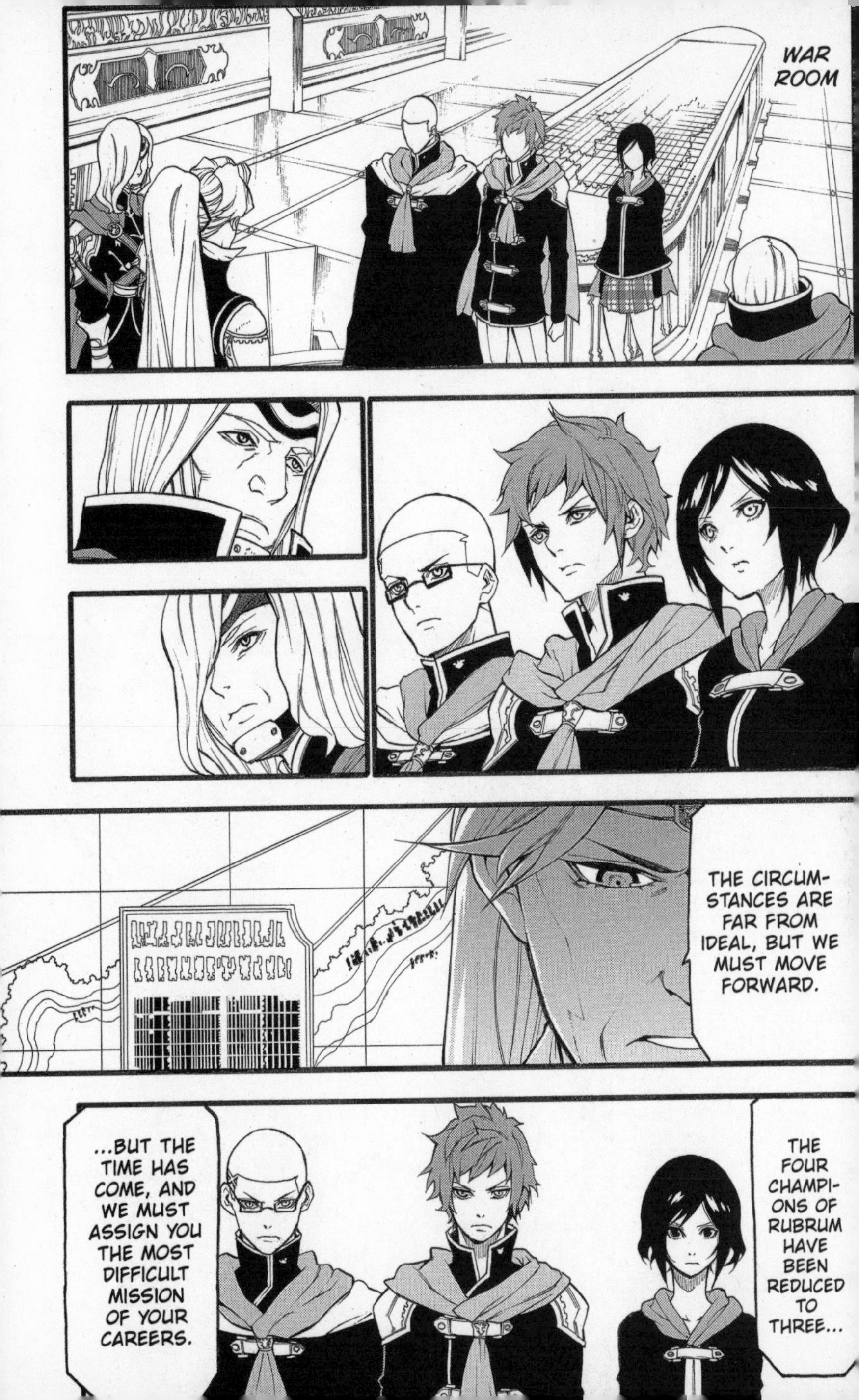
WAR ROOM
THE CIRCUMSTANCES ARE FAR FROM IDEAL, BUT WE MUST MOVE FORWARD.
THE FOUR CHAMPIONS OF RUBRUM HAVE BEEN REDUCED TO THREE...
...BUT THE TIME HAS COME, AND WE MUST ASSIGN YOU THE MOST DIFFICULT MISSION OF YOUR CAREERS.

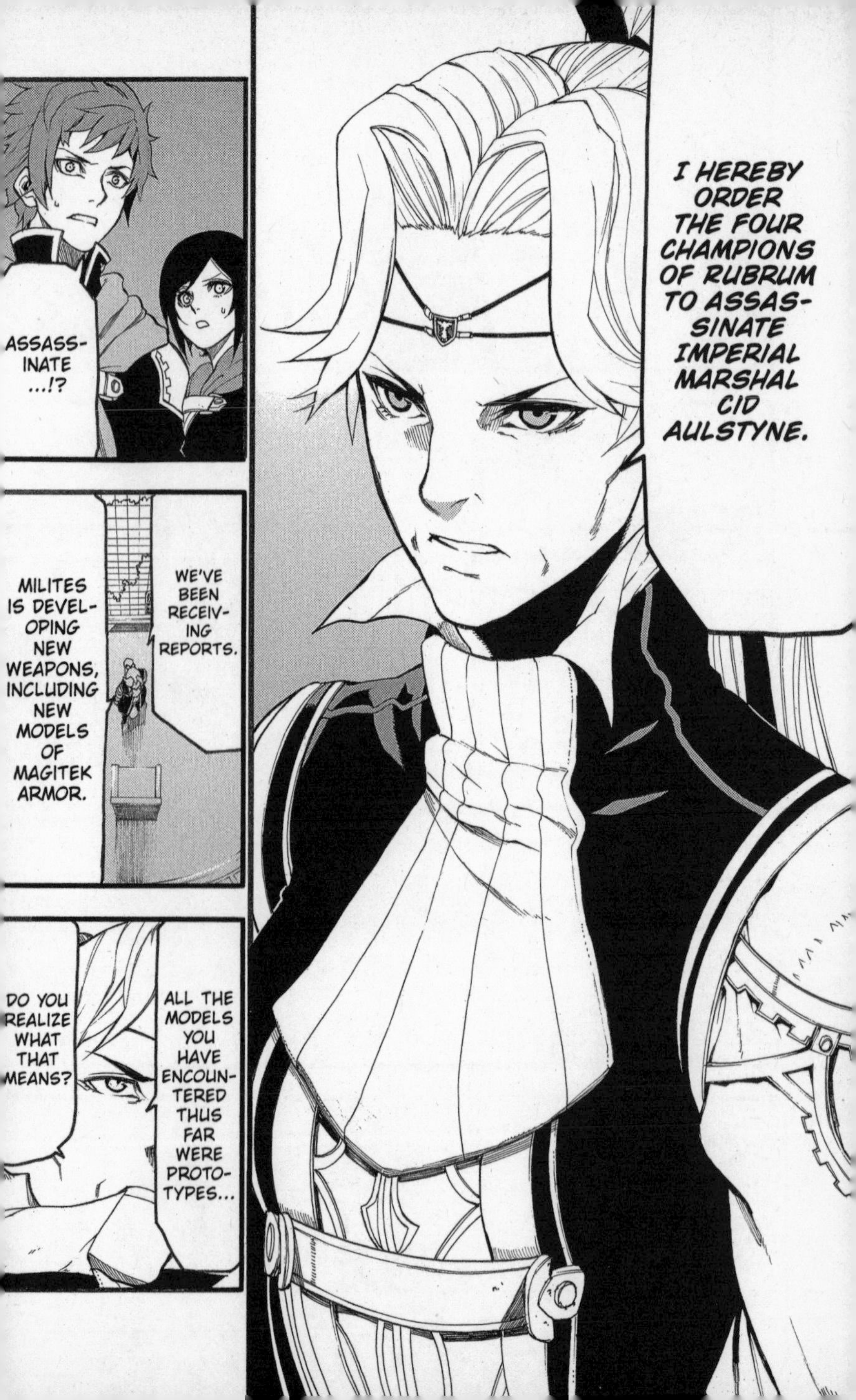
I HEREBY ORDER THE FOUR CHAMPIONS OF RUBRUM TO ASSAS-SINATE IMPERIAL MARSHAL CID AULSTYNE.
ASSASS-INATE ...!?
WE'VE BEEN RECEIV-ING REPORTS.
MILITES IS DEVEL-OPING NEW WEAPONS, INCLUDING NEW MODELS OF MAGITEK ARMOR.
ALL THE MODELS YOU HAVE ENCOUN-TERED THUS FAR WERE PROTO-TYPES...
DO YOU REALIZE WHAT THAT MEANS?

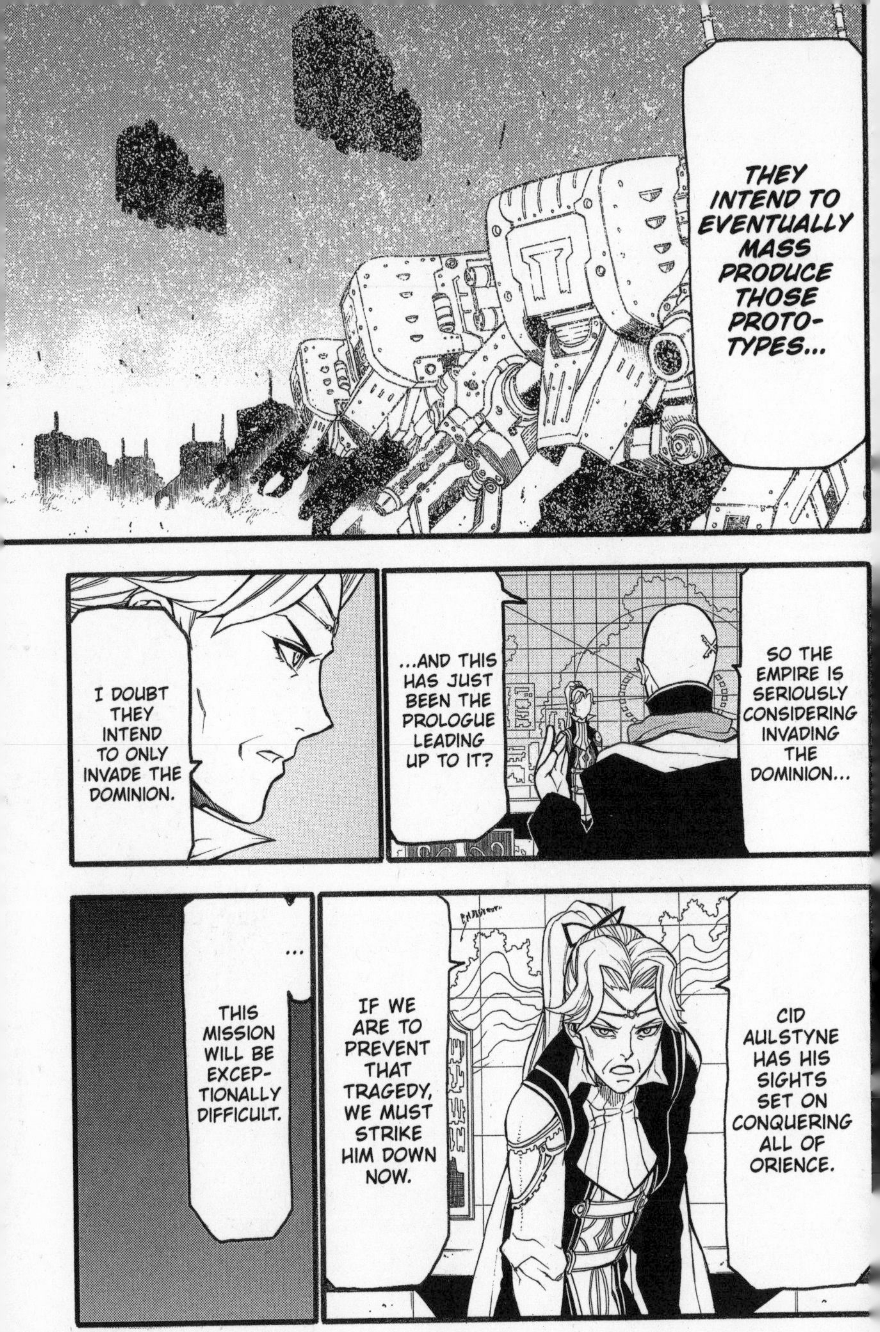
THEY INTEND TO EVENTUALLY MASS PRODUCE THOSE PROTO-TYPES...
SO THE EMPIRE IS SERIOUSLY CONSIDERING INVADING THE DOMINION...
...AND THIS HAS JUST BEEN THE PROLOGUE LEADING UP TO IT?
I DOUBT THEY INTEND TO ONLY INVADE THE DOMINION.
CID AULSTYNE HAS HIS SIGHTS SET ON CONQUERING ALL OF ORIENCE.
IF WE ARE TO PREVENT THAT TRAGEDY, WE MUST STRIKE HIM DOWN NOW.
...
THIS MISSION WILL BE EXCEP-TIONALLY DIFFICULT.

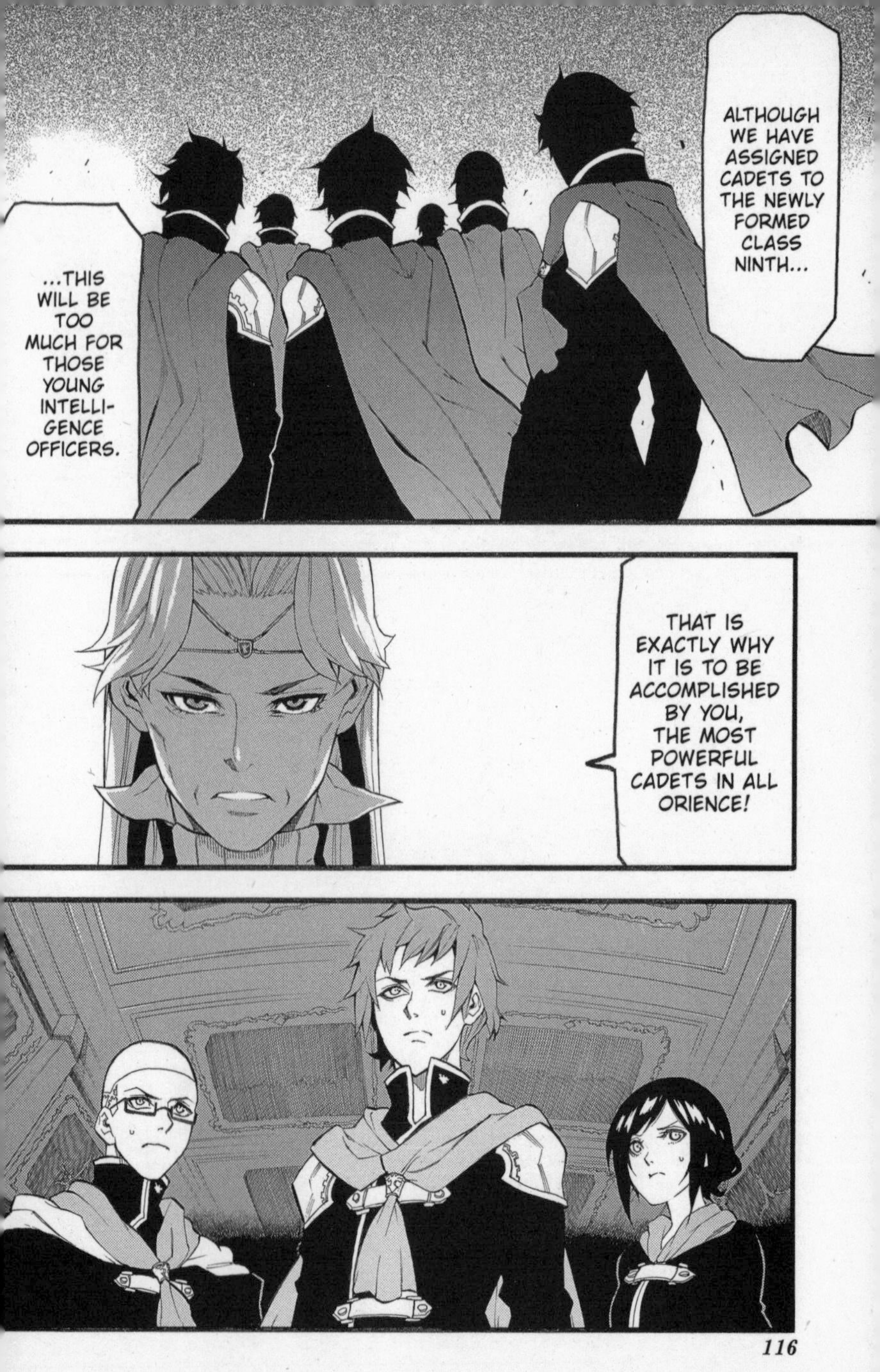
ALTHOUGH WE HAVE ASSIGNED CADETS TO THE NEWLY FORMED CLASS NINTH...
...THIS WILL BE TOO MUCH FOR THOSE YOUNG INTELLIGENCE OFFICERS.
THAT IS EXACTLY WHY IT IS TO BE ACCOMPLISHED BY YOU, THE MOST POWERFUL CADETS IN ALL ORIENCE!

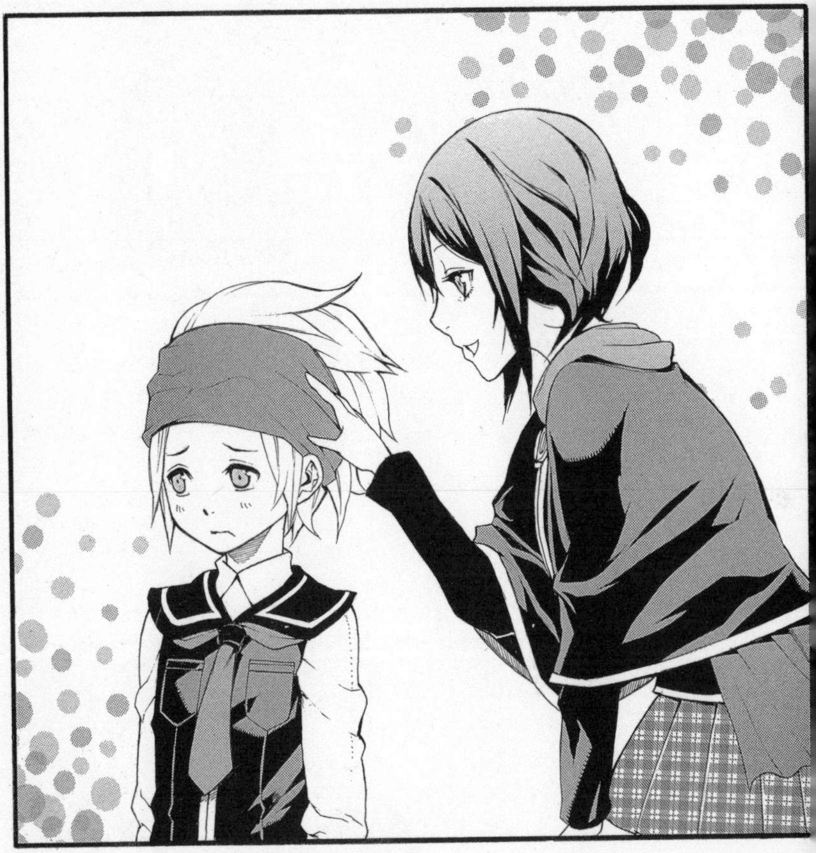

FINAL FANTASY 零式 TYPE-0™

SIDE STORY

The Ice Reaper

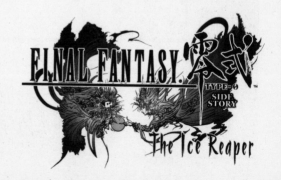

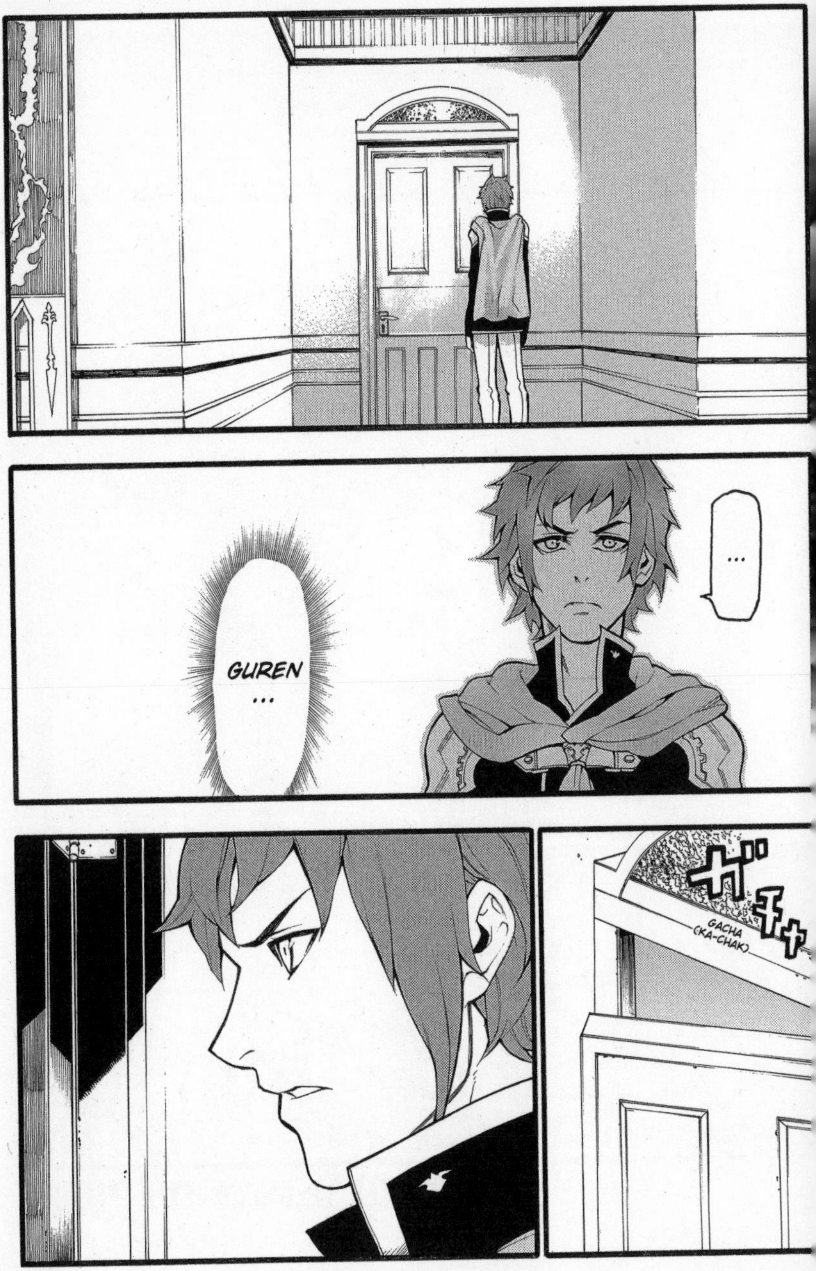
...
GUREN ...
ガチャ
GACHA (KA-CHAK)

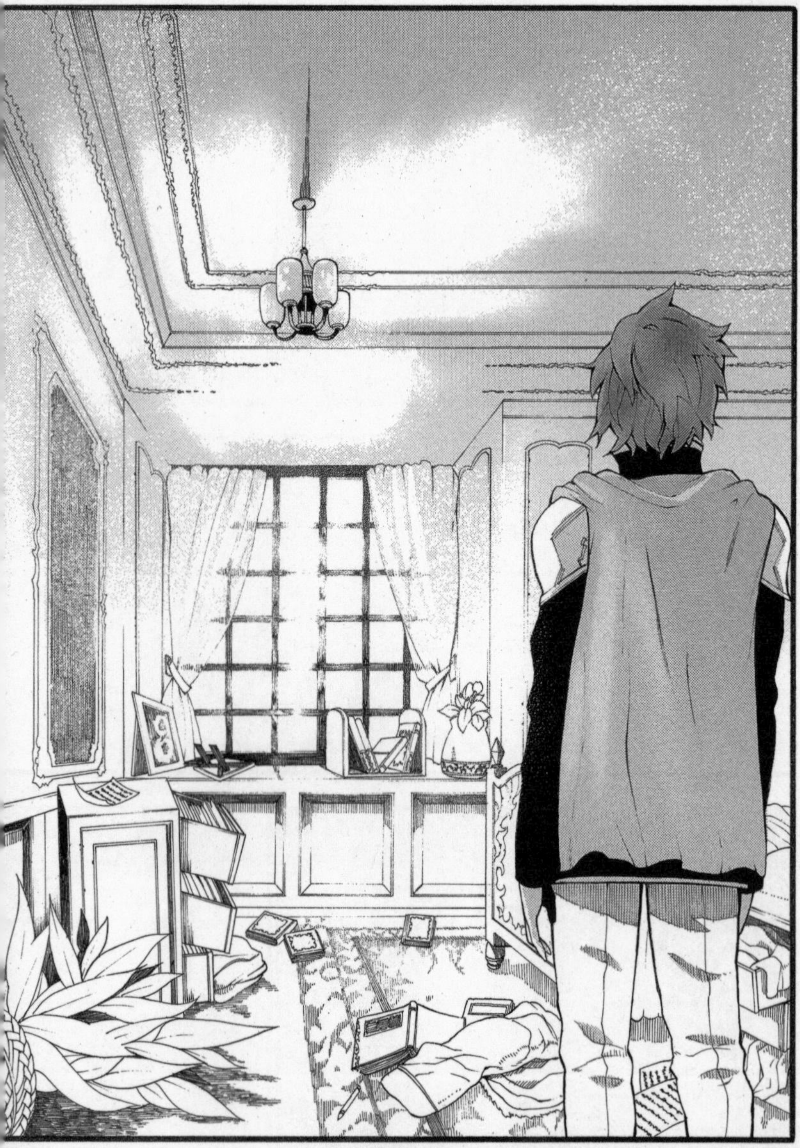

CHAPTER 17: UNCONVEYED FEELINGS

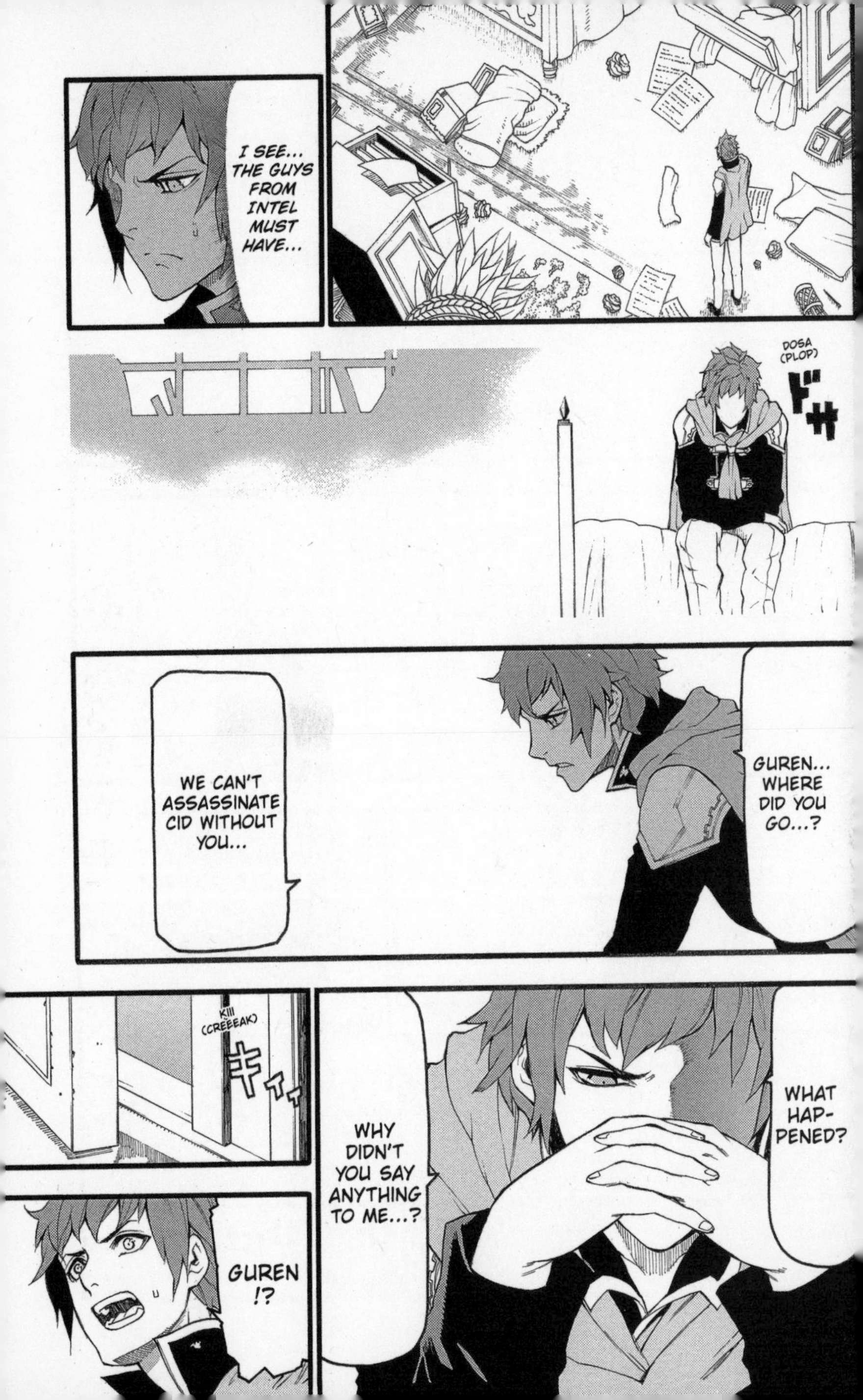

I SEE... THE GUYS FROM INTEL MUST HAVE...
DOSA (PLOP)
ドサ
GUREN... WHERE DID YOU GO...?
WE CAN'T ASSASSINATE CID WITHOUT YOU...
WHAT HAP-PENED?
WHY DIDN'T YOU SAY ANYTHING TO ME...?
KIII (CREEEAK)
キィィ
GUREN !?

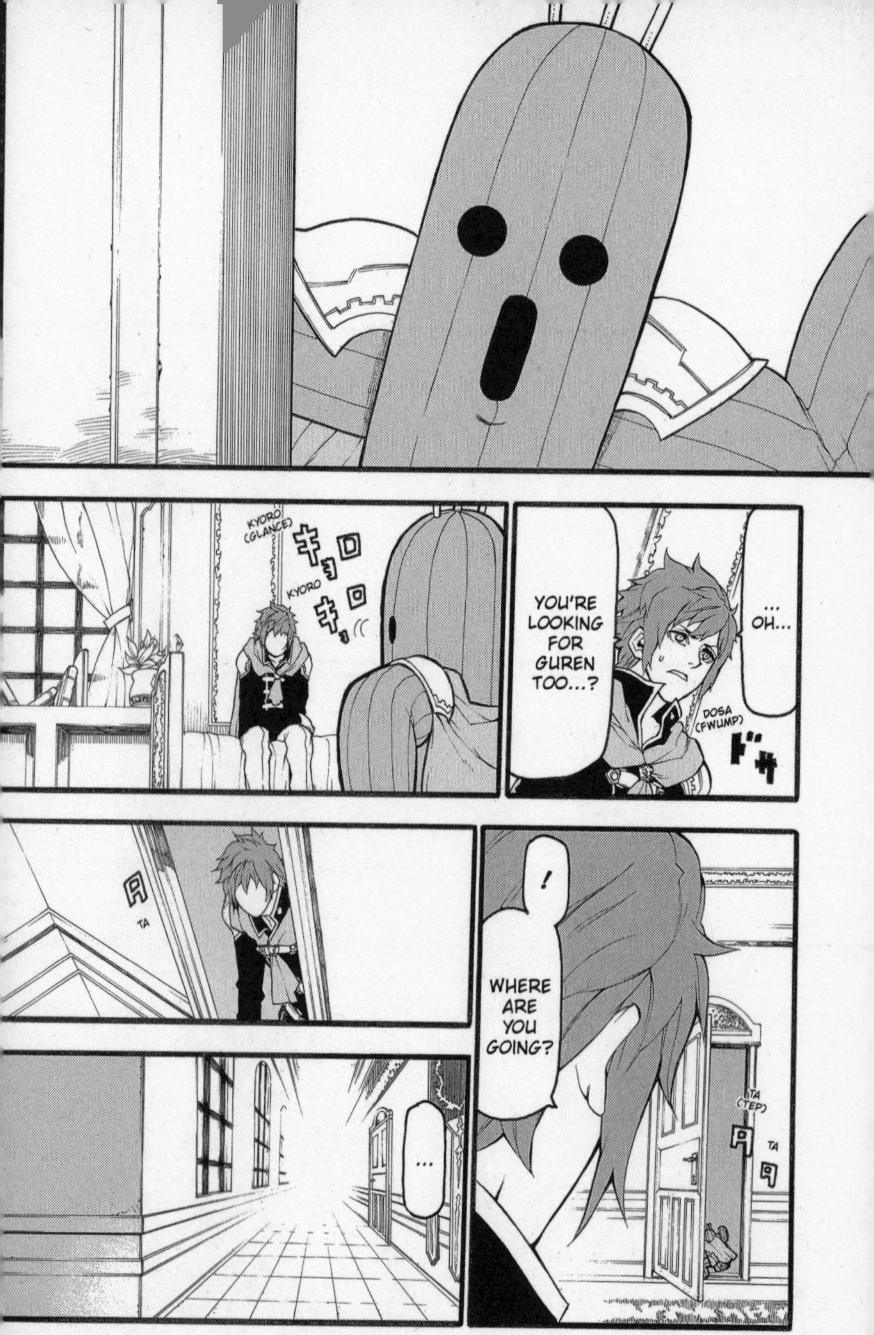

... OH...
YOU'RE LOOKING FOR GUREN TOO...?
DOSA (FWUMP)
KYORO (GLANCE)
KYORO
!
WHERE ARE YOU GOING?
TA (TEP)
TA
TA
...

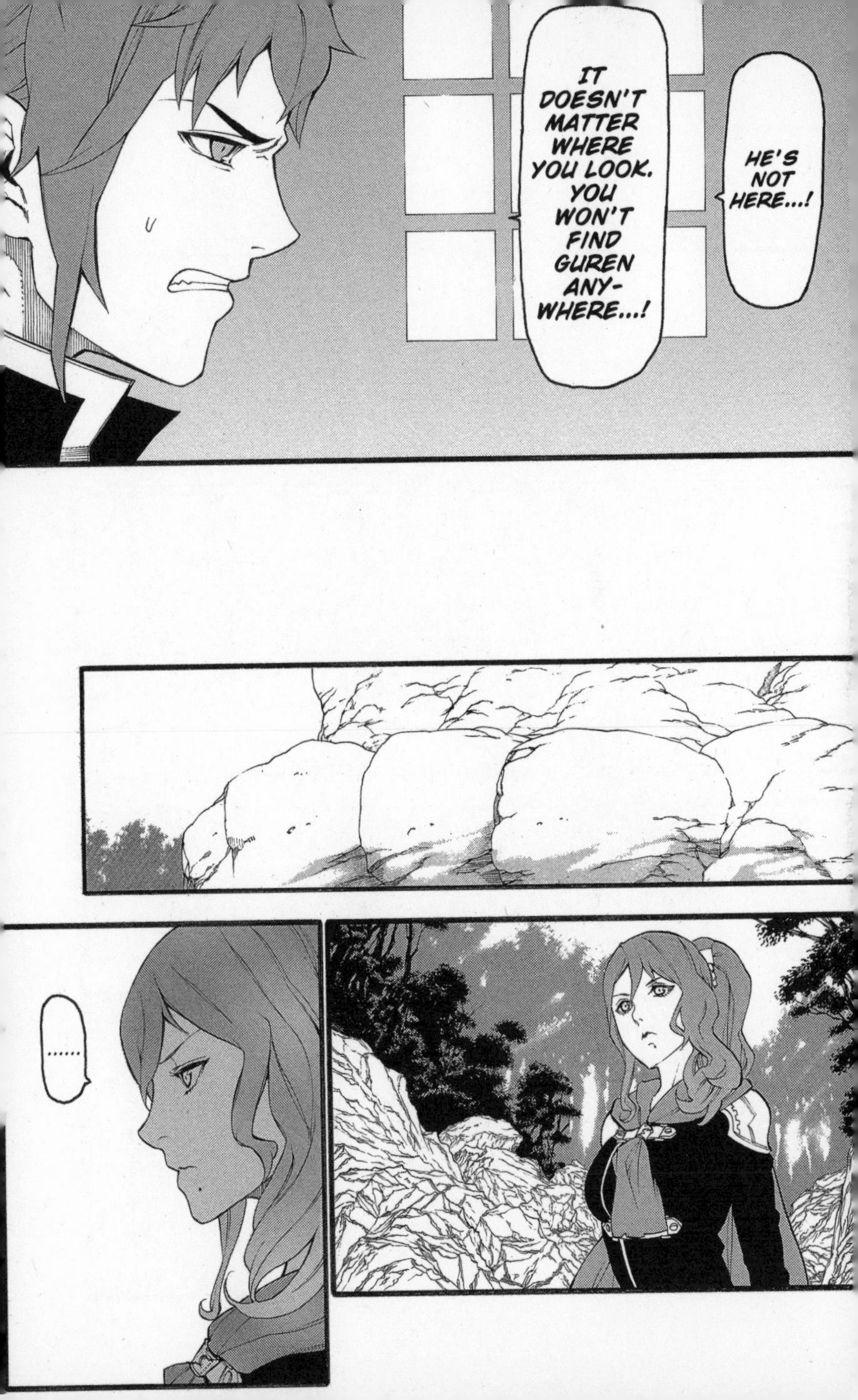
HE'S NOT HERE...!
IT DOESN'T MATTER WHERE YOU LOOK. YOU WON'T FIND GUREN ANYWHERE...!
......

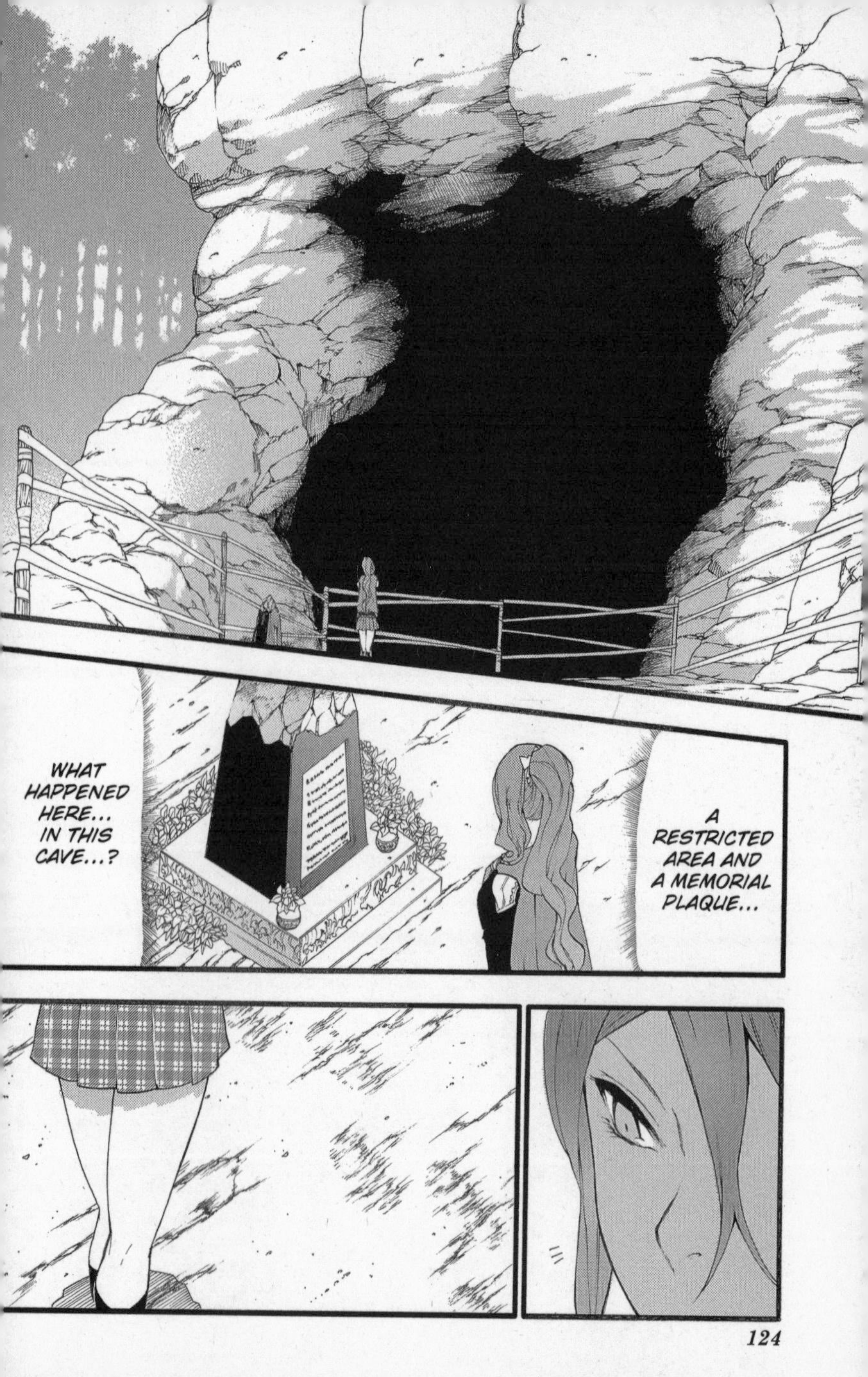
A RESTRICTED AREA AND A MEMORIAL PLAQUE...
WHAT HAPPENED HERE... IN THIS CAVE...?

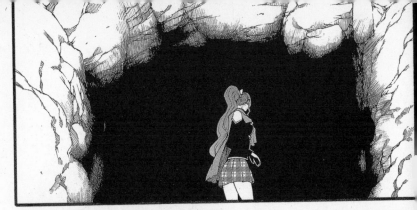

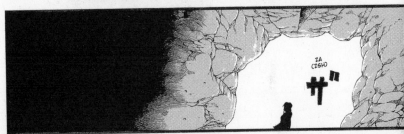

ZA (ZSH)
ザッ
!
...
I KNEW YOU WERE STILL IN THE DOMINION.
THERE WEREN'T ANY REPORTS OF YOU CROSSING THE BORDER.
...

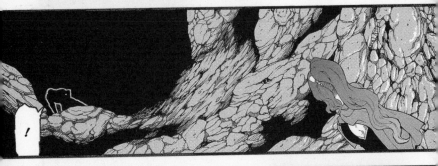

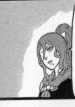

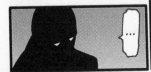

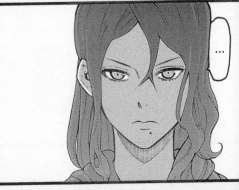

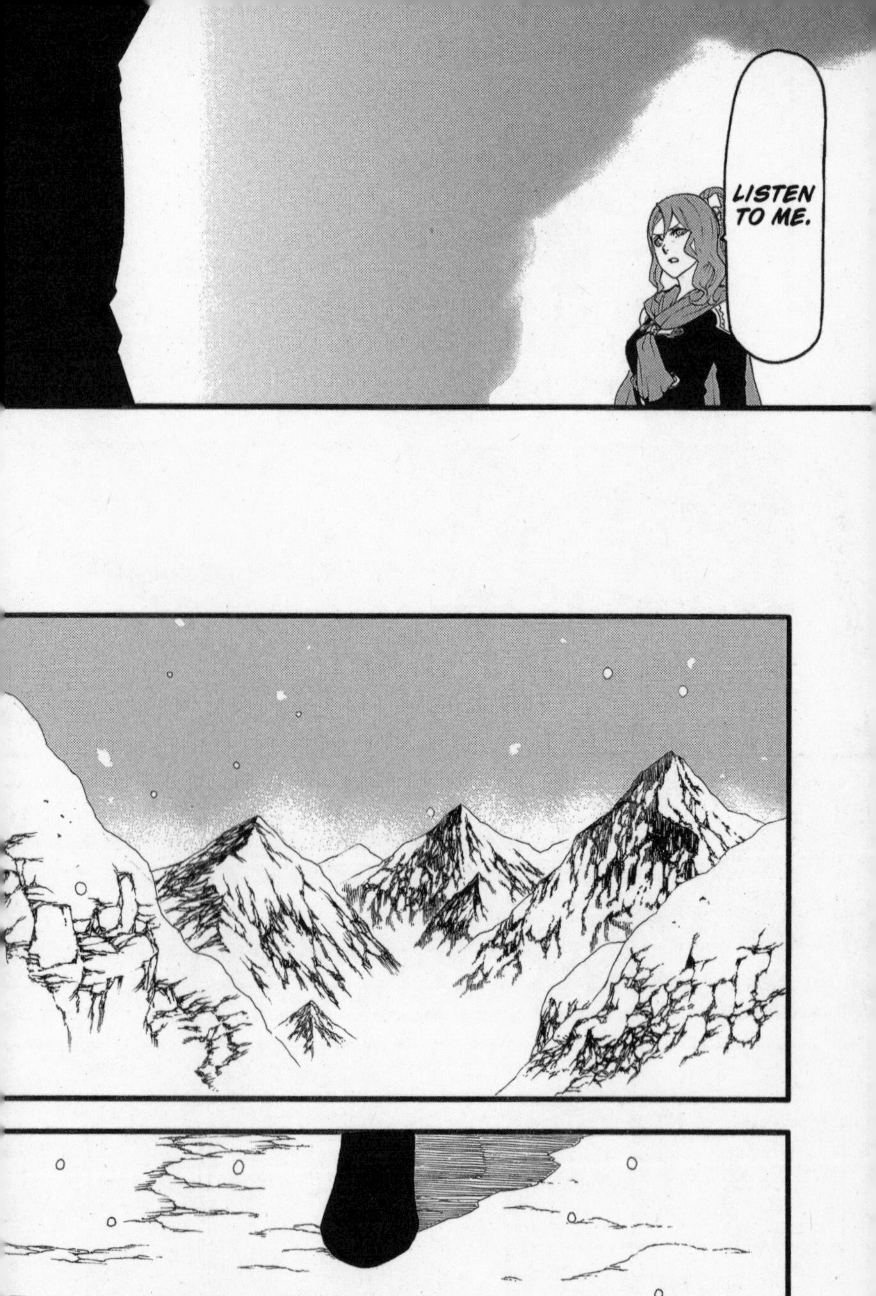
LISTEN TO ME.

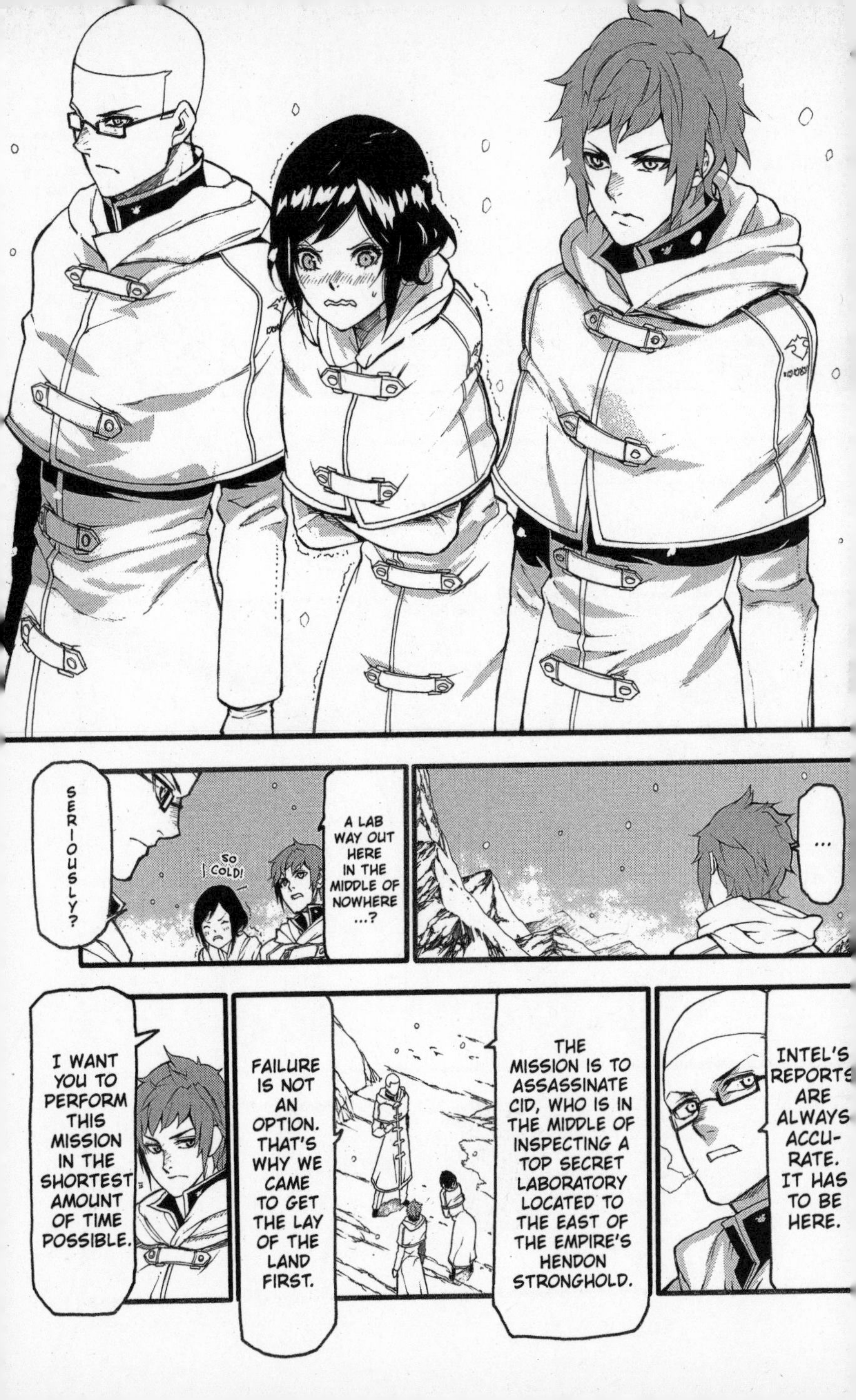
...
A LAB WAY OUT HERE IN THE MIDDLE OF NOWHERE ...?
SO COLD!
SERIOUSLY?
INTEL'S REPORTS ARE ALWAYS ACCU-RATE. IT HAS TO BE HERE.
THE MISSION IS TO ASSASSINATE CID, WHO IS IN THE MIDDLE OF INSPECTING A TOP SECRET LABORATORY LOCATED TO THE EAST OF THE EMPIRE'S HENDON STRONGHOLD.
FAILURE IS NOT AN OPTION. THAT'S WHY WE CAME TO GET THE LAY OF THE LAND FIRST.
I WANT YOU TO PERFORM THIS MISSION IN THE SHORTEST AMOUNT OF TIME POSSIBLE.

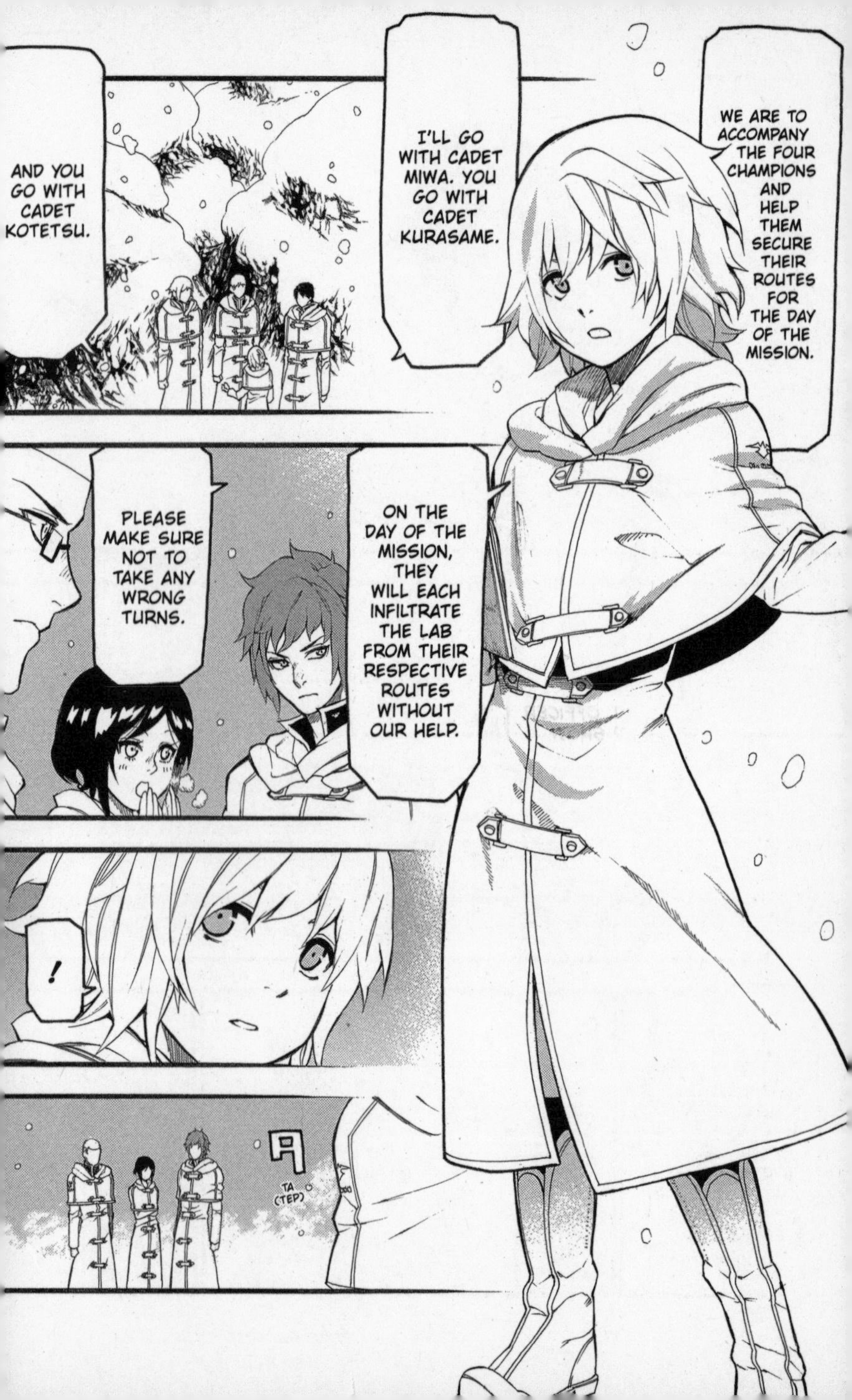

WE ARE TO ACCOMPANY THE FOUR CHAMPIONS AND HELP THEM SECURE THEIR ROUTES FOR THE DAY OF THE MISSION.
I'LL GO WITH CADET MIWA. YOU GO WITH CADET KURASAME.
AND YOU GO WITH CADET KOTETSU.
ON THE DAY OF THE MISSION, THEY WILL EACH INFILTRATE THE LAB FROM THEIR RESPECTIVE ROUTES WITHOUT OUR HELP.
PLEASE MAKE SURE NOT TO TAKE ANY WRONG TURNS.
!
TA (TEP)

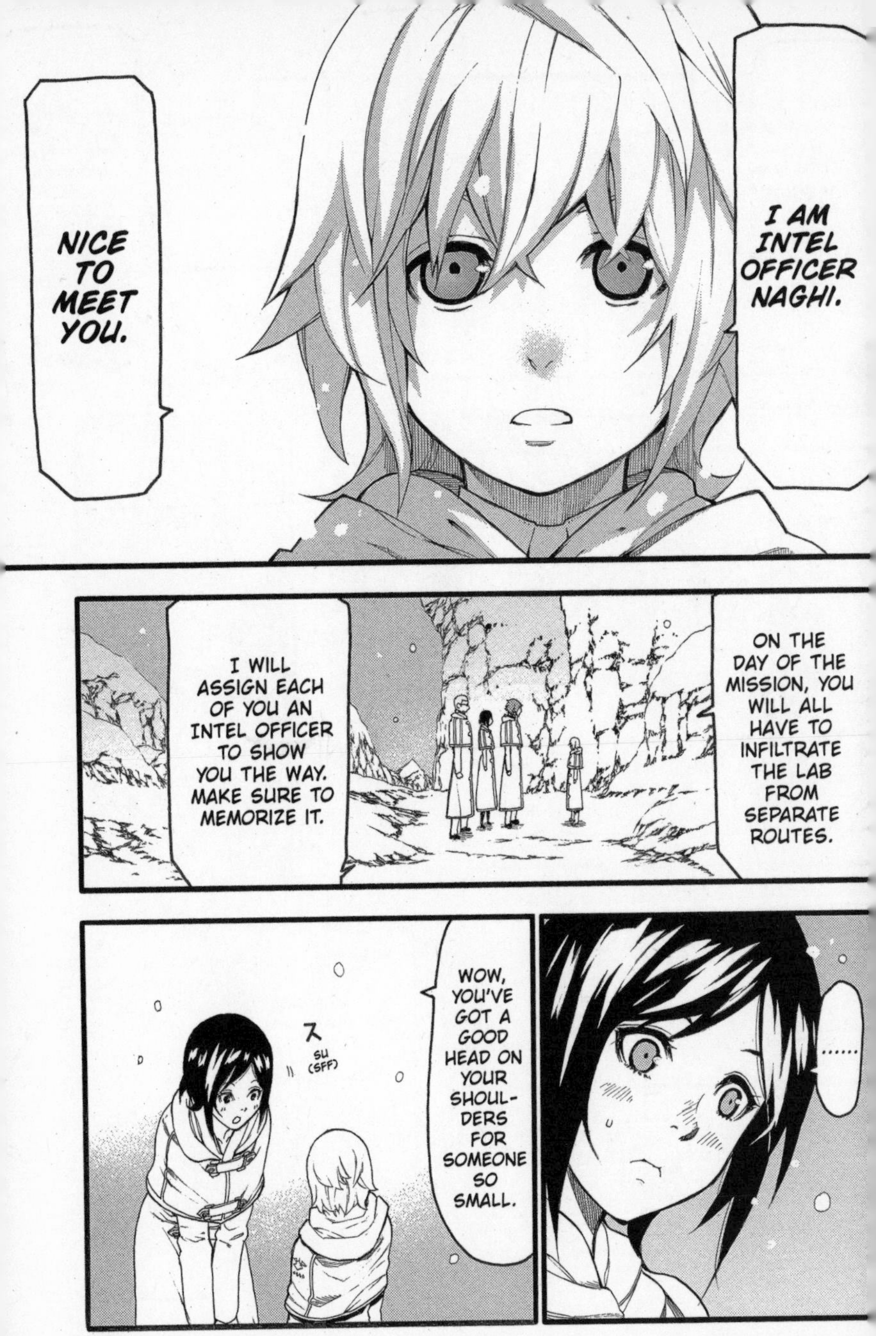
I AM INTEL OFFICER NAGHI.
NICE TO MEET YOU.
ON THE DAY OF THE MISSION, YOU WILL ALL HAVE TO INFILTRATE THE LAB FROM SEPARATE ROUTES.
I WILL ASSIGN EACH OF YOU AN INTEL OFFICER TO SHOW YOU THE WAY. MAKE SURE TO MEMORIZE IT.
......
WOW, YOU'VE GOT A GOOD HEAD ON YOUR SHOUL-DERS FOR SOMEONE SO SMALL.
ス
SU (SFF)

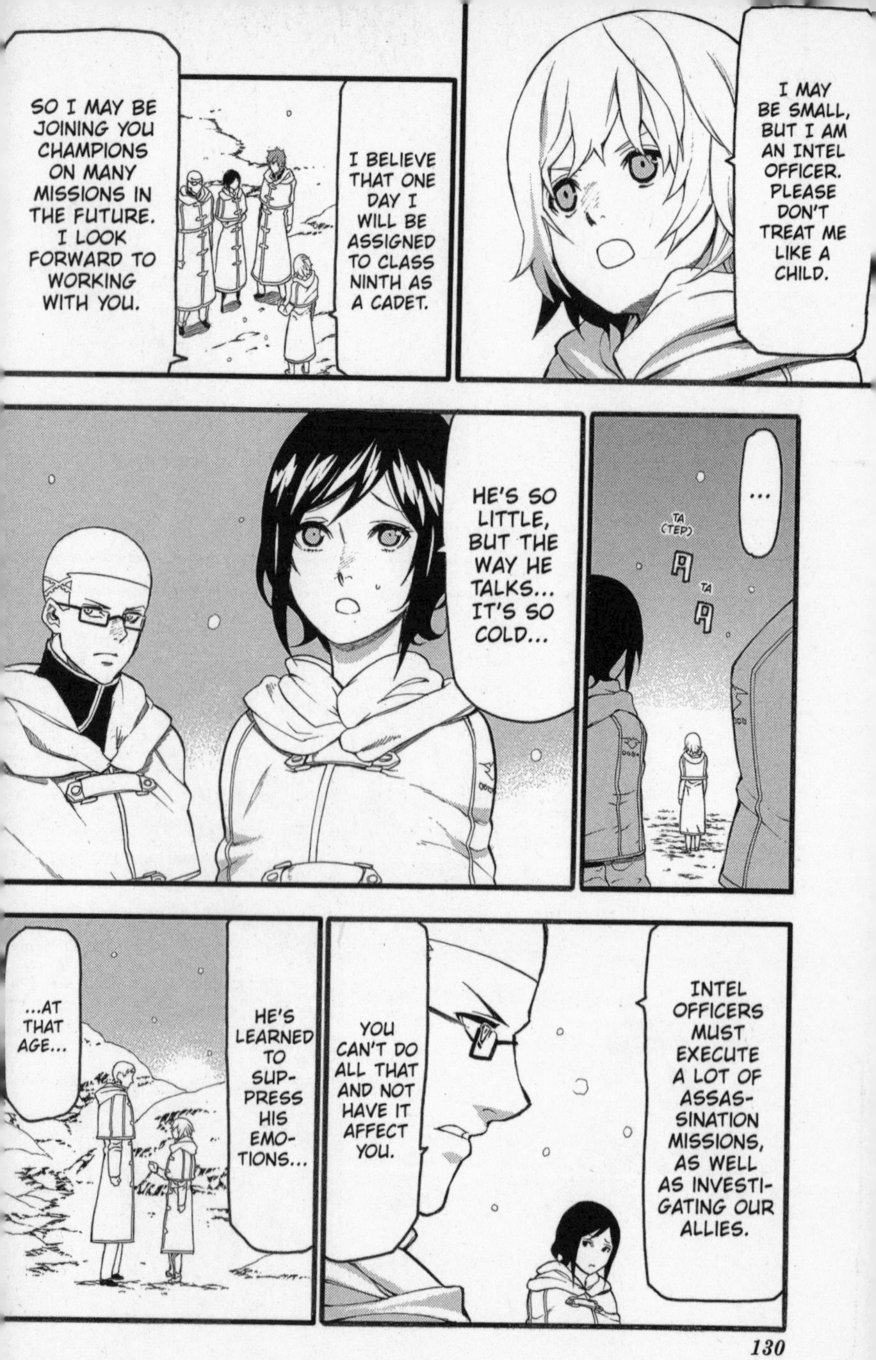
I MAY BE SMALL, BUT I AM AN INTEL OFFICER. PLEASE DON'T TREAT ME LIKE A CHILD.
I BELIEVE THAT ONE DAY I WILL BE ASSIGNED TO CLASS NINTH AS A CADET.
SO I MAY BE JOINING YOU CHAMPIONS ON MANY MISSIONS IN THE FUTURE. I LOOK FORWARD TO WORKING WITH YOU.
...
TA (TEP)
TA
HE'S SO LITTLE, BUT THE WAY HE TALKS... IT'S SO COLD...
INTEL OFFICERS MUST EXECUTE A LOT OF ASSAS-SINATION MISSIONS, AS WELL AS INVESTI-GATING OUR ALLIES.
YOU CAN'T DO ALL THAT AND NOT HAVE IT AFFECT YOU.
HE'S LEARNED TO SUP-PRESS HIS EMO-TIONS...
...AT THAT AGE...

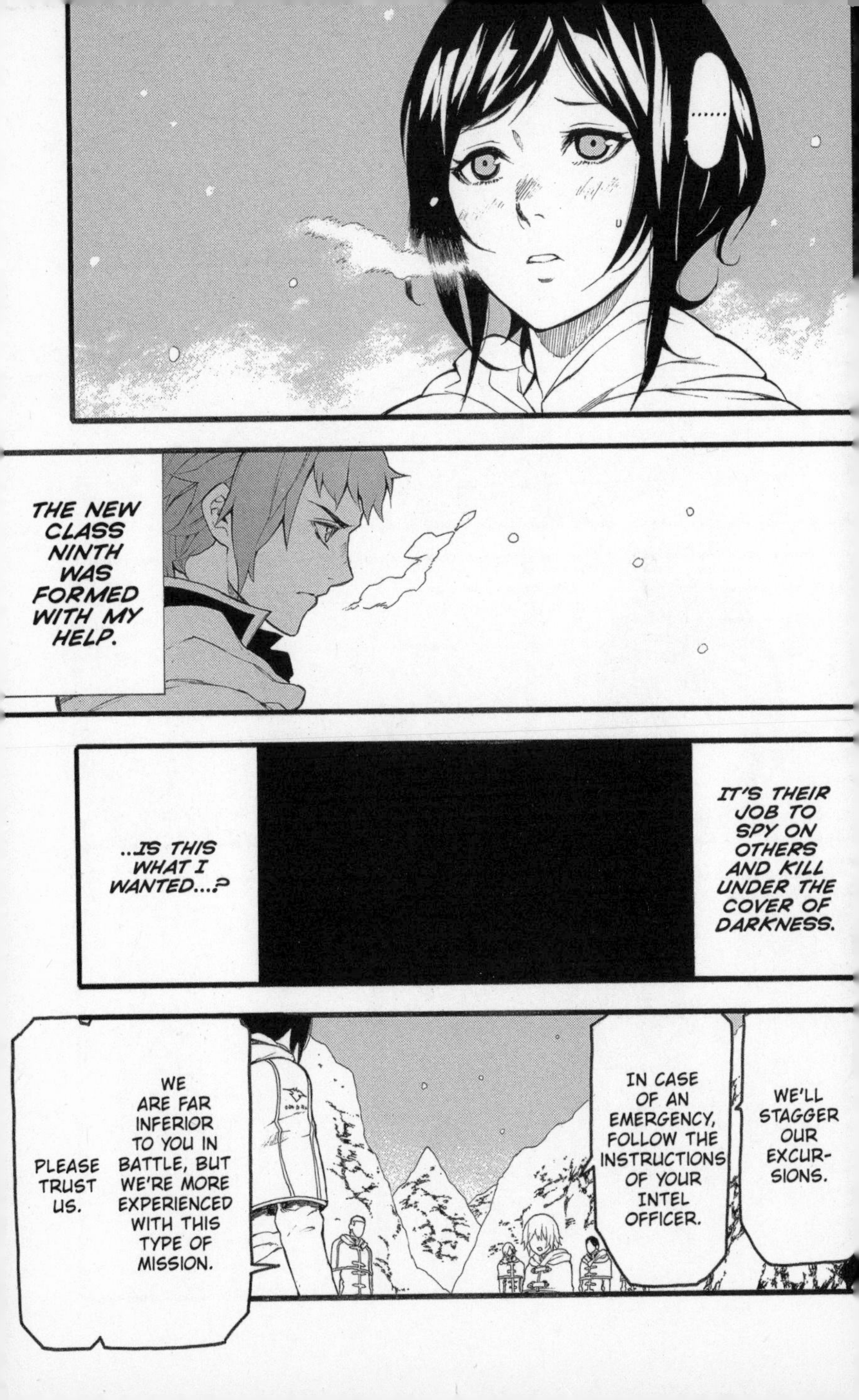
......
THE NEW CLASS NINTH WAS FORMED WITH MY HELP.
IT'S THEIR JOB TO SPY ON OTHERS AND KILL UNDER THE COVER OF DARKNESS.
...IS THIS WHAT I WANTED...?
WE'LL STAGGER OUR EXCURSIONS.
IN CASE OF AN EMERGENCY, FOLLOW THE INSTRUCTIONS OF YOUR INTEL OFFICER.
WE ARE FAR INFERIOR TO YOU IN BATTLE, BUT WE'RE MORE EXPERIENCED WITH THIS TYPE OF MISSION.
PLEASE TRUST US.

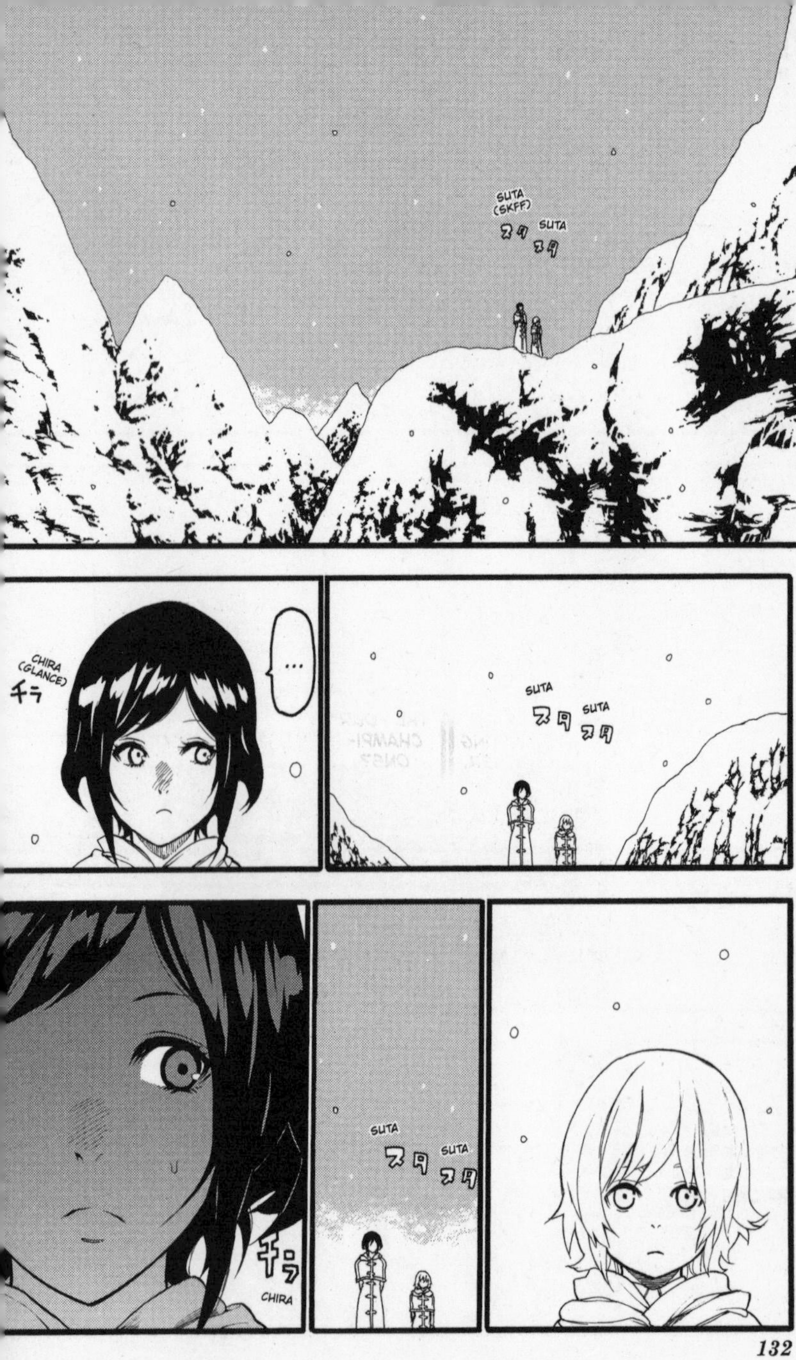
SUTA (SKFF)
スタ
SUTA
スタ
SUTA
スタ
SUTA
スタ
…
CHIRA (GLANCE)
チラ
SUTA
スタ
SUTA
スタ
チラ
CHIRA

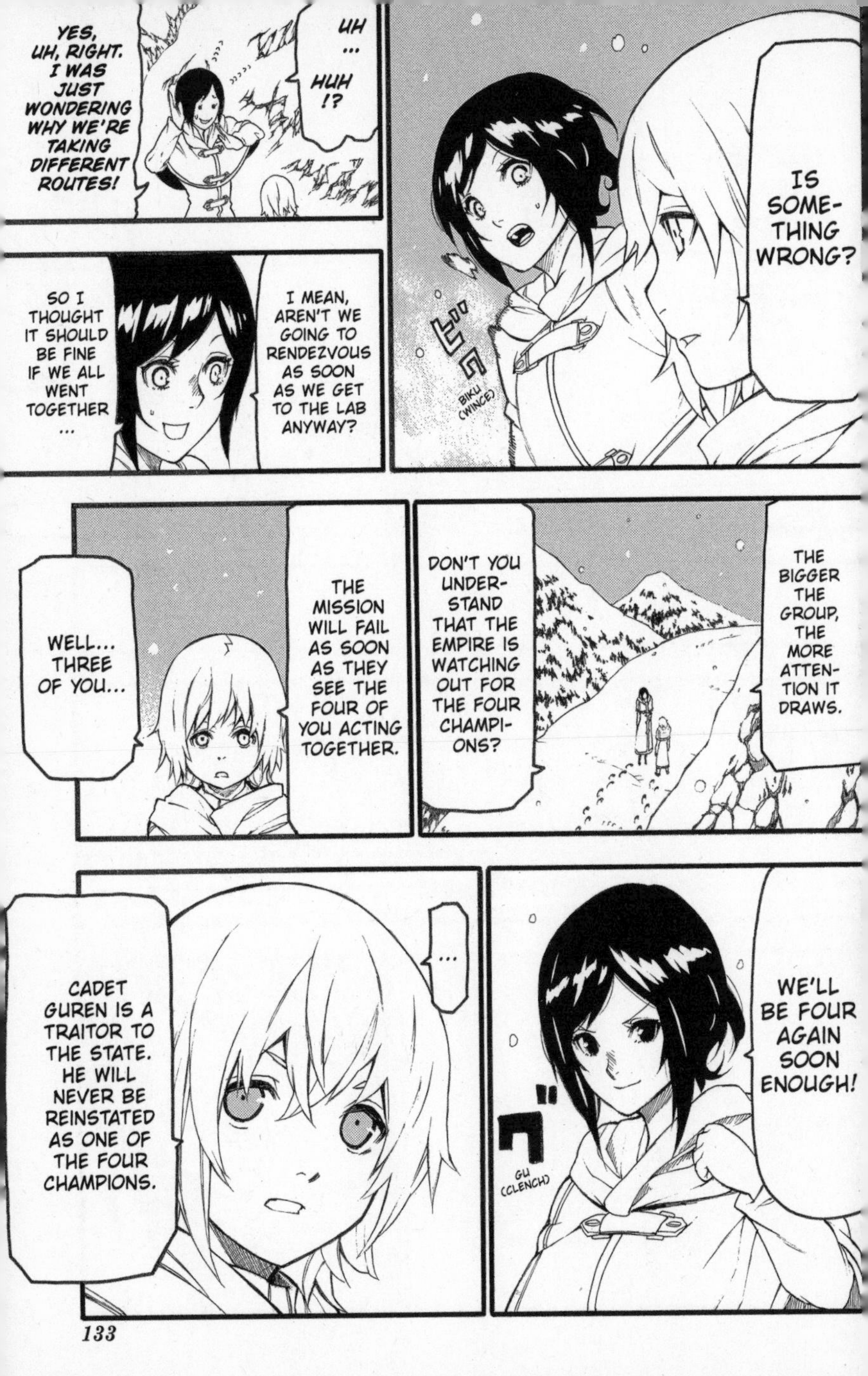
IS SOMETHING WRONG?
BIKU (WINCE)
UH ... HUH !?
YES, UH, RIGHT. I WAS JUST WONDERING WHY WE'RE TAKING DIFFERENT ROUTES!
I MEAN, AREN'T WE GOING TO RENDEZVOUS AS SOON AS WE GET TO THE LAB ANYWAY?
SO I THOUGHT IT SHOULD BE FINE IF WE ALL WENT TOGETHER ...
THE BIGGER THE GROUP, THE MORE ATTENTION IT DRAWS.
DON'T YOU UNDERSTAND THAT THE EMPIRE IS WATCHING OUT FOR THE FOUR CHAMPIONS?
THE MISSION WILL FAIL AS SOON AS THEY SEE THE FOUR OF YOU ACTING TOGETHER.
WELL... THREE OF YOU...
WE'LL BE FOUR AGAIN SOON ENOUGH!
GU (CLENCH)
...
CADET GUREN IS A TRAITOR TO THE STATE. HE WILL NEVER BE REINSTATED AS ONE OF THE FOUR CHAMPIONS.

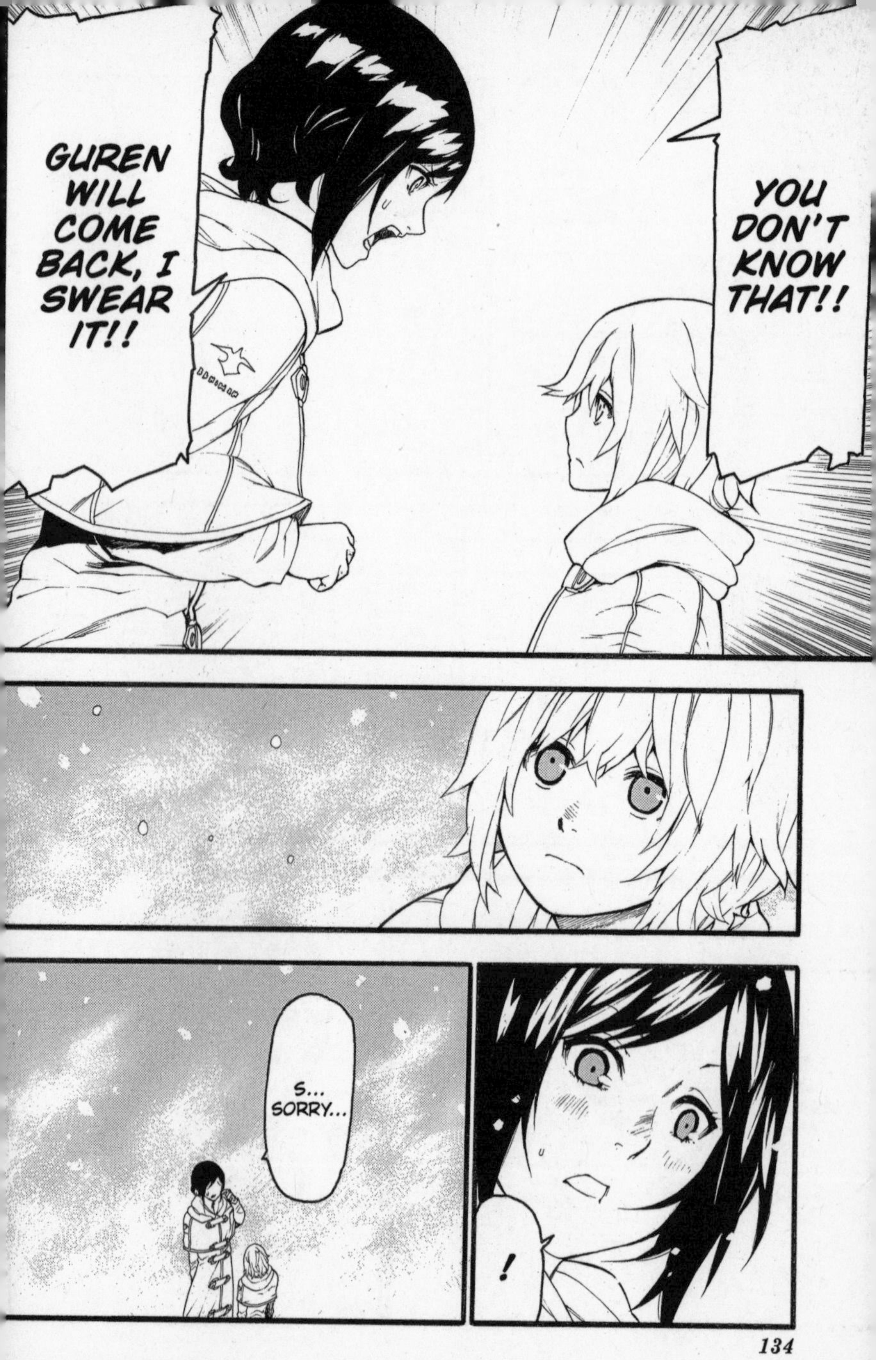
YOU DON'T KNOW THAT!!
GUREN WILL COME BACK, I SWEAR IT!!
!
S... SORRY...

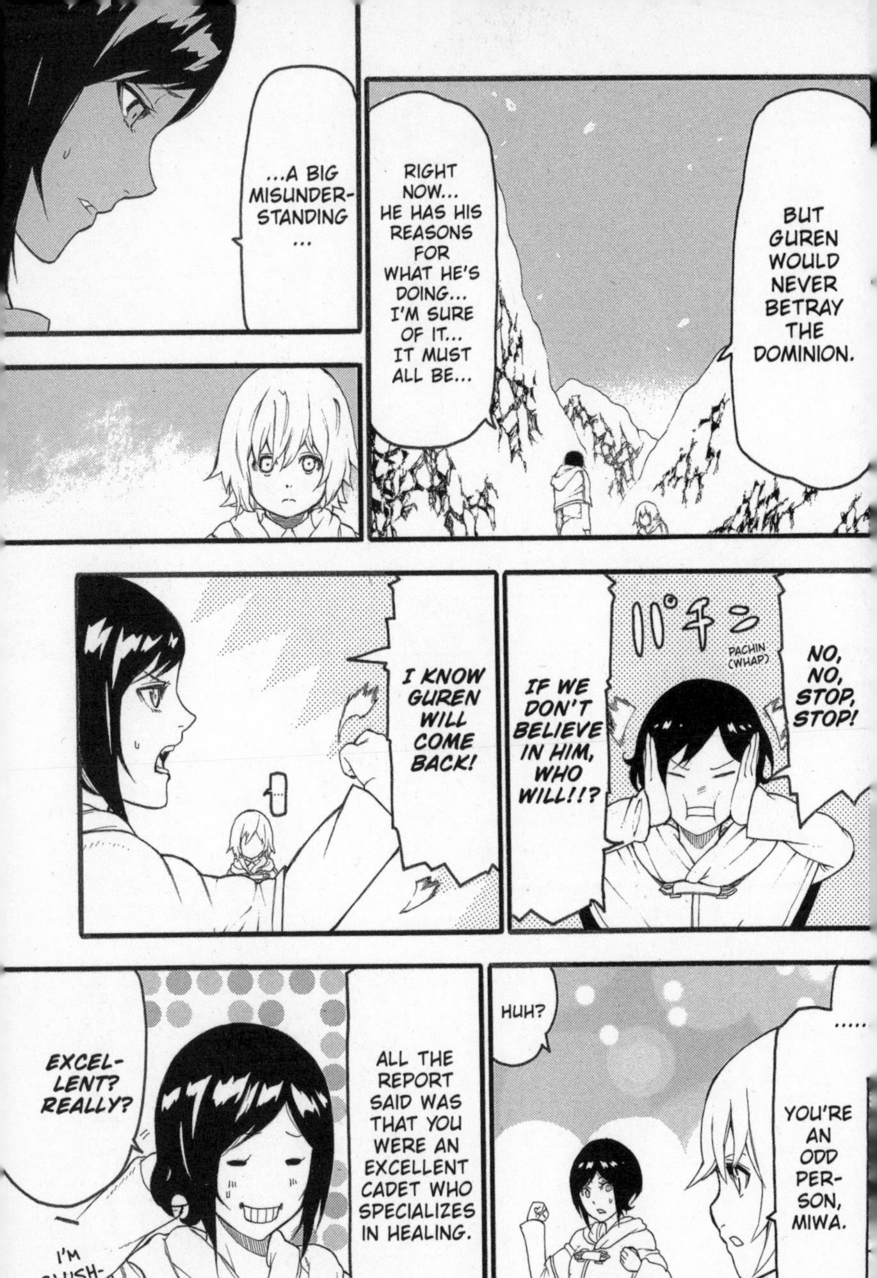
BUT GUREN WOULD NEVER BETRAY THE DOMINION.
RIGHT NOW... HE HAS HIS REASONS FOR WHAT HE'S DOING... I'M SURE OF IT... IT MUST ALL BE...
...A BIG MISUNDER-STANDING...
NO, NO, STOP, STOP!
パチン
PACHIN (WHAP)
IF WE DON'T BELIEVE IN HIM, WHO WILL!!?
I KNOW GUREN WILL COME BACK!
....
.....
YOU'RE AN ODD PER-SON, MIWA.
HUH?
ALL THE REPORT SAID WAS THAT YOU WERE AN EXCELLENT CADET WHO SPECIALIZES IN HEALING.
EXCEL-LENT? REALLY?
I'M BLUSH-ING...

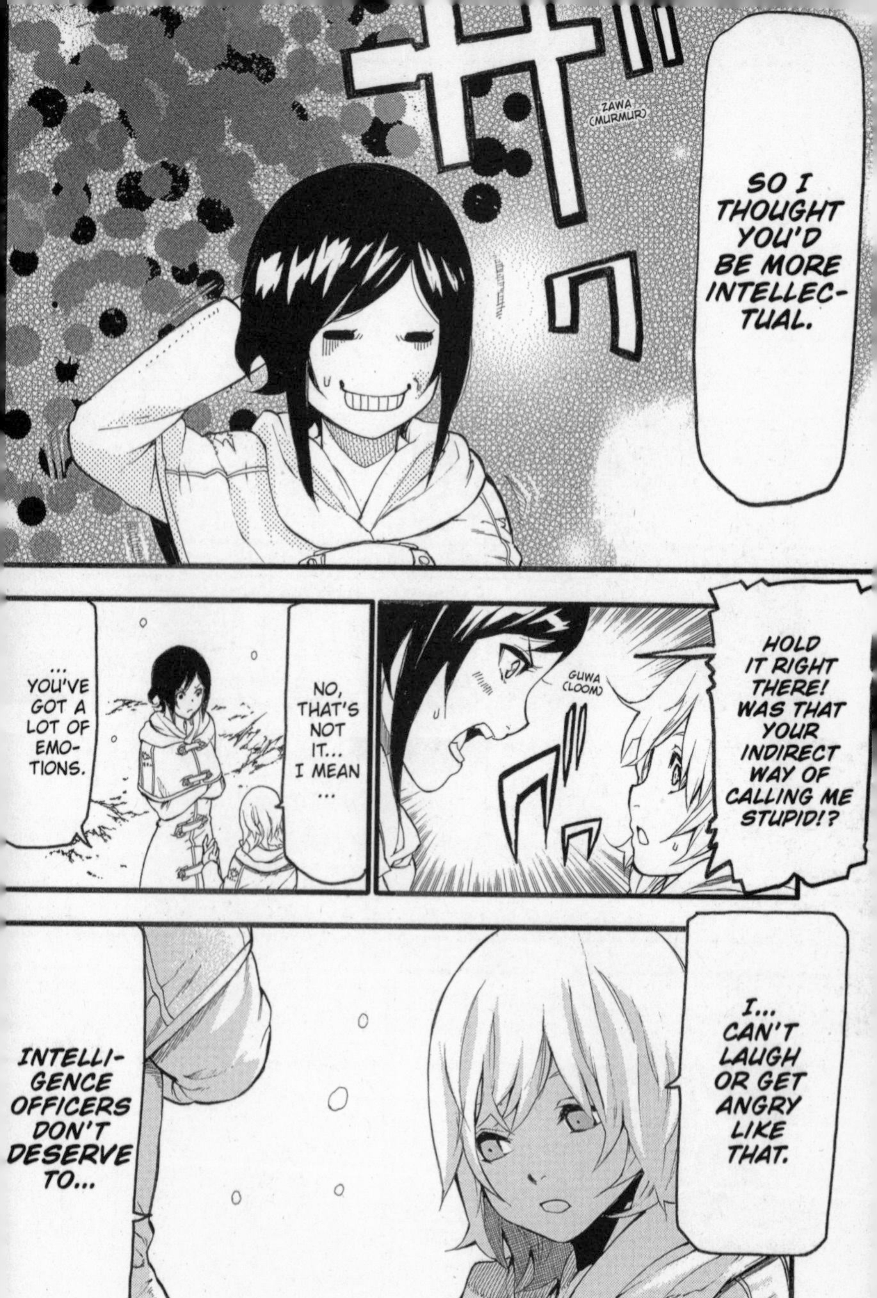
SO I THOUGHT YOU'D BE MORE INTELLEC-TUAL.
ZAWA (MURMUR)
HOLD IT RIGHT THERE! WAS THAT YOUR INDIRECT WAY OF CALLING ME STUPID!?
GUWA (LOOM)
NO, THAT'S NOT IT... I MEAN ...
... YOU'VE GOT A LOT OF EMO-TIONS.
I... CAN'T LAUGH OR GET ANGRY LIKE THAT.
INTELLI-GENCE OFFICERS DON'T DESERVE TO...

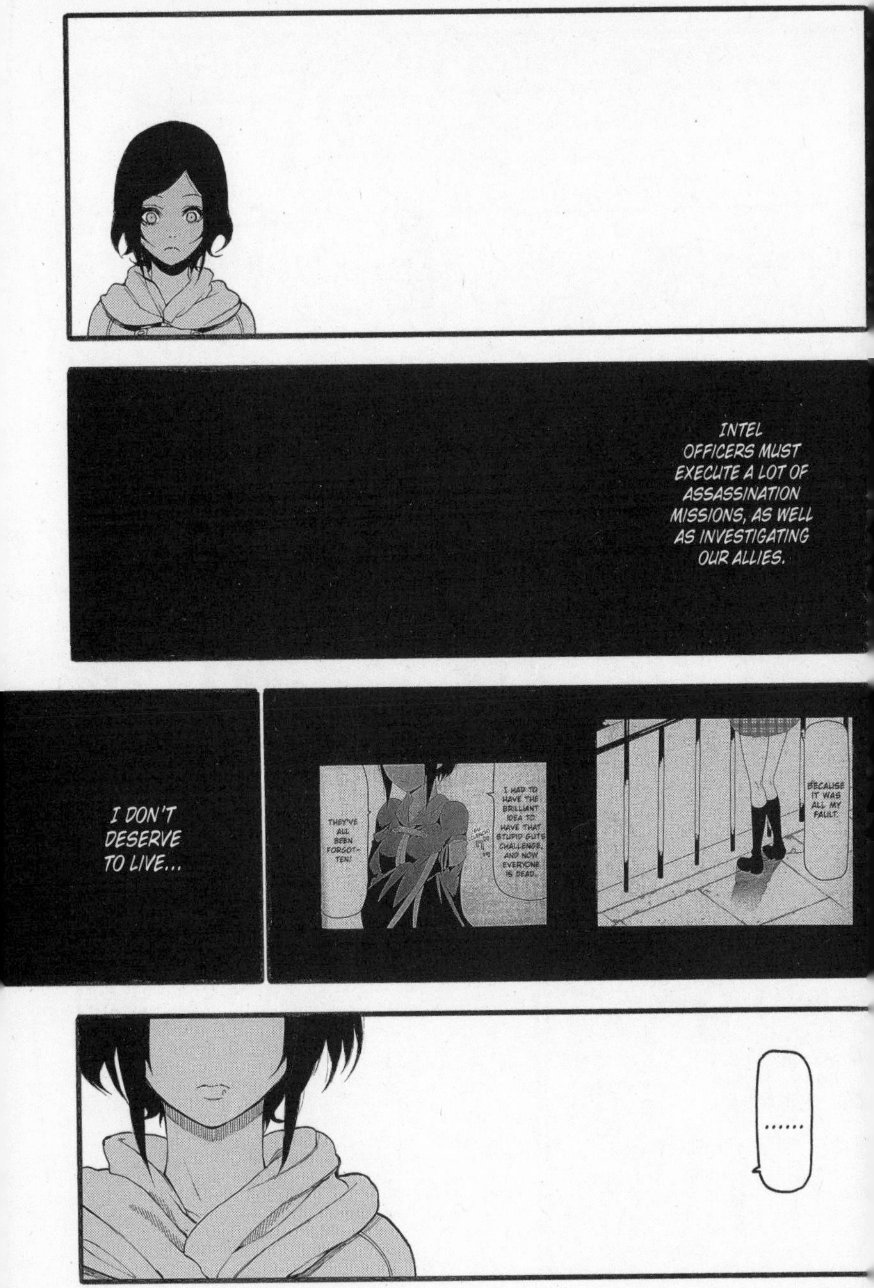
INTEL OFFICERS MUST EXECUTE A LOT OF ASSASSINATION MISSIONS, AS WELL AS INVESTIGATING OUR ALLIES.
BECAUSE IT WAS ALL MY FAULT.
I HAD TO HAVE THE BRILLIANT IDEA TO HAVE THAT STUPID GUTS CHALLENGE, AND NOW EVERYONE IS DEAD.
GU (CLENCH)
THEY'VE ALL BEEN FORGOT-TEN!
I DON'T DESERVE TO LIVE...
......

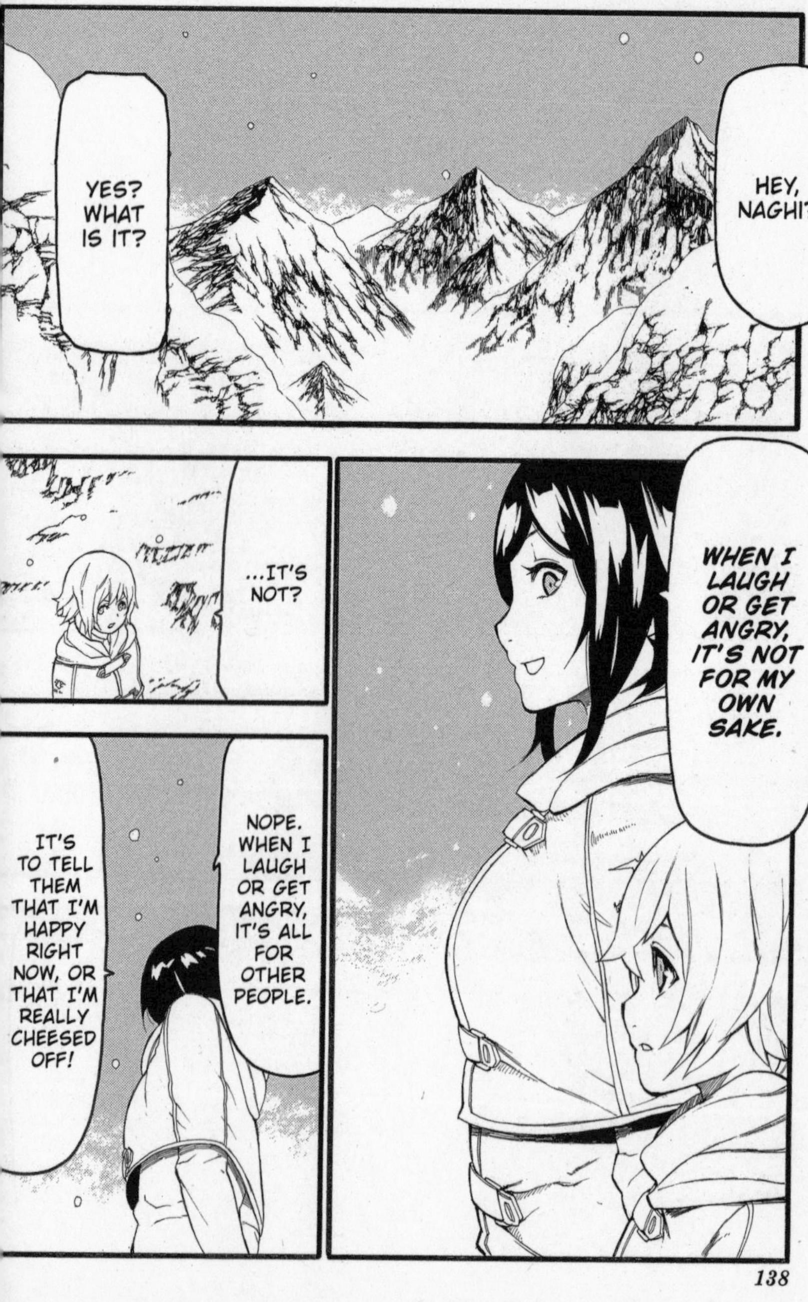
HEY, NAGHI?
YES? WHAT IS IT?
WHEN I LAUGH OR GET ANGRY, IT'S NOT FOR MY OWN SAKE.
...IT'S NOT?
NOPE. WHEN I LAUGH OR GET ANGRY, IT'S ALL FOR OTHER PEOPLE.
IT'S TO TELL THEM THAT I'M HAPPY RIGHT NOW, OR THAT I'M REALLY CHEESED OFF!

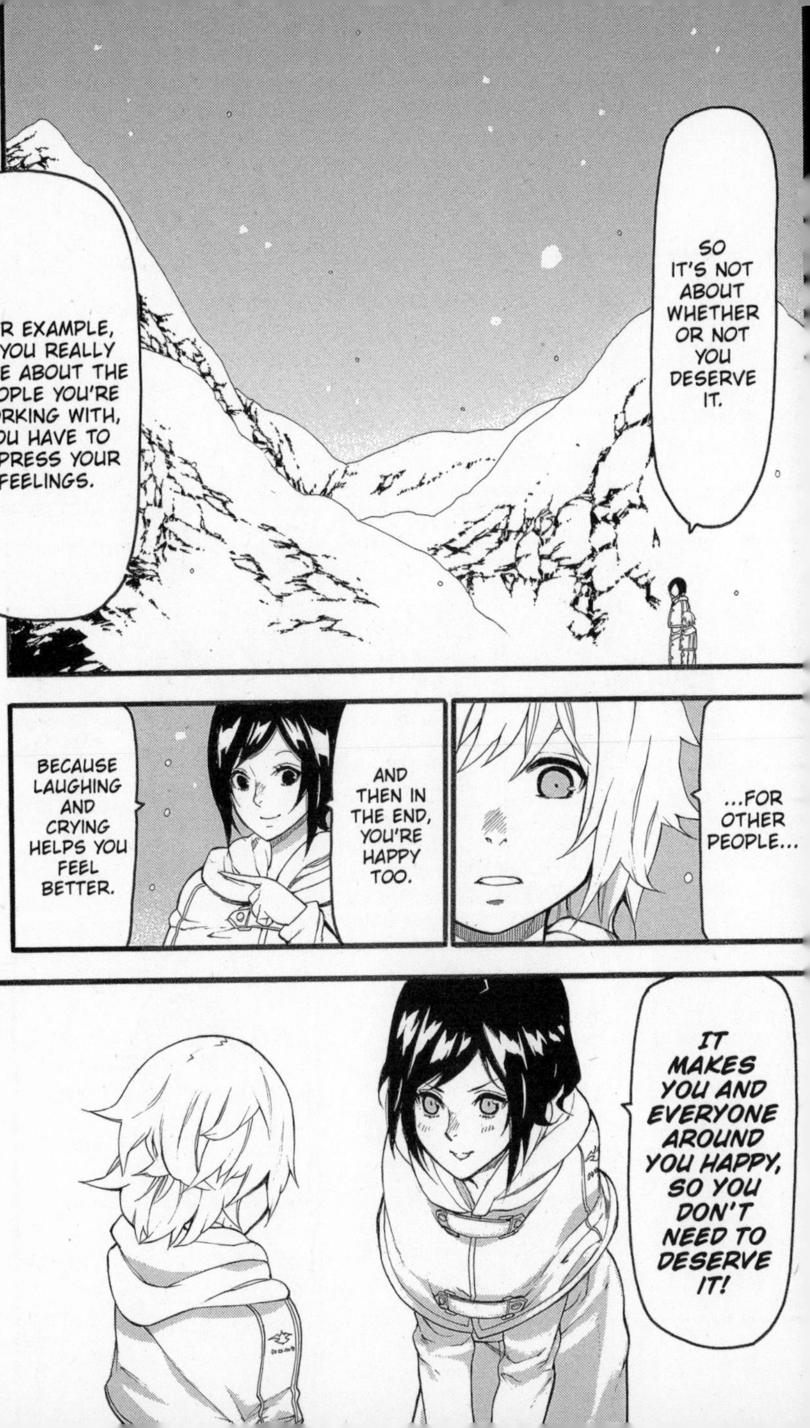
SO IT'S NOT ABOUT WHETHER OR NOT YOU DESERVE IT.
FOR EXAMPLE, IF YOU REALLY CARE ABOUT THE PEOPLE YOU'RE WORKING WITH, YOU HAVE TO EXPRESS YOUR FEELINGS.
...FOR OTHER PEOPLE...
AND THEN IN THE END, YOU'RE HAPPY TOO.
BECAUSE LAUGHING AND CRYING HELPS YOU FEEL BETTER.
IT MAKES YOU AND EVERYONE AROUND YOU HAPPY, SO YOU DON'T NEED TO DESERVE IT!

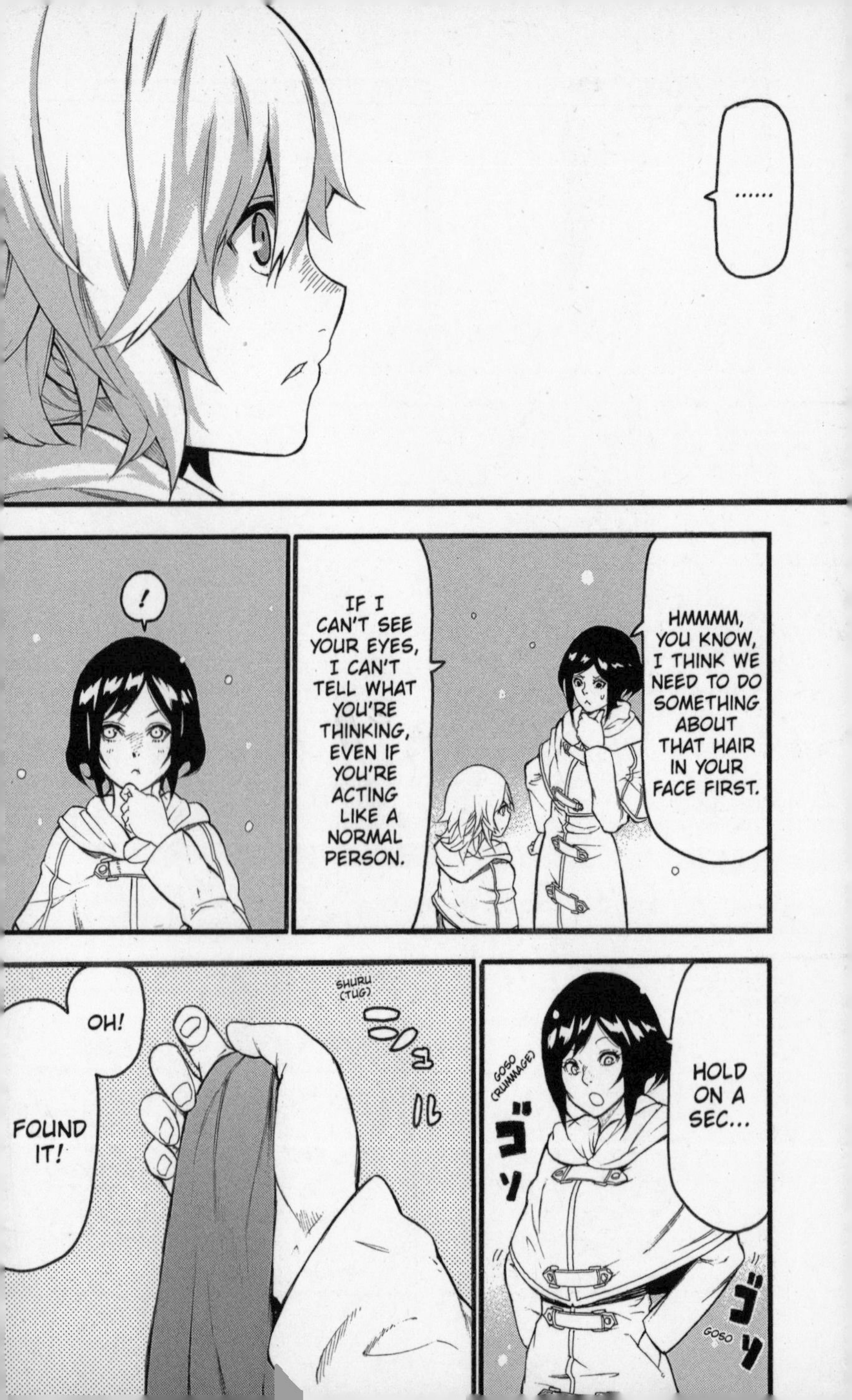
......
HMMMM, YOU KNOW, I THINK WE NEED TO DO SOMETHING ABOUT THAT HAIR IN YOUR FACE FIRST.
IF I CAN'T SEE YOUR EYES, I CAN'T TELL WHAT YOU'RE THINKING, EVEN IF YOU'RE ACTING LIKE A NORMAL PERSON.
!
HOLD ON A SEC...
GOSO (RUMMAGE)
ゴソ
ゴソ
GOSO
SHURU (TUG)
シュル
OH!
FOUND IT!

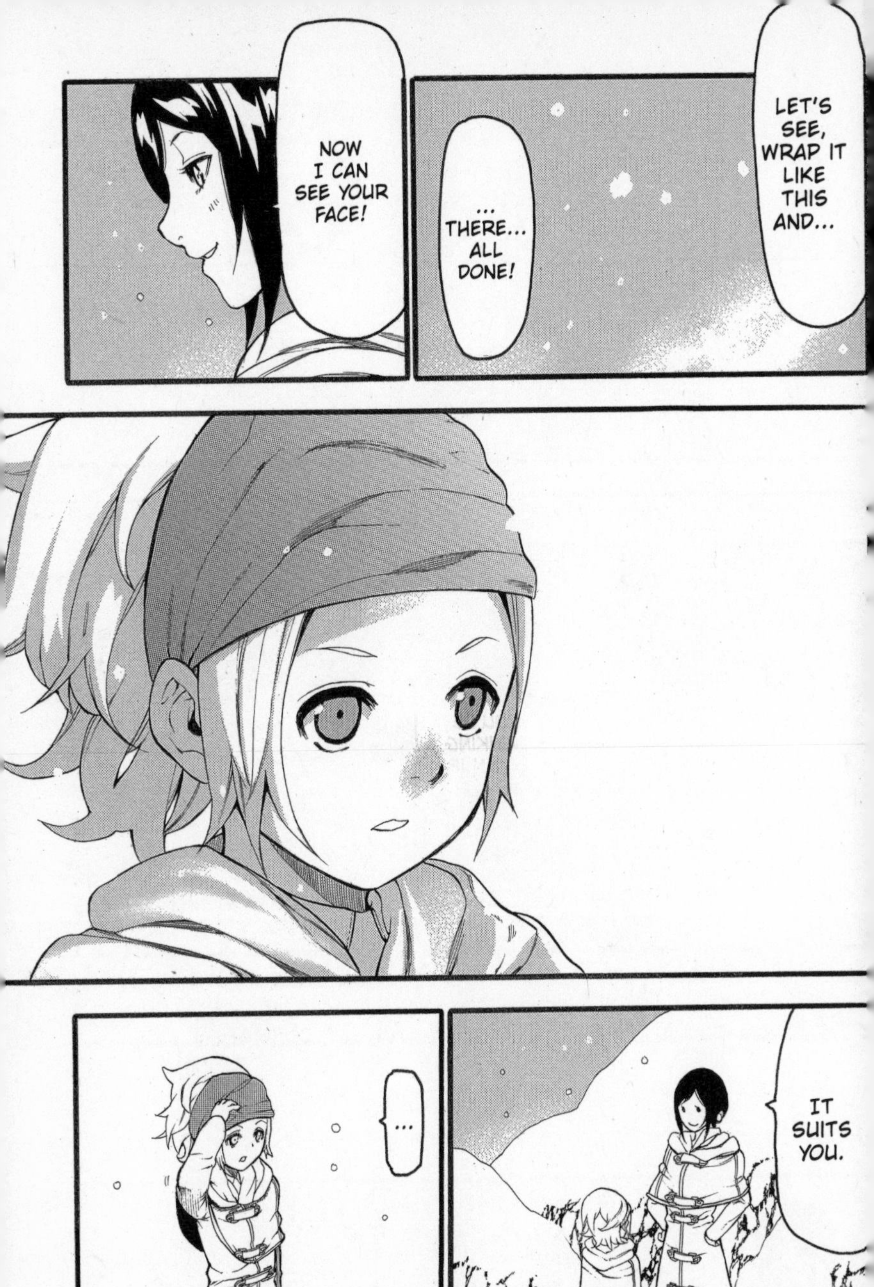
LET'S SEE, WRAP IT LIKE THIS AND...
... THERE... ALL DONE!
NOW I CAN SEE YOUR FACE!
IT SUITS YOU.
...

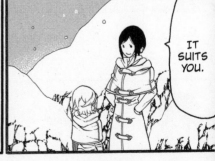

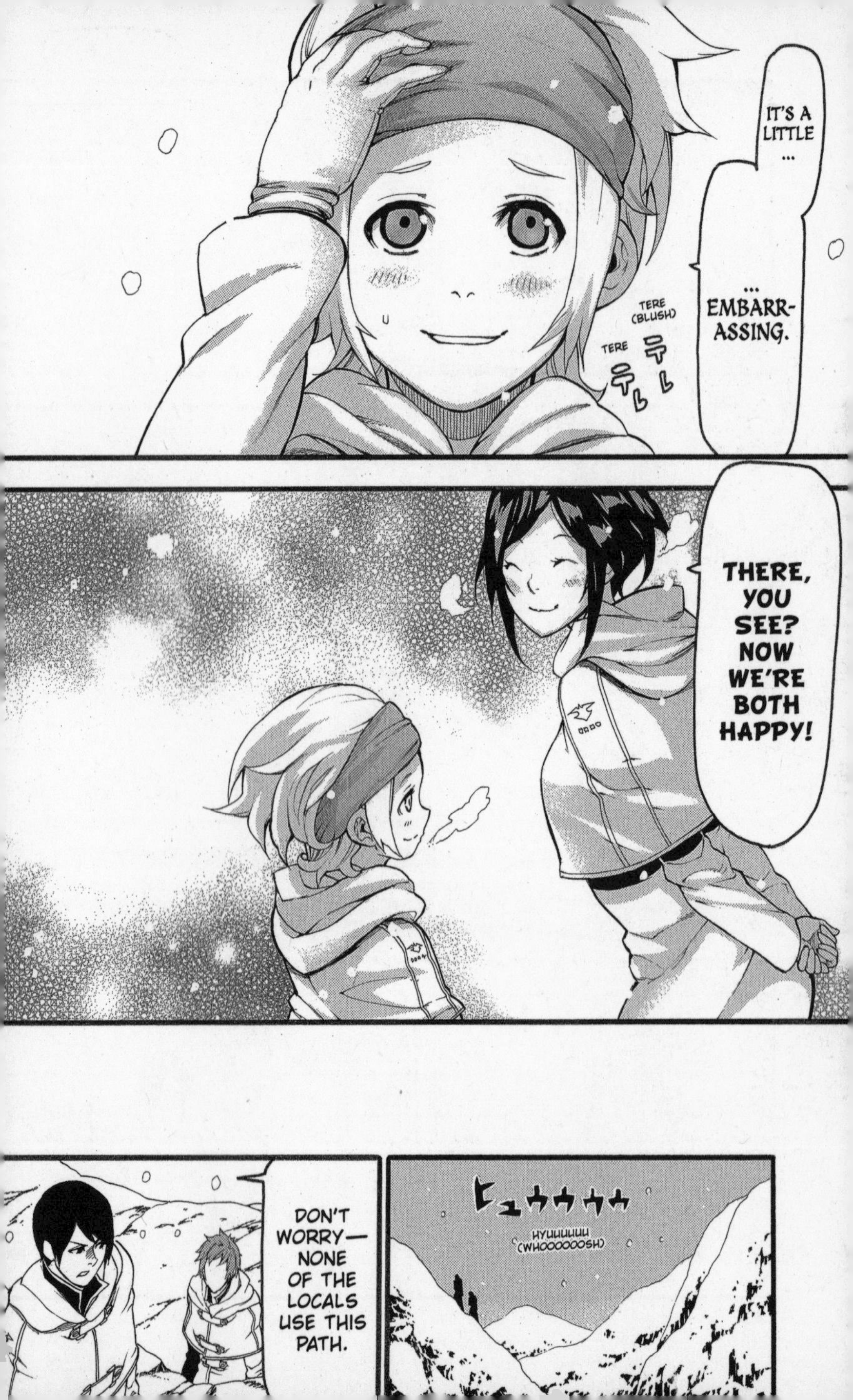
IT'S A LITTLE ...
... EMBARR-ASSING.
TERE (BLUSH)
TERE
THERE, YOU SEE? NOW WE'RE BOTH HAPPY!
HYUUUUUU (WHOOOOOOSH)
DON'T WORRY—NONE OF THE LOCALS USE THIS PATH.

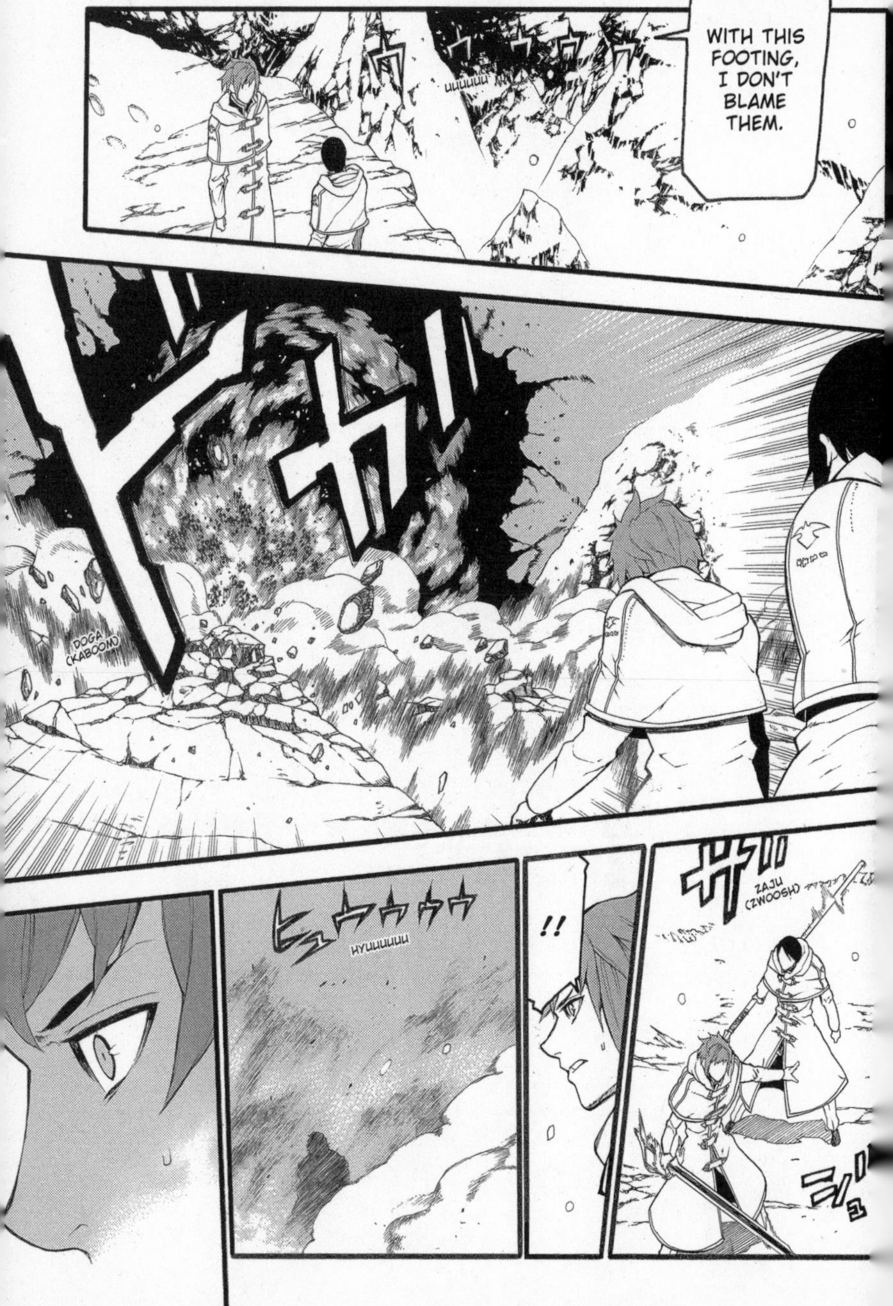
WITH THIS FOOTING, I DON'T BLAME THEM.
UUUUUUU
DOGA (KABOOM)
ZAJU (ZWOOSH)
!!
HYUUUUUUU

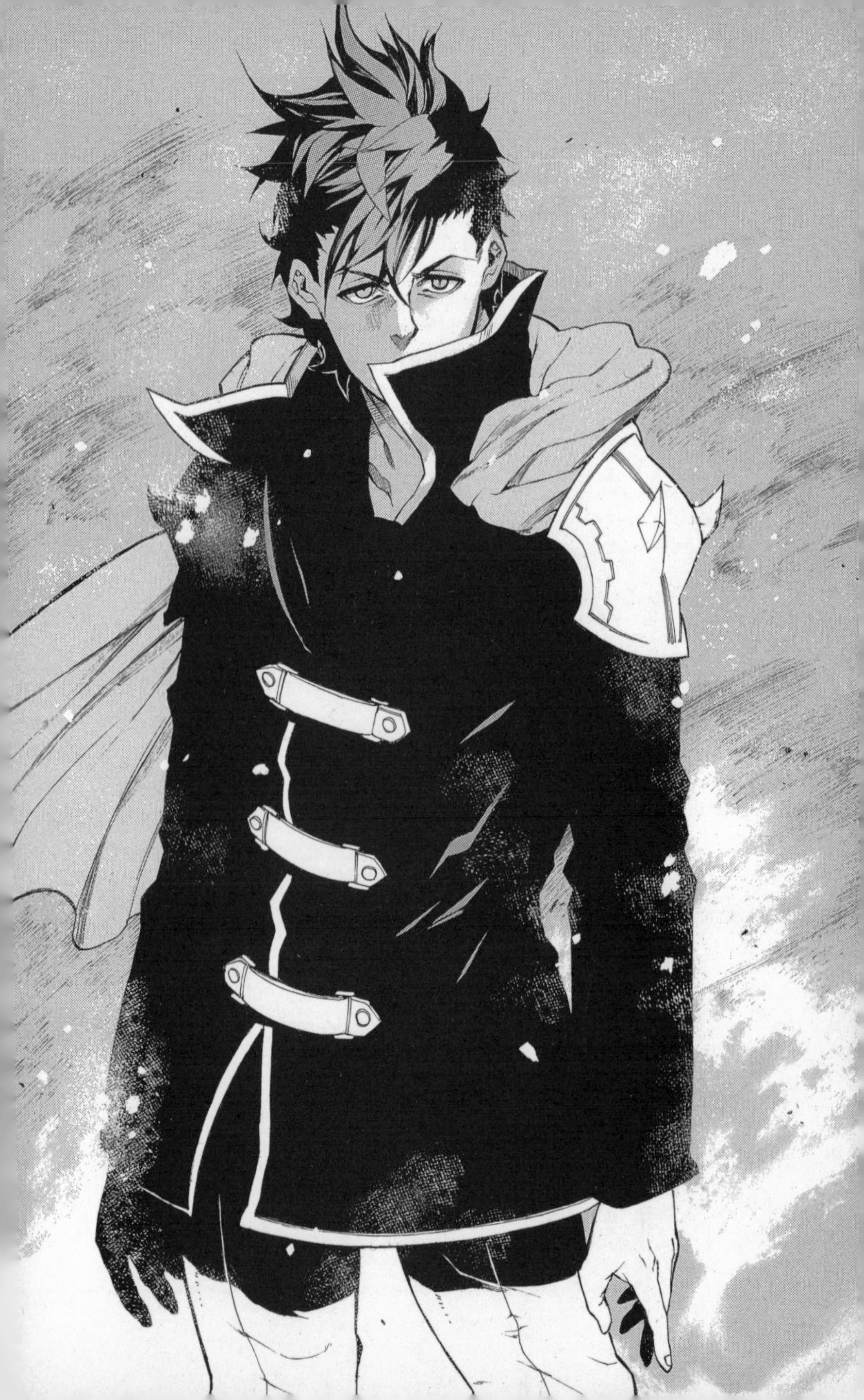

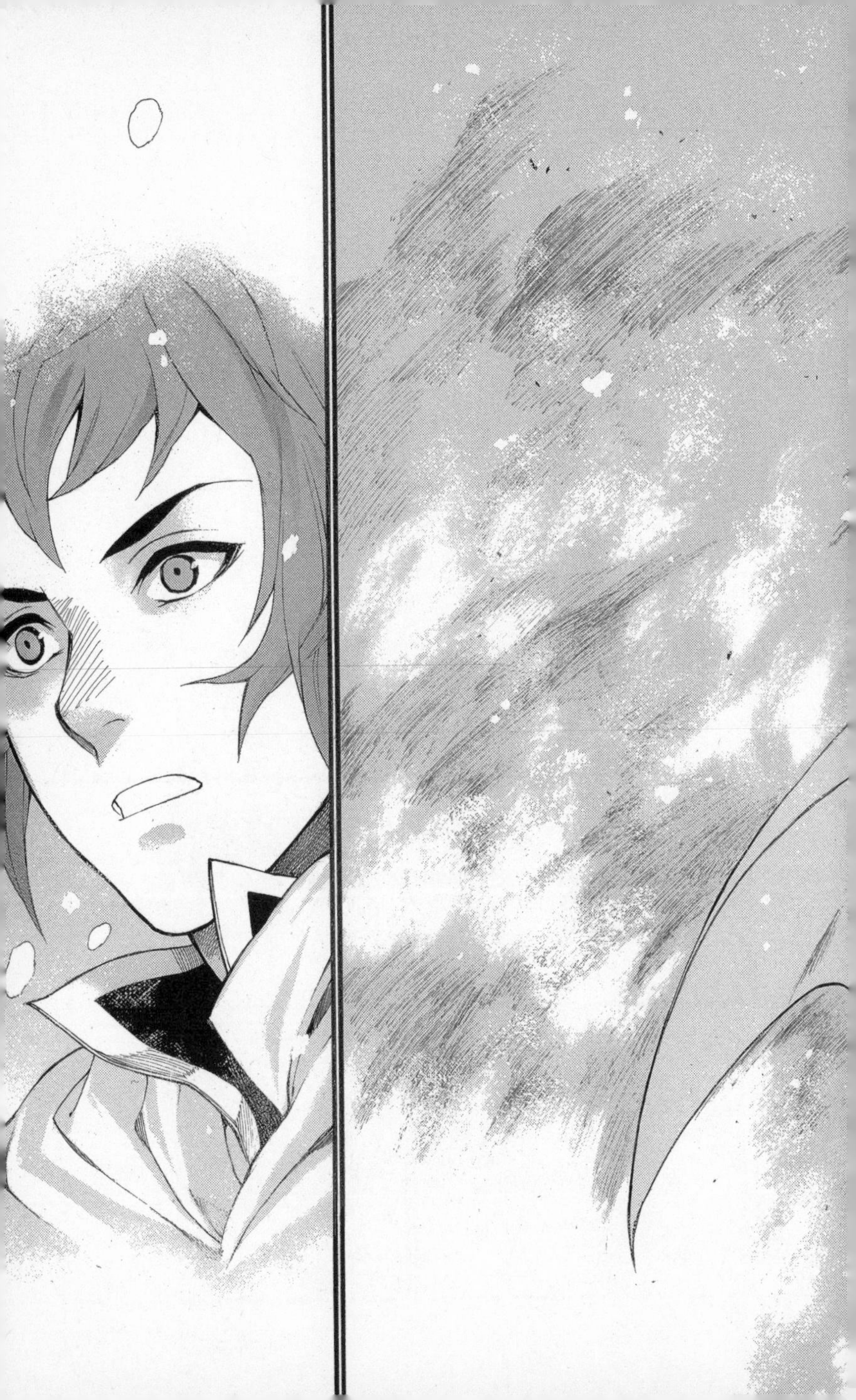

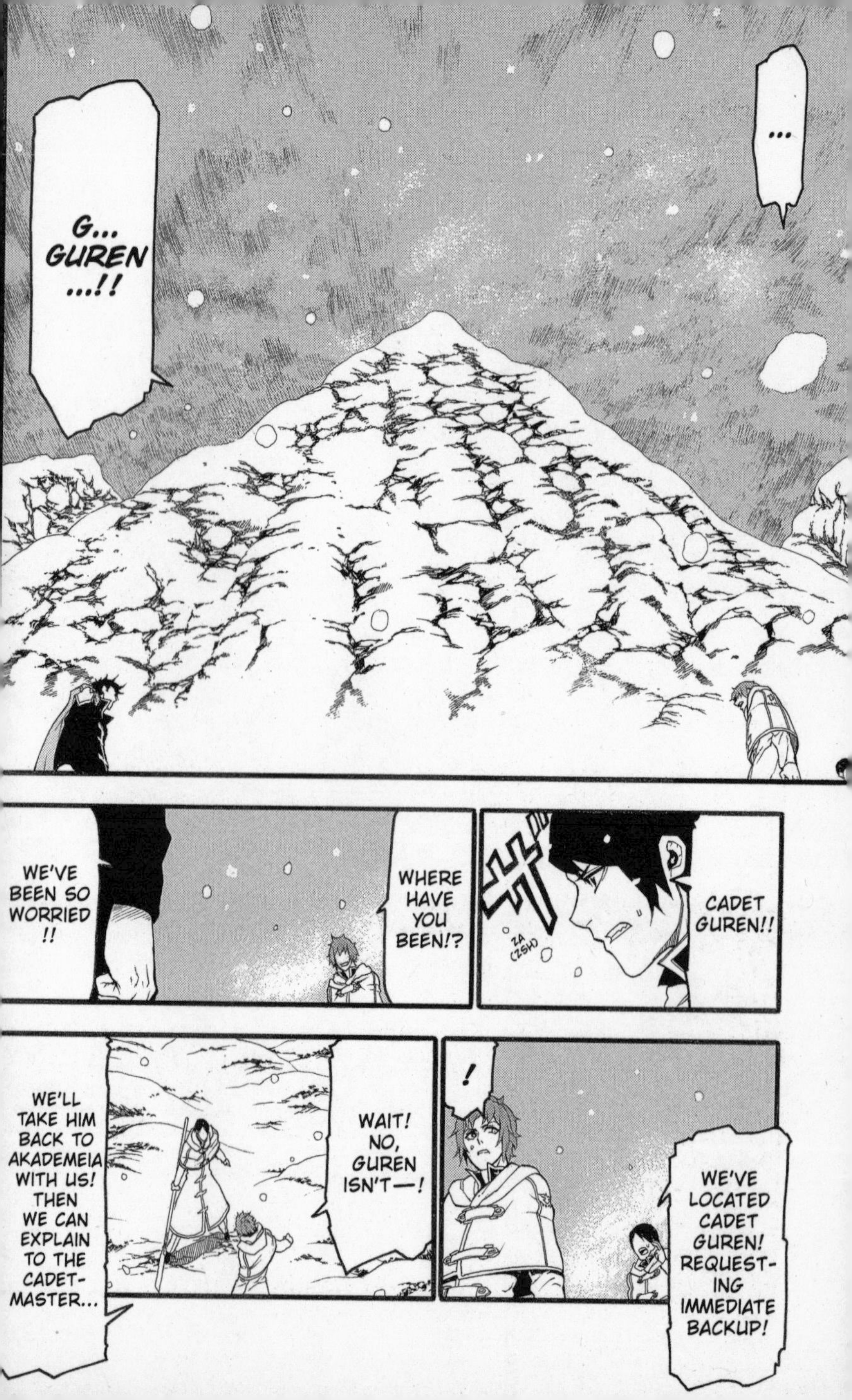
...
G... GUREN ...!!
CADET GUREN!!
ZA (ZSH)
WHERE HAVE YOU BEEN!?
WE'VE BEEN SO WORRIED !!
!
WE'VE LOCATED CADET GUREN! REQUEST-ING IMMEDIATE BACKUP!
WAIT! NO, GUREN ISN'T—!
WE'LL TAKE HIM BACK TO AKADEMEIA WITH US! THEN WE CAN EXPLAIN TO THE CADET-MASTER...

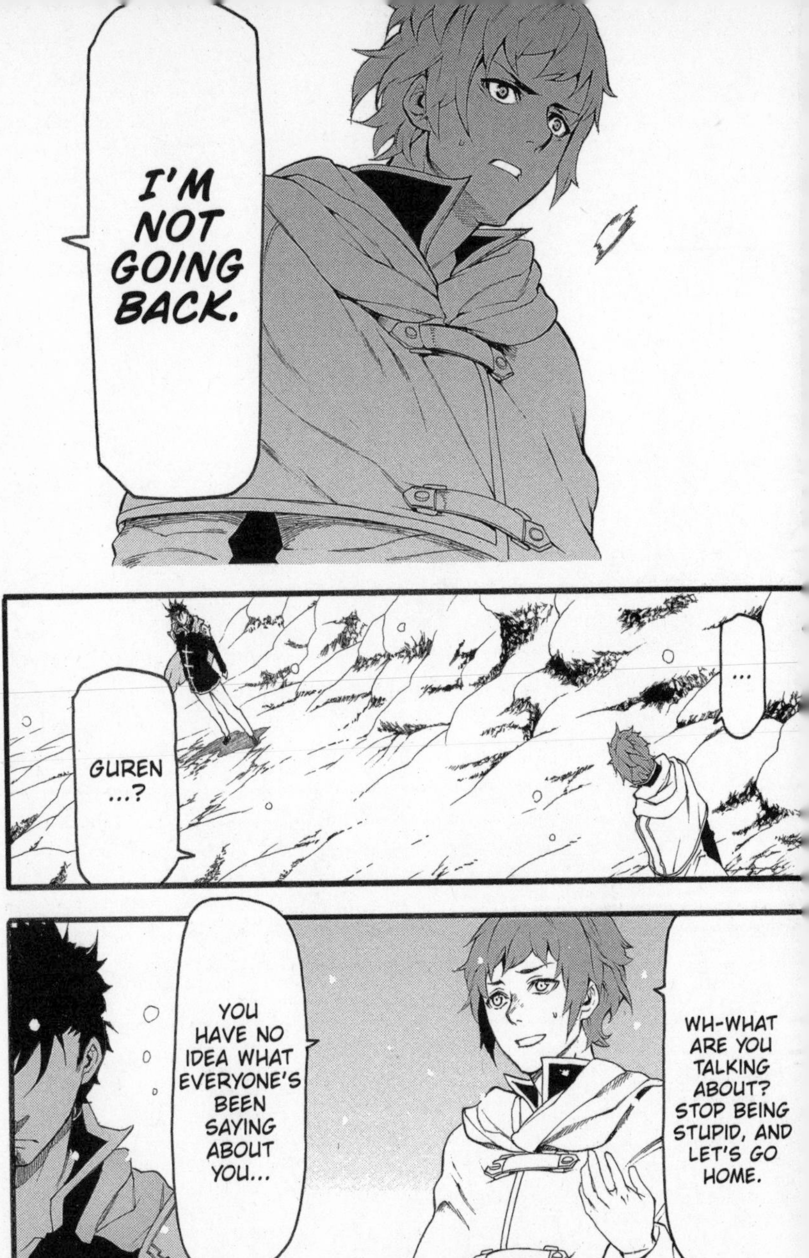
I'M NOT GOING BACK.
...
GUREN ...?
WH-WHAT ARE YOU TALKING ABOUT? STOP BEING STUPID, AND LET'S GO HOME.
YOU HAVE NO IDEA WHAT EVERYONE'S BEEN SAYING ABOUT YOU...

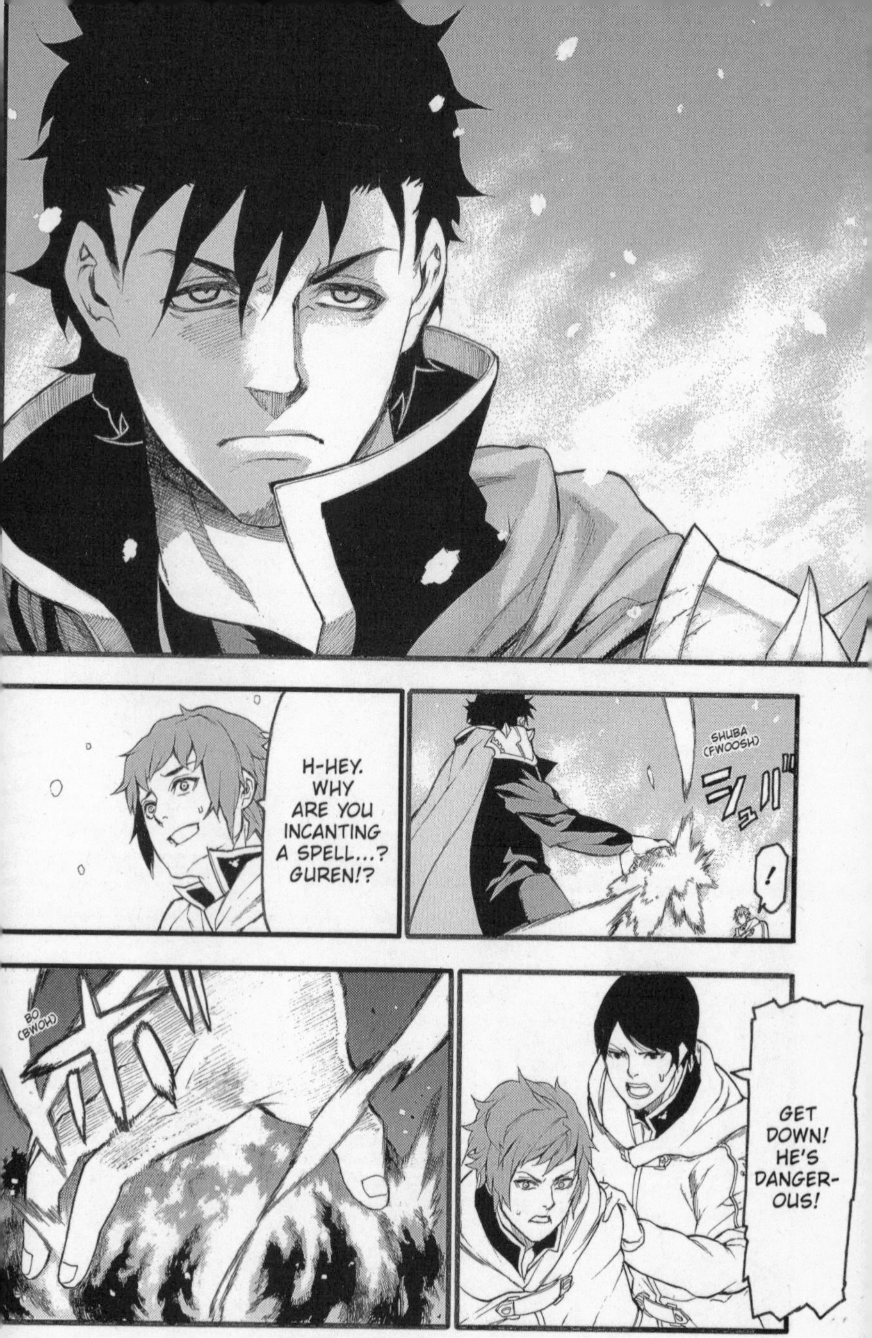
SHUBA (FWOOSH)
シュバ
!
H-HEY. WHY ARE YOU INCANTING A SPELL...? GUREN!?
GET DOWN! HE'S DANGER-OUS!
BO (BWOH)

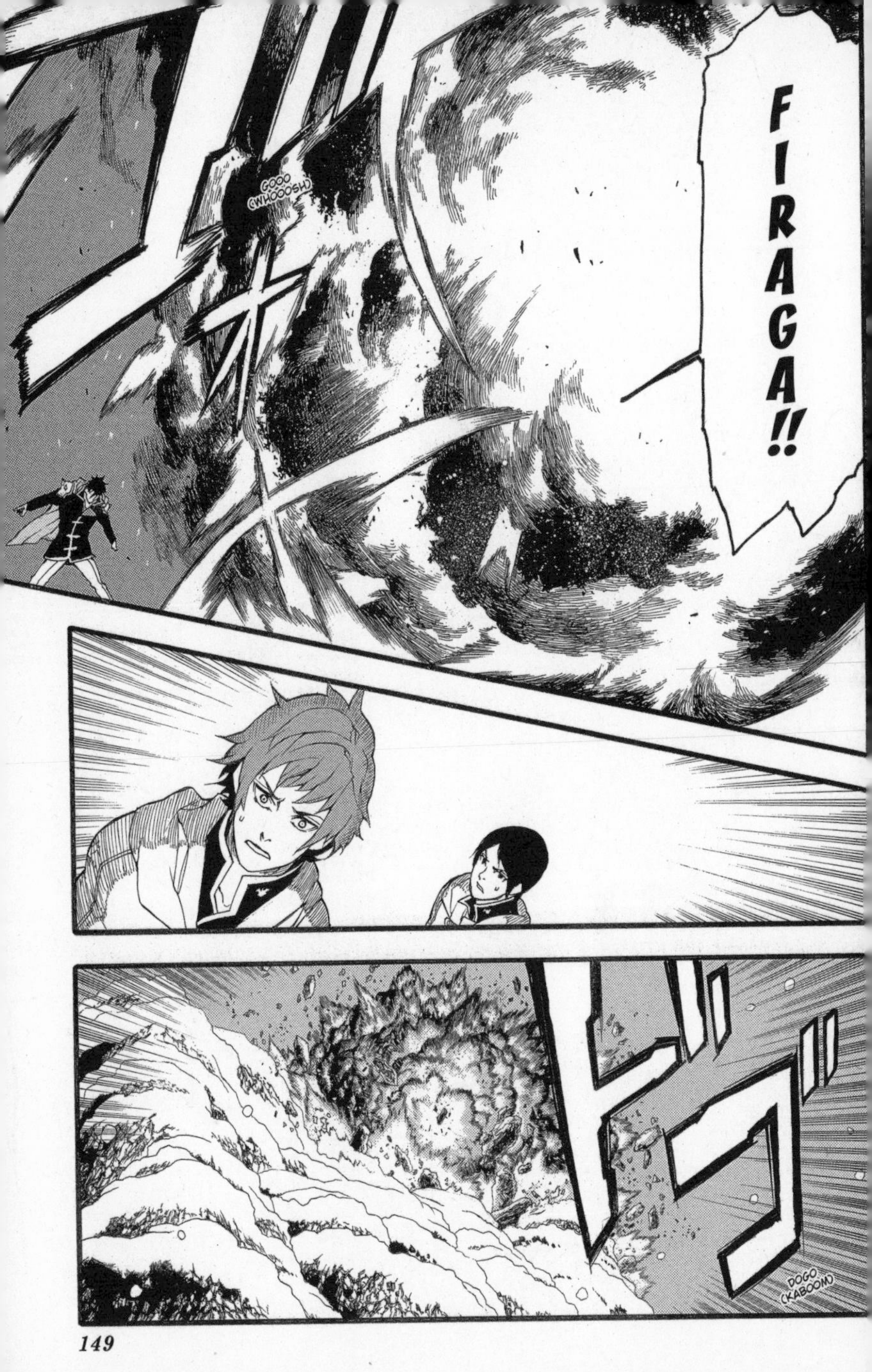
FIRAGA!!
GOOO (WHOOOSH)
DOGO (KABOOM)

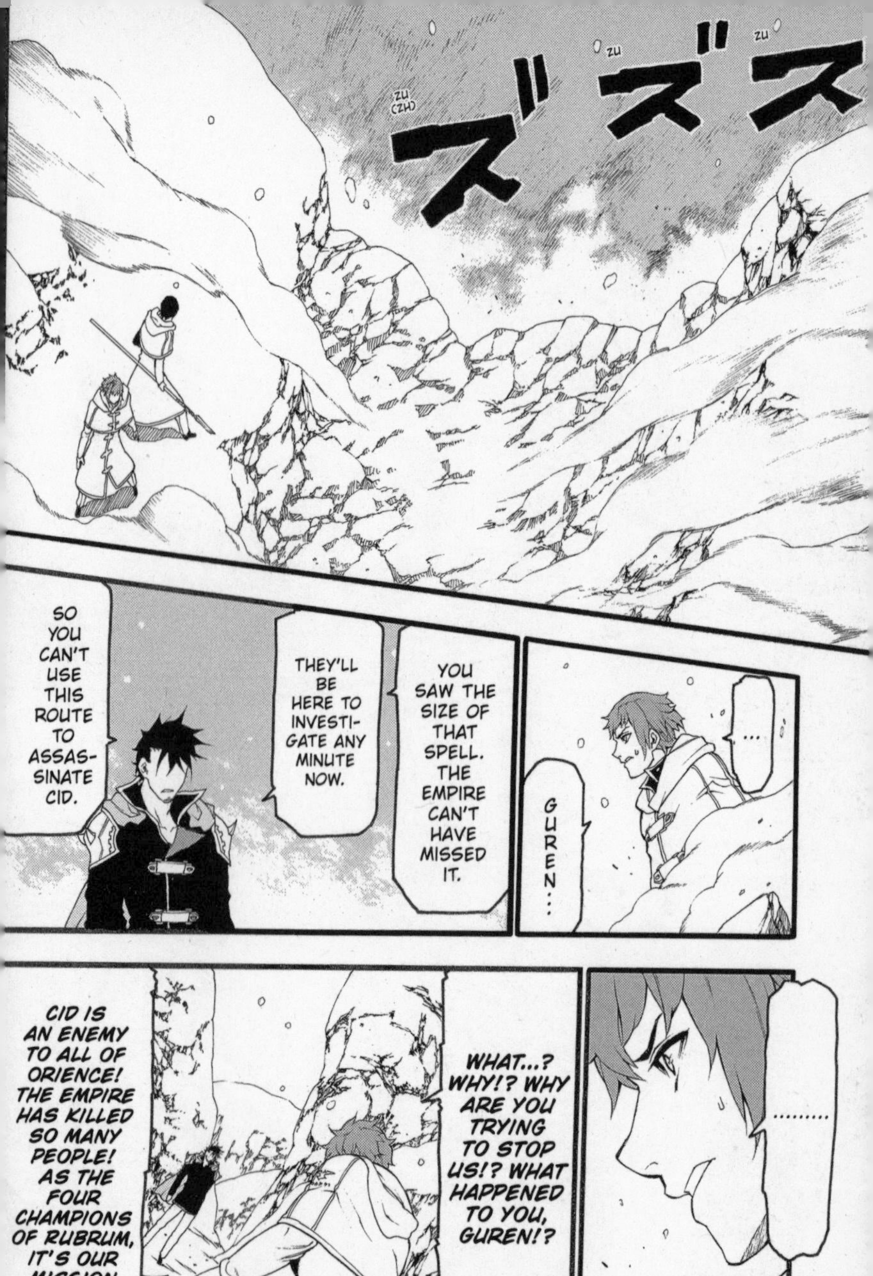
ZU (ZH) ZU ZU
ズズズ
...
GUREN...
YOU SAW THE SIZE OF THAT SPELL. THE EMPIRE CAN'T HAVE MISSED IT.
THEY'LL BE HERE TO INVESTIGATE ANY MINUTE NOW.
SO YOU CAN'T USE THIS ROUTE TO ASSASSINATE CID.
....
WHAT...? WHY!? WHY ARE YOU TRYING TO STOP US!? WHAT HAPPENED TO YOU, GUREN!?
CID IS AN ENEMY TO ALL OF ORIENCE! THE EMPIRE HAS KILLED SO MANY PEOPLE! AS THE FOUR CHAMPIONS OF RUBRUM, IT'S OUR MISSION TO STOP HIM!

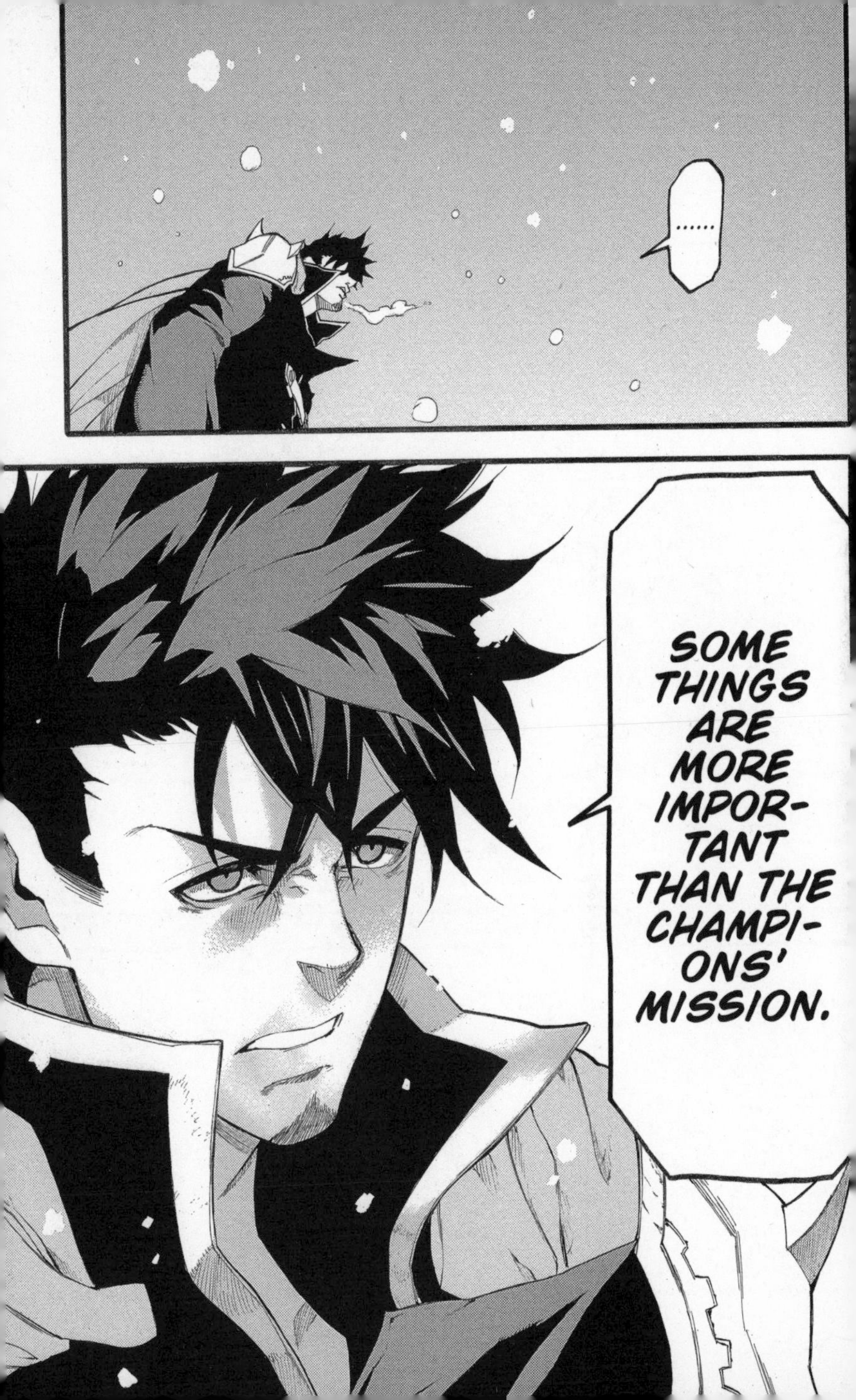
......
SOME THINGS ARE MORE IMPOR-TANT THAN THE CHAMPI-ONS' MISSION.

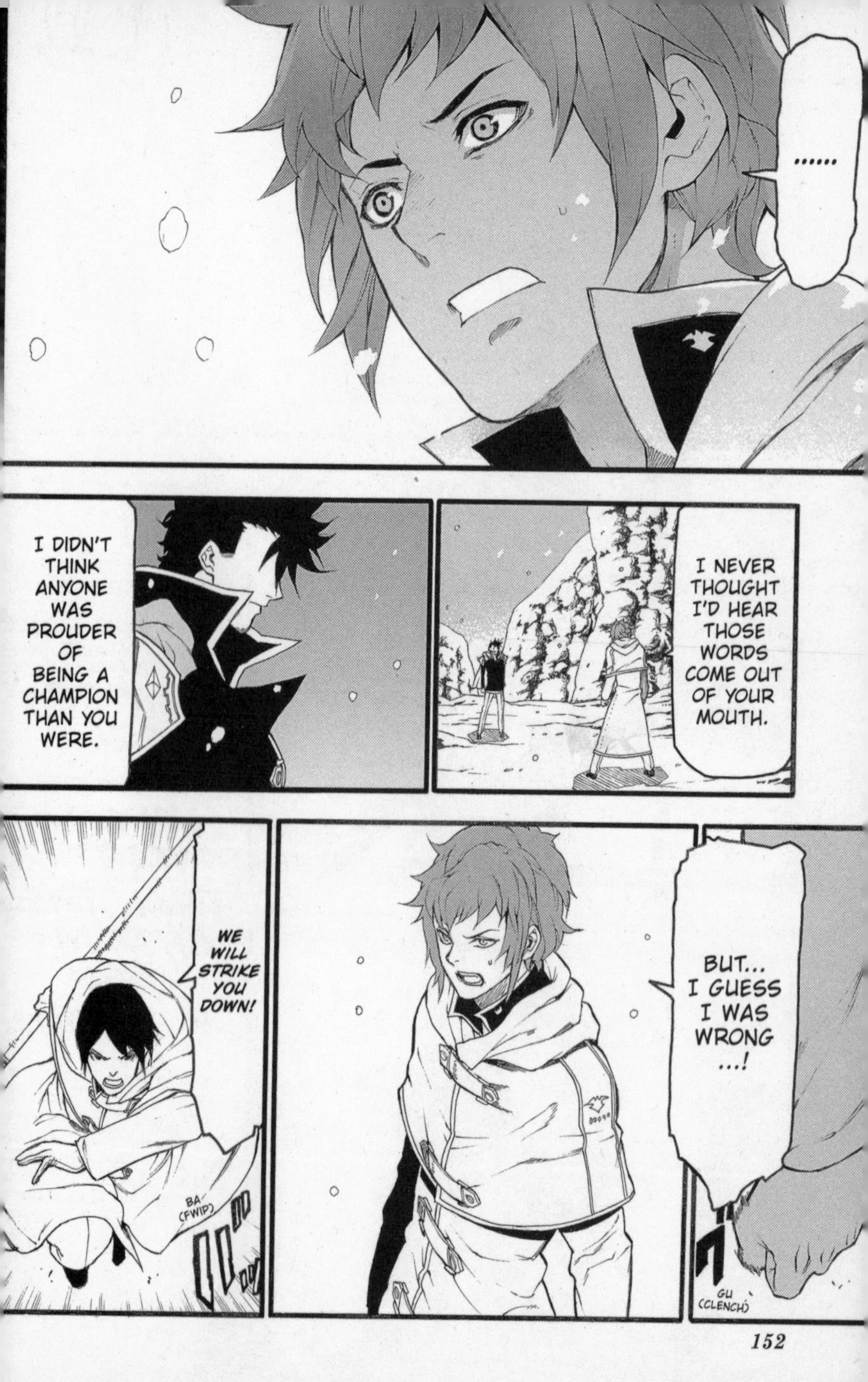
......
I NEVER THOUGHT I'D HEAR THOSE WORDS COME OUT OF YOUR MOUTH.
I DIDN'T THINK ANYONE WAS PROUDER OF BEING A CHAMPION THAN YOU WERE.
BUT... I GUESS I WAS WRONG ...!
GU (CLENCH)
WE WILL STRIKE YOU DOWN!
BA (FWIP)

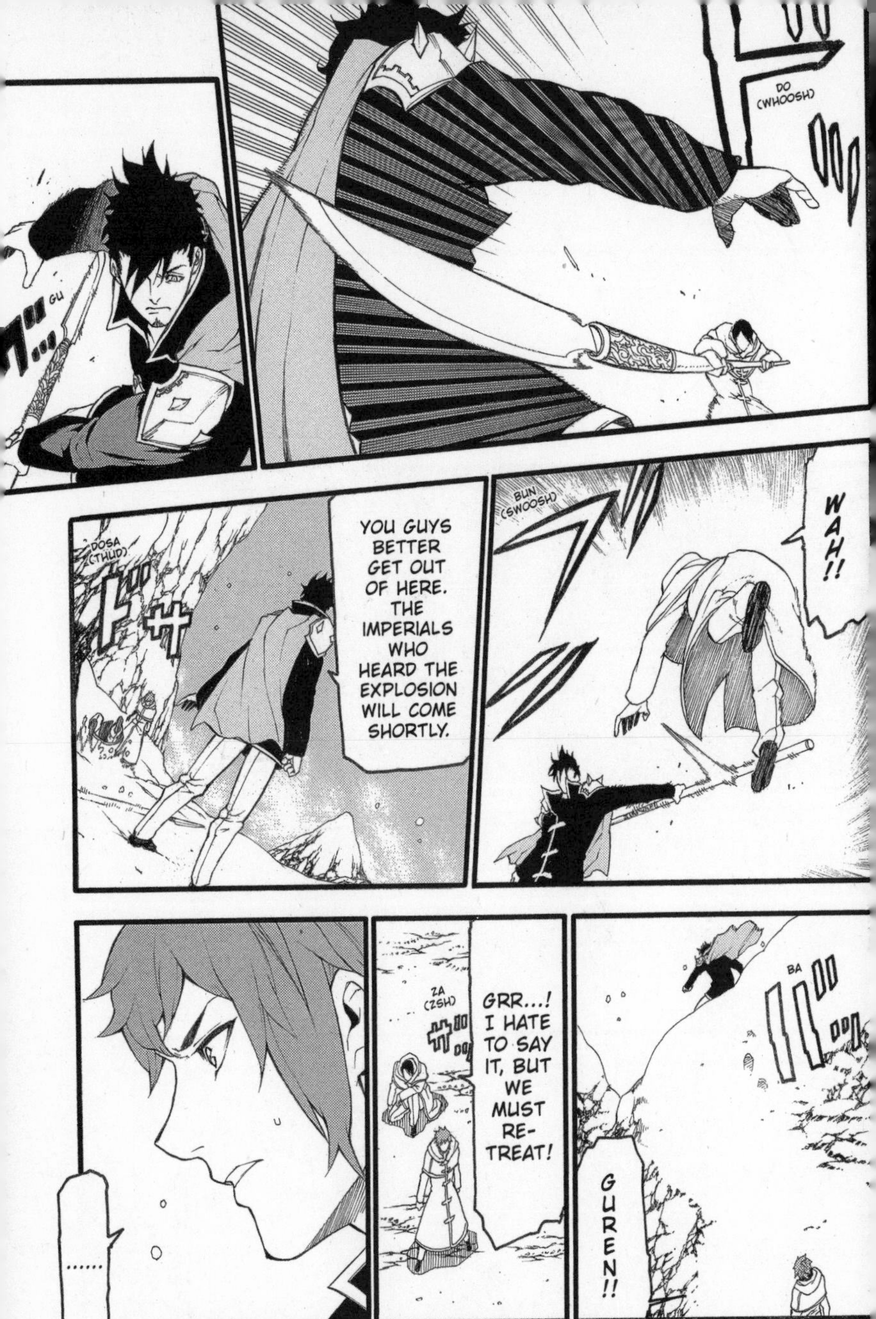
DO (WHOOSH)
GU
WAH!!
BUN (SWOOSH)
YOU GUYS BETTER GET OUT OF HERE. THE IMPERIALS WHO HEARD THE EXPLOSION WILL COME SHORTLY.
DOSA (THUD)
BA
GUREN!!
GRR...! I HATE TO SAY IT, BUT WE MUST RE-TREAT!
ZA (ZSH)
......

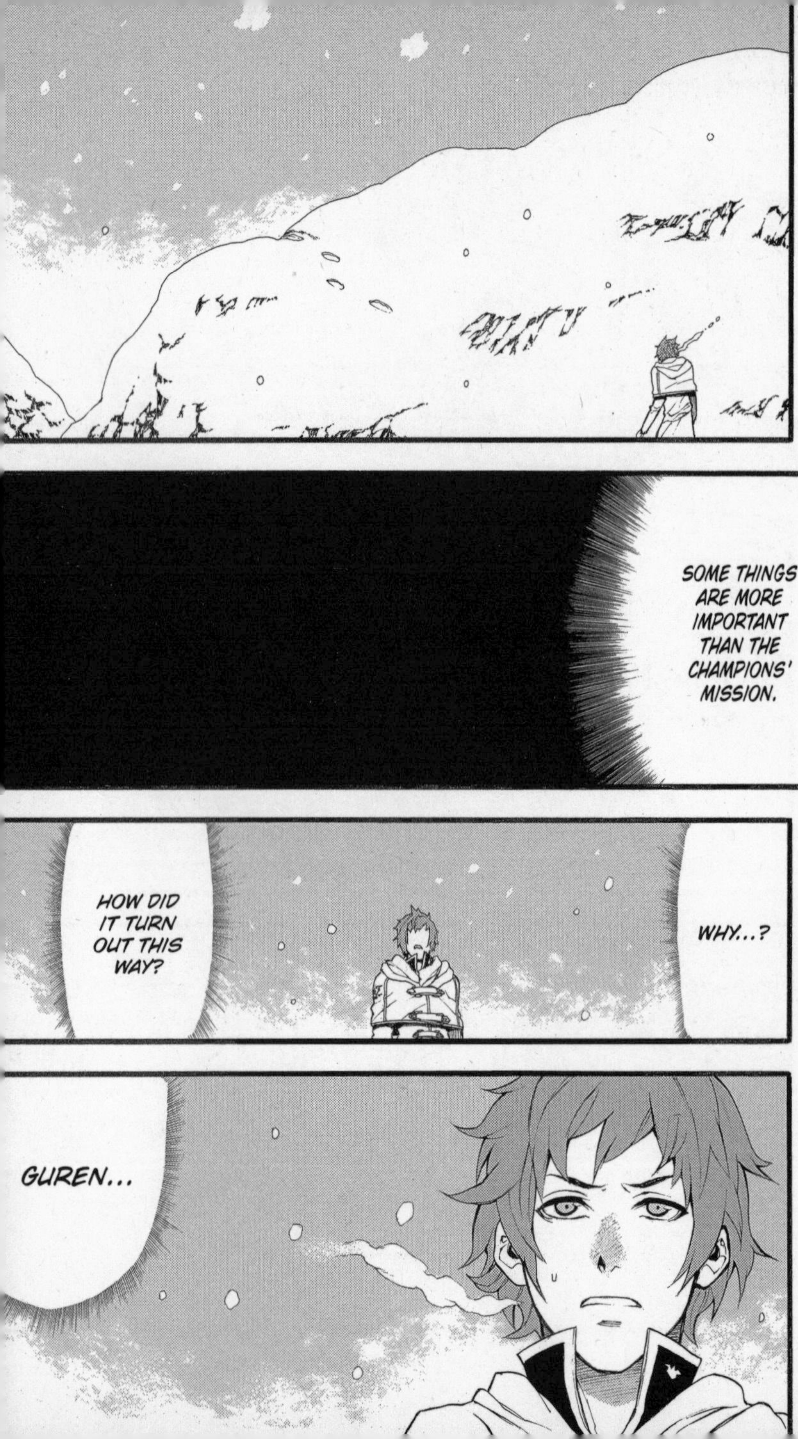
SOME THINGS ARE MORE IMPORTANT THAN THE CHAMPIONS' MISSION.
WHY...?
HOW DID IT TURN OUT THIS WAY?
GUREN...

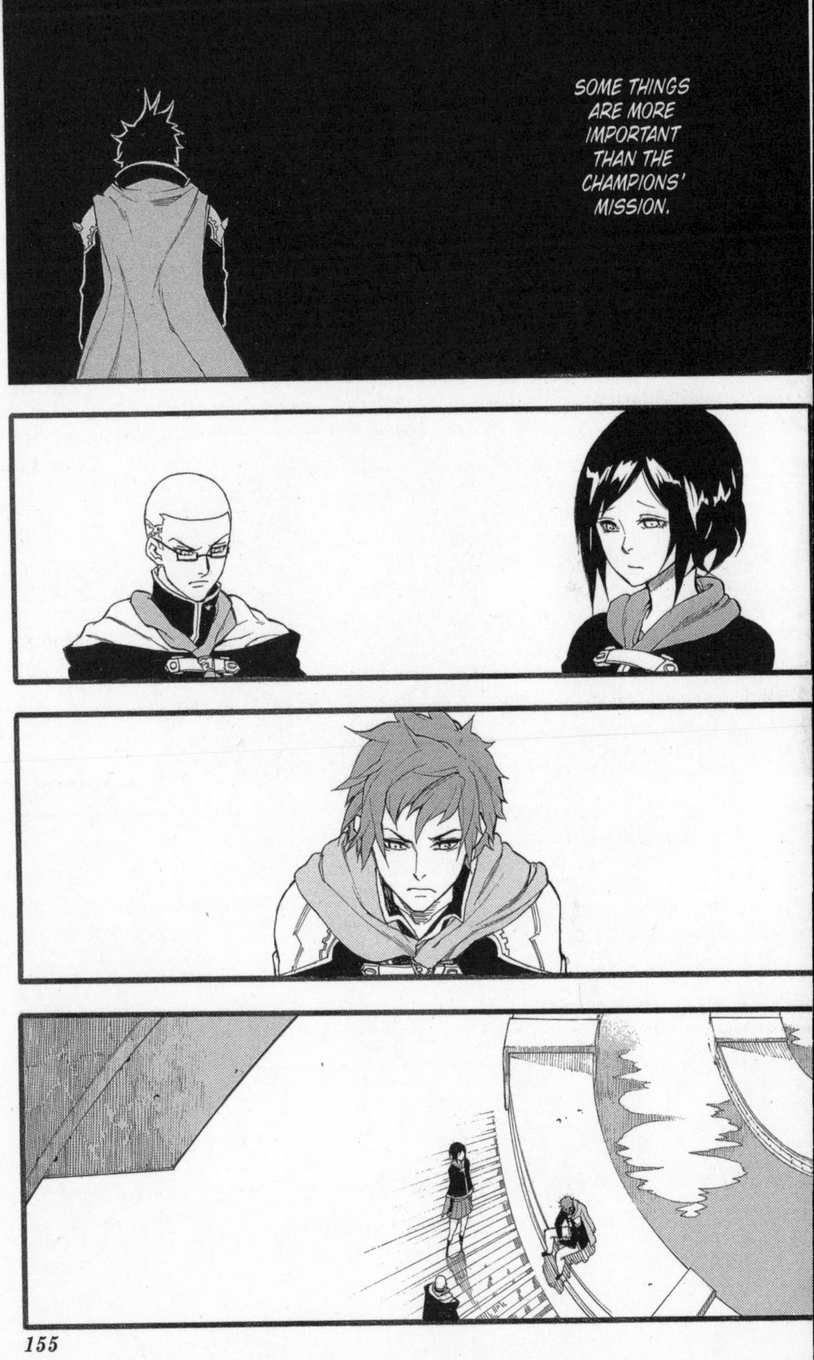
SOME THINGS ARE MORE IMPORTANT THAN THE CHAMPIONS' MISSION.

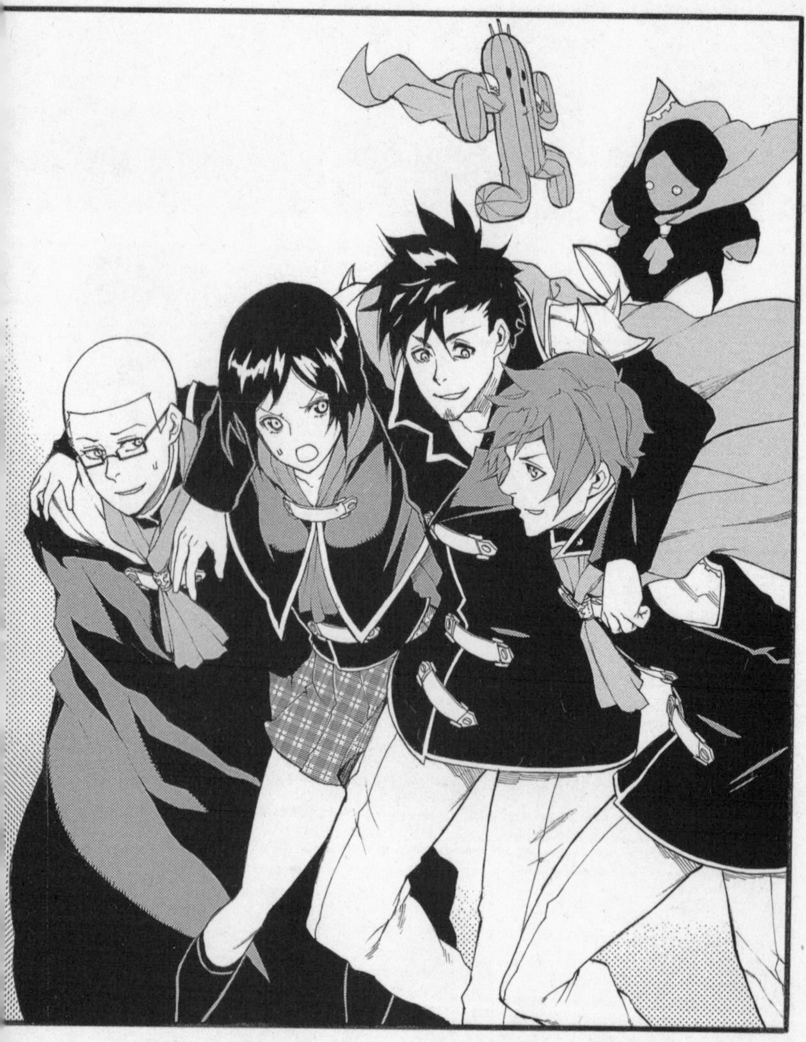

CHAPTER 18: THE FALLEN HERO

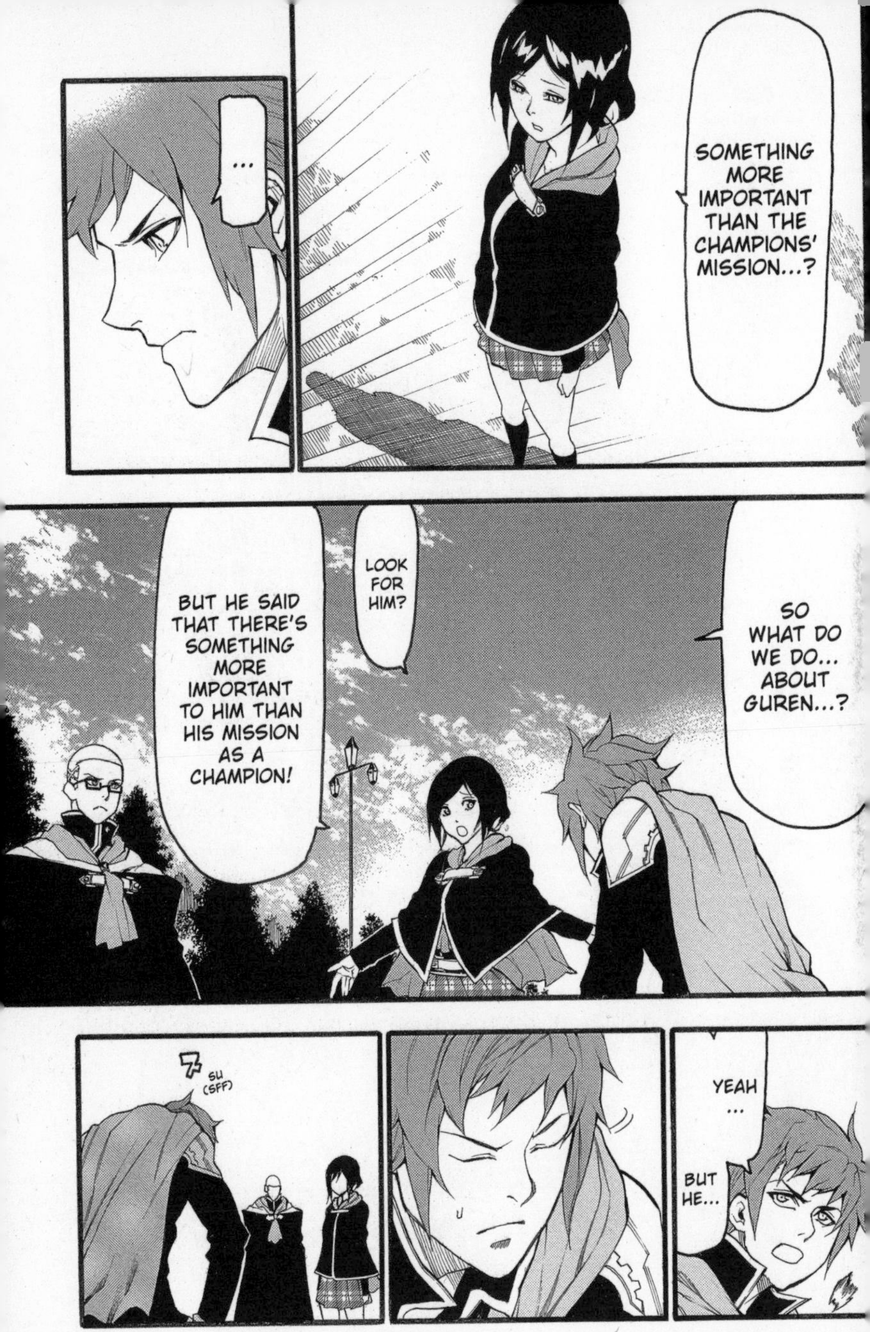
SOMETHING MORE IMPORTANT THAN THE CHAMPIONS' MISSION...?
...
SO WHAT DO WE DO... ABOUT GUREN...?
LOOK FOR HIM?
BUT HE SAID THAT THERE'S SOMETHING MORE IMPORTANT TO HIM THAN HIS MISSION AS A CHAMPION!
YEAH ...
BUT HE...
SU (SFF)

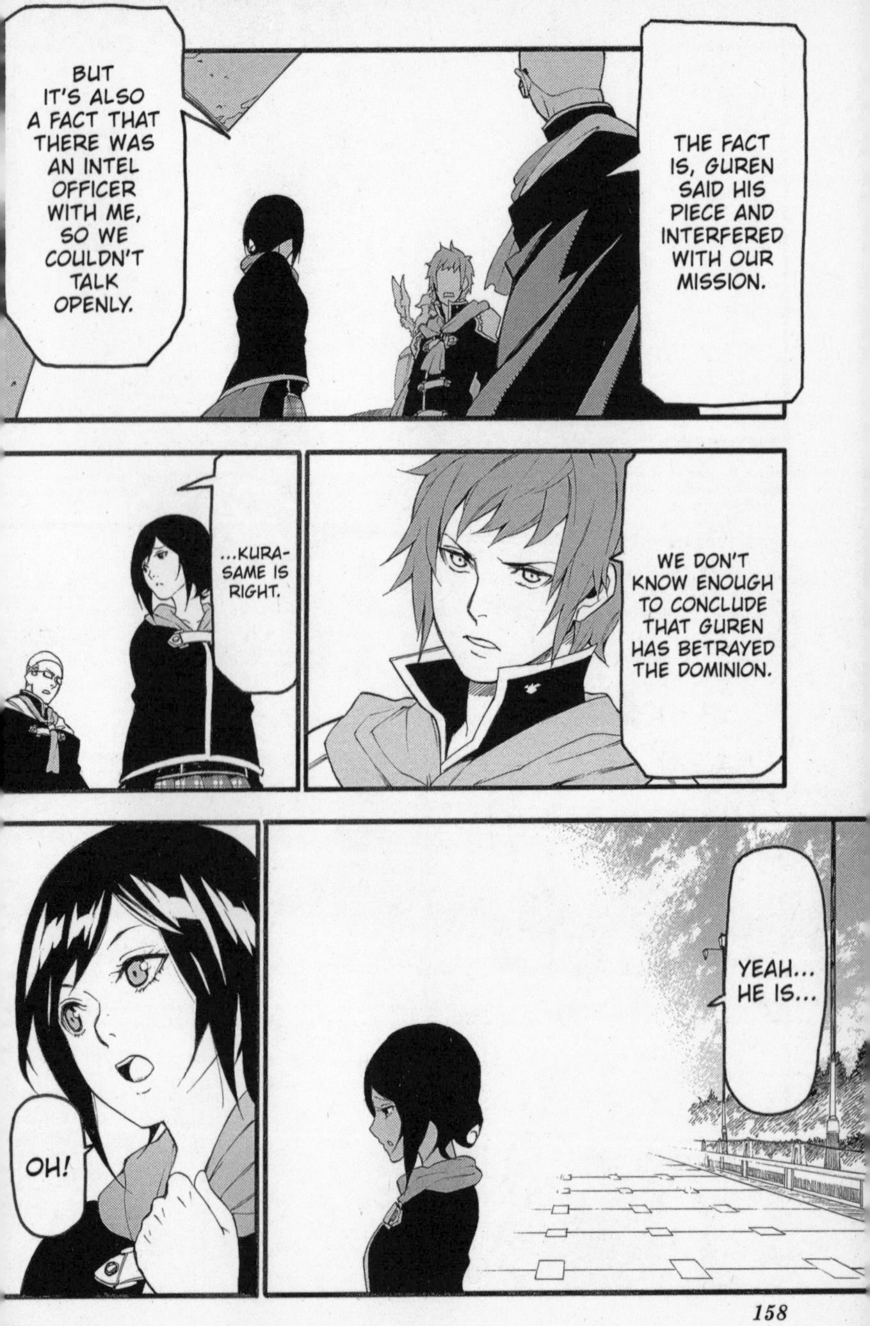
THE FACT IS, GUREN SAID HIS PIECE AND INTERFERED WITH OUR MISSION.
BUT IT'S ALSO A FACT THAT THERE WAS AN INTEL OFFICER WITH ME, SO WE COULDN'T TALK OPENLY.
WE DON'T KNOW ENOUGH TO CONCLUDE THAT GUREN HAS BETRAYED THE DOMINION.
...KURA-SAME IS RIGHT.
YEAH... HE IS...
OH!

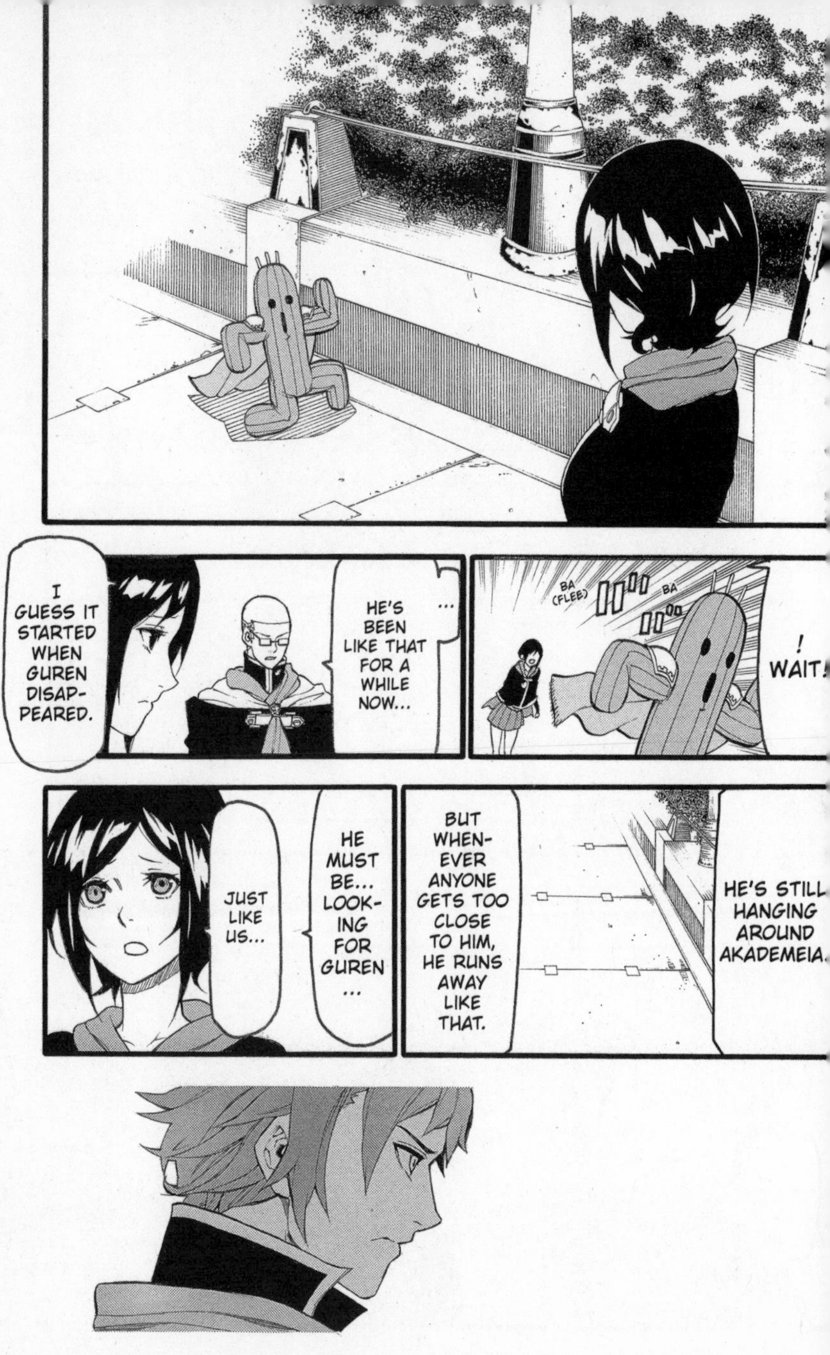
! WAIT!
BA (FLEE)
BA
...
HE'S BEEN LIKE THAT FOR A WHILE NOW...
I GUESS IT STARTED WHEN GUREN DISAPPEARED.
HE'S STILL HANGING AROUND AKADEMEIA.
BUT WHENEVER ANYONE GETS TOO CLOSE TO HIM, HE RUNS AWAY LIKE THAT.
HE MUST BE... LOOKING FOR GUREN...
JUST LIKE US...

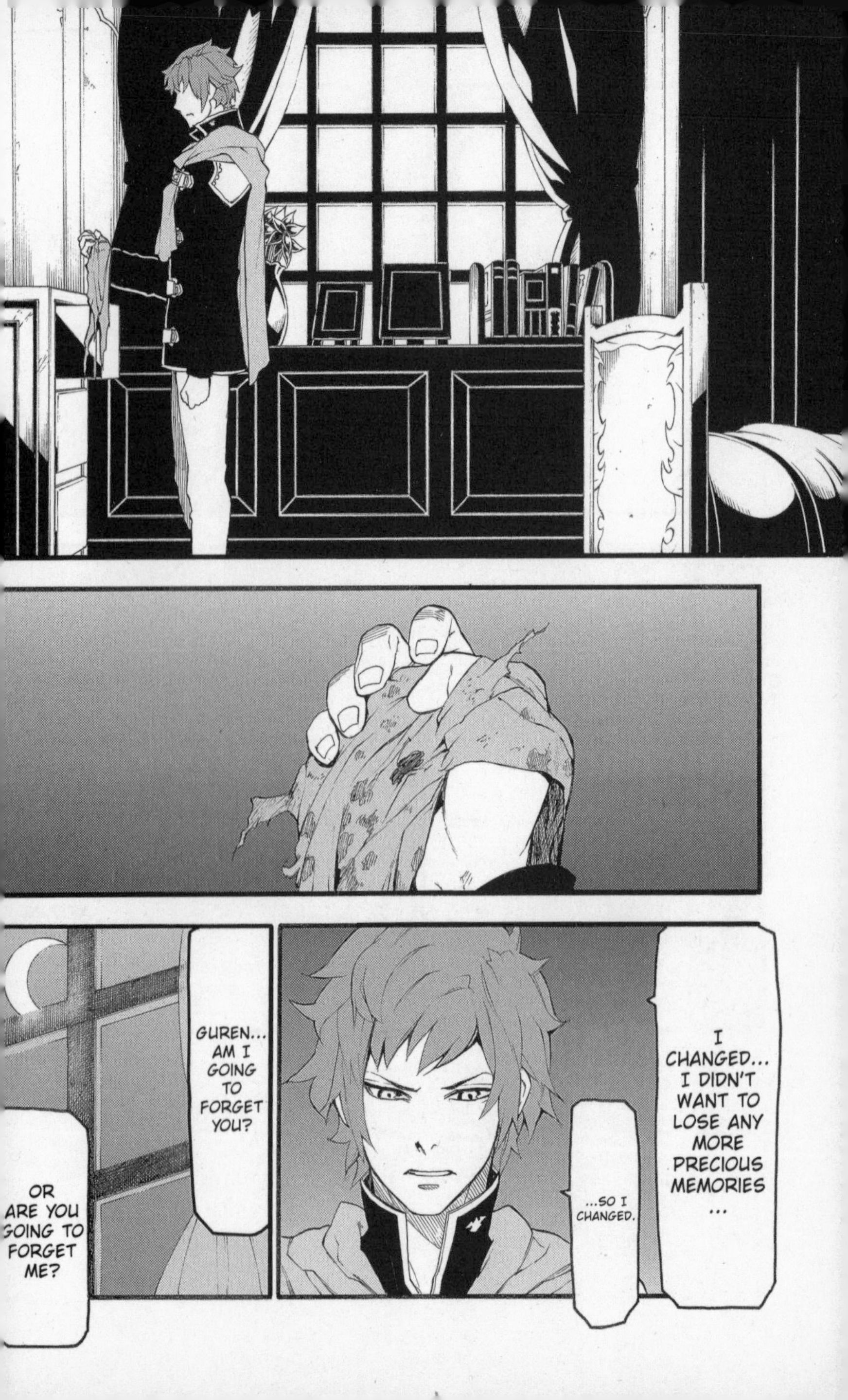
I CHANGED... I DIDN'T WANT TO LOSE ANY MORE PRECIOUS MEMORIES ...
...SO I CHANGED.
GUREN... AM I GOING TO FORGET YOU?
OR ARE YOU GOING TO FORGET ME?

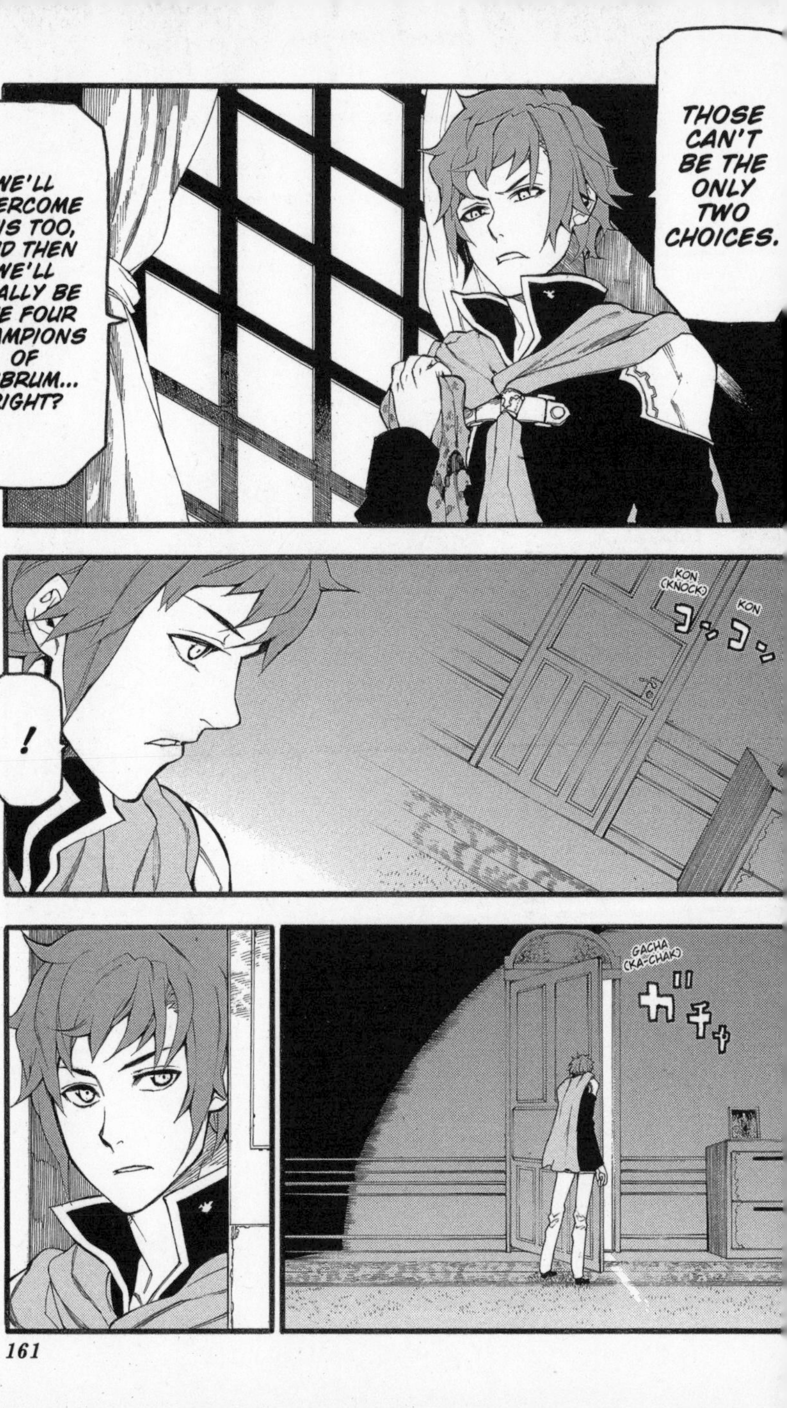
THOSE CAN'T BE THE ONLY TWO CHOICES.
WE'LL OVERCOME THIS TOO, AND THEN WE'LL REALLY BE THE FOUR CHAMPIONS OF RUBRUM... RIGHT?
KON (KNOCK)
KON
コッ コッ
!
GACHA (KA-CHAK)
ガチャ

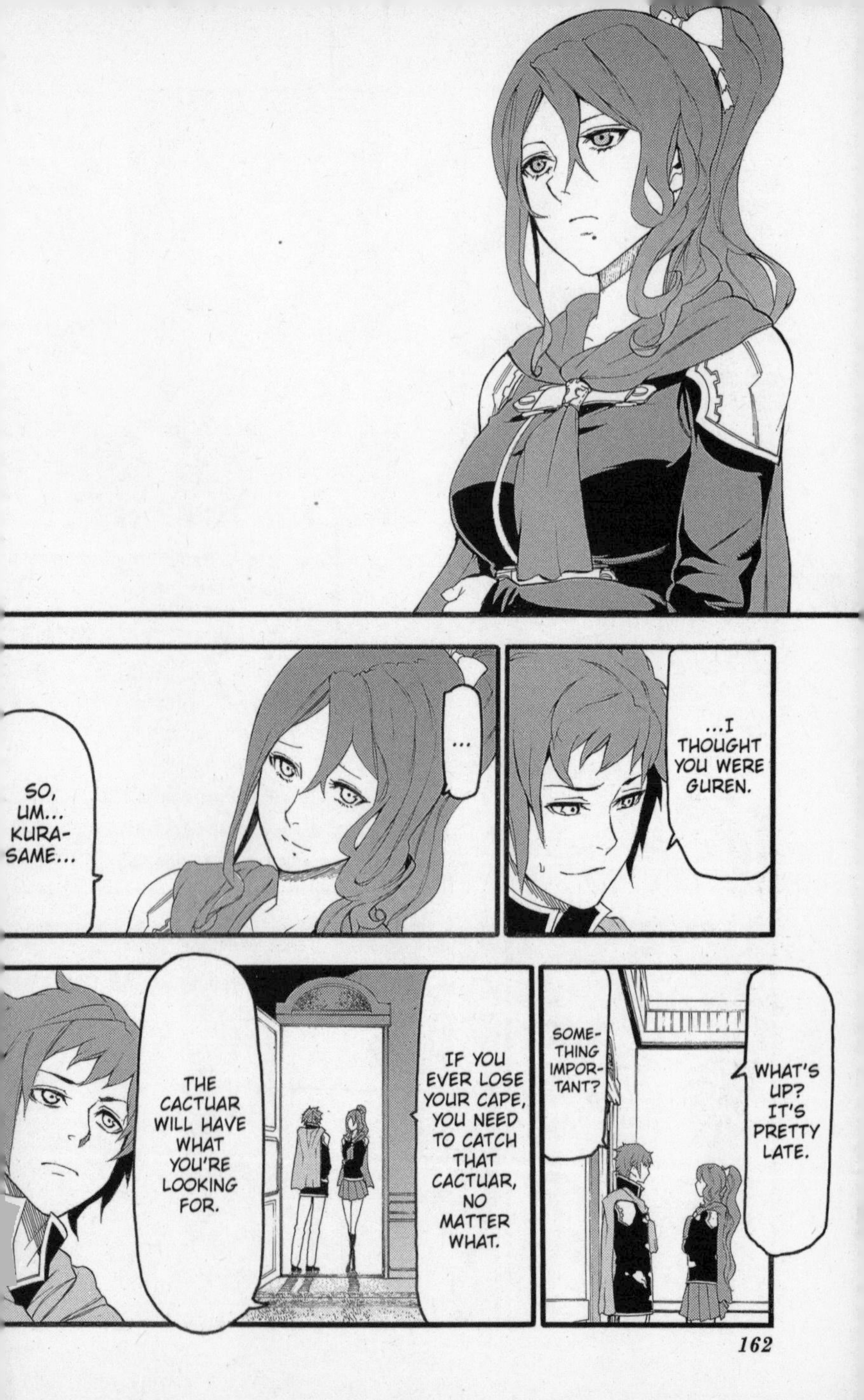
...I THOUGHT YOU WERE GUREN.
...
SO, UM... KURA-SAME...
WHAT'S UP? IT'S PRETTY LATE.
SOME-THING IMPORT-ANT?
IF YOU EVER LOSE YOUR CAPE, YOU NEED TO CATCH THAT CACTUAR, NO MATTER WHAT.
THE CACTUAR WILL HAVE WHAT YOU'RE LOOKING FOR.

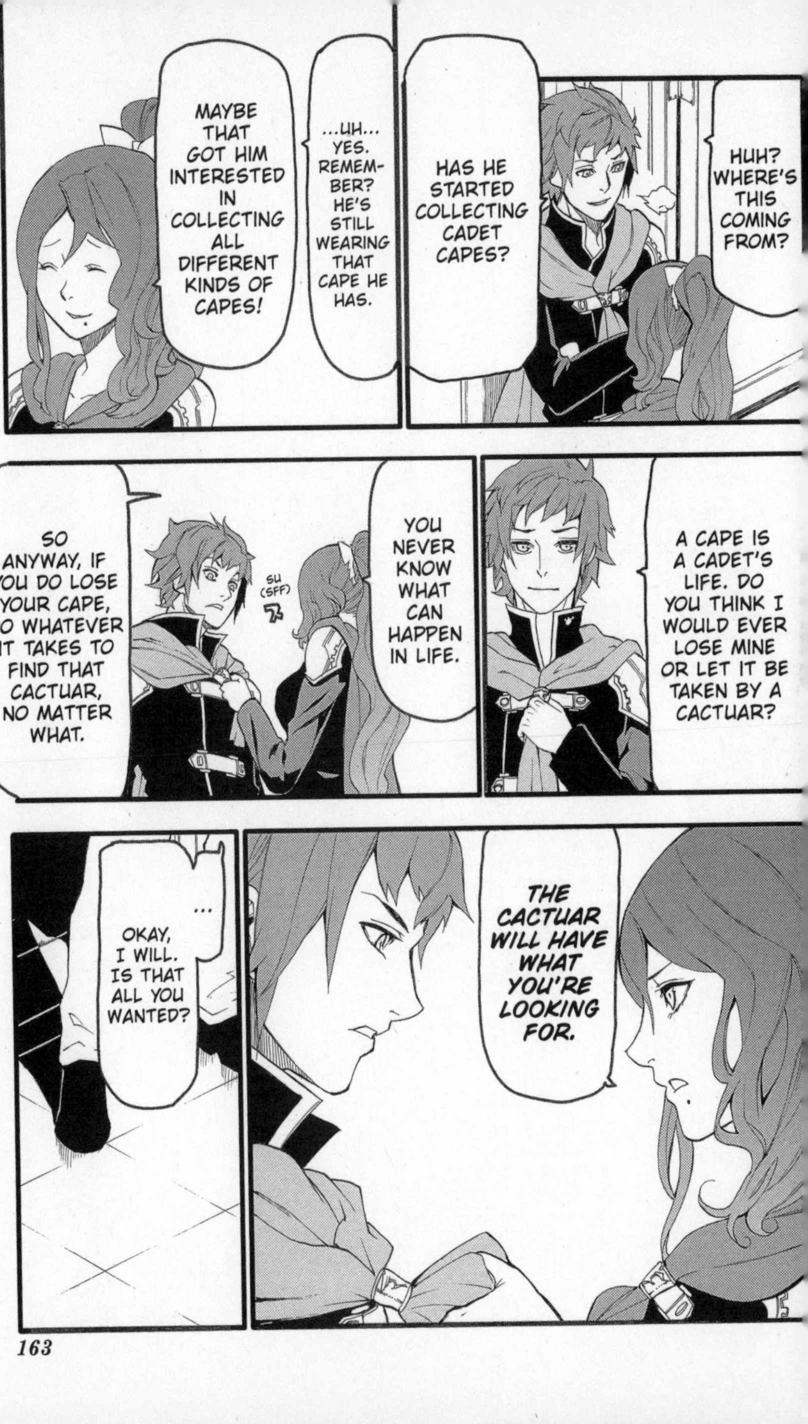
HUH? WHERE'S THIS COMING FROM?
HAS HE STARTED COLLECTING CADET CAPES?
...UH... YES. REMEMBER? HE'S STILL WEARING THAT CAPE HE HAS.
MAYBE THAT GOT HIM INTERESTED IN COLLECTING ALL DIFFERENT KINDS OF CAPES!
A CAPE IS A CADET'S LIFE. DO YOU THINK I WOULD EVER LOSE MINE OR LET IT BE TAKEN BY A CACTUAR?
YOU NEVER KNOW WHAT CAN HAPPEN IN LIFE.
SU (SFF)
SO ANYWAY, IF YOU DO LOSE YOUR CAPE, DO WHATEVER IT TAKES TO FIND THAT CACTUAR, NO MATTER WHAT.
THE CACTUAR WILL HAVE WHAT YOU'RE LOOKING FOR.
...
OKAY, I WILL. IS THAT ALL YOU WANTED?

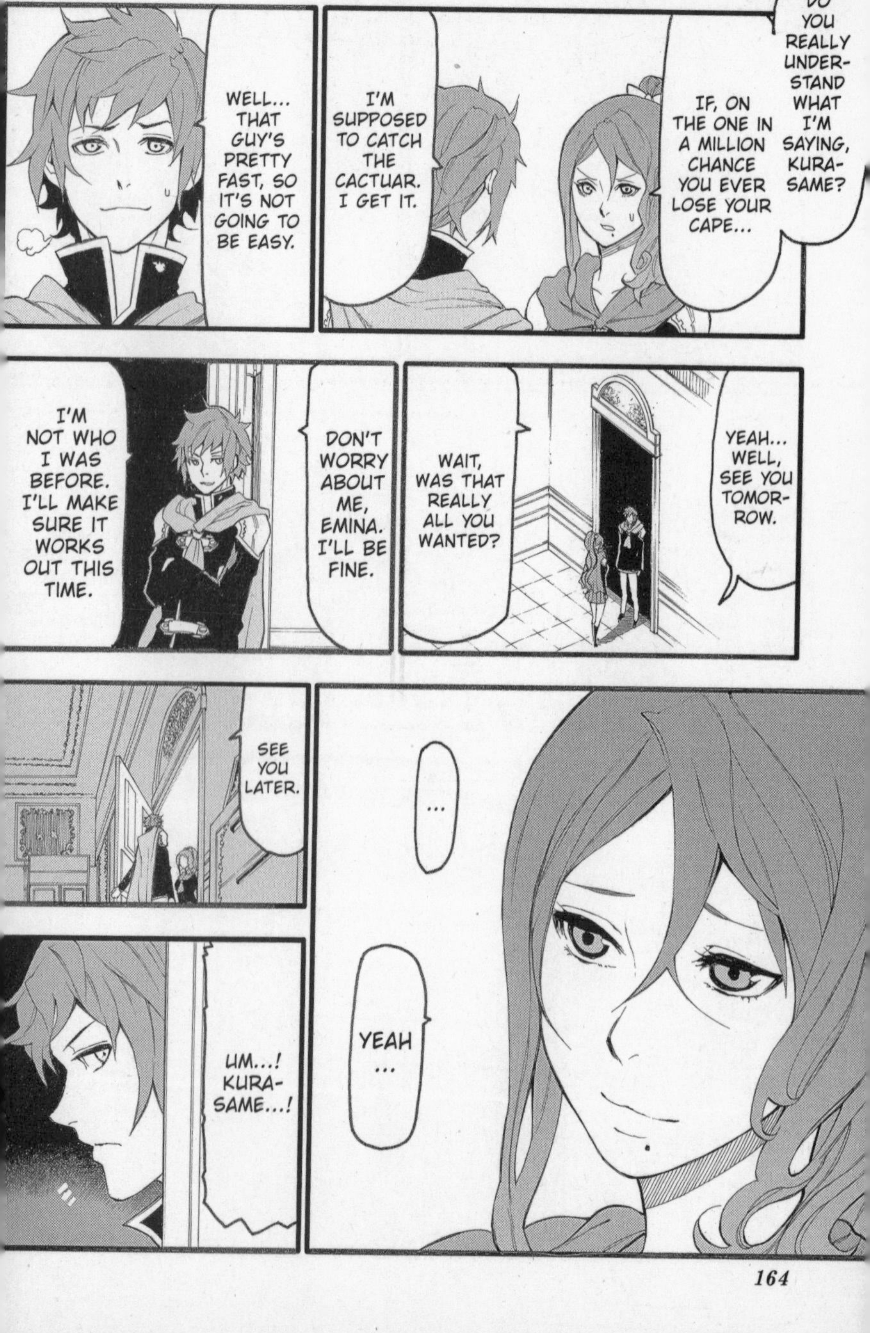
DO YOU REALLY UNDERSTAND WHAT I'M SAYING, KURASAME?
IF, ON THE ONE IN A MILLION CHANCE YOU EVER LOSE YOUR CAPE...
I'M SUPPOSED TO CATCH THE CACTUAR. I GET IT.
WELL... THAT GUY'S PRETTY FAST, SO IT'S NOT GOING TO BE EASY.
YEAH... WELL, SEE YOU TOMORROW.
WAIT, WAS THAT REALLY ALL YOU WANTED?
DON'T WORRY ABOUT ME, EMINA. I'LL BE FINE.
I'M NOT WHO I WAS BEFORE. I'LL MAKE SURE IT WORKS OUT THIS TIME.
...
YEAH...
SEE YOU LATER.
UM...! KURASAME...!

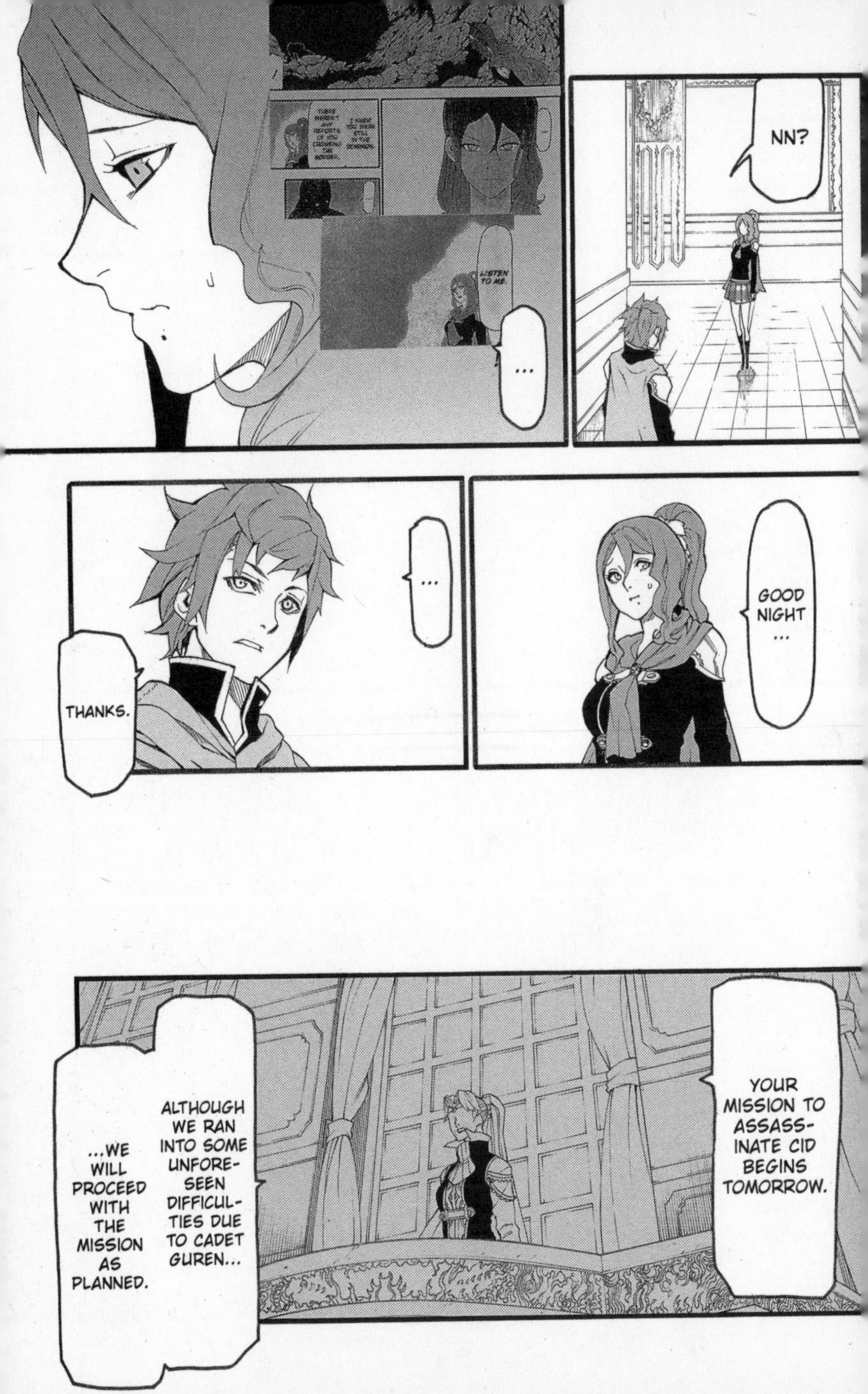
NN?
THERE WEREN'T ANY REPORTS OF YOU CROSSING THE BORDER.
I KNEW YOU WERE STILL IN THE DOMINION.
LISTEN TO ME.
...
GOOD NIGHT ...
...
THANKS.
YOUR MISSION TO ASSASS-INATE CID BEGINS TOMORROW.
ALTHOUGH WE RAN INTO SOME UNFORE-SEEN DIFFICUL-TIES DUE TO CADET GUREN...
...WE WILL PROCEED WITH THE MISSION AS PLANNED.

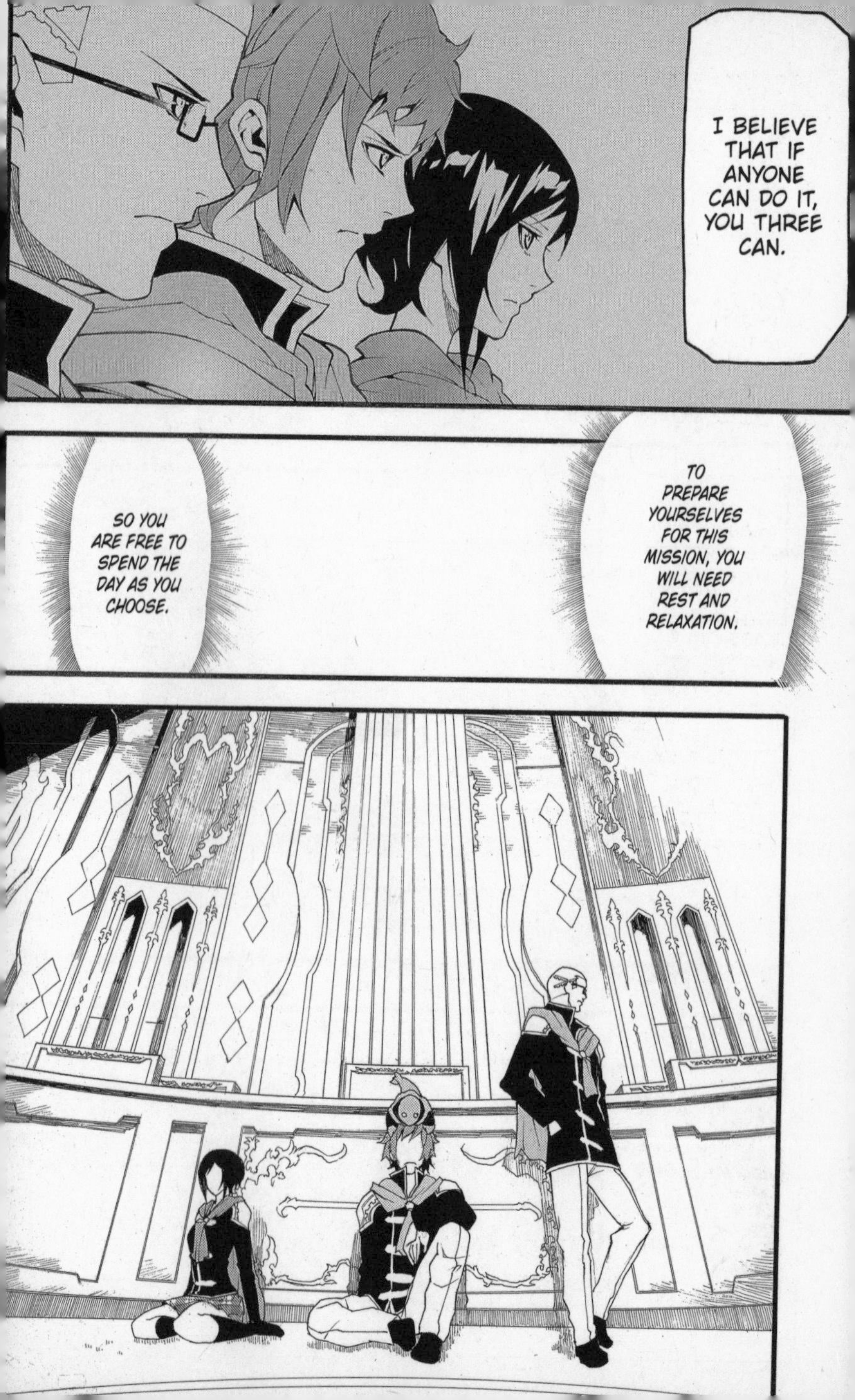
I BELIEVE THAT IF ANYONE CAN DO IT, YOU THREE CAN.
TO PREPARE YOURSELVES FOR THIS MISSION, YOU WILL NEED REST AND RELAXATION.
SO YOU ARE FREE TO SPEND THE DAY AS YOU CHOOSE.

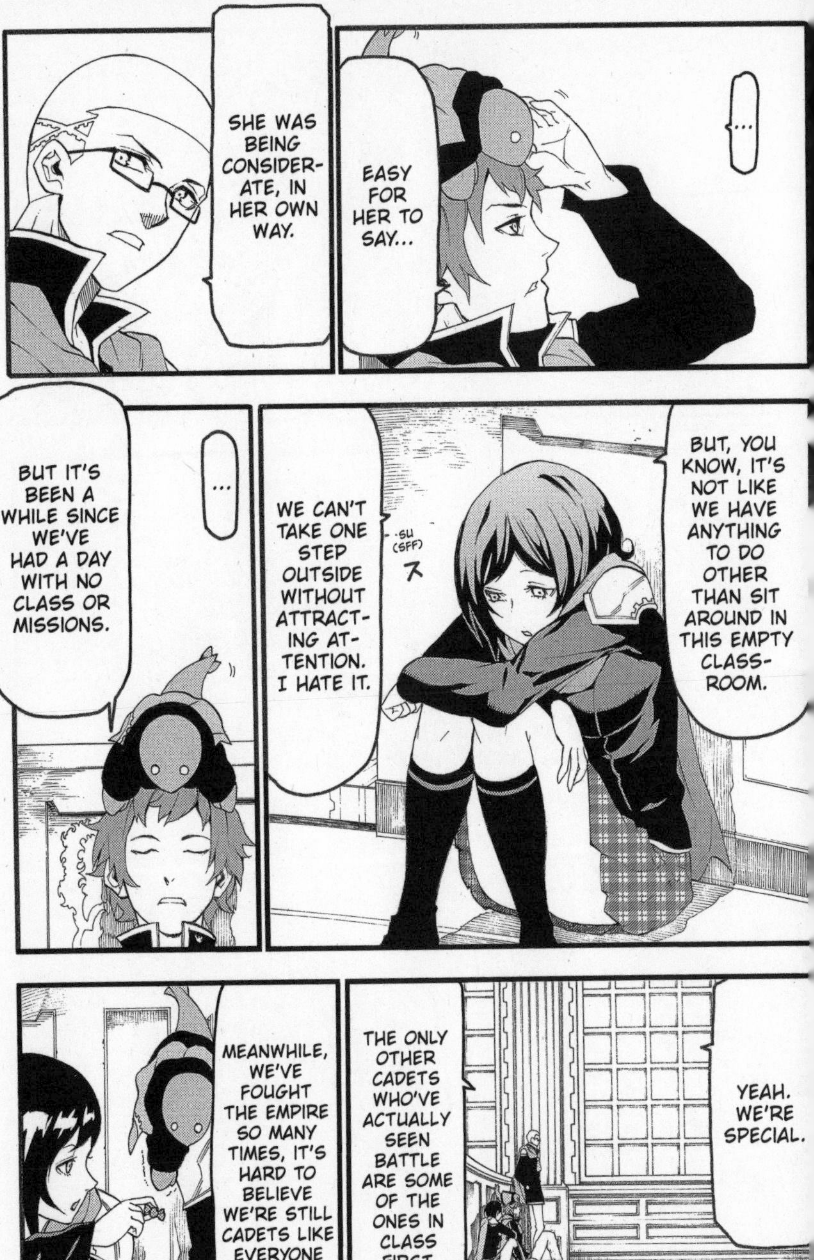
...
EASY FOR HER TO SAY...
SHE WAS BEING CONSIDER-ATE, IN HER OWN WAY.
BUT, YOU KNOW, IT'S NOT LIKE WE HAVE ANYTHING TO DO OTHER THAN SIT AROUND IN THIS EMPTY CLASS-ROOM.
ス
SU (SFF)
WE CAN'T TAKE ONE STEP OUTSIDE WITHOUT ATTRACT-ING AT-TENTION. I HATE IT.
...
BUT IT'S BEEN A WHILE SINCE WE'VE HAD A DAY WITH NO CLASS OR MISSIONS.
YEAH. WE'RE SPECIAL.
THE ONLY OTHER CADETS WHO'VE ACTUALLY SEEN BATTLE ARE SOME OF THE ONES IN CLASS FIRST.
MEANWHILE, WE'VE FOUGHT THE EMPIRE SO MANY TIMES, IT'S HARD TO BELIEVE WE'RE STILL CADETS LIKE EVERYONE ELSE.

WELL...

THAT'S BECAUSE IT'S OUR MISSION AS THE FOUR CHAMPIONS OF RUBRUM.

...

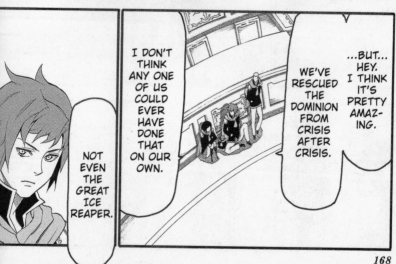

...BUT... HEY. I THINK IT'S PRETTY AMAZING.

WE'VE RESCUED THE DOMINION FROM CRISIS AFTER CRISIS.

I DON'T THINK ANY ONE OF US COULD EVER HAVE DONE THAT ON OUR OWN.

NOT EVEN THE GREAT ICE REAPER.

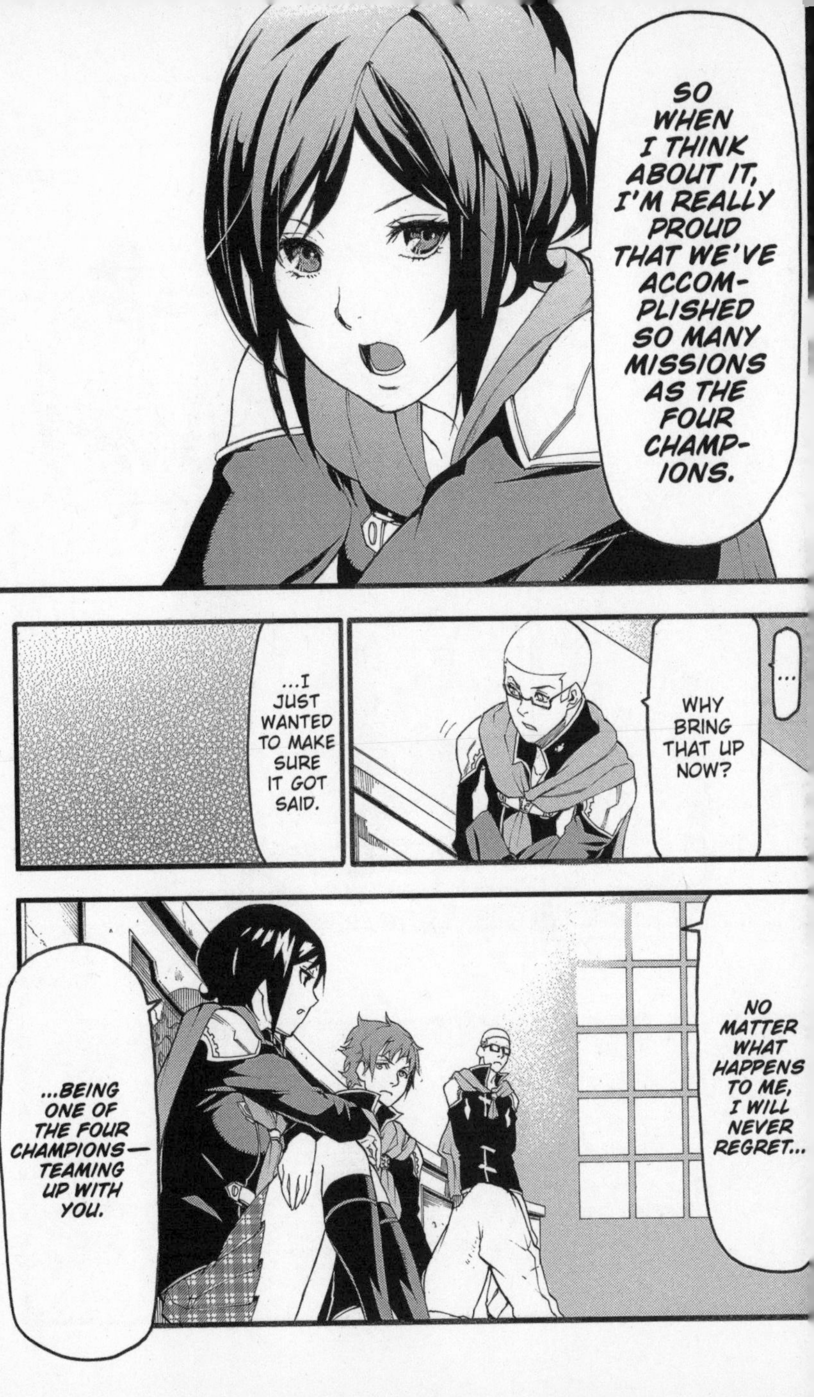
SO WHEN I THINK ABOUT IT, I'M REALLY PROUD THAT WE'VE ACCOMPLISHED SO MANY MISSIONS AS THE FOUR CHAMPIONS.
...
WHY BRING THAT UP NOW?
...I JUST WANTED TO MAKE SURE IT GOT SAID.
NO MATTER WHAT HAPPENS TO ME, I WILL NEVER REGRET...
...BEING ONE OF THE FOUR CHAMPIONS—TEAMING UP WITH YOU.

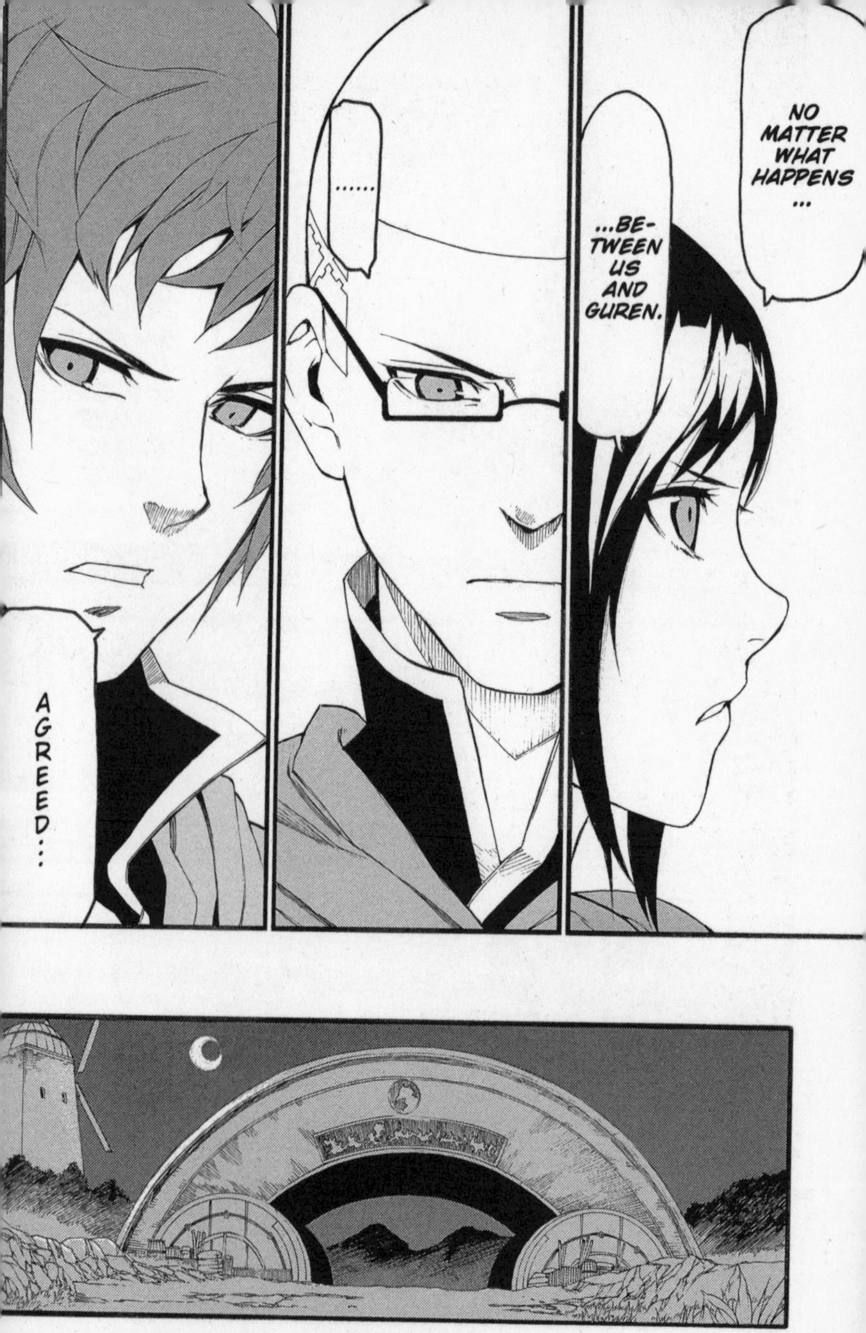
NO MATTER WHAT HAPPENS ...
...BE-TWEEN US AND GUREN.
......
AGREED...

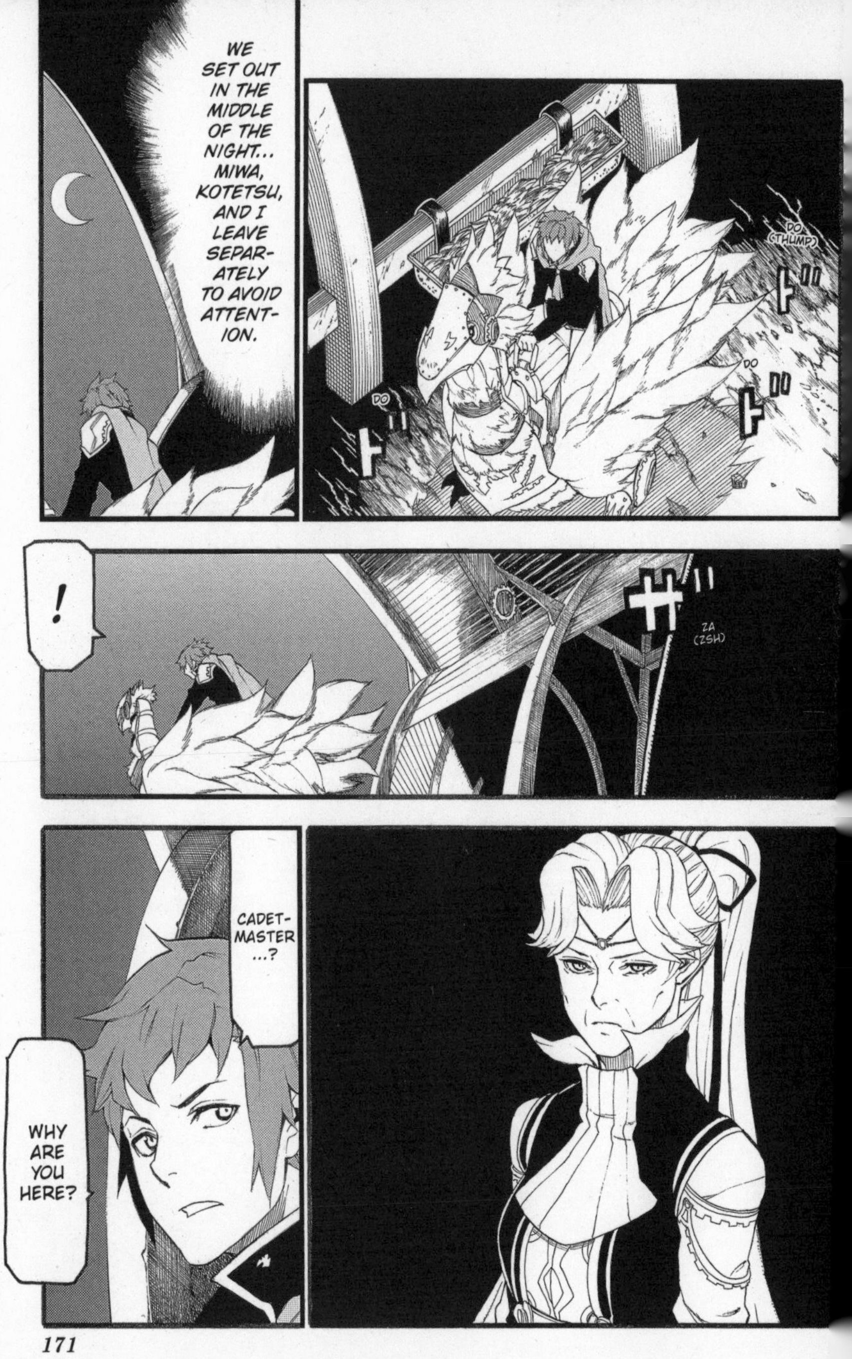
DO (THUMP)
DO
DO
WE SET OUT IN THE MIDDLE OF THE NIGHT... MIWA, KOTETSU, AND I LEAVE SEPARATELY TO AVOID ATTENTION.
ZA (ZSH)
!
CADET-MASTER...?
WHY ARE YOU HERE?

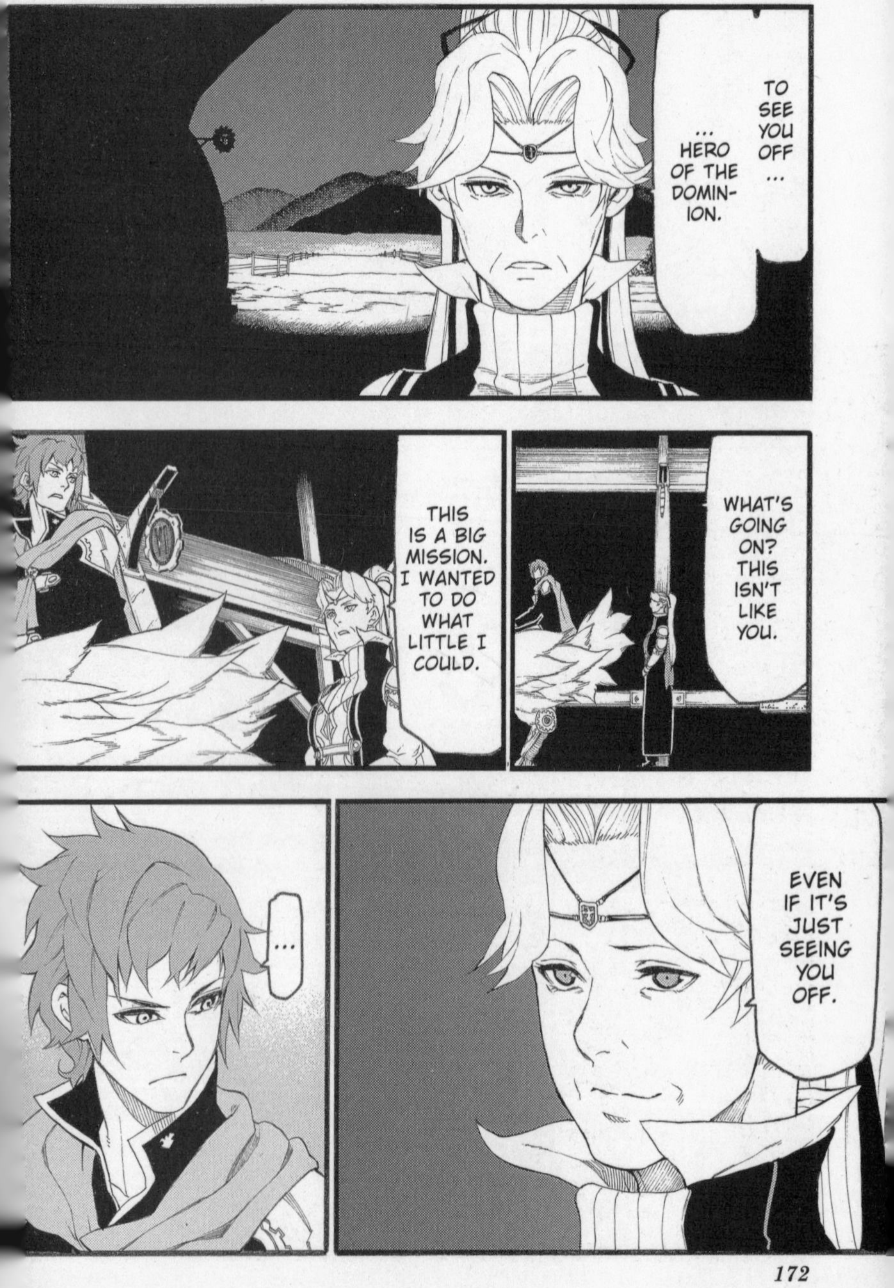
TO SEE YOU OFF...
...HERO OF THE DOMINION.
WHAT'S GOING ON? THIS ISN'T LIKE YOU.
THIS IS A BIG MISSION. I WANTED TO DO WHAT LITTLE I COULD.
EVEN IF IT'S JUST SEEING YOU OFF.
...

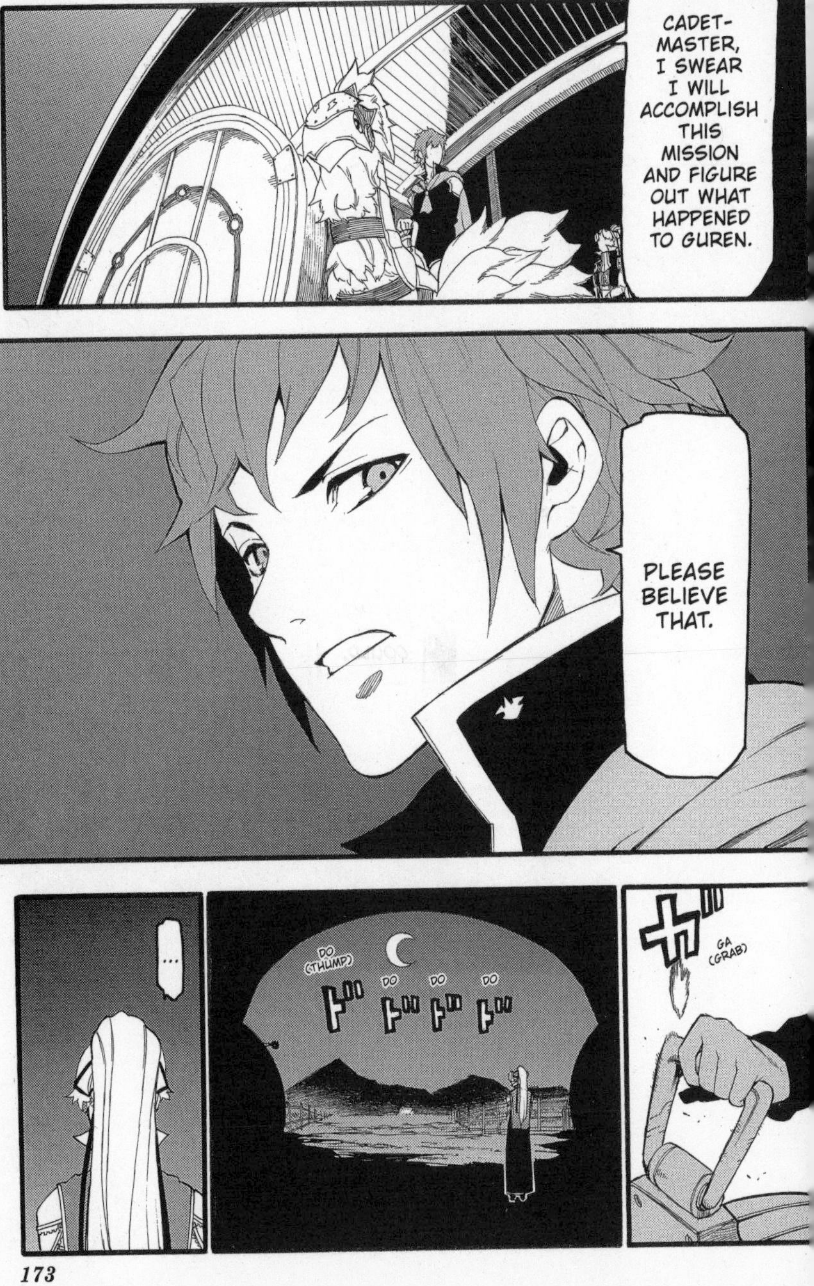
CADET-MASTER, I SWEAR I WILL ACCOMPLISH THIS MISSION AND FIGURE OUT WHAT HAPPENED TO GUREN.
PLEASE BELIEVE THAT.
ガッ
GA (GRAB)
DO (THUMP)
DO
DO
DO
...

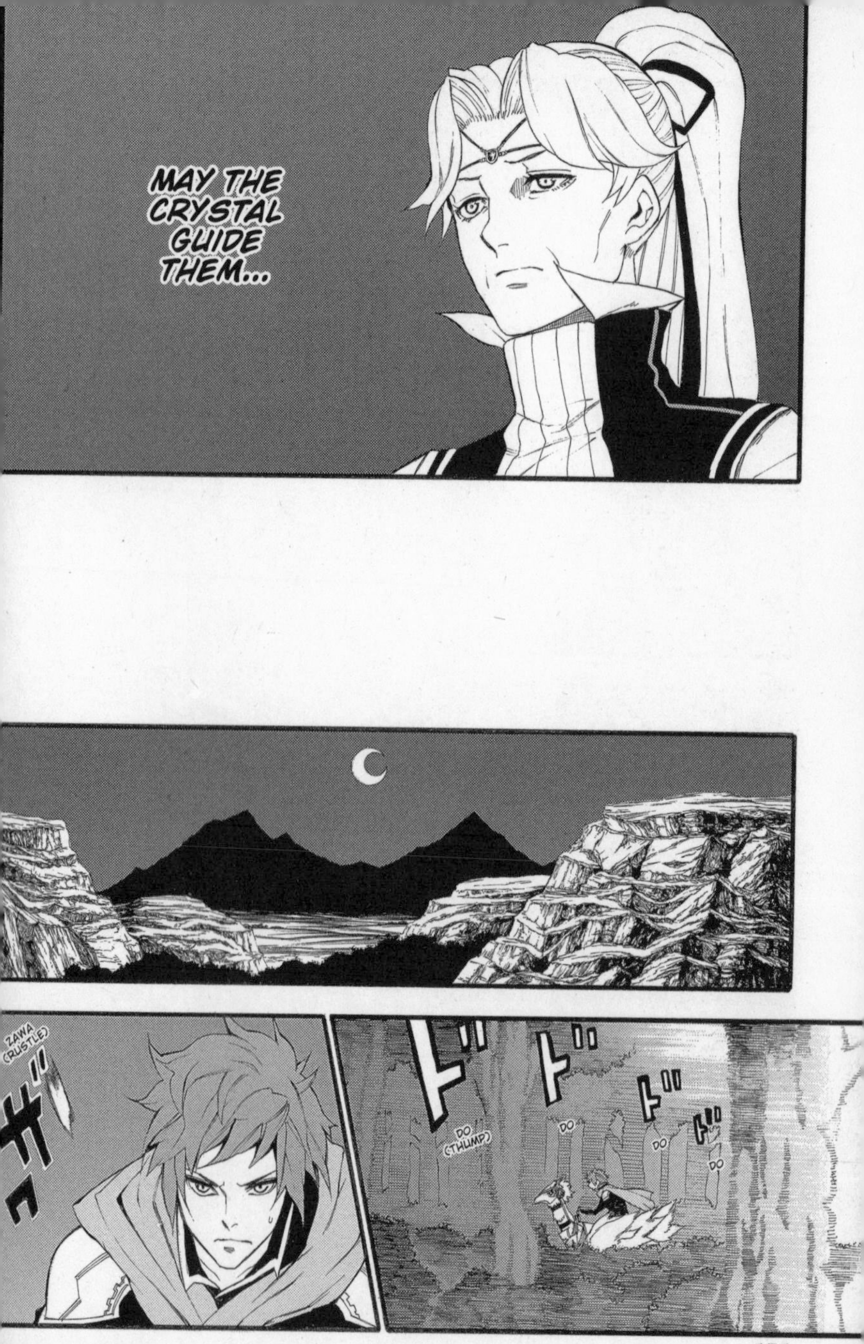
MAY THE CRYSTAL GUIDE THEM...
DO (THUMP)
DO
DO
DO
ZAWA (RUSTLE)

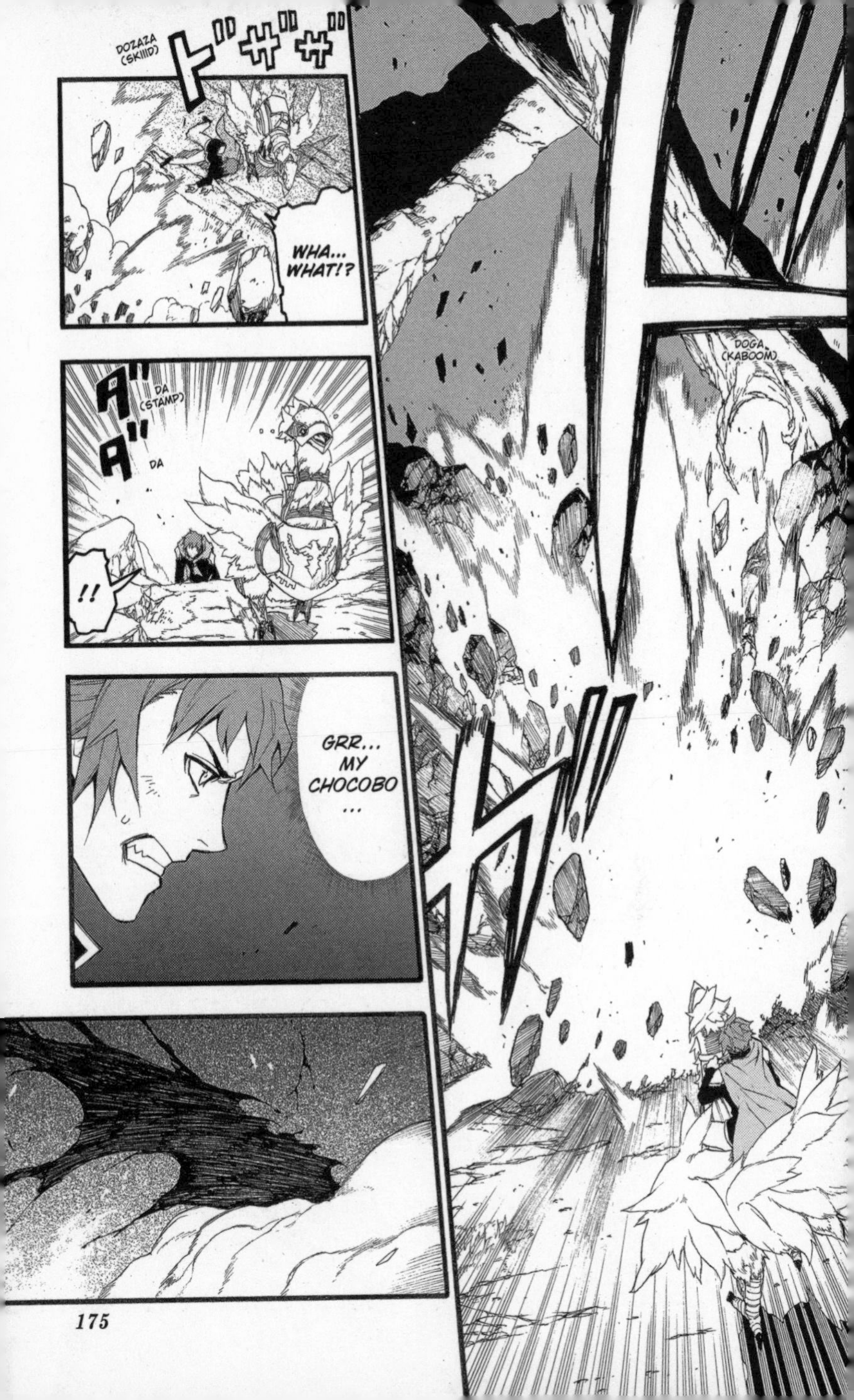
DOGA (KABOOM)
DOZAZA (SKIIID)
WHA... WHAT!?
DA (STAMP)
DA
!!
GRR... MY CHOCOBO ...

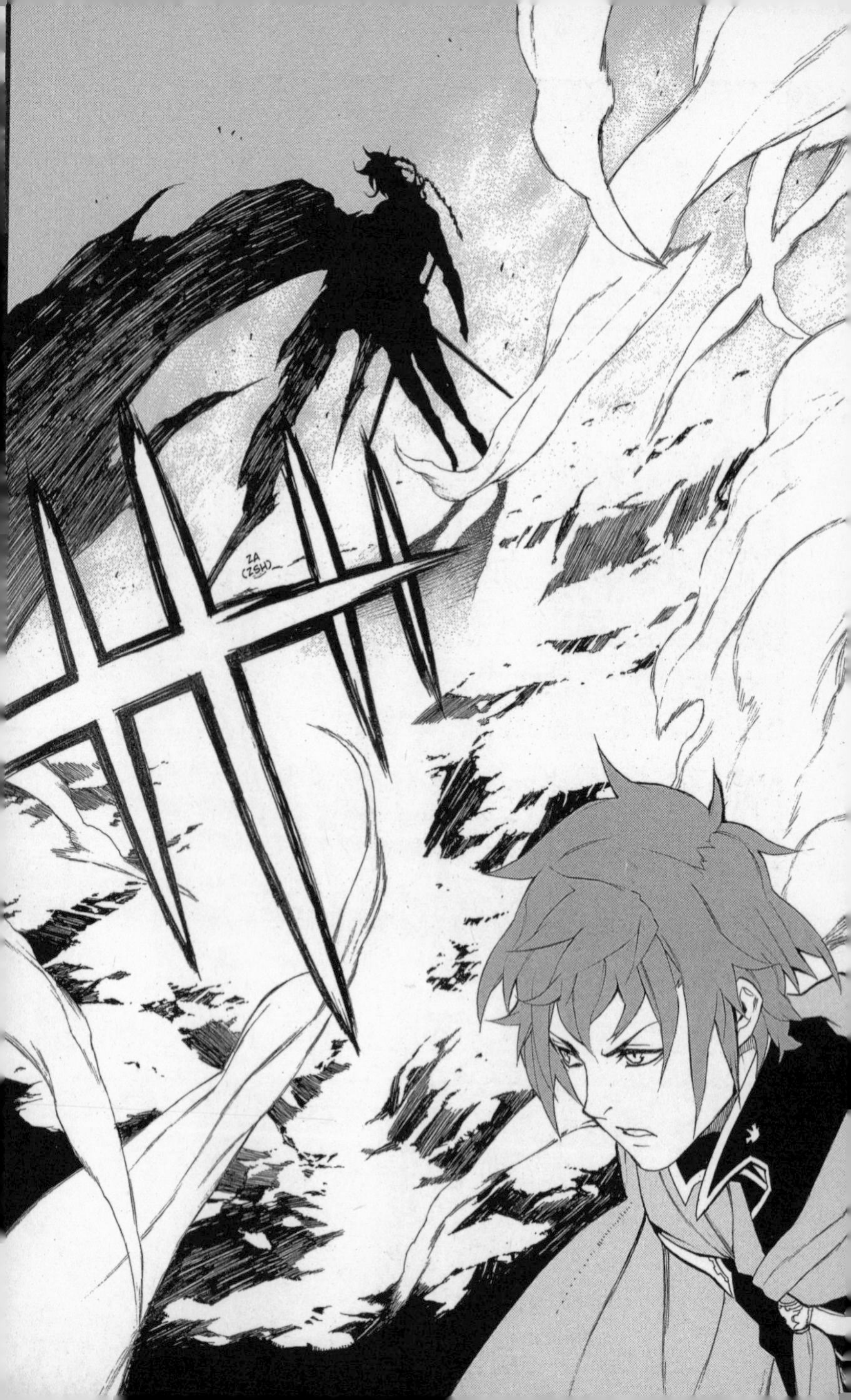
ZA
(ZSH)

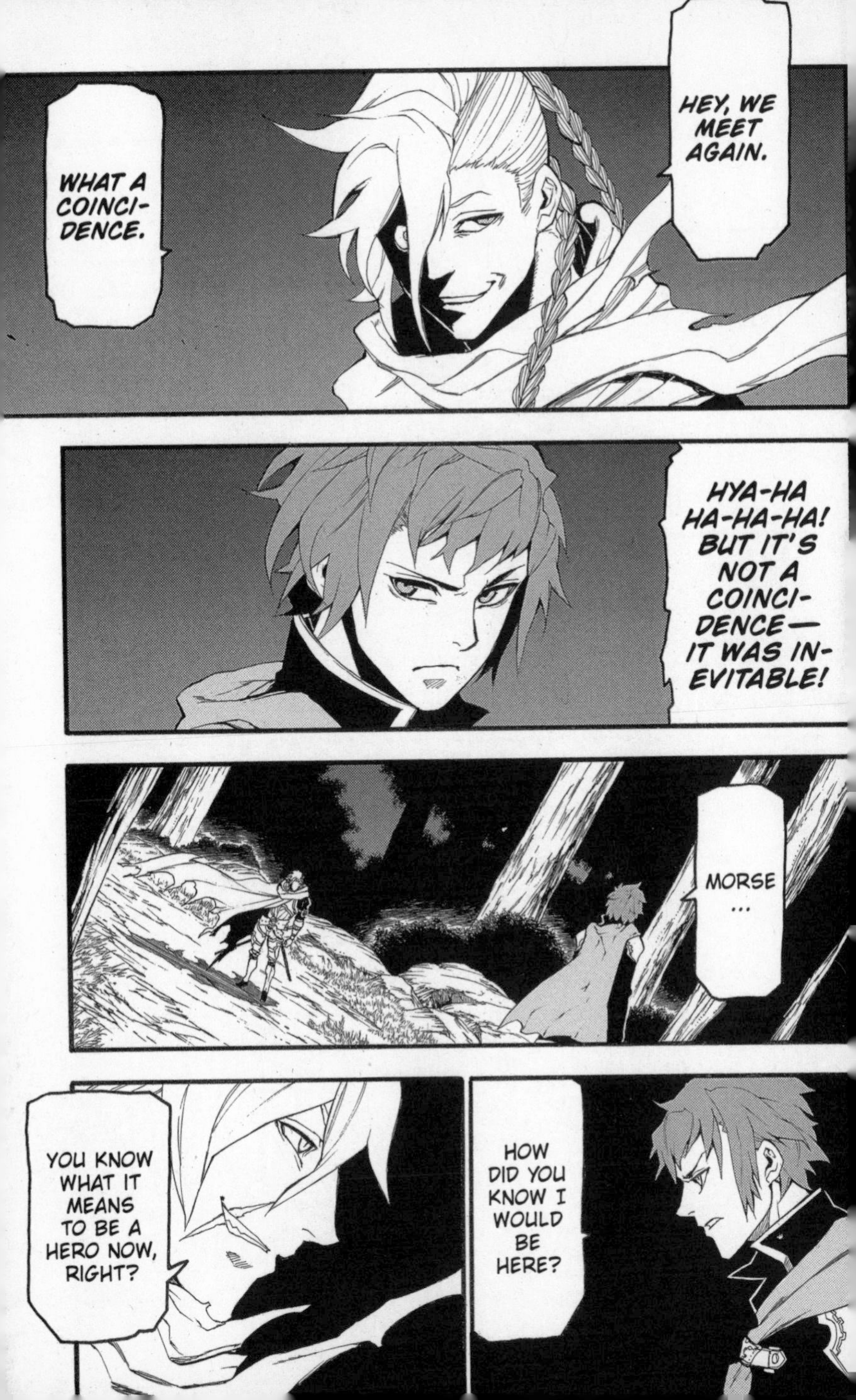
HEY, WE MEET AGAIN.
WHAT A COINCI-DENCE.
HYA-HA HA-HA-HA! BUT IT'S NOT A COINCI-DENCE—IT WAS IN-EVITABLE!
MORSE...
HOW DID YOU KNOW I WOULD BE HERE?
YOU KNOW WHAT IT MEANS TO BE A HERO NOW, RIGHT?

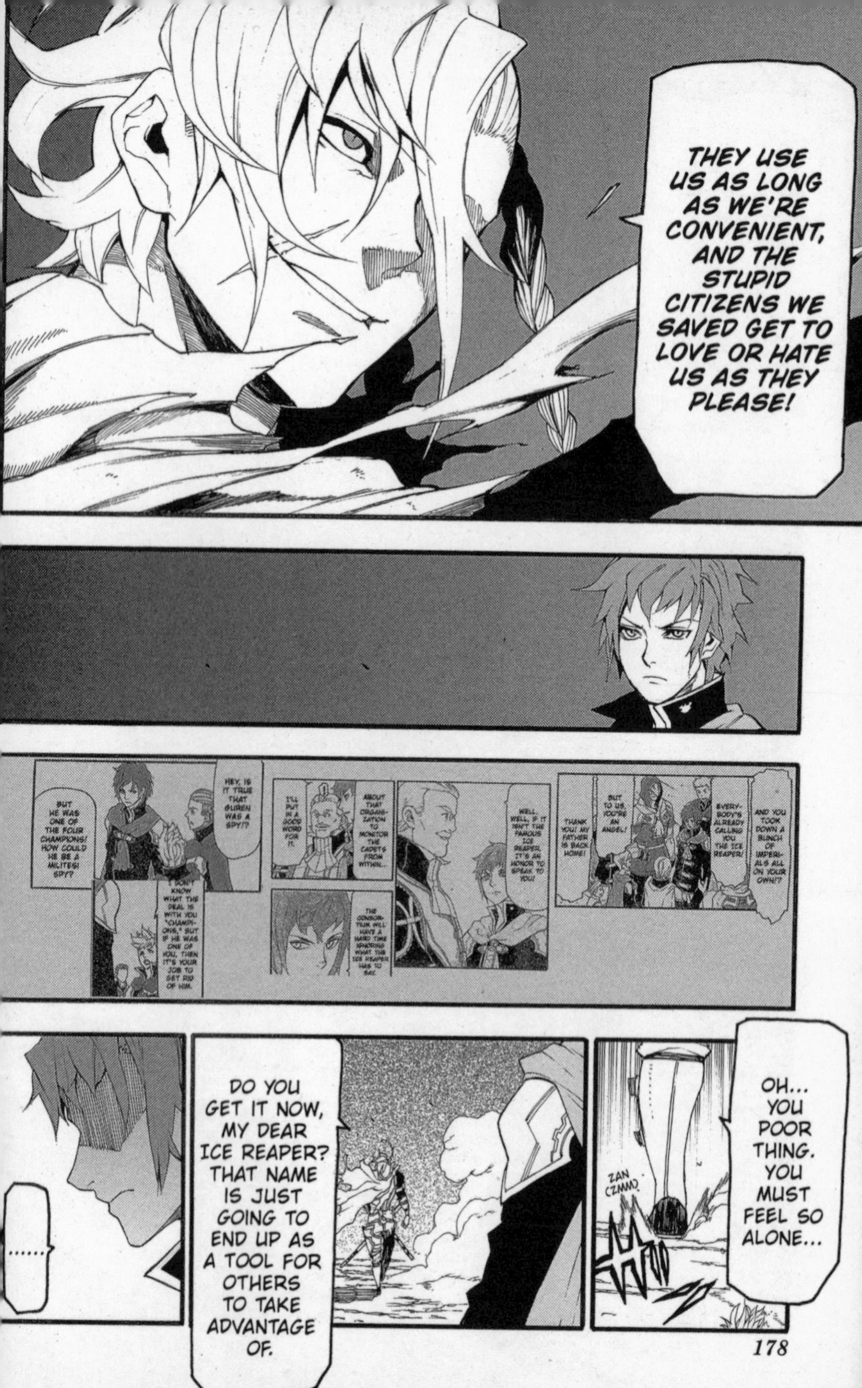
THEY USE US AS LONG AS WE'RE CONVENIENT, AND THE STUPID CITIZENS WE SAVED GET TO LOVE OR HATE US AS THEY PLEASE!
AND YOU TOOK DOWN A BUNCH OF IMPERIALS ALL ON YOUR OWN!?
EVERYBODY'S ALREADY CALLING YOU THE ICE REAPER!
BUT TO US, YOU'RE AN ANGEL!
THANK YOU! MY FATHER IS BACK HOME!
WELL, WELL, IF IT ISN'T THE FAMOUS ICE REAPER. IT'S AN HONOR TO SPEAK TO YOU!
ABOUT THAT ORGANIZATION TO MONITOR THE CADETS FROM WITHIN...
I'LL PUT IN A GOOD WORD FOR IT.
THE CONSORTIUM WILL HAVE A HARD TIME IGNORING WHAT THE ICE REAPER HAS TO SAY.
HEY, IS IT TRUE THAT GUREN WAS A SPY!?
BUT HE WAS ONE OF THE FOUR CHAMPIONS! HOW COULD HE BE A MILITESI SPY?
I DON'T KNOW WHAT THE DEAL IS WITH YOU "CHAMPIONS," BUT IF HE WAS ONE OF YOU, THEN IT'S YOUR JOB TO GET RID OF HIM.
OH... YOU POOR THING. YOU MUST FEEL SO ALONE...
ZAN (ZMM)
DO YOU GET IT NOW, MY DEAR ICE REAPER? THAT NAME IS JUST GOING TO END UP AS A TOOL FOR OTHERS TO TAKE ADVANTAGE OF.
......

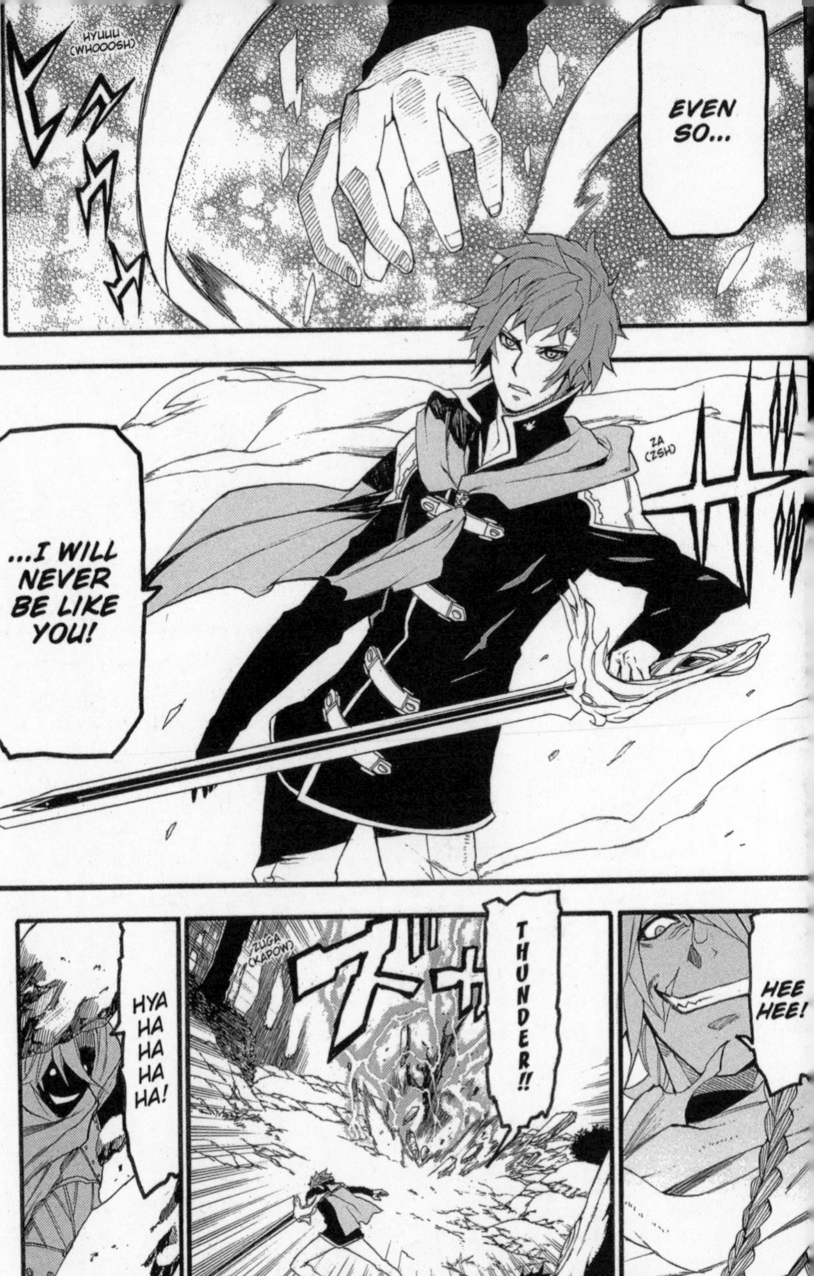
EVEN SO...
HYUUU (WHOOOSH)
ZA (ZSH)
...I WILL NEVER BE LIKE YOU!
HEE HEE!
THUNDER!!
ZUGA (KAPOW)
HYA HA HA HA HA HA!

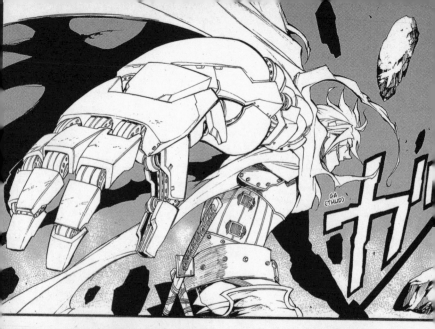

GA
(THUD)

GACHA
(KA-CHAK)

A MECH-ANICAL ARM!?

!?

JUST BE A GOOD BOY AND LET ME KILL YOU! IT'S FOR YOUR OWN GOOD!

YOU DON'T UNDER-STAND! THIS IS A KINDNESS, HYA-HA-HA-HA!

DO
(BLAM)

DO

DO

DO

DO

DO

DO

180

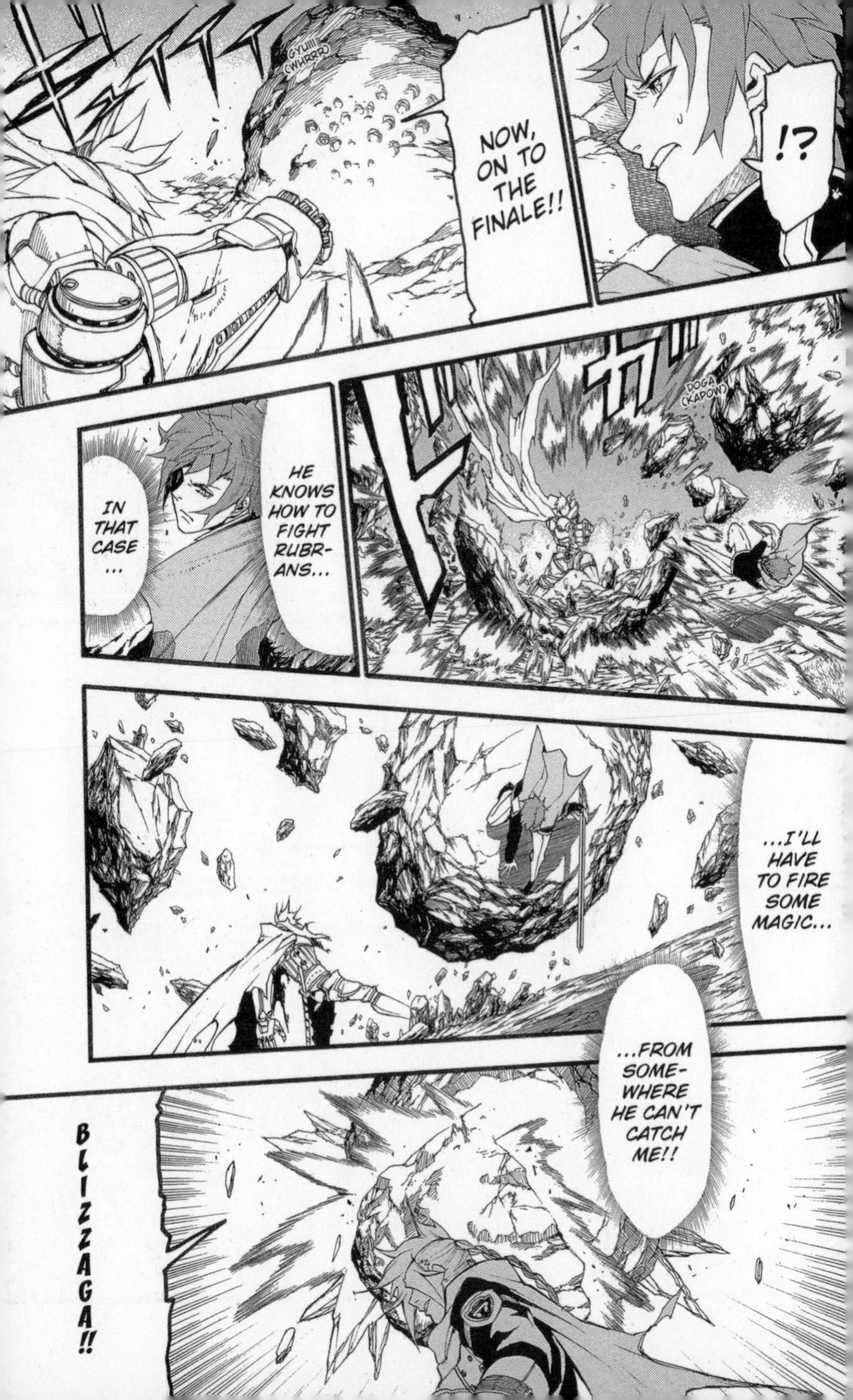
!?
NOW, ON TO THE FINALE!!
GYUIII (WHRRR)
DOGA (KAPOW)
HE KNOWS HOW TO FIGHT RUBRANS...
IN THAT CASE...
...I'LL HAVE TO FIRE SOME MAGIC...
...FROM SOMEWHERE HE CAN'T CATCH ME!!
BLIZZAGA!!

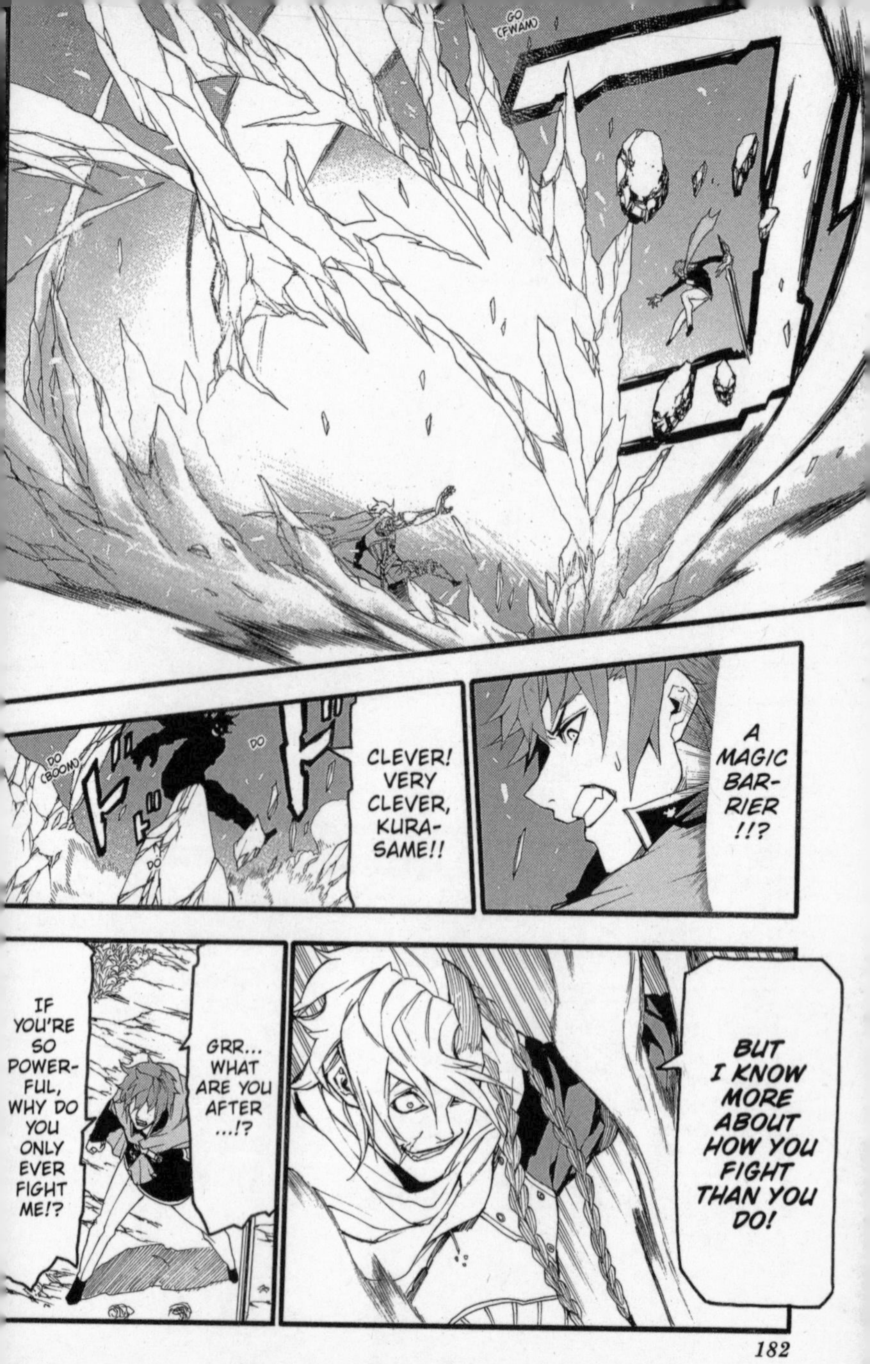
GO (FWAM)
A MAGIC BAR-RIER!!?
CLEVER! VERY CLEVER, KURA-SAME!!
DO (BOOM)
DO
DO
BUT I KNOW MORE ABOUT HOW YOU FIGHT THAN YOU DO!
GRR... WHAT ARE YOU AFTER ...!?
IF YOU'RE SO POWER-FUL, WHY DO YOU ONLY EVER FIGHT ME!?

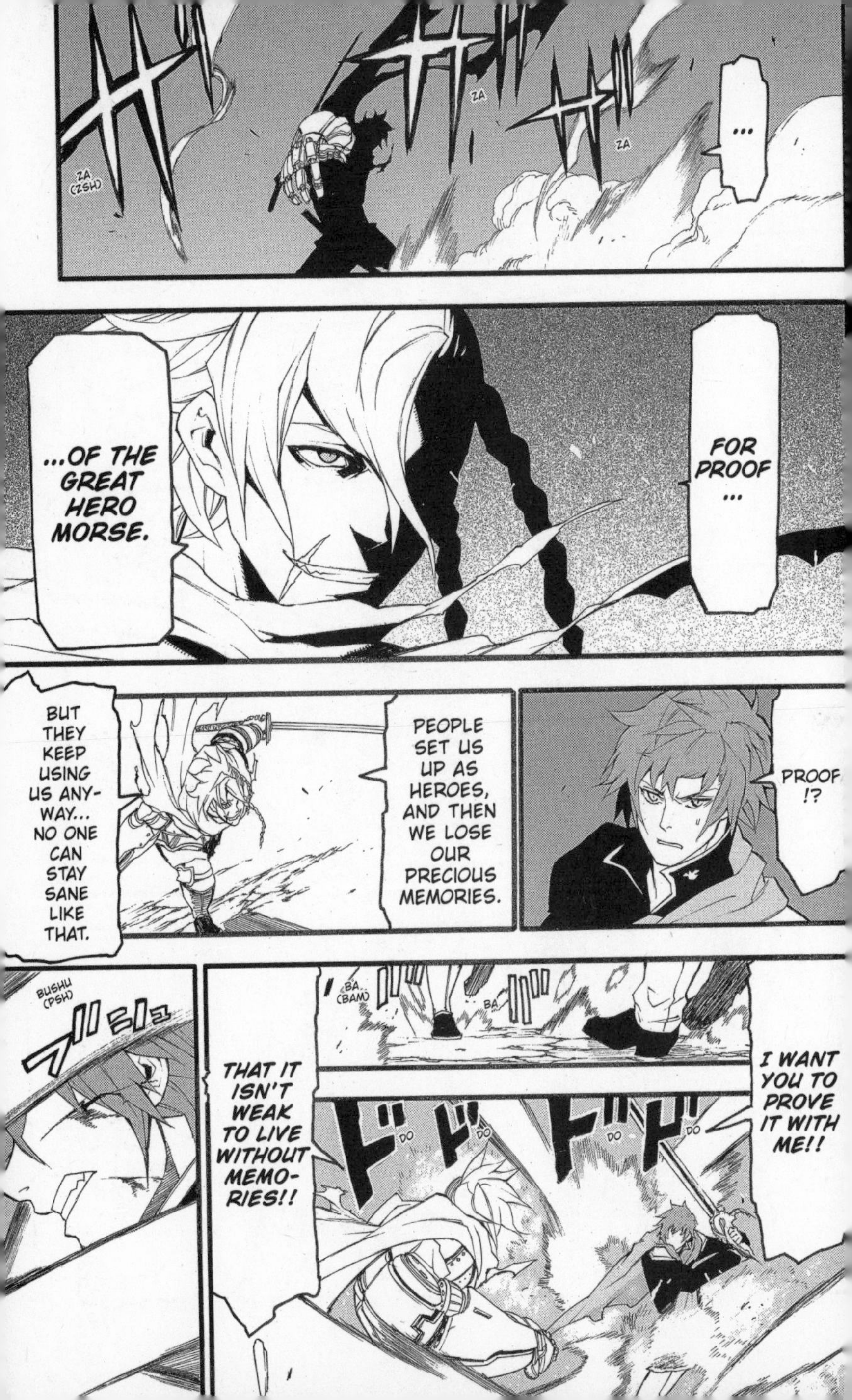
...
ZA
ZA
ZA (ZSH)
FOR PROOF ...
...OF THE GREAT HERO MORSE.
PROOF !?
PEOPLE SET US UP AS HEROES, AND THEN WE LOSE OUR PRECIOUS MEMORIES.
BUT THEY KEEP USING US ANY-WAY... NO ONE CAN STAY SANE LIKE THAT.
BA (BAM)
BA
I WANT YOU TO PROVE IT WITH ME!!
DO
DO
DO
DO
THAT IT ISN'T WEAK TO LIVE WITHOUT MEMO-RIES!!
BUSHU (PSH)

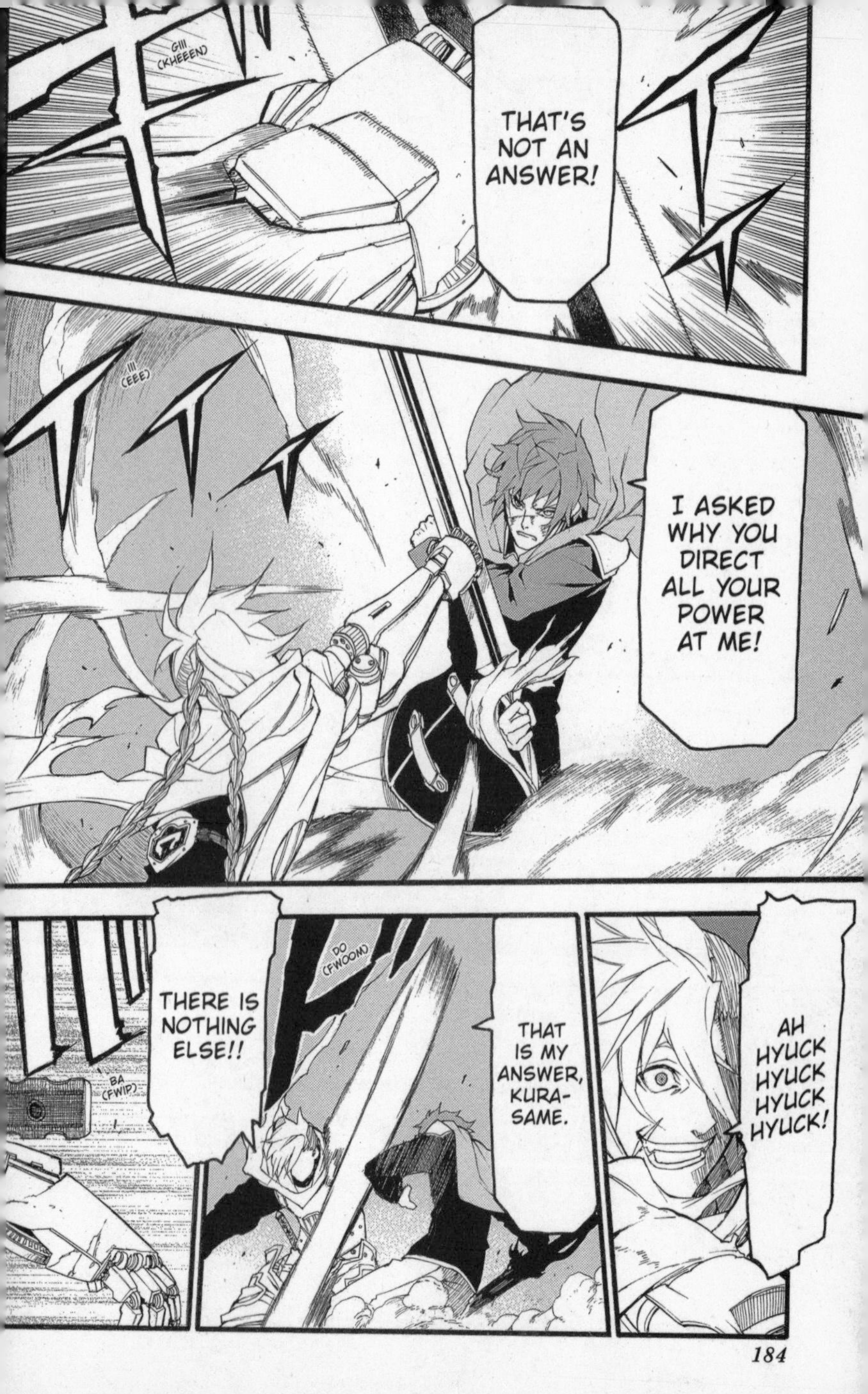
THAT'S NOT AN ANSWER!
GIII (KHEEEN)
I ASKED WHY YOU DIRECT ALL YOUR POWER AT ME!
III (EEE)
AH HYUCK HYUCK HYUCK HYUCK!
THAT IS MY ANSWER, KURA-SAME.
DO (FWOOM)
THERE IS NOTHING ELSE!!
BA (FWIP)

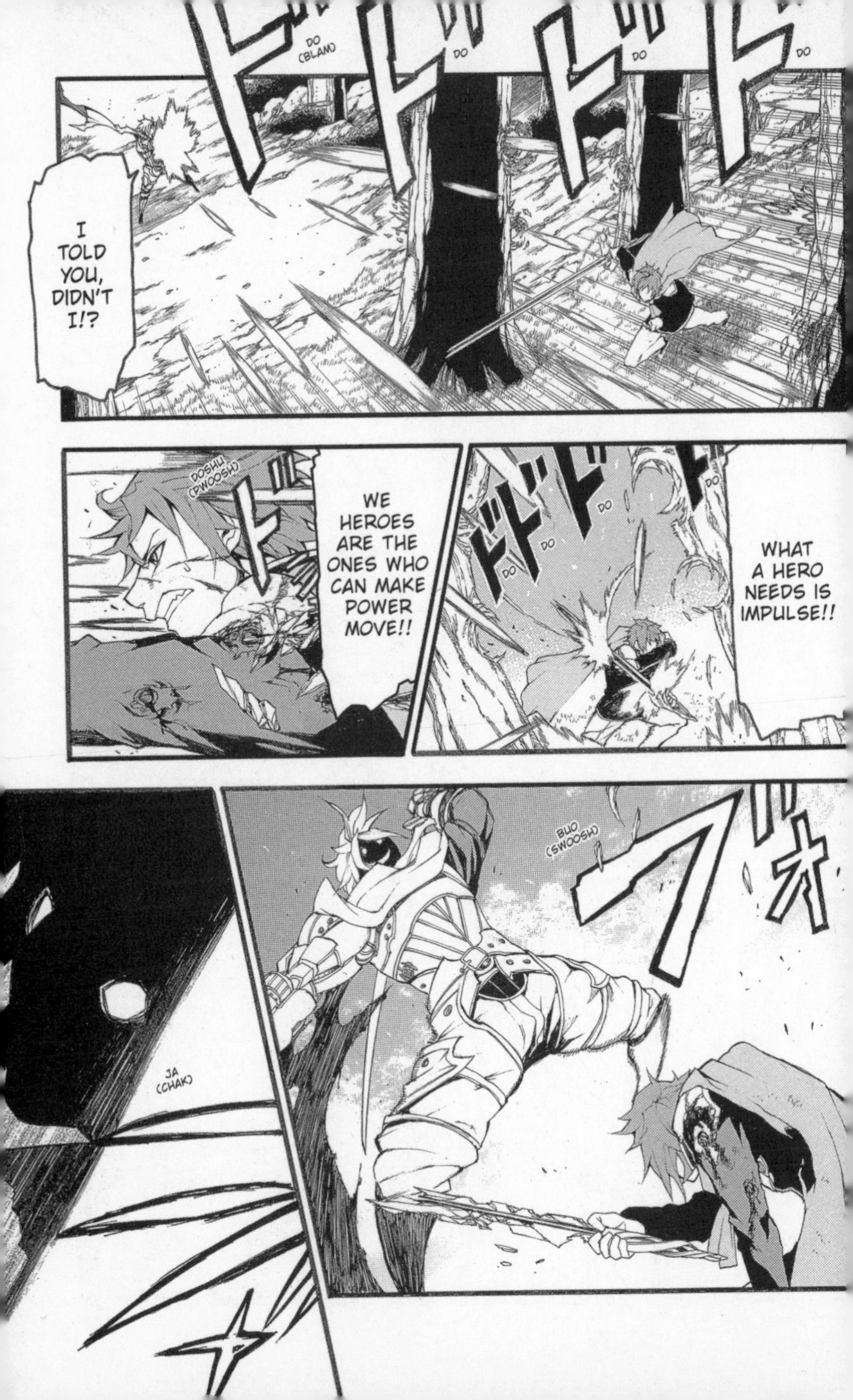
DO
DO
DO
DO
(BLAM)
I TOLD YOU, DIDN'T I!?
WHAT A HERO NEEDS IS IMPULSE!!
DO
DO
DO
DO
DOSHU
(PWOOSH)
WE HEROES ARE THE ONES WHO CAN MAKE POWER MOVE!!
BUO
(SWOOSH)
JA
(CHAK)

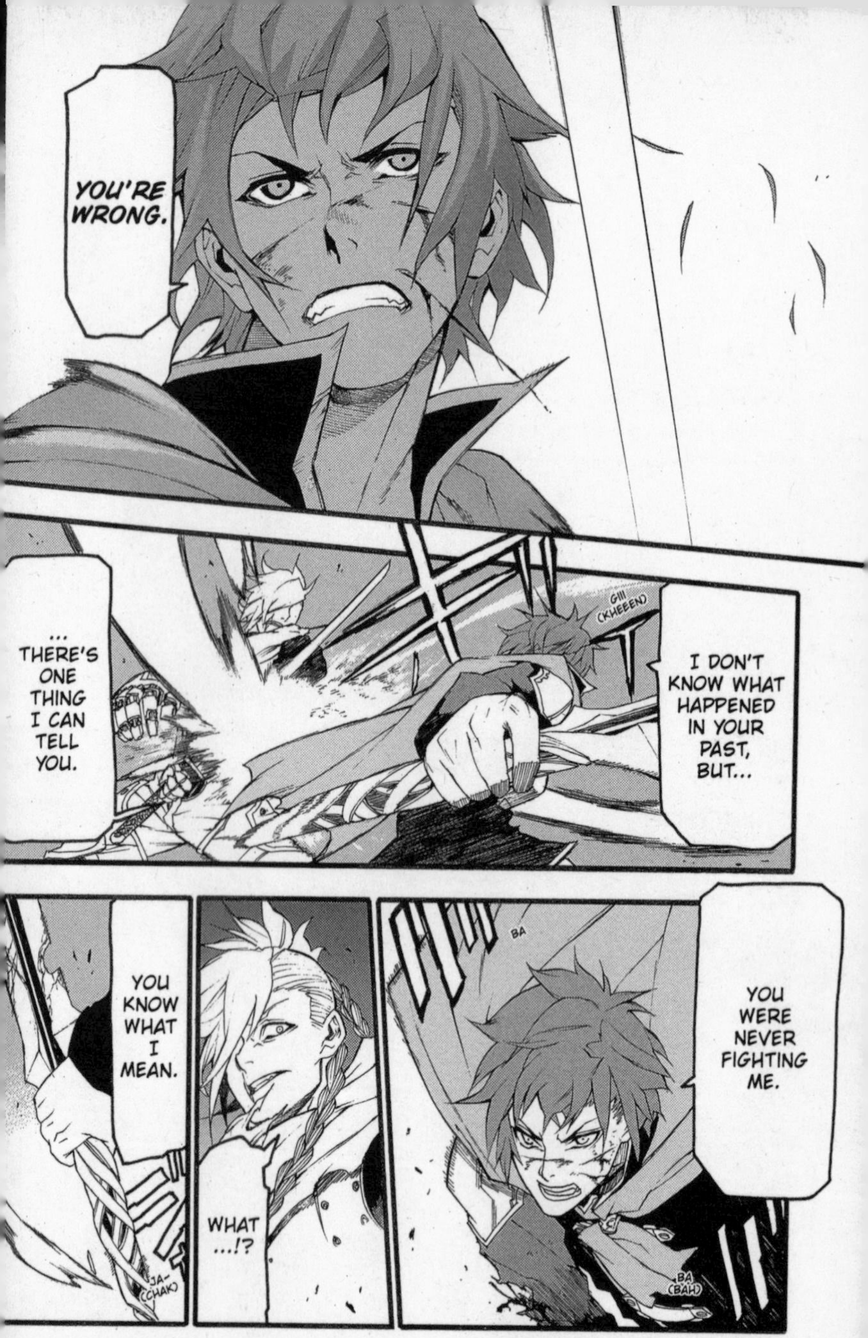
YOU'RE WRONG.
GIII (KHEEEN)
I DON'T KNOW WHAT HAPPENED IN YOUR PAST, BUT...
... THERE'S ONE THING I CAN TELL YOU.
BA
YOU WERE NEVER FIGHTING ME.
BA (BAH)
WHAT ...!?
YOU KNOW WHAT I MEAN.
JA-(CCHAK)

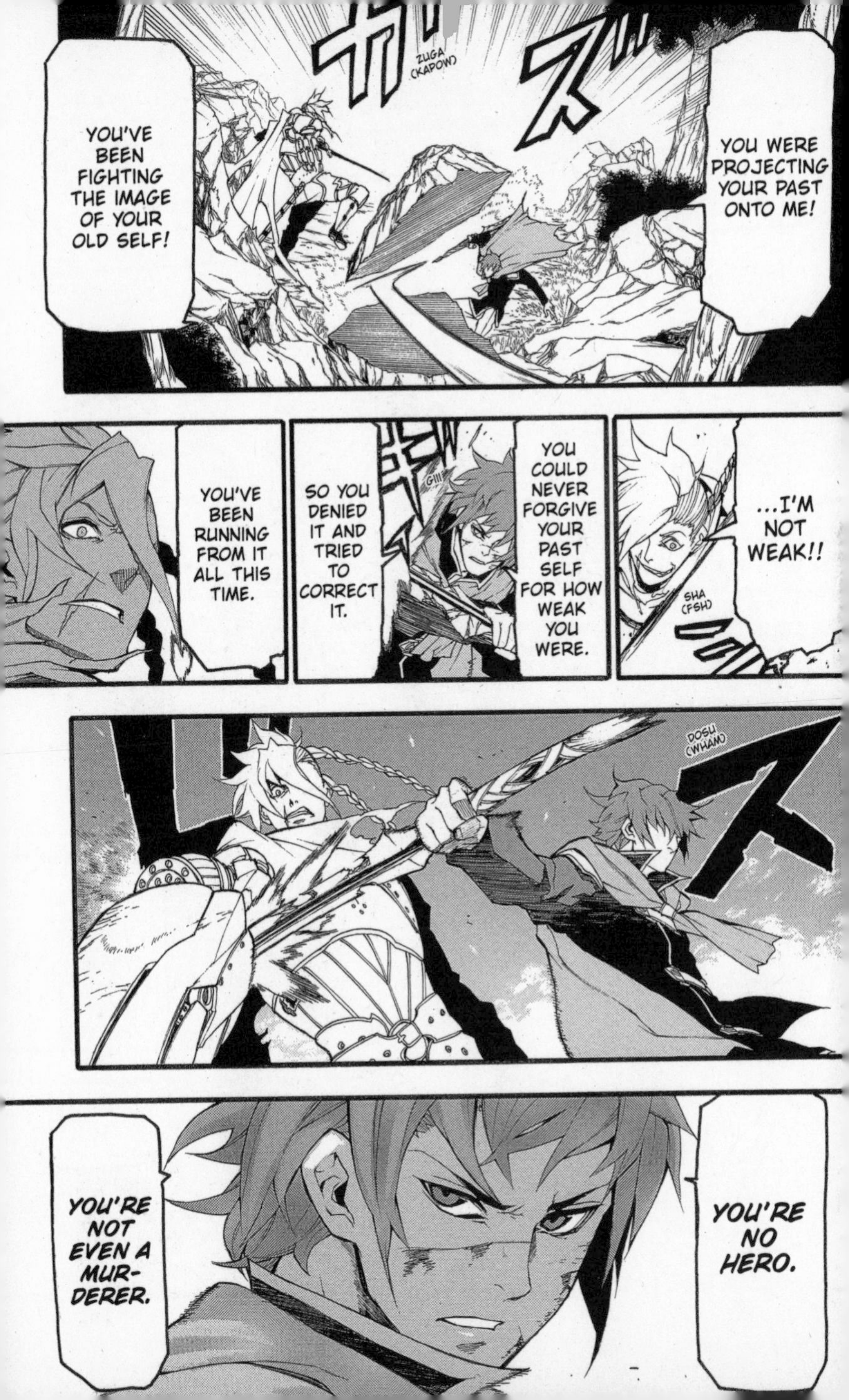
ZUGA (KAPOW)
YOU WERE PROJECTING YOUR PAST ONTO ME!
YOU'VE BEEN FIGHTING THE IMAGE OF YOUR OLD SELF!
...I'M NOT WEAK!!
SHA (FSH)
YOU COULD NEVER FORGIVE YOUR PAST SELF FOR HOW WEAK YOU WERE.
GIII
SO YOU DENIED IT AND TRIED TO CORRECT IT.
YOU'VE BEEN RUNNING FROM IT ALL THIS TIME.
DOSU (WHAM)
YOU'RE NO HERO.
YOU'RE NOT EVEN A MURDERER.

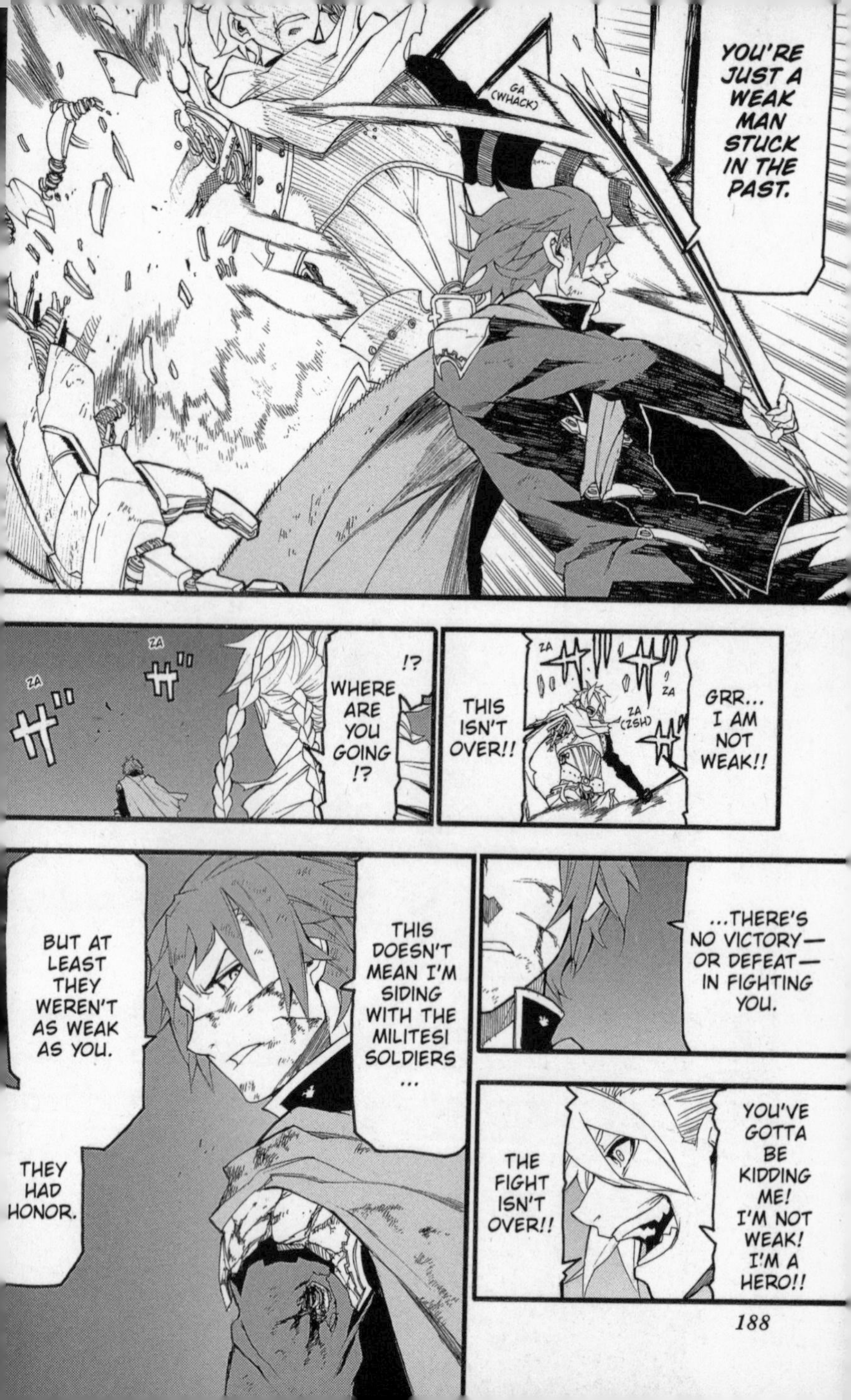
YOU'RE JUST A WEAK MAN STUCK IN THE PAST.
GA (WHACK)
GRR... I AM NOT WEAK!!
ZA
ZA
ZA (ZSH)
THIS ISN'T OVER!!
!? WHERE ARE YOU GOING !?
ZA
ZA
...THERE'S NO VICTORY— OR DEFEAT— IN FIGHTING YOU.
YOU'VE GOTTA BE KIDDING ME! I'M NOT WEAK! I'M A HERO!!
THE FIGHT ISN'T OVER!!
THIS DOESN'T MEAN I'M SIDING WITH THE MILITESI SOLDIERS ...
BUT AT LEAST THEY WEREN'T AS WEAK AS YOU.
THEY HAD HONOR.

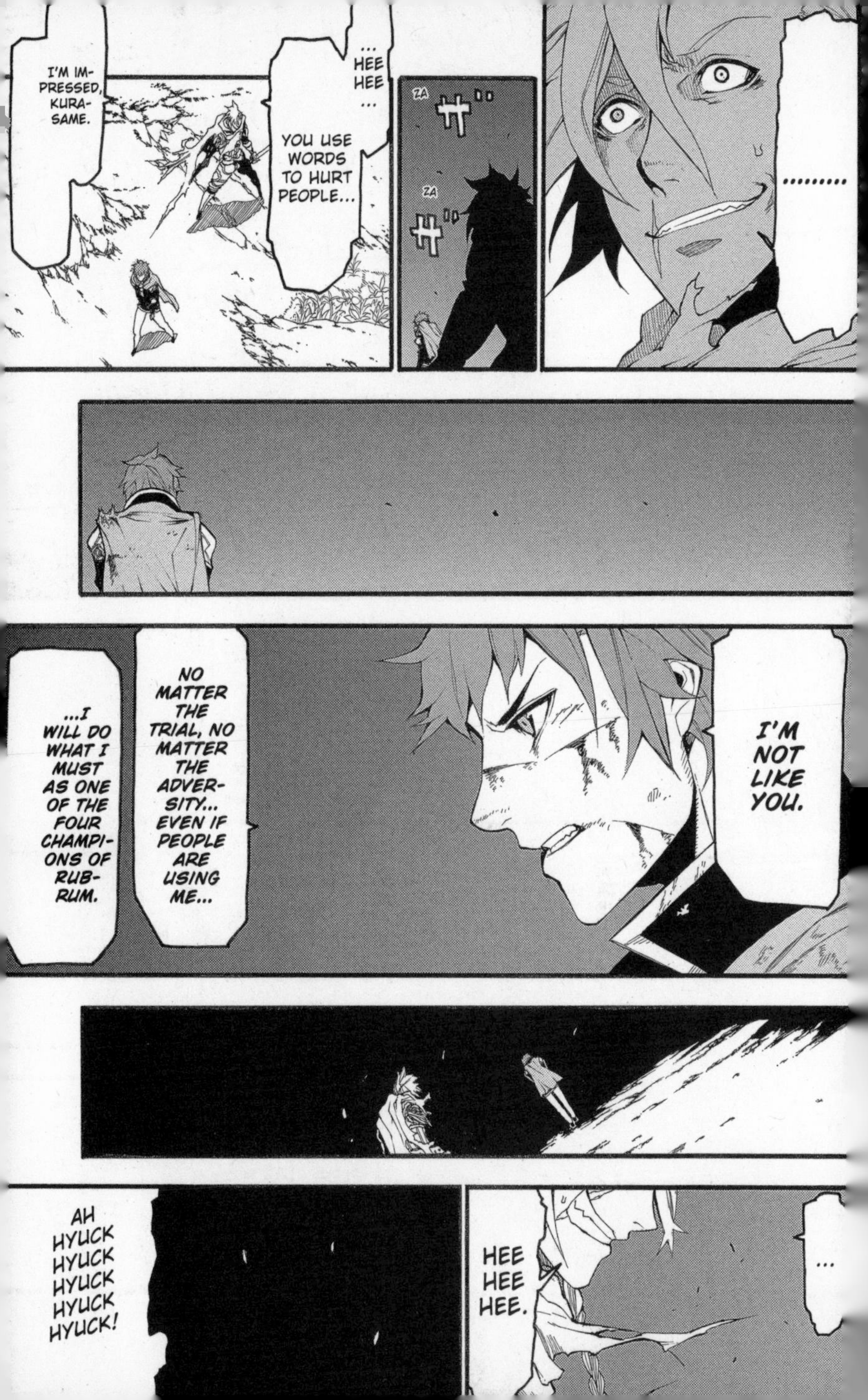
....
ZA
ZA
... HEE HEE ... YOU USE WORDS TO HURT PEOPLE...
I'M IMPRESSED, KURASAME.
I'M NOT LIKE YOU.
NO MATTER THE TRIAL, NO MATTER THE ADVERSITY... EVEN IF PEOPLE ARE USING ME...
...I WILL DO WHAT I MUST AS ONE OF THE FOUR CHAMPIONS OF RUBRUM.
...
HEE HEE HEE.
AH HYUCK HYUCK HYUCK HYUCK HYUCK!

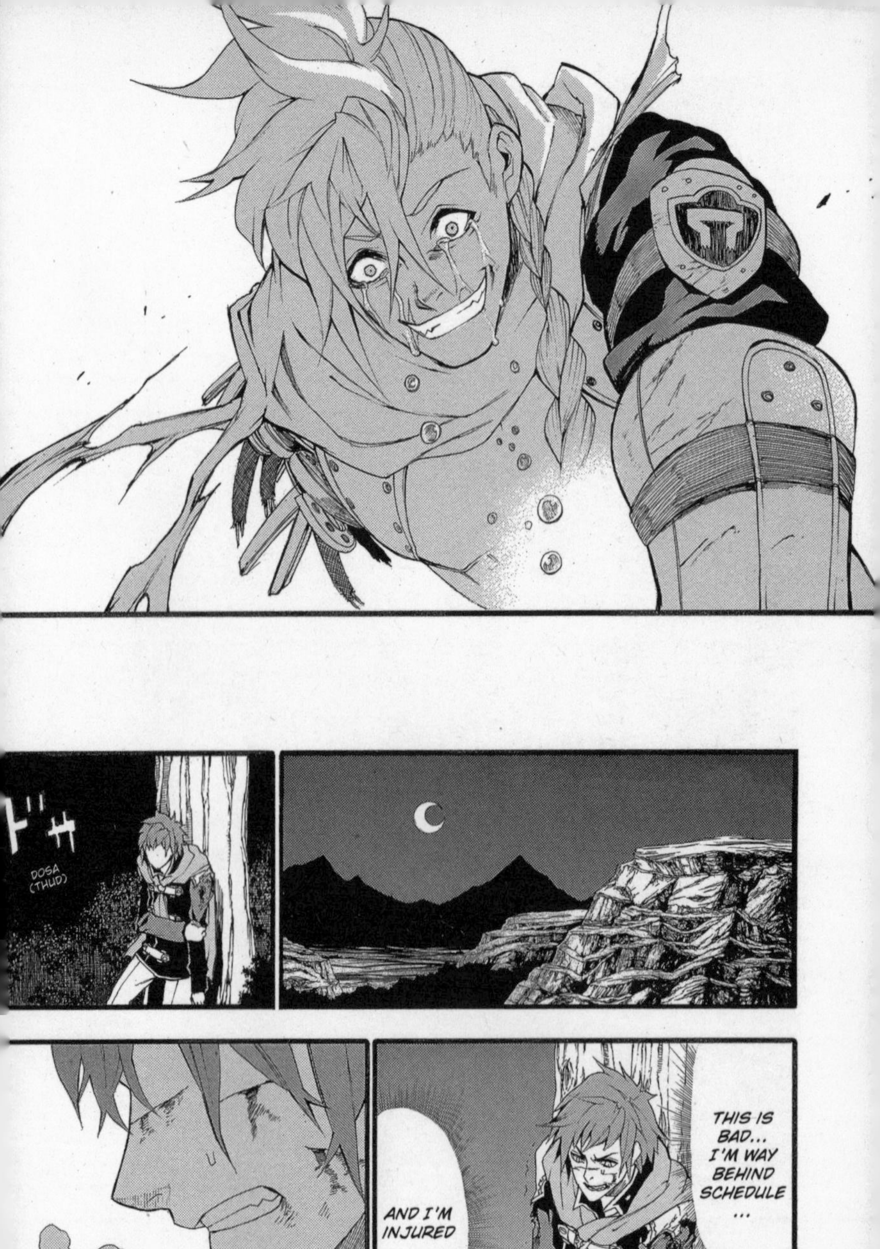
ドサ
DOSA (THUD)
THIS IS BAD... I'M WAY BEHIND SCHEDULE ...
AND I'M INJURED ...

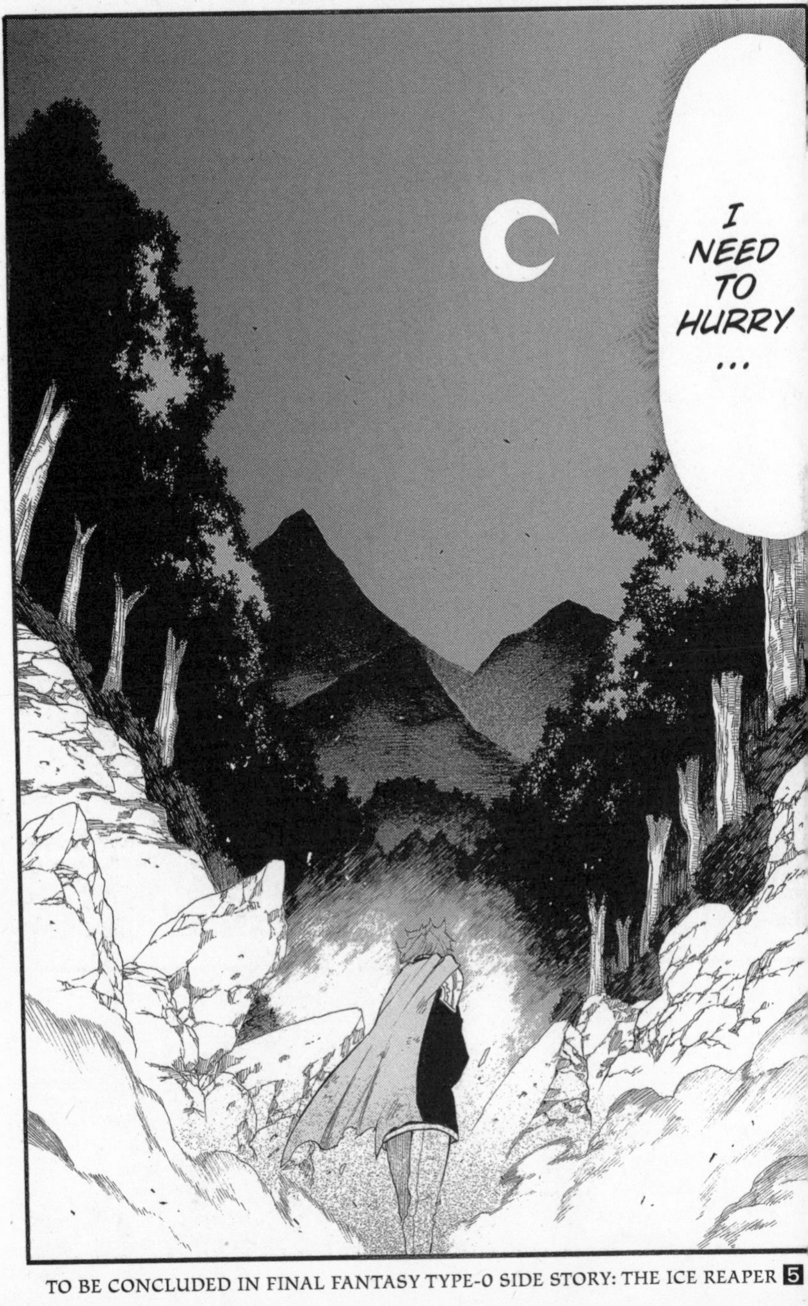
I NEED TO HURRY ...

TO BE CONCLUDED IN FINAL FANTASY TYPE-0 SIDE STORY: THE ICE REAPER 5

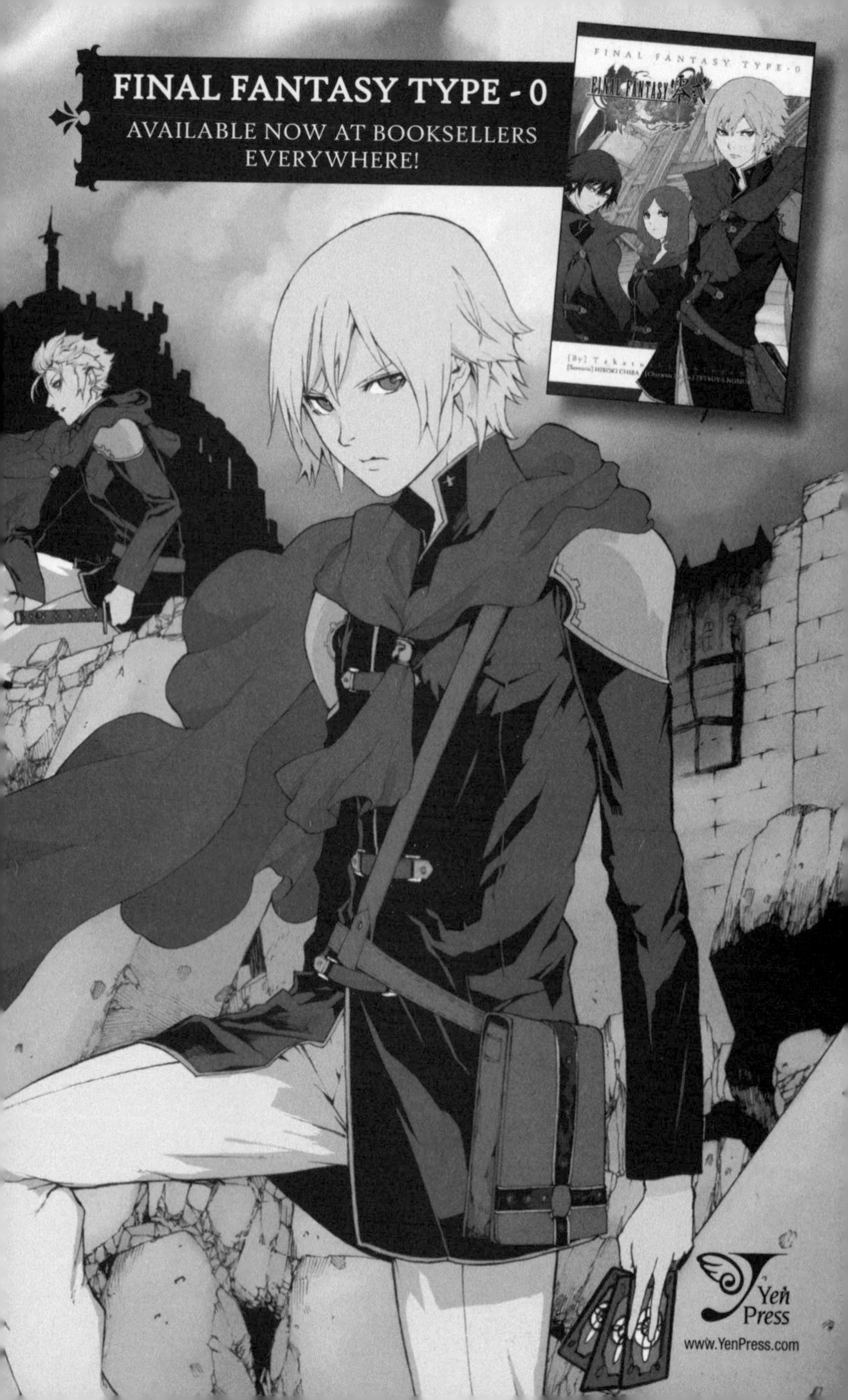
FINAL FANTASY TYPE - 0
AVAILABLE NOW AT BOOKSELLERS EVERYWHERE!
FINAL FANTASY TYPE-0
Yen Press
www.YenPress.com

FINAL FANTASY 零式 TYPE-0

Art: TAKATOSHI SHIOZAWA
Character Design: TETSUYA NOMURA
Scenario: HIROKI CHIBA

The cadets of Akademeia's Class Zero are legends, with strength and magic unrivaled, and crimson capes symbolizing the great Vermilion Bird of the Dominion. But will their elite training be enough to keep them alive when a war breaks out and the Class Zero cadets find themselves at the front and center of a bloody political battlefield?!

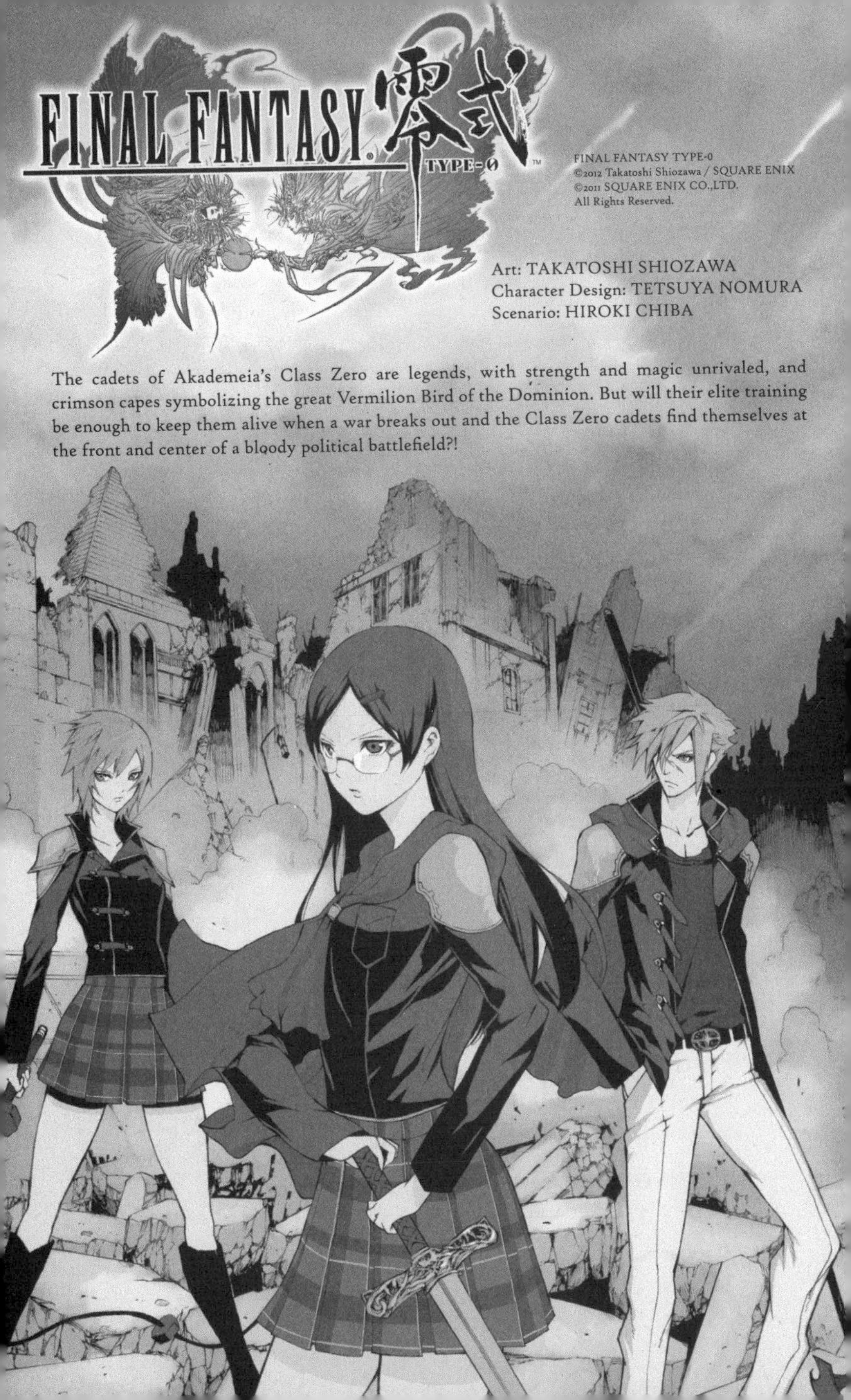

FINAL FANTASY TYPE-0 SIDE STORY:
THE ICE REAPER ④

TAKATOSHI SHIOZAWA
CHARACTER DESIGN: TETSUYA NOMURA

Translation: Alethea and Athena Nibley

Lettering: Katie Blakeslee and Lys Blakeslee

FINAL FANTASY TYPE-0 GAIDEN HYOKEN NO SHINIGAMI Vol. 4
© 2013 Takatoshi Shiozawa / SQUARE ENIX CO., LTD.
© 2011 SQUARE ENIX CO., LTD. All rights reserved.
CHARACTER DESIGN: TETSUYA NOMURA
First published in Japan in 2013 by SQUARE ENIX CO., LTD. English translation rights arranged with SQUARE ENIX CO., LTD. and Hachette Book Group through Tuttle-Mori Agency, Inc., Tokyo.

Translation © 2016 by SQUARE ENIX CO., LTD.

Yen Press
Hachette Book Group
1290 Avenue of the Americas
New York, NY 10104

www.HachetteBookGroup.com
www.YenPress.com

Yen Press is an imprint of Hachette Book Group, Inc. The Yen Press name and logo are trademarks of Hachette Book Group, Inc.

The publisher is not responsible for websites (or their content) that are not owned by the publisher.

Library of Congress Control Number: 2015960111

First Yen Press Edition: April 2016

ISBN: 978-0-316-26922-3

10 9 8 7 6 5 4 3 2 1

BVG

Printed in the United States of America